All The RAGE

BY IAN 'MAC' McLAGAN

BILLBOARD BOOKS
An imprint of Watson-Guptill Publications
New York

For Kim, who makes it all possible.
Goodnight, Ronnie.

Cover design by Robin Lee Malik, Buddy Boy Design.

Senior Acquisitions Editor: Bob Nirkind
Editor: Jacqueline Ching
Designer: Cheryl Viker
Production Manager: Ellen Greene

Cover: Kenney, Woody, Rod, and Mac at the Los Angeles Forum, 1975, © Ed Finnell.
Back cover: Photo of Mac, © Todd V. Wolfson.

The text of this book is set in 11-pt. Berthold Baskerville.

First published in the U.K. in 1998 by Sidgwick & Jackson, an imprint of Macmillan Publishers, Ltd.

U.K. edition edited by John Pidgeon, Chris Welch, and Ian McLagan.

Copyright © Ian McLagan 2000

Published in 2000 by Watson-Guptill Publications, a division of BPI Communications, Inc., 1515 Broadway, New York, NY 10036

Visit us at http://www.watsonguptill.com

Library of Congress Cataloging-in-Publication Data

McLagan, Ian.
    All the rage/by Ian 'Mac' McLagan.
      p. cm.
    Includes discography and index.
    ISBN 0-8230-7842-6
    1. McLagan, Ian. 2. Rock musicians–England–Biography. I. Title.
ML417.M46 A3 2000
782.42166'092–dc21   00-023675
                                                                  CIP

Printed in the United States of America.

First printing, 2000

1 2 3 4 5 6 7 8 9/08 07 06 05 04 03 02 01 00

Contents

Contents *(continued)*

Acknowledgments

Thanks to John Pidgeon for aiding and abetting, and then ultimately leaving me to get on with it, and Pete Townshend, Chris Welch, Rob Patterson, and Chesley Millikin for encouragement and thought-provoking suggestions along the way. Big Love to Ronnie "He would if he could and he often does" Wood, in spite of the lack of any useful memory whatsoever; the same goes to Kenney "Damn his hands and rot his bones" Jones for no memory, but a very good heart all the same; and Rod Stewart for wanting all the filth to be left in; to Jason Cooper for managing to manage me as well as he did; Tetsu Yamauchi, wherever he is; Pete Buckland, for reliable Faces tour itineraries and for going out with women nearly his own age; Bill German for Stones itineraries; Royden "The Chuch" Walter Magee III for being Royden "The Chuch" Walter Magee III for so many years of my life; Tom Wright, The Faces official photographer; Jody Denberg, Nico Zentgraf, and Dave McNarie for considerable research and development, and Albert Lee, Zigaboo Modeliste, John Hellier, Bernie Boyle, Don Archell, Kent Benjamin, and Kate Harvey for information no library could provide.

Written over a two and a half year period in Austria, Belgium, Brazil, Brunei, Canada, Denmark, England, France, Germany, Holland, Ireland, Japan, Korea, the Philippines, Romania, Scotland, Singapore, South Africa, Sweden, Switzerland, Taiwan, Thailand, Turkey, and the USA, on planes, trains and buses, in airport terminals, hotel rooms, dressing rooms, bathrooms, toilets, and pissholes, on tour, on vacation, and at home near Austin, Texas.

Foreword

All the Rage is such a perfect memoir of the rock 'n' roll world of our time, there's very little to add. Mac (no one who's known him more than five minutes could possibly think of him by any other name) turns out to be, as well as a great keyboard player and charming companion on adventures of virtually any sort, a world-class storyteller. Since the story he's telling is about a life lived amidst the most exciting and honored parts of the pop music world, it's almost immediately engrossing.

He did leave out something important, though, and that is a sense of his own place in the scheme of things. I don't mean the bare facts of the matter, playing with the Small Faces, The Faces, Rod Stewart, The Rolling Stones, Bob Dylan, Bonnie Raitt, Bobby Womack, Bruce Springsteen, and you name it. Chances are, those names are part of the reason why you've come to this book.

What you mightn't know is that this all didn't just happen. Oh, the run of events was as random and fortuitous (or not) as in any factual story. But the fact is that you don't get to play with the best unless you bring something very special to the process. In the professional pop music world, mere virtuosity is a cheap commodity because there's so much of it around. What the best musicians look for is someone who combines chops with personality. Mac continually gets all these great gigs because he brings something special to them, and it's not just from his fingers but from his whole being.

I'm stressing this because if there's one problem with *All the Rage* it's that Mac is overmodest about his musical achievements. Since I'm a fan, let me fill in that blank.

Mac was sometimes a sideman. He was never a bit player. The best evidence is on the records where he played as a full-fledged band member, especially with The Faces in their various combinations on "Flying," "My Way of Giving," "Afterglow," "Tin Soldier," "Cindy Incidentally," "Sweet Lady Mary," "Maybe I'm Amazed." And with Rod Stewart, solo, and on his great remake of the Temptations' "I'm Losing You." He's a master of the deep, sensuous grooves of the B3 organ and its kin, and he's a first-rate rollicking piano player too-something like Ian Stewart of the Rolling Stones, whom he portrays here so lovingly.

Also like Stu, Mac has the perfect personality to fit into a group. He is hysterically funny, not only as a retailer of anecdotes (which is what makes *All the Rage* so much fun), but also as a master of the spontaneous, laconic one-liner. (The last good one he got off in front of me came as he and his band were discussing changing the arrangement of a tune they were playing with Bill Bragg. "They can play what they want to," he said to me, with a raised eyebrow. "I'm playing 'Roll Over Beethoven.'" Sounded perfect when he did too.) But he's also observant and intuitive about the needs of others. He'll stand up for what he believes is right—ask Rod Stewart—but he'll also try to figure a way to make almost any reasonable situation work.

I think all this comes across especially clearly in the parts of *All the Rage* that have, superficially, almost nothing to do with rock 'n' roll: the scenes set in the Irish village where he spent summers with his mother's family. Unconstrained by any need to be hip, just being himself, he draws a wonderful and tragic portrait of his dear Uncle Ned, one that just about any writer would be proud to have created.

Another thing that makes the book special is its utter honesty about sex, drugs, and monotony. Their effect on a musician's life is well known, but the specifics have never, to my knowledge, been presented as realistically as they are, as openly and so matter-of-factly. There's no scandal here, nor any intent to scandalize, just the bare-bones truth of how those in the rock world lived their lives. Then.

As to now, Mac is also dead straight about his career, the opportunities bypassed or wasted as well as the days of heady success, the embarrassing moments (funny and otherwise) as well as the proud triumphs. There's a sense of confidence in doing that that takes an impressive measure of the man. So as well as a load of laughs, he is, in the end, sagacious, too.

It's not any less than I would have expected from my old friend, but it is a lot more moving to read it than an art school dropout has any business pulling off. He's lucky there's not a rock writers' union or we'd have to file a grievance. It's all well and good for musicians to publish their weeded-out diaries, but Mac's gone and done a real book!

In the course of it, we're granted a set of rare privileges. We get to see rock 'n' roll life from the inside, we get to know a variety of spectacularly talented and fascinating characters the way Mac knows them, and we get to know the extraordinary man who wrote it. If you love the music, there's not a better way to find out about how it seems on the inside.

And if I was Bob Dylan, I'd have given him the million too.

Dave Marsh
Oct. 27, 1999

Preface

Some memories brought a tear, and some left a bitter taste. Some needed recalling to fully understand what really had happened, and not what I thought had happened. Some villains have character, where most only have character flaws, and some angels can be devils when they're given half a chance. Laugh? I'd thought I'd never stop. Cry? I almost always bought my own beer. There were acid flashbacks, stoned euphoria, bouts of obscene drunkenness and taste sensations from as far back as the cradle. If I'd known how long this collection of stories was going to take to write, I might never have begun, but then again if I'd known how much fun I was going to get out of the writing, I would have started years ago. If there are mistakes it's not that I haven't tried very hard to nail down the facts, but sometimes the collective memory of pals makes liars of us all.

Since its publication in the U.K., I've made additions throughout the book, corrections where mistakes were found, updated the last chapter and added a discography that will be incomplete as long as I have breath. Now, all you have to do is start at the beginning–like I did.

Ian McLagan
February 2000
Austin, Texas

Check out my Website, www.macspages.com.
Have a look, have a laugh, have a listen.

PART ONE
1945-1969

CHAPTER ONE

Green Onions

It's September 1995 and I'm on my way home to Austin, Texas, from Bangkok. Breaking the journey in Los Angeles, I spot an ad for an organ in the classifieds. It's a 1954 Hammond B2. I can't resist this little gem, so I buy it–sight unseen–and arrange to have it collected, crated, and trucked to Texas.

Sometimes a smell can trigger a memory so strong and true, it unravels years in an instant, like the smell of a pub at opening time, or a whiff of oil paint, which takes me straight back to my art school days in Twickenham. So, as they unbolt the crate, even before I get to see how beautiful this instrument is, the combination of furniture polish and Hammond oil wafts up my nose and I get a flashback to 1964, when I was nineteen and caught that odd mixture for the first time.

Ever since I heard "Green Onions" by Booker T. and the MG's on the radio, the sound of a Hammond organ has moved me. Although at the time I didn't know exactly what Booker T. was playing, I knew I wanted to make that noise. I didn't even know how to play an organ, but the way it swirled and swam and bit your ears off, I knew somehow I had to have one. Later, after seeing Georgie Fame and The Blue Flames at the Flamingo, I found out Georgie played a Hammond L100, and he made it sing just like Booker T.

So I did my research in the music shops, and found out that the coolest-sounding organs were all Hammonds but that the L100, while it still had that special sound, was lighter and cheaper than the other models. Not that any of them were cheap, which didn't much matter, because I had no money. Then, thumbing through the back pages of the *Melody Maker,* I noticed an ad for Boosey and Hawkes, on Regent Street, who were offering to let me: "Try a Hammond organ in your own home on two weeks' free approval." Yeah, right, I thought. Pull the other one. I tried to figure out what the catch could be, because I couldn't believe they'd let me get my sweaty hands on a genuine Hammond without money changing hands or at least making a promise to buy.

But when I called them up, they were very helpful. There was no catch. The only thing I could not do was move it, once they'd set it up. That wasn't going to be a problem. The problem would be explaining the arrival of this beautiful monster to Mum and Dad. But I wasn't thinking that far ahead. I wasn't really thinking at all, apart from wondering-when could it be delivered?

"Tomorrow."

"Okay."

And that was it.

The next morning at about 10 A.M. there was a knock at the door and two men in white coats were standing on the doorstep. Though it wouldn't have surprised me if they were coming to take me away, they were from the store, of course, and after signing the papers and promising not to move it, we pushed the dining table and chairs back against the wall. Very carefully they wheeled in a brand new walnut Hammond L101 spinet organ and matching bench with the Playing Guide and connecting cables tucked inside the lid, and a brand new Leslie 147 speaker cabinet, which filled up the entire room. My face must have been a picture. This was the gear! It was all polished and shiny and made our dining room suite look quite tatty. They showed me how to start it up and we shook hands. It couldn't have been simpler.

"See you in two weeks then."

"Yes, okay, bye." Slam.

"Aarrgh!" I screamed and ran upstairs to get the Dansette from the bedroom, set it up on top of the bookcase, plonked "Green Onions" on the turntable and cranked it up! Yes, yes, yes, nothing could stop me now. I had lost my mind and I'd never find it again. Now I had to figure out how to play the beast and get that Booker T. sound. Carefully listening to sustained notes on the record, I pushed and pulled the drawbars in and out until I got the same sound. Then if I played the part right, the sound would change-just like the record. The next thing was to master was the Leslie cabinet. This was where the sound came out. The Leslie is a combined amplifier and speaker cabinet, but it has two speakers that point up and down. The sound travels through revolving rotors which throws the music out in waves. It's what makes the sound of every Hammond bite and swim in your ears. You can regulate the speed at which it rotates and it's very powerful!

Well, I noodled around with it for hours that day and played with it until I got some results. Basically, I just taught myself. The wonderful thing about the Hammond is it sounds good without too much effort. It's not like the bagpipes or the violin, where even after a lot of work it can still sound bad! When Dad came whistling his way up the path after work, I went to the door to head him off.

"Hello, Dad."

"What's up?"

"Nothing much. Well, I've got something to ask you."

"Yes."

"Er, Dad, you'll never guess what I've got."

"What have you got?"

"A Hammond organ."

"What's a Hammond organ?"

"It's free. I've got it for two weeks, then they'll come and take it away and no charge whatsoever."

"Where is it then?"

"It's in the back room, it's fantastic, and it's not costing a penny."

He was down the hall and peering round the door suspiciously before I could stop him. "Blimey, Lord luvaduck," he said. "Well, I'm blowed, where's the dining room table gone?" He was in the doorway, trying to squeeze past the monster organ and the Leslie.

"It's great, isn't it?"

"Well, it's big…how are we going to eat with this thing in here, and why didn't you ask me or your mum?"

"Sorry, but it'll only be here for a couple of weeks. Listen to this." I played the first part of "Green Onions." "Not bad, eh?"

"I dunno." He was thinking. "Here, don't say a word, let me break it to your mum." Somehow I knew it was going to be all right. The men in white coats came to take it away two weeks later and my new mahogany L102 and matching Leslie cabinet arrived the following week. I bought it on the "never never." Dad co-signed the hire-purchase forms for me because I was under age.

I never had any ambition as a kid to play the piano, let alone the organ. It was all my mum's fault. She'd had a dream of playing the piano since she was a kid, but growing up in the little town of Mountrath in the centre of Ireland, as one of eleven kids, there was hardly money for shoes let alone piano lessons. And as she hadn't been able to afford them when she was young, I was going to get them whether I wanted them or not.

When I was twelve, Mum found a piano teacher for me. Mrs. Morgan lived in Cranford, next to Heathrow airport, and I started going to her house every Saturday afternoon for lessons. I hated it and just wasn't interested. She was probably a good teacher but I considered it all a waste of my time.

It didn't take her long to realize it was a waste of hers too, even though she was being paid for it. She had an annoying habit of putting her coffee cup and saucer on the ivories while I was playing, and I was always worried they'd fall off. Every three minutes a BEA Vickers Viscount airliner would scream overhead as it came in to land, rattling the french windows and the cup and saucer too.

She taught me "The Vicar of Bray" and "London Bridge Is Falling Down" which were bad enough, but I had to play scales up and down the keyboard and I knew she wasn't going to teach me anything I might want to play. After a few weeks, instead of getting on the bus to Cranford, I'd hang out with Alan Worrell and Terry Munro, my mates from Spring Grove Grammar School.

The Temperance Billiard Hall was above a car showroom opposite Hounslow bus garage. They had a dozen great tables, and it was usually empty in the daytime. It was a very dignified and quiet place. No alcohol was served, which was why it was called the "Temperance" billiard hall, and for only a few pennies you could get a delicious cheese roll, a cup of tea, and enjoy a pleasant afternoon playing snooker. None of us was very good, but we took it seriously and played to win. We all liked the look and sound of Gene Vincent and The Blue Caps, but Terry was a big fan, and he wore a flat cap like them. Later Alan and I bought chequered flat caps as well, which we wore when we played snooker together, thinking we were Jack-the-Lads. It was as if they were our first group uniforms, although we weren't actually in a group yet.

Of course, when the bill for the lessons came in, Mum found out I hadn't been going and she sent me out to the garden for what she called a "switch." The bush had long, thin spiny leaves with tufts every few inches and it grew conveniently just outside the back door. She'd whip the backs of my legs with it whenever it was felt to be necessary. Ouch! I don't regret not having lessons; the music I love could hardly be taught by a white, English, classically trained music teacher. But I don't know why I couldn't have been shown Fats Domino's "Blueberry Hill," Little Richard's "Good Golly Miss Molly," or Jerry Lee Lewis's "Great Balls of Fire." Now that would be an education with a capital "E."

Though she never had a lesson in her life, my grandmother was a natural musician and could play any tune on her concertina. I was lucky enough to hear her play many times when I was a kid on my summer holidays in Ireland. Dad was a car mechanic, and Mum worked full time in the glove department of Derry and Toms on Kensington High Street, which meant that when the summertime came my elder brother, Mike, and I would be at home getting into trouble. So from an early age we were split up for the holidays. He was put on a train to South Wales to spend the summer with Mum's friends, Gwennie and Ivor in Llanbradach, and I was taken "home" to Ireland by any one of several aunties and in September brought back by another.

These were idyllic days of seemingly endless sunshine, and because of that I now realize I saw only the best of the country, since the winters could be very harsh. Gran had twelve children in the little house on Main Street, Mountrath. Eleven survived, the third eldest being Susan, my mum. All but two of the children crossed the Irish Sea to England to find work. Willie managed to move eight miles away to Portlaois, but Ned missed his chance altogether and was forced to stay at home and look after Gran. He was a vital part of my wonderful summers.

Ned was a farm worker without a farm of his own. When he was helping a neighbour bring in the hay he'd be up at the crack of dawn, and if I was awake in time, which was not as often as I would have liked, I'd go with him on the "bogey," a flat, square, wooden, horse-drawn cart, built for carrying whole haystacks. I'd play with the other kids while he attached the chains around the haystack and then jacked them up, which pulled the stack onto the bogey while we watched, thrilled. Then, we could climb up on the top, ready for the ride home, a piece of straw in our teeth, kings of the castle and as happy as lambs.

Sometimes, I'd oversleep and wake up to the clattering of cart wheels on the cobblestones outside in the yard. I'd run across to the little window set deep in the thick, stone walls only to see Ned, the horse and cart, and Vera, his greyhound, turning into the street from the yard below me and disappear out of sight on a radiant sunny morning. I wouldn't see him again until supper-time, and I'd feel lost and lonely for a few minutes, not knowing what to do with myself. This mood never lasted long because there were a thousand things to do and all the time in the world to do them.

The cobblestone yard went from the front gate on Main Street down the length of the house. It went past the open barn on the right side, the horse stable, the cow shed, with chickens and chicken shit everywhere you stepped, to the high wire-mesh fence surrounding the cabbage patch, built in a vain attempt to prevent the turkeys getting at them. There was a stone wall the length of the yard on the left all the way to the back with every conceivable bit of rusted old iron, including tools, horseshoes, buckets, tractor seats, and cans of nails.

Further down the yard there was a dung heap where the pigs would toss me when I tried to ride them, and a good hundred yards down, at the back, was the pigsty and the chicken house. Next to the chicken house was a door in the high stone wall leading to the stream, which ran along the other side of a path. There were stepping-stones across the stream and the hurling field on the other side where Gran would sometimes take me to pick mushrooms for breakfast. I was never bored.

Sometimes, when he went to cut the turf from the bog, Ned would take me with him on his bike, his shovel tied underneath the crossbar and a sack wrapped around it for my comfort. The smaller of the dogs was in the basket on the handlebars, and Vera trotted behind us effortlessly.

He'd take a kettle with some water in it, a bottle of milk plugged with a cork, sugar, tea, tin mugs, and a sandwich or two, all stuffed in an old potato sack which he'd have slung over his shoulder. The crossbar was uncomfortable and the road was bumpy, but I wouldn't miss going to the bog for anything. The bog was a strange place. It was totally wild, windy, and wet, covered in heather and you'd have to watch where you put your foot, because it was quite spongy to walk on. I slipped into a muddy puddle up to my knee once and had a very wet Wellington boot all day as a result. There were frogs which I'd try and catch, but they'd hop into the deep bog water to avoid me, and Ned warned me to stay well away from the edge of the bog because it was deep and murky and you'd never get back out if you ever fell in. He must have painted a sinister picture because I believed it to be bottomless.

Whether he said it or not, I kept well away. While I was chasing frogs or just wandering about, he'd be cutting the turf into rectangular shapes with the long, narrow shovel he'd brought, stacking the sopping wet, heavy chunks of peat into small piles along the ridge for them to dry. This was backbreaking work, but he was well used to it. He was a hard worker and a popular man around town. Ned would take me threshing now and then. The neighbouring farmers would take turns helping each other bringing in the hay and threshing it, whatever that was. For the men it meant a very hard morning's work interrupted by a good lunch, followed by a long afternoon and a hearty meal and a booze-up, the crates of bottled Guinness sitting in the shade in the house while they sweated in the sun. But for us kids it was play all day in the hay and unlimited crisps and Corcoran's lemonade. It was quite a social gathering for everyone, and I bet that beer never tasted better. Ned was a drinker, but he didn't drink well. He'd drink until he was unconscious. Gran was always stopping passers-by and giving them orders from the street door.

"Go across there now, and tell Ned Young to come home this minute."

He was a grown man, but she wouldn't let him be. I was sent to search for him sometimes in the evenings, and it could take a while. There were thirteen bars in Mountrath's Main Street and he could be in any one of them. He was a happy drunk, never mean spirited, and once I found him, he'd welcome me with a smile and try and buy me off with crisps and lemonade. I'd sit quietly out on the kerb, munching and drinking, but all the time I knew Gran would still be waiting for us with the street door open.

"Sure, I'm coming, I'm coming. Can't she leave me alone at all?" he'd grumble. One evening, I went to several bars before somebody said he was there. I went into a tiny back room and he was out cold on the floor, drunk as he could be and singing to himself. There were a couple of other drunkards making fun of him and I burst into tears, not knowing what was happening. To see him out of control made me feel I was lost too. I couldn't understand how Ned could be this way, although he was just drunk.

Maybe he drank to forget what he thought was a hopeless existence. The fact is, he had no future. He was a very shy man, he'd never marry, and anyway, he couldn't leave Gran. It was all he could do to leave the house and drink his sorrows away. I remember him being teased about some woman who lived over somewhere beyond the bog, as if there was some danger of him ever getting married and moving away. But was not to be.

Occasionally, there'd be a gathering at the house. It didn't happen often, but when it did, all hell broke loose. If Gran thought the company was grand enough, it would be held in the sitting room at the front of the house. It was the only room downstairs with a carpet covering the painted concrete floor and had fine mahogany tables and chairs. It was for "best" only and the fire wasn't lit unless there were guests. She'd play the concertina at the drop of a hat for any audience, which was why she was so popular, and she could play any tune from memory.

More often than not, the party was held in the kitchen, which was bigger anyway, and as the large fire burned all day, it was a very cosy room. One night a crowd gathered and a man with a lovely voice sang a verse of a song about Ned. Of course, he must have made it up as he went along, but I was impressed at how famous Ned was, not surprised, but impressed. Then Ned sang "The Wild Colonial Boy" in his reedy, thin voice and an old codger came in late from the pub and pulled a dozen pint bottles of Guinness stout out of secret pockets in his poacher's overcoat, to shouts and cheers. It was sheer magic and the music was all around me, and yet my ears weren't fully open.

rate English actors doing bad American accents, didn't stop me and my brother from cringing with embarrassment. Whenever a rotten British film came on, we dreaded it.

Of course, there were some great films made in England and he liked some of them. *Genevieve* was a jolly romp in the sunshine, but the first one that made the most impression on me was *The Blue Lagoon*. I was only about four or five at the time, but I remember the awful loneliness I felt when the ship went down and the children's parents drowned. Come to think about it, that's a horrible start to any picture.

Dad would have enjoyed living in the States. And Texas would have suited him because of the space and the friendly people. He was a dreamer and he would have loved life in America. My romance with the United States began with the films he took us to see on Friday nights–those American "flicks" and the rock 'n' roll and blues records I heard on the BBC and Radio Luxembourg.

After leaving catalogues out in my room, dropping hints, and whining for the best part of a year, I was given a guitar for Christmas. I knew I was going to get it for about a week because that package hidden in Mum's wardrobe was guitar-shaped after all! It was a Spanish guitar, and unfortunately the novelty wore off quite soon when I realized I had to tune it and learn how to play it and I don't think I ever got it in tune once. I went back to roller-skating, though I still liked to sing Johnny Duncan's "Last Train to San Fernando" with that catchy chorus: "If you miss this one, you'll never get another one–iddy-biddy-bum-bum–to San Fernando."

Who could resist saying "bum" twice in every chorus? Certainly not me.

I was a cheeky little sod at school, and it got me into trouble more than once. In my second year at Spring Grove Grammar School, when I was eleven or twelve years old, Mr. Reynolds, the biology teacher, gave me four black stars for handing in rotten homework or something equally stupid. I was always getting into trouble for the silliest things. My mind wasn't running on a track, it was constantly derailing. Now, normally, you'd be given one black star for being naughty and if you managed to be so bad as to get four in any one term then you'd get a detention as well, which meant you'd be kept in for an hour after school that day.

Unfortunately, I'd already got a detention from another teacher that day, so when Mr. Reynolds gave me four more black stars, I knew I'd be imprisoned for the next two evenings, and I wasn't thrilled about that. We called him "Josh" behind his back, after Sir Joshua Reynolds, the famous painter, and I was so pissed off at him I chalked JOSH IS A SOD on a blackboard on the wall in the changing rooms. The other kids laughed, and I thought nothing more of it until the next day, when the senior master, Mr. Lyneham, dismissed all but four forms at the end of morning assembly.

When the others had gone he called for whoever had chalked a message on the blackboard the previous afternoon to come forward and receive the cane. He knew it had to be one of us, as we were the only kids in there that day. Receive the cane? Feel the pain, more like. There was silence in the school hall and I looked around nervously to see if anyone was going to tell on me, but no one did. I couldn't admit guilt there and then, surely, I thought, there had to be some way out. After a short silence he said that if the culprit didn't go to the headmaster's study by the end of the school day, all four forms would have to stay in detention that evening. When I'd left home the previous morning I had no idea I was going to get four black stars, two detentions, and the cane, in just over twenty-four hours! I drifted to the classroom in a daze. I was a wanted man and was about to feel the cane for the first time. I had no choice; I had to own up before somebody snitched on me, but I got through the morning and most of lunchtime before I plucked up the courage.

The school was originally built as the home of Sir Joseph Banks, the famous botanist who sailed with Captain Cook and brought back many rare plants from all over the world. It was a grand old building set in acres of grounds with tall cedars, a fountain, and two massive domed greenhouses behind the main building, that housed the art room and the biology laboratory. The headmaster's study was at the foot of the main staircase in the panelled entrance hall, so I'd been past his door many times but had never been inside.

Terrified, I knocked on the imposing oak door. L.T. Brown, the headmaster, opened it and before he could say anything, tears streaming down my cheeks, I blurted it all out, "It was me, sir. I'm the one who wrote on the changing room wall. Sorry, sir."

He was an inscrutable old character, almost bald with a big, kind face. He took his glasses off, looked down at me for a second, and said quietly, "Will you come in for a minute and have some tea?"

"Thank you, sir, yes," I sniffled.

He must've thought I'd suffered enough. He handed me his handkerchief and offered me a seat by the fire, and sent his secretary off to make tea, closing the door behind her. He sat down in the armchair across from me and asked me if I understood the meaning of the word I'd used. I told him I didn't, and he said he thought as much. He explained that it was a shortened version of sodomite, and that for me to accuse Mr. Reynolds of buggery was a serious matter. I told him I was angry at him for giving me the four black stars, and I lost control. What a gentleman he was. He didn't cane me, he didn't even scold me, he just talked and reasoned with me and made me understand why it was wrong. Of course, I had to promise to apologize to Mr. Reynolds, but other than that there was no punishment given at all, and I had tea and biscuits with the headmaster as well.

Things didn't get much better, though. I eventually broke the school record for getting the most black stars in one term, twelve, and managed to be absent for fifty-three days. It was the only thing I excelled at in those dark days.

Lonnie Donegan and skiffle were all the rage in England between 1956 and 1957. Lonnie played guitar and banjo in Ken Colyer's Jazzmen and then Chris Barber's Jazz Band, which were Dixieland outfits, and his hit records, like skiffle itself, seem to have happened by accident. A few years later, another guitarist in Chris Barber's band, Alexis Korner, almost single-handedly spawned the British blues boom when he formed Blues Incorporated with Cyril Davies as an offshoot of that band, which makes Barber the John Mayall of his day, or the other way around.

Skiffle sounded so simple that anybody could do it and kids all over England were strumming guitars, scrubbing washboards with thimbles, and making tea-chest basses. Passed on from tea importers for use as cheap packing cases, they now played a key role in the biggest homegrown musical craze of the decade. You would turn the plywood box upside down, nail a broom handle to one side, stretch a piece of string from the end of the handle to the other side of the box, and away you'd go.

Not wanting to be left out, Alan Worrell, Terry Munro, and I formed a group of our own. We had the flat caps as a uniform already, so we called ourselves The Blue Men—a fabulous name, I think you'll agree. We were all replaceable except Terry, who could play a bit of guitar. Alan scratched away at the washboard because he had good rhythm and I played tea-chest bass because that's all that was left. I painted it blue with our group name in large white capital letters.

We weren't good, but we were available, and we actually played at some function at school once, thumping away like good'uns:

"It takes a worried man to sing a worried song. It takes a worried man to sing a worried song. It takes a worried man to sing a worried song. I'm worried now but I won't be worried long."

This was Lonnie's anthem, sung at breakneck speed. It was kind of "speedfolk" not rock 'n' roll at all, but it was fun if nothing else and it started countless young musicians on the path to fame, fortune, and early retirement.

Although I could tune a radio, I still couldn't tune my guitar, which had been gathering dust in the wardrobe. But I was determined to have another go, because Terry, who was getting comfortable on the guitar by then, taught me the E, A, and elusive B7 chords. He showed me G, C, and D7 too and pretty soon I could hit them, as long as I had a couple of seconds to get my fingers in place. I was learning what anybody who's ever picked up a guitar will tell you, it's not what you know, it's if you can play it!

Alan and Terry had a pal, Johnny Eaton, who had a good voice and played a bit of guitar too. The first tune that I ever played with Terry and

only five people turned up anyway, and they sat against the back wall stone-faced, waiting for us to start. It was a total bring-down. We could tell they didn't think much of us, because in the middle of "Hoochie Coochie Man" one of them threw a chair at the stage. It was such a shock, and though it wasn't meant to do any harm, the mood was broken. Nick shot me a startled eyebrow above his hands, as he wailed on the harp, but there was nothing we could do but carry on and ignore the muttering from the back of the room. It wouldn't have been so bad, but we outnumbered them, and of course we didn't get paid or get the residency.

Soon after that we tried for another residency, this time at a pub on the corner of King Street in Twickenham, just a hundred yards from the foot-bridge leading to Eel Pie Island. One of the other bands up for the gig was The Detours. They were basically The Who before Keith joined them, but they were still awesome. Pete hadn't started using feedback yet, but he used a very exaggerated tremolo effect I'd never heard before that was the sound equivalent of a strobe light, and it floored me. Going on after them was a mistake for us because they were so dynamic and we were more laid back and, sure enough, they got the gig. But Pete told me later that the gig only lasted for one night, presumably because it was so close to the Island, which was such a happening place.

Blistering Sunday nights at the Station Hotel or Eel Pie Island begat sluggish Monday mornings on the bouncy 73 bus route through Whitton, and I was meant to be at college by 9:30 A.M. Occasionally I'd turn up a little late and if I got there half an hour or so late, well, what could I do? I couldn't breeze in late every morning of my life, could I? I owed it to myself to take the morning off, regroup, have a spot of lunch, and go in revitalized.

So, I'd stay on the bus until the next stop, cross the bridge at Twickenham Station, hop down the steps by the railway and into the Rugby Tavern, a very welcoming establishment that like a lot of old pubs has since been demolished. It was the sort of place where for something like sixpence you could get a half-pint of rough cider and no questions asked about your age. Ah, I can smell those beery floorboards now!

Other mornings, I'd go farther along the train tracks to The Albany, a grander pub altogether, where I might run into Martin Brock, another student on the lam who got himself a full-time, early morning milkman's job with every intention of going into classes afterwards. Of course, he was much too tired by the time the bus passed the college. Once I saw him fast asleep on a bench by the river across from Eel Pie Island. We'd have a drink, and then the amateur drinkers from college would arrive at lunchtime, so we'd have another couple, and by the time the pub shut its doors at 3 P.M. we weren't good for anything but getting the bus home.

The Beatles' "Love Me Do" had just come out, and the first time I heard it was in the corridor by the main hall. Some girls had set up a record player at lunchtime and they played it to death. Hearing a harp on an English pop record for the first time knocked me out, and I was an instant fan. But after the press had gone on and on about them, I wondered why they didn't blaze the name of The Rolling Stones across their pages. I was jealous for my band.

One morning, in the *Daily Mirror,* there was a photograph spread across the middle pages that made it look as if The Beatles were wearing lipstick! That was it. I'd had enough, and that's what gave me the idea for a spiffing wheeze and I thought up the slogan "Exit Beatle." Yeah, that would show them!

With the help of Dave Pether, Nick Tweddell, Pete Brown, and Martin Brock, we printed posters with the slogan underneath the photograph, and exaggerated the lipstick with bright red paint. We wanted everybody to get the message, but as we'd never be allowed to stick them up, we decided on a terrorist-style attack. As the Students' Union Official Party Boy, I had an office, so we locked ourselves in with a case of beer, sandwiches, buckets of paste, brushes, a pile of posters, and a ladder. All we had to do was to make ourselves comfortable, pass around the beer and sandwiches, and wait quietly for the caretaker to do his rounds, and then we'd have the whole college to ourselves.

What a laugh. The magic part of it for me was that everybody would see the posters. They couldn't avoid them, because we plastered them everywhere. We stuck the largest poster on the ceiling above the lockers and the art department noticeboard. When the caretaker opened up the school in the morning he was really pissed off, because it made him look stupid, but as we'd used flour and water paste there was no damage to the walls. But, to make us look bad, he unstuck one and Sellotaped it to an expensive art poster. The bastard! He also ripped down as many as he could, but we had had the advantage of time and numbers.

Although our mates were impressed, it backfired when Osmund Caine, the senior lecturer, summoned me to his office first thing that morning. It must've been a bit of a giveaway me being at college that early. I explained that we hadn't used any Sellotape, and promised to take them down straight away, but by then they must have been seen by most of the students, so we had a partial success.

To be honest, I was bored with classes by then, and fell into another decline. Just like school, I was now playing hookey most of the time. It was all too easy, but that was about to change. The end of the summer term was coming, and at the end of every term we got our beer money! Every Monday, we'd travel by bus to the Victoria and Albert Museum or the Natural History Museum to draw, then we'd bus it back to the college, paying the fare out of our own pockets. On the morning of the last day of term we'd line up and get our "disbursement money" for the bus fares we'd paid out. Of course, I didn't get as much as the rest of the students because I hadn't been there quite as often, but still, it was enough to get well and truly plastered.

The last day was always very relaxed, there were no classes, we'd go to the pub at lunchtime, and then we'd watch a film in the lecture theatre and go home for the holidays. They'd lined up *Jour De Fête* by Jacques Tati this particular day, and I was looking forward to it. Unfortunately, it all turned to rat!

I got very pissed at The Albany, wobbled back to the college, went for a pee, decided to light a Woodbine, dropped the packet in the urinal, and pissed all over my cigarettes. Naturally, I fished them out and placed them on the radiator to dry. What a sensible chap! Having had a pee, I was ready to see the film, so I weaved my way along the corridor to the lecture theatre. Osmund Caine's leg was stretched across the doorway when I got there.

"Go home boy!" That was all he had to say. I was speechless. Actually, I was legless, and in no state to argue with his clever use of the English language. I went home, though how I got there I'll never know. Caine was a tall, bald, bearded old coot, and not a favourite with any of the students I knew. We used to be interviewed by him at the end of each term and most of us dreaded it. He'd sit you in a low chair in front of his desk, while he sat looking down on you, silhouetted against the window behind him. It was obviously arranged to make you feel small, which in my case took no effort at all. My interview usually involved him complaining about my absences or my lack of interest, but I wasn't interested.

His wife also taught at the college but she could hardly have been less like him. She was a very warm and compassionate woman, an innovative teacher with an open attitude to everything art could be, who would let a class develop and allow you to discover things for yourself. Unfortunately, I didn't pay much attention to her either. One day she came up to me and without any malice whatever, said, "You know, Mac, one day you'll find out what it is that you want to do and you'll do well at it, but until then you're just wasting your time." She was right, and she was a great teacher. I was just pissing it away, and after that incident at the end of term I was thrown out.

However, my lovely mum, feeling I'd been treated unfairly, took the case to Caine's superior, the college principal, who granted me a reprieve of sorts. If I excelled in my summer work–and there was a lot of it to do–I'd be allowed back in for another year. But I got myself a summer job packing electrical switches at a factory in Southall, and it became all too easy to put off doing my homework until the last two days before I went back. I shouldn't have left it so late, because all my interest had shifted to the band, which was starting to happen. Anyhow, I really applied myself and worked and worked for two whole days making up for the weekends that I'd wasted. The last night I bought six bottles of Watney's Red Barrel. It was horrible beer, but it was all that was left in the off-licence, and I ploughed through until four in the morning, falling asleep flat-out on the bedroom floor. When I got up, I ached and had a rotten hangover. But it was finished, and it was good!

For the second time in a year I got to college on time and eagerly awaited the "criticism" which took place in Mr. Shields' large studio. All the students' work was on display on one wall, and chairs and benches were arranged along the opposite wall, so that everyone could see and hear the comments. The lecturers took turns discussing the work they had set for us and I was singled out for good work in two categories and the others got decent mentions too. Hoo-fucking-ray!

The hard work of the last two days had actually paid off. It was a relief and a triumph for me. I lined up at the disbursement office to collect my £120 grant and then I cleared out my locker. Then I went to the bank and cashed the cheque. It was the first day of term, but I'd left art school to become a professional musician at the same time or, to put it another way, become unemployed.

CHAPTER FOUR

Muleskinner Blues

I had more front than Jayne Mansfield back in 1964, and no shame whatso-
ever. I'd go up to The Stones' manager Eric Easton's office, just off Regent
Street, as often as possible and lig about hoping something would turn up for
The Muleskinners. Andrew Loog Oldham, as co-manager, also had an office
there, but he and Eric were too big-time to deal with us themselves, so Eric
put Bob Knight on our case. Bob was more than helpful and a very nice man.
He not only got us a gig backing Julie Grant, a pop singer who covered
American hits of the day, but also set up a deal with Vox and took us down
to the Jennings Musical Industries (JMI) factory in Dartford, Kent. He got us
kitted out with AC 30 amplifiers, a bass amp, a small P.A. system, and some
Reslo microphones and stands, and all for nothing. It was incredible. But best
of all, he booked us to open for The Rolling Stones on their first U.K. tour
since their trip to America, and for decent money. I remember being in total
awe as Stu drove their lipstick-covered van up to the backstage door, girls
screaming and running after it down the alley, as he screeched to a stop.
"Bloody girls," Stu would mutter unmoved, as he opened the back doors that
were thick with warpaint to unload the equipment.

We wouldn't have minded being chased by a gang of girls, though The
Stones had probably had enough of it by then. Backstage, Mick and Brian were
friendly and outgoing. Brian came to our dressing room and offered round cigarettes. It meant a lot to a band like ours to feel we were on the same path,
whether we were or not, and wherever it was leading.

Johnny Eaton had left the band to pursue a serious singing career on the
stage, so I was left to handle the vocals, which is quite embarrassing to think
about now, especially as I was even shaking a pair of maracas like Mick. I
put it down to a lack of a proper lead vocalist, too much youthful exuber-
ance, and too many purple hearts.

Oddly enough, our first recorded attempts were made around this time in
a basement studio at Southern Music on Denmark Street with me singing. As

The Stones had worked their magic on Buddy Holly's "Not Fade Away," we recorded Buddy's "Love's Made a Fool of You" with a young Glyn Johns engineering, hoping for similar success. But listening back, it was obvious we needed a real vocalist. So, after holding auditions, we took on Terry Brennan, a soulful singer from Wimbledon who'd been in The Roosters with Eric Clapton and Tom McGuinness before they joined The Yardbirds and Manfred Mann respectively. He had an incredible collection of blues, R&B, and soul records and kept a tiny photograph of Etta James wearing a blonde wig in his wallet. This geezer was serious. Soon after, we recorded with Terry, and Fontana Records liked it enough to put out our first and only single, our version of Willie Dixon's "Back Door Man," made famous by the great Howlin' Wolf.

Terry and a couple of us went to see The Yardbirds at the new Crawdaddy Club, which had moved down the street from the Station Hotel, where The Stones had held court. I didn't like the building. It was an athletic ground's premises and it had no character. The audience was younger, what we called "pseudos" or weekend ravers. Keith Relf's voice left me cold. But if that wasn't bad enough, when he wasn't singing, he was thumping on a set of congas. Their main claim to fame, and the reason we went, was to meet and hear Eric Clapton. What a fabulous player. He played long, brilliant guitar solos that soared. Plus, he looked great. He was a sharply dressed Mod–the real dog's bollocks!

Thanks to the constant barrage of phone calls to agents and bookers, we got to play at the Marquee Club on Wardour Street, Soho, quite a few times, opening for Graham Bond or Gary Farr and the T-Bones or, more usually, Jimmy James and The Vagabonds, whose bass player Phil Chen is still my old mate. The Jamaican Chinaman or Chinese Jamaican, whichever way you look at him, never seems to get any older, or like me, any taller. Years later he toured with Rod Stewart and in 1979 joined The New Barbarians for our final gig at Knebworth in England.

The scene was opening up all the time, and I'd scour the club ads in the back pages of the *Melody Maker,* hustling for an opening slot, which is how we opened for John Mayall at Klooks Kleek in Hampstead, and for the American all-girl band, Goldie and the Gingerbreads, at the Fishmonger's Arms in Wood Green. Although they were seen as a novelty and only had one hit in the U.K., "Can't You Hear My Heartbeat," they were a really good band, and Margo Lewis played the Hammond B3 organ like she was on fire. By now, I'd dropped the Hohner Cembalet and was using my Hammond L100. But apart from changing our sound for the better, the only drawback was humping the organ and the Leslie cabinet into clubs.

The Leslie wasn't made to be transported, and I realized soon enough that there would always be a problem finding band members before a gig to help me lift the organ. My fingers would be cramped in an arthritic state, because you could only pick it up by its thin wooden case. On the good side, now I had "the sound" and it was loud, although still not quite as loud as Dave's guitar. We got our own night at the Golders Green Refectory, but we didn't do very well and, finally, we got our own residency every Friday night at a club in Eastleigh, near Southampton, seventy miles from London on the south coast. I'd hire a van and driver to take us there. We'd set up, have a bite to eat, and then play to a younger crowd than we were used to. They weren't a hip crowd at all, and they were slightly indifferent at first, but they got into it as the weeks went by, and we started to make a little money.

As I was booking the gigs, I was in charge of the cash flow, which was more of a trickle then, so every penny counted. Van rental, petrol, and—as none of us drove—the driver's bunce, all had to come off the top before we got any cash. We were getting fifteen pounds a night at most of the places, sometimes only twelve pounds ten, so we were barely scratching by. But thanks to Alan, a friendly guy who had a Thames van and liked the look of the girls who came to see us, most weeks we had a little more in our bins than we should've done.

The point when I really felt we were a pro band came when Marquee Artists, who were the agents for the Marquee Club, booked us to back Howlin' Wolf in Sheffield on a Sunday night. For a start, just travelling all the way to Sheffield felt professional. The farthest we'd gone until then was the hundred miles or so to Birmingham University, so this was almost like being on tour. It was also a thrill to play with the legendary Howlin' Wolf, and his equally legendary guitarist, Hubert Sumlin.

It was our first time in Sheffield and it had snowed that day. The snow had turned into slush and was starting to freeze again as night fell. We hadn't planned on bad weather, so we were only wearing jackets and the grim industrial part of town was very depressing. Even more depressing was the poster outside the Mojo Club, where we were supposed to be playing:

Tonight THE PRETTY THINGS

Next Sunday HOWLIN' WOLF

What a royal fuck-up! Of course, the agency would hear all about it on Monday morning, but we'd run out of cash on the way up, and I'd been counting on paying for the petrol for the journey back out of the night's earnings. Now we were fucked! The people in the club weren't very helpful, though it wasn't their mistake, but we were so disappointed not to get to play with The Wolf. Luckily, one of the band had a borrowed AA card, which meant we could get petrol, but we had to run out before they'd let us have any.

We ran out twice and had to walk miles each time to get to a phone. They say it's tough at the top, well, it's rough on the side of the road.

We got another chance to play with The Wolf later though, when Marquee Artists brought him, Sonny Boy Williamson, and Little Walter over from the States. As a rule, The Yardbirds backed Sonny Boy, and if they weren't available, The Authentics got the job. This pecking order for backing blues legends ended when it eventually reached The Muleskinners. We didn't mind. We were more than honoured to get to play with such fabulous players. Let's face it, we had a lot to learn and who better to learn it from than the greats?

The second time we were booked to back The Wolf was at the Ricky Tick Club, Reading, and we were due to rehearse with him and Hubert Sumlin on the afternoon of the show. All Wolf's photographs showed him looking very stern, so we set up early, worked over a few of his numbers, and waited nervously for him to arrive.

He was a huge man, and when he came through the door wearing a large tweed overcoat down to his ankles, he seemed to block out the light. There he was, the legend, all the way from Chicago. Hubert was behind him, smiling.

"Hi boys!" The Wolf's unmistakable voice boomed at us from the other end of the empty hall. We introduced ourselves, and I think he could see we were nervous and in awe of him. But he relaxed us immediately, leaning down, putting his enormous arms around all of us, and announcing with a big hug and gold-toothed smile, "My boys."

And we were his boys all right. We would've done anything for him at that point. Hubert, who looked like he could've done with some of The Wolf's teeth, was introduced to us, and a lovely man he was too. They'd just arrived from Berlin, and he told us how odd he thought the people were there. "They speak funny," he said, "and when I spoke to them, they couldn't understand me!" He was astounded at this. He might not have seen the language barrier coming up, but when he plugged in his brand-new, cheapo Italian guitar, he spoke pure Esperanto to us. The amazing thing was it sounded just like his records. It didn't sound at all like a tacky plastic guitar. That night The Wolf was a blinder to play with. He was menacing on stage. He'd lean out over the audience and howl, and to play "Smokestack Lightnin'" with him was such a thrill. He roared when he sang, like no one else, but he could sing sweet too and played a mean harp. What a night! It was a wonderful gig, and we talked about nothing else all the way home in the van.

We also played a double with them at the Chelmsford Corn Exchange and the Club Noreik, in Tottenham, north London. It wasn't unusual to play two shows in one night then, considering that the audience were high as kites anyway, pills being all the rage. The Club Noreik, being an all-nighter, was an easy place to get uppers, or leapers, as we knew them, and we became very partial to them, especially when we had more than one show to do. We'd score some French Blues or Purple Hearts, and stay up all night, no problem. It was a cheap drug you could get easily, but it had one big drawback. When they wore off, they'd give you a comedown. You'd feel terrible and nauseous and the only way to counter that was to take more pills. Clever how it works, isn't it?

After the Chelmsford gig, in December 1964, The Wolf invited Nick and me to join him in his car on the drive back to London, but the shine was taken off the experience when he picked up the *Evening News* that night in December 1964 and read that Sam Cooke had been shot and killed in Los Angeles. The Wolf had known him well; they'd served in the military together, he told us, and the big man was obviously shaken up by his untimely death.

It was a fantastic experience to have played with those guys, and Pete, Nick, Dave, and I went out to Heathrow Airport to see them off. They were both pleased to see us again, and I asked The Wolf if he'd sign my copy of his *Moanin' in the Moonlight* album. He and Hubert both signed it, then The Wolf handed me a $100 bill—the first I'd ever seen—and asked me to get him a bottle of Jack Daniels. But as there was nowhere to buy American whiskey at the airport, I gave it back and after one more big hug from the big man, off they went. It's incredible that we were the only people who bothered to go to the airport to say goodbye to them.

I don't know where my autographed album went, but I managed to keep hold of a Muleskinners' business card they signed. Hubert even wrote to us a few months later keeping us up-to-date with news of their gigs and recording plans. Little Walter was a different kettle of fish. Although he was a fabulous harmonica player, you'd never confuse him with Mister Warmth. It was another Ricky Tick Club gig—in Guildford this time. It was a beautiful, sunny Sunday afternoon as we waited anxiously on the street for him to arrive. We'd set up our gear but were nervous about meeting the man, not least because we hadn't rehearsed with him at all. It wasn't going to be easy. We knew a few of his tunes, like "My Babe" and "Key to the Highway," but there wasn't a soul out there on the wide streets of Guildford, let alone a blues fan.

I said to the guys, "I wonder who thought this little lot up?"

It was unusual to play on a Sunday afternoon, and it felt like we were at the wrong place on the wrong day. Was this going to be another Sheffield? Eventually, a grey Ford Cortina with a kid who looked even younger than us at the wheel pulled up, and I saw Little Walter Jacobs in the shadows of the back seat, apparently asleep. When he stepped out into the bright sunlight of middle-class England, he was clutching a pint bottle of whiskey, his bug-eyes not yet fully open. Although he didn't look drunk, he wasn't in a great mood either, but then he had just woken up.

The kid introduced us. Walter mumbled something and walked out of the daylight into the hall and the gloom of the dressing room, where he slumped down on the sofa, evidently looking to catch up on his sleep and leaving us feeling a bit unnecessary, to say the least. We did the verbal equivalent of twiddling our thumbs, talking amongst ourselves, while we waited to see what was what.

"Hey Walter, d'ya wanna rehearse with the band?" The kid asked a little too helpfully. I would've let him sleep.

"Plenty of time. Let me sleep, okay?"

"There isn't much time, actually. You go on in about an hour and a half. The band needs to rehearse."

"Okay then, let's get to work." He turned his attention to us. "D'you know any of my tunes?"

I told him we knew "My Babe" and mentioned "Boom, Boom, Out Go the Lights."

"Okay, how 'bout 'Juke'?"

We'd heard it, didn't know it, but said we did. Rule one: never let on you don't know the tune. He took a harp from his jacket pocket, brought it up to his mouth and started to play "Key to the Highway" right there and then. It was great. Just to hear his unmistakable sound that close was something I'll never forget. Dave, who'd brought his guitar in, picked out a rhythm part unamplified and Walter turned mere sound into beauty with his soulful wailing. The rest of us were all smiles, grinning at each other in case we were dreaming. This was as good as it got for five white boys on a Sunday afternoon in Guildford, Surrey. But the kid was about to bring us back to earth with a bump.

"Pretend you're a slave on a chain gang," he suggested.

Walter stopped playing abruptly as he pulled the harp away from his mouth, glared coldly, and pointed a long-nailed finger at the kid.

"Wha'd'you say?" Little Walter was wide awake now. "What the fuck do these kids know, or ever have to know about a fuckin' *chain gang*, you motherfucker? They're from England, you asshole! Get the fuck outta here!"

This was just the start. He tore into the kid, telling him to mind his own business, just drive the car, and leave the band and the music to him. Then he told him to get in the car and stay there until he needed him. Oh boy, we were glad to have that moment pass, but the mood passed too.

The gig was a bit of a shambles. He'd had a few and we hadn't. Maybe we should have. But it wasn't just the bad taste left from the scene in the dressing room; the lack of rehearsal, our inexperience, and the fact that Walter had changed the keys of some of the numbers guaranteed it wouldn't have been great. Guildford was hardly the home of the blues, and even the twenty or thirty youngsters who came to this echoing hall didn't know what they were missing. The crowd, if you can call them that, didn't come down to the stage. They stood at the back and the sides of the hall as if they were hiding. It was a bloody shame that this incredibly talented bluesman had come all the way from Chicago to play to such a disinterested audience. I was and still am a big fan of Little Walter and it should've been so much better. It didn't stop him signing a card, "To my pal from Little Walter," which I treasure to this day.

We got to play with Sonny Boy Williamson twice. The Yardbirds, who normally backed him, were too busy with their own career by then, and The Authentics were presumably backing someone else. The first time was on December 28, 1964, at the Basingstoke Town Hall. Sonny Boy was a feisty old character, very dapper in a two-tone City suit with a bowler hat tilted at a jaunty angle. He wore a goatee beard, and there was the sweet smell of Johnnie Walker on his breath. He walked into the dressing room carrying the leather briefcase full of harps and his whiskey bottle and started playing immediately. We went through "Don't Start Me to Talking" and "Fattening Frogs for Snakes," and I was knocked out when I realized he was going to do "Help Me," because it was basically "Green Onions" with him on top. Then he just started making them up. He was on good form and ready to go. Before we left the dressing room, something he said made us all laugh, but he misunderstood our laughter and got the needle as if he thought we were taking the piss out of him. Turning on us, he snapped, "I taught John Lee Hooker how to play the guitar," as if that would impress us, then walked off. Now John Lee Hooker is one of the blues greats, but he's no guitar virtuoso, so I couldn't help thinking that wasn't something you'd boast about—like you wouldn't boast about being Sonny Boy's dentist. But his bad mood passed and he gave a blinding show.

We did another date with him at the Riverside Club in the Cricketers Hotel, a pub by the Thames in Sunbury. It was a beautiful night, the stars were out, but sadly, so was the piano. And although Sonny Boy was in tune, he kept changing the length of every twelve-bar section, which confused the hell out of Mick Carpenter. He had one number that was a basic twelve-bar measure but every time round he'd sing it slightly differently. It wasn't a problem for me, but Mick couldn't latch on to what was going on so easily because, being at the back behind the drums, he couldn't hear him as well as us. Sonny Boy sang thirteen bars, he sang eleven; one time he carried on for fourteen bars before he came back around. It was a fiasco. In another song he got lost and ended it very abruptly. But the show went down well because he'd make songs up as he went along, like a true folk poet. He could do anything with a harp too.

He'd walk around the stage with it sticking out of his mouth, playing it endwise without using his hands. The audience always got their money's worth with Sonny Boy, and he had more of a following in the U.K. than in the States. He toured for several weeks on the Ricky Tick circuit and made a lot of friends, even recording live albums with both The Yardbirds and The Animals.

Nick Tweddell, our harp player, was in seventh heaven, having jammed with Howlin' Wolf, Little Walter, and Sonny Boy Williamson, each one a distinctly different stylist, and all in the space of a few short months. It would be something to tell his children and grandchildren in years to come. We saw John Lee Hooker put on a great show at the Ricky Tick in Reading, and afterwards I asked him for his autograph, which he graciously gave me. I handed him the only scrap of paper I had on me, which was a reminder from the finance company that my electric piano payment was overdue. It took him ages to sign it, because his handwriting was so shaky, and I watched fascinated, as he laboriously drew the "H," formed the two "o"s and then the "k" and the "e." Then he must've had enough, because he didn't bother with the "r." He added his initials underneath and handed it back to me without a word.

Talking about those days with Nick recently, he said: "It's hard to believe it ever really happened." And he's right. For white boys in West London to even find those blues recordings back then was difficult enough, but to get the opportunity to actually play with the legends themselves was beyond our wildest expectations.

Dave, Nick, Pete, me, and a few others were at an all-night party, after which we all went camping in the New Forest for a couple of days. Riding back to London on his scooter, Dave was hit by a car. His leg was broken in several places and he was hospitalized for several weeks. We had to get other guitarists to replace him until he was fit to play again, but it wasn't the same without him, and that's when I started to lose interest in the band.

CHAPTER FIVE

Small Faces Abound

Some time in June 1965, Jack Barrie, who worked at Marquee Artists, asked me if I'd be interested in joining a group he was managing called Boz and The Boz People. My first feeling was that it was a rotten name for a band. I wasn't sure I wanted to be a Boz Person! But as I was absolutely determined to make a go of being a musician, and the rest of The Muleskinners were either working or intending to get work in the design world, I jumped ship without a second thought. Boz Burrell later went on to play bass with Bad Company, but in those days he was the front man and singer of his own band. He and his "People" were a nice bunch of blokes and talented musicians, but they were very jazz-influenced and I'd been playing blues.

Boz sang in the "shoe-bop-a-rhubarb" scat style that only Ella Fitzgerald could manage with any conviction and it left me cold. I'd keep trying to get him to listen to Otis Redding and Wilson Pickett, but he couldn't figure it out. He was into head music, not the soulful, gutsy stuff I wanted to play. It was all too clever for me, I was lost. But for a while I hung in, because I was learning and I was sensible enough to know I had a lot to learn. Despite the musical differences of opinion, we did have a laugh. The first time I smoked dope was with The Boz People. We were at a U.S. Army base and were booked to play four sets of an hour each, which is plenty long enough. After the first set Bernie offered me a doozie of a reefer, I took a drag, and as the pot smoke expanded it filled my lungs and came out of my mouth and nose with a snort. This tasted all right, I thought, and it crackled and popped as I took another puff, then we went back on stage. The second set flew by, although some songs seemed to last forever. Sadly, it only heightened my awareness of the music Boz was playing, but again, when we played a song I liked, I found I liked it even more.

As well as our own, we did several gigs backing Kenny Lynch, a black Cockney singer who had been around for a while, had enjoyed a couple of hits, and was playing a series of Sunday concerts at seaside resorts. He was really easygoing and a lot of fun to be around. He also had a Rolls-Royce which he drove to the gigs, and he'd take one member of the band each time. My turn came on the way to Scarborough. It was a pleasant drive up, but when we got there, Boz phoned in a panic to say the van had broken down and they and the equipment wouldn't be able to make it in time for the show.

What a shame, I thought. We won't be able to play now. Think again, Mac. Kenny wasn't fazed. In fact, he didn't seem to give a toss.

"Come on, Mac. It'll be a doddle."

I was horrified. There would only be Kenny, me, and a piano on stage. Worse, I wasn't even sure of the songs and worst of all, the opening act was Billy J. Kramer and The Dakotas with Mick Green, who was a fabulous slack-string Telecaster player, on guitar. But Kenny was a trouper, who loved to entertain. He also liked to take home some readies. So he went out there and gave them the full performance, happy as a pig in shit. As for me, embarrassment was my middle name. If the floor could've opened up and swallowed me, I would have been eternally grateful. I prayed the building would collapse or a fire would break out. Instead, I broke out in a cold sweat! I must've lost pounds. "Up on the Roof" went all right, but the Elvis classic "Can't Help Falling in Love with You" seemed like a minefield of chords. It was horrendous; even thinking about it more than thirty years later makes me itch and shudder. I got through it but I don't know how. Time eventually passes. I'd look at my hands, wondering what they were going to do next, and then I'd watch, horrified, as they played something so obviously wrong that I'd be screaming the silent scream. No one can help you in that situation, you just have to play through.

One Sunday, up north on another of Kenny's gigs, the headliner was Mrs. Mills, a very popular piano player who, it turned out, suffered from chronic stage fright. Waiting for the curtain to go up, she was sitting at her piano, when all of a sudden she wailed, "I can't go on, dear Lord, I can't!" Someone with her, who must have seen this before, was trying to calm her down, but Gladys wouldn't have it. She was in a terrible state. "No, no, I won't go!" she cried. But the moment the curtains started to open, blow me if she didn't go straight into her first tune with a big smile and a twinkle in the eye, as if she was having the time of her life.

The Boz People's finest hour was opening for The Byrds on their first British tour. When I say we opened for them, I mean we played three short numbers, then five other acts went on before The Byrds appeared. David Crosby, in a green suede cape, was the Brian Jones of the band, meaning he was the outward, friendly guy in the group who came to our dressing room offering us something to smoke. But whereas Brian had fags, David had weed. This was obviously some sort of progression. Thirty odd years later, I was waiting to board a flight to Memphis at Los Angeles airport, when I saw David across the lounge with Graham Nash, who I'd known since 1966, when The Hollies and Small Faces were on the same British tour. I waved and went to say hello to Graham, who introduced me to David. Though I'd bumped into him a couple of times since those early days, I didn't expect him to remember me. He didn't. We chatted until it was time for my flight, then I went back to the line of people waiting to board. As I turned to wave, I caught David pointing at me with a knowing look and saying something I was too far away to hear across the airport lounge. Graham beckoned me back.

"David didn't recognize you, I told him you're Ian McLagan of the Small Faces."

"We loved you," David said, pointing a fat finger at me, his big face beaming. "In 'Eight Miles High' that line was about you guys!"

You could've knocked me down with a feather! Whenever I'd heard that song, the two words "small faces" had always stuck out, even if I wasn't paying attention, but I'd never worked out exactly what it was about. Now I knew. The line was "In places, Small Faces abound" and was meant as a salute from one band to another. It had taken a long time to find that out. But the moment I got to Memphis I bought a Byrds *Greatest Hits* CD so I could hear it, knowing what it meant, for the first time. I wish Steve Marriott had known.

The Boz People were booked to play for three nights in Scotland, but the van broke down on the Friday morning and couldn't be fixed in time for us to make the gig that night. But Jack Barrie reckoned if we could get up there by Saturday night, we could still walk away with a few quid and maybe even cover the cost of the van repairs.

Now, Boz wasn't one to lose sleep worrying over minor details like a career or money, simply because he didn't have either–and wouldn't have been able to get himself moving even if he did. He liked a laugh more than anything else, and although he was an amusing bloke, he could be very exasperating if, like me, you actually wanted to get on in the music business. Finally the van was fixed–Scotland here we come–but after several traffic holdups it broke down again on the North Circular road, heading for the start of the MI motorway. Boz wasn't bothered a bit, but found it hilarious, giggling like a schoolgirl. I was not amused, and suddenly I saw the significance of the most fundamental rule of show business: just show up. If you're not there, you can't play and you don't get paid. It's that simple. In a blinding flash I saw everything clearly.

"I've had enough of this shit!" I said, and reached for my bag. "See you later." I got out of the van and thumbed a lift home. I didn't think it out, I just knew I couldn't carry on like that. But even later that night when I felt depressed, I knew I'd done the right thing.

The next night, Sunday, I went to see my girlfriend Irene, who lived in Manor House at the far end of the Piccadilly Line from Hounslow. Not surprisingly, I was in a foul mood. After pouring my heart out to her, travelling back across town to Hounslow, I bumped into our neighbour, Gillian's cousin Phil Weatherburn.

"Hello, Mac. How's the band?"

"Rotten–I just quit."

"You should join the Small Faces."

"Bloody funny, Phil." Yeah, Ha Bloody Ha.

"Have you seen them? They're really great."

Actually, my dad had turned me on to them a few months before. They'd been on ITV's "Ready, Steady, Go!" one Friday night, as I was getting ready to go out.

"Here, Ian, look at this lot, will you?" He'd shouted up the stairs. And when I came down to see what he was on about, he'd pointed at Ronnie Lane and said, "He looks just like you." He did. I could see the likeness and waited for a decent camera angle to check him out again. The Small Faces looked and sounded incredible.

They were playing their first single "What'Cha Gonna Do About It." It was August 1965 and they were rocking. And they were real Mods, not like me, the art student type in brown corduroy jacket and blue jeans without a pot to piss in.

"Yes, Phil I've seen them. They're brilliant, but they've got an organ player." And I'm thinking, What's Phil's problem? By the time I said good-night to him I was really depressed. I was adrift. I had no idea what to do next. Home. To bed. To dream.

I woke up on Monday morning unemployed and deflated. What a fucking idiot. I'd left the band without thinking it out. If they'd thrown me out I might've felt better, but I'd done this to myself. It was November 1, 1965, and the phone call came about 10 A.M.

"Hounslow 7353."

"Is Ian McLagan at home?" the question came in a thick Manchester accent.

"Er, yes."

"This is Don Arden. I'd like to talk to him about a job." I'd only been out of work since Saturday.

"I'm Ian," I said.

"I've got a band that needs a keyboard player. Can you come in to the office today?"

"Yes," I mumbled. My brain was turning to jelly. This was Don Arden. I'd heard the name and knew he was an impresario, whatever that was. But he was somebody in the business, and I was impressed. I agreed to meet him at his office at noon. I'd have met him in Timbuktu at ten if he'd asked me to. Who the hell did I think I was? Actually, I thought of myself as a professional musician, which is why I'd moved on from The Muleskinners and why I'd walked out on The Boz People. Let's face it, I wasn't doing anything else and I could dream, couldn't I? Mum and Dad might have thought otherwize, but if they did, they never said a word. It was a long time after when I realized they'd put me through art school when most kids had to go straight out to work at fifteen or sixteen, and this after my brother Mike had gone to university. I took many things for granted in those days, Mum and Dad allowing The Muleskinners to rehearse five nights a week in our back room being only one of them. God Bless 'em.

I raced up to Carnaby Street on the Tube, found the entrance to 52/55 next to John Michael's shop, and climbed the stairs to the outer office of Don Arden's little empire. The receptionist asked if she could help me, but as I didn't know which band Arden wanted me to work with, or whether it was a session or a full-time job, I told her I didn't know anything other than he had called. She offered me a seat while she went to enquire. There were eight-by-tens of the artists he managed on the wall: The Animals, The Nashville Teens, Small Faces, and The Clayton Squares.

I knew The Animals' organist Alan Price had been replaced by Dave Rowberry only a few months before and John Hawken, who played with The Nashville Teens, was a fantastic piano player, and it couldn't possibly be the Small Faces, could it? So I thought it had to be The Clayton Squares, though I didn't know anything about them. When she came back, she told me somebody would be out to see me shortly and offered me a cup of tea, so I sat down again to wait and wonder what it was all about. The phone rang every now and then. She'd answer it and then carry on with her typing. She wasn't particularly friendly and hardly spoke to me, so I sat quietly reading magazines. Three times that afternoon different faces peered round the office door, gave me the once over, and disappeared. It was all very strange. And all the time I'm thinking: "Which band?"

Hours passed. It must have been 4:30 P.M. when Arden called for her to take me in to his office. He stood by the door at the end of the long corridor, greeting me with all the warmth it was possible to put into a professional smile, shook my hand, and ushered me into his office. He was a short, chubby man, and after offering me a chair, he introduced me to Ron King, who ran the agency, a beady-eyed, cold fish called Pat Meehan, who ran the office, and Bill Corbett, a large, stern-looking man wearing a camel-hair overcoat. I was intimidated by them eyeing me up and down, but they seemed pleased enough with what they saw and shook my hand, one at a time. Don, sitting behind his desk, asked me the only question. "What are you earning at the moment?" About a fiver a week was the right answer, but with a straight face I said, "Twenty pounds," because that's what my dad was earning at the time, which was a fair wage.

"Twenty pounds? You start at thirty, but you'll be on probation for a month. After that, if everything goes well, you'll be on an even split with the lads."

"Which lads?" I asked.

"The Small Faces, of course." I was in heaven. "But you're not to tell anyone, okay?" I nodded. "Right, you can go now, but I want you back here at six o'clock sharp, all right?"

"Yes." A sudden thought. "Can I tell my parents?"

"Just tell them you'll call them in a couple of weeks and explain everything then." They obviously wanted time to thoroughly check me out before they made any announcement to the press. I intended to show them they'd picked the right face. I walked back down the stairs, my knees wobbly and my head in a spin, and wandered down Carnaby Street without knowing where I was going or what I was going to do for the next hour. I must have turned left, walked along Beak Street, and taken another left, because I found myself on Broadwick Street. I knew where I was going then. Wardour Street was straight ahead of me, and The Ship just a few yards up from the Marquee.

I walked up to the bar, ordered a pint of bitter and a packet of crisps. I hadn't had anything to eat since breakfast, so I was starving, but I was thirsty too. While I wolfed down the crisps and sipped my beer, I tried to get to grips with what had just happened to me. I was buzzing with excitement, and though Arden had told me not to tell anyone, I was dying to give Dad a hint. But he wouldn't be home before 5:30 P.M. so I drank my pint and kept an eye on the clock. I didn't know exactly what lay ahead of me, but I knew my life had just taken a turn for the better, and I was going to be very rich. When Dad picked up the phone, I was so worried about ruining my chances that all I said was that I'd got a job with a band, that it was good money, that he and Mum shouldn't worry, and that I wasn't allowed to tell anyone anything, but that I'd call them in a couple of weeks. He was great.

"Are you all right?"

"Oh yes!" I almost spilled the beans, but caught myself in time. "I'll call you when I can, and tell you all about it."

"Okay, take care of yourself."

Dad was used to me disappearing for days on end. I walked back to Carnaby Street on a cloud, my head spinning from the beer and the prospect of meeting the band, although I wasn't sure when that was actually going to happen.

Since my last visit, the receptionist, who'd just been uninterested in me before, had turned unmistakably cold. There was a reason for her hostility, as I soon found out. It was her boyfriend I was going to replace in the band. I don't know why she had it in for me, though. It wasn't me who kicked him out. It was obvious to anyone who'd seen or heard the Small Faces that Steve Marriott was an incredibly gifted singer and natural front man, but this was not apparent to their organist Jimmy Winston, and his efforts to hog the stage had become an embarrassment to the rest of the band for the few months they'd been together. But getting rid of him was complicated by the fact that his brother owned the group's van, which explained the cloak-and-dagger way I'd been brought in. Don Arden wanted to get the van back in case Jimmy claimed the band's equipment. Of course, I didn't know this at the time. All I knew was she wasn't very friendly when she told me to go straight into Don's office.

My new manager shook my hand, gave me another professional smile, then Steve, Ronnie, and Kenney Jones popped their heads round the door, laughing and grinning at me and each other. Then they picked me up. It was so silly. What a funny bunch, and what a smartly dressed bunch as well, like professional Mods. The three of them were short like me, we were all between five-feet-five and five-feet-six inches. I hadn't realized from watching them on TV or photos that they were short-arses too. Even the significance of the name had slipped by me. From that moment we clicked, we couldn't have got on better. In the car, while Bill Corbett drove us to the hotel, we talked about the music we liked and influences we shared, like Muddy Waters, Booker T. and the MG's, Ray Charles, Tamla Motown, and Stax in general, so I knew without any doubt we were going to get on well.

I'd only stayed at bed and breakfast places with The Muleskinners and The Boz People, but the band, which now included me, was booked into the Russell Square Hotel in the West End. This was a big deal to me, but the others were past being excited about fancy hotels, and were more excited about talking to me. We quickly got to know each other better that night. They were all over me, asking questions, calling room service and pouring drinks, and I was a bit intimidated at first. No one had scrutinized me like this before and I wasn't used to the attention.

Steve was larger than life. A cartoon of a person. He'd studied drama as a kid and had played the Artful Dodger in the original West End production of Lionel Bart's *Oliver*. The more I got to know him, I realized he'd been typecast. He was a natural for the part and you can hear it on the original live recording of that show. He was also a very intense person. Whenever he said something funny he'd scream with laughter before you could properly grasp what it was he'd said that was so funny. It was exhausting trying to keep up. Ronnie, or "Plonk" as some people called him, was a funny guy too, and even though he could be excitable, he was a lot more relaxed than Steve, and much easier to get to know, which is probably why I felt closer to him. Kenney was quieter, but once he got started, and when he got a word in edgewise, he was hilarious.

Their excitement wasn't just to do with me. The three of them were on leapers, and just as I'd taken them for innocents, they had assumed I was too. They didn't have to worry though, they hadn't done anything I hadn't done already. Once we'd got past that hurdle, there was another problem, which was almost as easily solved. My hair was not happening. It might have been modern–it wasn't greased back–but it certainly wasn't Mod. Ronnie came to my rescue, blow-drying my barnet* and giving it some height. As he worked on my hair, I watched him in the mirror and saw what Dad had seen, that we did look alike, almost like brothers. It was uncanny, and they all found it funny that it was my dad who had turned me on to them.

I wondered how they'd found me. Ronnie explained they'd seen a review of a Boz People gig in *Beat Instrumental* magazine, which raved about my organ playing. What they hadn't known was that the photo wasn't of me, it was of Boz, although it was my name in the caption. It didn't faze them that I didn't look much like the photograph. Maybe that was another reason for the ducking and diving in Don's office. We laughed a lot that night and it took a long while for me to get to sleep, as I relived each moment of that day.

The next morning "Old Bill" Corbett, as the guys called him, drove us back to Don's office on Carnaby Street, the Mecca of the Mods. After a brief hello it was time to get me kitted out from head to toe, and that was when I became aware of just how well known they were. They were recognized everywhere, people pointing and staring, and because I was with them, pointing at me as if I was famous too.

They handled it well, but it was all new to me, and I found it a little daunting at first, to say the least. We went from John Michael to Topper's, and then on to Lord John. It was incredible. Although Steve, Ronnie, and Kenney already had lots of new clothes, they weren't above picking up more gear while I was getting togged up. Little Steve, one of the sales assistants, knew them from previous visits, and being a short Mod himself was eager to show us all the new clothes and where I was inclined to get one shirt or one pair of pants, Ronnie would push me to get more. "No, go on, get 'em while you can. You're goin' to need a lot of clobber for all the TV shows and gigs we've got lined up." He'd grab another five shirts and put them on my already large pile on the counter and go off looking for sweaters for me. He was having almost as much fun as I was. Kenney egged me on to get more too, and then Steve brought a butterscotch suede jacket

* *Cockney rhyming slang: Barnet Fair-hair.*

over and asked me what I thought of it. I'd never owned real suede before, only synthetic "suedette," but this was as soft as a baby's bum. I slipped it on and didn't take it off the whole day.

If the day before had been a dream come true, then it felt like I was still sleepwalking. I didn't even try to take it in. How could I? The money I was spending in a couple of hours–not that any actually changed hands–was more than I'd spent on clothes in the previous five years.

Topper's was the place to buy wild Italian shoes in London; no other shoe shop came close. I walked out of there with four pairs of their very finest footwear in my possession. They sold some really unusual shoes and kept coming up with something new. There's a photograph of the Small Faces with me in a pair of Topper's open-weave, two-tone, brown and tan leather shoes that I would give a bundle for today.

The only clothes I'd ever bought before on Carnaby Street were the seersucker band jacket, black pants, and plastic belt that had been The Muleskinners' group uniform. This was different. I could take anything off the shelves, and if it didn't fit they would alter it, there and then. I was in heaven. I got every colour of the John Michael pastel button-down-collar shirts, a couple of leather belts, some wool sweaters, a wool overcoat, and a pair of leather gloves. We piled the bags into a taxi and drove to Sound City, on Shaftesbury Avenue, to buy me a brand new cream Fender Telecaster, so I could learn the guitar part of "I've Got Mine" in time to mime the new single that night on the Radio Luxembourg show "Ready, Steady, Radio."

My dizzy flight into outer space crash-landed that evening when Jimmy Winston started banging on the dressing room door. I suppose he had to turn up eventually. He was really pissed off with them and though I felt very awkward, what could I say? I just kept in the background and left it up to them. He wanted his job back, but that wasn't going to happen and he seemed to realize it had nothing to do with me and that it wasn't my fault. But he was understandably upset, so they took him into another room to talk to him and calm him down.

Eventually, he left, but it was a sobering experience for me to see the other side of the coin, and realized there was very little job security that went along with all the jollity. I couldn't wait for my month of probation to be over.

"Ready, Steady, Radio" was broadcast live in front of an audience with bands miming to their records. It was an odd concept, but it was a popular show. I'd spent most of the afternoon practicing on the Telecaster, so I felt confident playing the song, but when I heard Keith Fordyce the presenter introduce the four of us as "the Small Faces!" I felt a tingle of excitement and then, as we walked out onto the brightly lit stage, the entire audience screamed so loud it gave me a fright. I'd never heard screams like that before, and I could hardly hear the record from the monitor speakers. In three minutes flat we were on and off the stage, into the Jag and away.

The following morning Bill Corbett, who I now knew was our road manager, driver, and bodyguard, drove us to Swindon for my first proper gig. Bill was an ex-boxer and one-time chauffeur for The Beatles, who never smiled. Although it didn't occur to me at the time, it must seem odd to read that a band would recruit an organ player on the strength of a review and a wrongly captioned photograph, but it wasn't until we rehearsed at Swindon Town Hall that they heard me play. Luckily for me, it went well.

We played "Green Onions" and "Plum Nellie," both Booker T. and the MG's instrumentals, and it flowed as if we'd been playing together for years. Kenney was a loud, solid drummer, Ronnie had a great ear for simplicity in a bass line and was locked into Kenney, and Steve was a dynamic guitarist and the most soulful singer. He had an old man's voice. There was no looking back; we jammed for a long time and Steve decided we'd play some of the instrumentals that night. I wasn't prepared for the audience though. They went nuts, screaming so loud it was hard to concentrate on the music, but you can get used to anything and eventually I used to blank them out or I couldn't have got through it night after night.

CHAPTER SIX

"Happy Boys, Happy!"

Days became nights and nights turned into days and nothing was ever the same again. I had found my band. On November 5, instead of being invited to someone's house for a Guy Fawkes' night party, we stopped on the way to a gig, went into a corner shop, and bought fifty pounds worth of fireworks. We found an empty space outside of town, Steve threw a match into the box and jumped clear. We stood there for a moment, watching the whole lot go up in a noisy rainbow of booms, crashes, bangs, and wallops, then we drove off. We gigged every day–sometimes twice a night–and travelled all the time, especially in the north of England.

We seemed to be permanently in or around Manchester, Leeds, and Sheffield and played in Burnley, Bury, Bolton, Bradford, Blackburn, and Barnsley a hell of a lot. The first two weeks passed very quickly.

We were at a hotel in Nelson, north of Manchester, playing at the Imperial, when I asked Bill if it would be okay to phone my parents, seeing as the two weeks I'd promised to stay silent were up–and I'd kept my word to Don that I wouldn't say a word to them. I had to ask Bill if he could let me have the price of the call, because in spite of my new-found fame and fortune, and since he took care of everything, I didn't have a penny on me. But I was surprised when he handed me thirty pounds with no questions asked. That was half as much again as Dad was earning, though I didn't mention it to Dad. I suddenly felt rich for the first time in my life and Dad and Mum were as excited as I was when I told them all the news. Dad, being a wise guy, had guessed already that I was a Small Face. I was happy, they were happy, and finally I seemed to be doing something right in their eyes, so I was very happy!

I'd been popping pills for a while and had smoked hash a few times before but these guys made a religion out of a doozie. On the way to a promotional appearance at the Tottenham Royal a couple of days after I joined, Steve turned to me in the car and asked me mischievously if I wanted a smoke.

When I said "yes" he passed me a very strong, three-skin spliff. I took a few puffs and was initiated into the Small Faces proper. We arrived at the gig, slipped past the screaming fans held in check by the bouncers, and were led into a cordoned-off bar area. After we sat down with the manager of the place, I found myself going through waves of elation, sadness, stupid giggling, introspection, depression and extreme happiness, each emotion repeating itself over and over. It took me a while to realize my mood changes were directly related to the changing coloured lights around the ceiling of the bar. Every time they turned red, I felt warm to everybody. When they changed to yellow, I felt withdrawn; blue, miserable; purple, giggly; green, awkward and afraid. How very unusual. I was very stoned. I was incredibly stoned! And I liked it.

We were very suss. From then on we were out of it all the time, unless we ran out of gear, which was very rare. Occasionally, after getting back into London after a gig, we'd go round to score at a girl's flat near Harley Street. We were there one night listening to sounds, dissecting the music like we always did, checking out "Jelly Bread" by Booker T. and the MG's over and over again, when our roadies, Dave Clark and Dennis, turned up for a smoke. Dennis always looked like he was on leapers, and it didn't take much persuading to get them to hump the guitars, amps, and my Hammond and Leslie up two flights of stairs at two in the morning. Then Ronnie, Steve, and me could jam on the tune, switching instruments every once in a while, me learning the guitar lines and Steve the organ. Kenney, by this time, would be tucked up in bed, as he wasn't much into smoking dope or staying up all night getting ripped, when he could be at home.

Though "I've Got Mine" was a great song, and an instrumental version would later resurface on *Ogdens' Nut Gone Flake,* it had hit the charts with an anchor, and as Steve and Ronnie had written it Don wanted outside writers for the next single to ensure a hit. Kenny Lynch had brought him his and Mort Shuman's "Sha-La-La-La-Lee" and he thought it couldn't miss. This was to be my first time in the studio with the guys, and as they'd recorded the two previous singles at IBC Studios in Portland Place, that was where we cut "Sha-La-La-La-Lee" as well. Kenny was quite surprised to see his ex-pianist so soon, and as good as it was to see him, I didn't reckon the song's chances on the charts, it sounded too corny to me. But then, what did I know? The track was a doddle to record but Kenny insisted on singing the choruses with us, and though he's got a pleasant enough singing voice, it was a high part to sing and as soon as he put the headphones on he started to screech because he couldn't hear himself well enough. He was even louder than Steve, and that's saying something. The engineer got him to move back from the mike, but he was still too loud. Then they heard someone grunting between the choruses, and it turned out to be Kenny again, doing an Erroll Garner, mumbling along with the track. We fell about laughing but he couldn't help it, and you can't hear the grunts, but the high voice on the choruses is him. Ever since then if anyone shouted or grunted while wearing head-phones we've always called it "Kenny Lynching."

We didn't have a B side ready, but Steve had an idea for an instrumental twelve-bar that became "Grow Your Own." He loved the sound of the Hammond so much, he gave me free rein to go nuts in a solo. Surprisingly, hardly anyone caught on to the references to pot, our audiences possibly being too young, although we considered ourselves to be such devils. Not that our pot smoking was that much of a secret, but the dream was to have our fans turn on without society turning on us. Once we'd recorded "Grow Your Own" we listened to it a few times and never played it again after that. It wasn't unusual that if a song didn't turn out to be an A side it would more than likely never get performed live at all. Paul Weller was surprised to hear that I couldn't remember anything about one of his favourite Small Faces songs, "Get Yourself Together" until I listened to it again. I remembered it then, of course, but as we probably only played it a few times in the studio, and more than thirty years have passed since then, well...

We toured nonstop until Christmas Eve, occasionally making it back to London, but never long enough to get home to see our girlfriends or mums and dads, and rarely having a day off. We knew we had to "strike while the iron was hot," as Don had put it, and anyway we loved to play. But every few days we'd have photo sessions and seemingly endless interviews with magazines and local papers, which became tedious very quickly. The questions were so stupid, like, "What's your favourite colour, or favourite food?" It was so silly that you'd have to give a different answer each time or you'd nod off with boredom.

I hadn't realized how much work was involved in staying popular, but it was still new and exciting then, and I knew that anything was better than a real job. The band were my brothers, we had money and clothes. Everything was perfect. Except we had no home base. We were all still living with our parents, and as I lived on the other side of London, I would spend the night at one of their houses whenever we got back to town. In fact, I never stayed at home again. I'd left home the day I joined the band, though I hadn't known it at the time. Don solved the problem when he found us a four-bedroom, four-storey house at 22 Westmoreland Terrace, Pimlico, near Victoria Station. As soon as we looked it over we knew this was our party house. There were steps up to the front door, then there were two bedrooms on the ground floor and a large bathroom at the rear of the house. From there stairs led down to the basement kitchen and dining room. The main staircase in the front hall led to the sitting room, which took up the whole of the first floor and from there the stairs led up to the top floor and two more bedrooms.

We were set to move in after Christmas, because we'd had no time to buy any furniture. But when I got home on Christmas Eve I felt terribly restless being back with my parents again in the straight world. I couldn't handle it. It was the first time I'd been home since I'd joined the band. I'd only managed to see Irene once in that time and that was a total disaster. I'd arranged to meet her after a gig, but when Bill dropped me off at her parents' flat it was well past midnight and she was rightfully pissed off. All I got for my efforts was a goodnight kiss and cuddle on the door step. I'd figured on staying at her place, but because of the cold reception I caught a cab to take me into central London, where I found a hotel for the night. I'd been looking forward to seeing her at Christmas, hoping I might get more than a kiss and cuddle this time, but when she came to the house on Christmas Day I started to explain how difficult it was getting time off to see her, and it developed into an argument and after Christmas dinner she went home. It was all over, but I was relieved really, and as we rarely had days off, things weren't going to get any easier.

When I called Ronnie and Steve, it turned out they were both going through similar situations. They'd both had rows with their girlfriends and couldn't wait to move into the new pad, so we agreed to meet that night and move in there and then. Having only just turned seventeen, Kenney was the youngest of the band, and an only child, so he wasn't ready yet to move away from the Jones family seat in Stepney, but for us, this was freedom. Steve, typically, had chosen the biggest bedroom at the top of the house, Ronnie took the front bedroom on the ground floor, and as I was the new boy in town who hoped for some peace and quiet, I took the small room next to Steve's on the top floor.

Apart from the beds, the only furniture we had were a couple of wooden chairs and an old sofa, but Ronnie brought his Dansette record player and a pile of sounds with him. I took a bottle of brandy from home and Steve's contribution was to bring some black Afghani, some Rizla rolling papers, and Mick O'Sullivan, a pal of his from Loughton. He was supposed to be an actor and though I never actually saw him act, he could roll a decent joint and pour a fair glass of brandy, as long as he didn't have to pay for it.

Mick was permanently unemployed, and became little more than a ligger and a freeloader, but it was handy to have someone at the house while we were out of town, though what he did for his free bed and board, I'm not at all sure. We moved in that night, and he took over Kenney's room, as Kenney was still living at home. That first night was magical. Hunched over the record player in the sitting room of our new home, we listened to Booker T. and the MG's, Yusef Lateef, and Smokey Robinson and The Miracles, passing joints and amazing ourselves by discovering a subtle bass lick here, and the faintest percussion sound there, and then screaming with laughter at Lord Buckley preaching "Here Come Da Nazz." Over the next week or so we raided furniture shops, until the house was filled with a hodge-podge of styles: a modern orange revolving chair in the shape of an egg, an oak stereo unit, pseudo-antique sofas and chairs, Mexican-style rugs from Casa Pupo, and all on credit, because the only cash we ever had was what Bill Corbett gave us each week. As wild as our furnishing ideas were, the wallpaper in the sitting room, which had Greek statues in black on a white background, was so bloody awful nobody noticed our combined lack of taste in interior design.

By January, I'd been with the band for two months, and I was starting to worry that maybe this wasn't going to be the permanent arrangement I had hoped for after all. Was I in, or was I out? As I felt closest to Ronnie, I eventually plucked up the courage to ask him what the deal was, explaining that Don had told me I was on probation for a month and then if all went well…

"What are you talkin' about?" he said, jumping in before I'd finished. "Of course you're in the band. 'Ere Steve, listen to this." They hadn't known about Don's deal and couldn't believe I still wasn't on an even footing with them. "Come on," he said, and the two of us cabbed it to Don's office on Carnaby Street. Plonk was my man. Funny thing, that name, Plonk. Most people assume he got it because of the sound he made on the bass, and others think it was because he was a wine drinker. It had nothing to do with that, he had a big knob, that's all!

After Ronnie poked his head round Arden's door and told him what was what, I finally became a permanent member of the Small Faces. But to my horror my money dropped from thirty to twenty pounds a week, which is all they'd been earning and all we were ever going to get. This was a time of enormous earnings from records that were constantly in the Top Ten and live shows that sold out night after night wherever we played, so naturally we assumed that the real money we were making on top of our weekly cash-in-hand was being looked after for us. We were young and inexperienced in business, and wasn't this all a dream anyway? I was the oldest at twenty, Ronnie was nineteen, and Steve was still eighteen, but we weren't stupid, and we were beginning to see the kind of people we were dealing with. Steve was the realist of the bunch. He always picked up more shirts than anyone else when we raided Carnaby Street, as if he was collecting his money in advance, in the form of clothes.

One week in 1966, I remember playing ten gigs. One particular Friday we started off with an appearance on "Ready, Steady, Go!" at ATV Studios in Wembley, drove to the Princess Club in Birmingham, played there, drove across town to the Domino Club, played there too, then drove on to a hotel in Manchester, where we did another double the next night. But we were on top of the world, having so much fun, playing to screaming fans wherever we went, getting stoned and generally living the life of Riley. And on days off we partied even more.

Arden hired Liesel, a German lady, to cook and clean for us at number 22, as well as drop off and collect the laundry and dry cleaning on a daily basis. She came in Monday to Friday, and Marge came in two or three times a week to do the polishing. Marge was getting on in years and her doctor had put her on "mother's little helpers," not an uncommon prescription then and she would rabbit* all day if you let her. We soon learned to try and avoid her in the mornings, because she'd nail you on the stairs, on the way to the bathroom. She used to rattle on about nothing in particular and just as you thought you'd escaped, she'd start on about something else.

"Bloody Russians," she'd complain, blaming them for the weather.

So we'd wait for her to start polishing the door knocker, which would take her a while, and then creep down the stairs in turn while she was out on the front step, but if she saw you, you didn't have a chance.

"Oh, Mac, did I tell you about my Bert's lumbago?" Which is how Steve got that line for "Lazy Sunday."

"Oh, he's in terrible pain. What he goes through. Oh, you've no idea. Well, as I always say, you never know what's going to happen next, do you? What with the weather and all. Well, I never did, I must say, blah, blah, blah."

Liesel was a different kettle of fish. First, she was a fantastic cook, although she would cook heavy meals early in the day, until we got her organized. We used to stay up half the night, getting stoned, listening to sounds, and laughing

* *Cockney rhyming slang: Rabbit and pork-talk.*

at the silliest things. We were the stonedest men in town! We'd get stoned, go to sleep stoned, wake up stoned, and find ourselves staring at a breakfast of Wiener schnitzel and mashed potatoes. It wasn't easy at first to explain what we were all about, and poor Liesel used to get so upset with us, before we told her what was going on and she adapted to our hours and appetites. In fact, once she had, she even agreed to cook us some hash brownies and did a wonderful job, as well as getting very stoned making them. We turned quite a few people on with Liesel's magical hash brownies. They became legendary, and people would come to the house, have a nibble, leave, then tell us weeks later how they'd had the weirdest things happen to them, partly because Liesel would put more rather than less hash in and also because the effect crept up on you. Even experienced smokers like Georgie Fame were surprised at how stoned they could be hours after they left our place.

After a gig one night, Dave and Dennis dropped some equipment off at the house and had come upstairs to the sitting room for a smoke. As I was about to pass the joint, the sitting room door opened and a policeman's helmeted head appeared in the haze of hash smoke.

"You don't want to lose this do you?" He was looking straight at me, so I had no time to hide the freshly rolled, three-skinned doozie I was holding. I didn't know if he meant the house, the joint, or my way of life.

"No, officer," I muttered.

"Well, you should close your van doors, or someone'll steal your equipment."

"Oh, right, thanks a lot." Ronnie blurted with relief. We were stunned into a useless silence as the policeman said goodnight and shut the door behind him. Dave, our head roadie, had not only left the van doors open, he'd left our street door wide open too. Luckily, the friendly copper wasn't looking for drugs, so he hadn't seen or smelled anything. He went on his way without realising he could've busted the lot of us and had his face and name plastered all over the front page of the *Daily Mirror*.

In the year after I joined, we must have played everywhere in the British Isles, always touring in a Mark 10 Jag driven by Bill Corbett. We made ourselves as comfortable as possible and had a record player under the dash and a box of our favourite singles that we'd play over and over while we rolled doozie after doozie, sinking into the leather upholstery as we drifted off to the sounds. We had a ton of singles, but we played the hell out of Smokey and The Miracles' "Tracks of My Tears," Freddie King's "Hideaway," Booker T.'s "Green Onions," and Fontella Bass's "Rescue Me."

Kenney was the DJ *de jour* because he always sat up front. In fact, he was the disc jockey and heating engineer, come to think of it, because he was the nearest to the controls. Kenney spent a lot of the time sleeping, or as Steve would put it sarcastically, "workin' it" because the heater would get to him before it reached us in the back, where we'd be so dry in the mouth from the hash anyway, that our eyes would be puffy and half-closed from smoking so much.

We'd take turns rolling spliffs and award them points out of ten, the idea being to roll such an unsuss joint you'd be able to smoke it in broad daylight, passing a policeman in the street. It was a tall order, but it was attainable. Steve and I were pretty consistent but Ronnie's heart wasn't really in it, and he never got a better score than a seven. As any druggie will tell you, the buzz is as much to do with the preparation as the smoking, and even though the Jag had joint-rolling tables set into the back of the seats, if you weren't careful and didn't roast the hash well enough you'd end up with little hard lumps amongst the tobacco.

These would catch fire, drop in your lap, and burn tiny holes in your strides. Ronnie would never weed the seeds out properly in a grass joint, so when you puffed on one of his masterpieces, the hot seeds would pop out, and before you knew it you'd have another little hole in your jacket. On long drives at night, we'd stuff the corners of a blanket into the windows to keep Bill from getting too stoned, but all the smoking in the dark left our jackets and strides dotted with little hash and seed burns. Having chauffeured The Beatles before us, Bill would go on about how they "were from another planet" and "never needed to do drugs and take pills like you lot." Although we knew they were smokers and tried to explain that "fab gear" started out as their term for good hash, he wouldn't hear of it.

The best pot you could get in London then was from Jamaica. As the dealers preferred that we went to them, and I loved cabbing around London at night, I would volunteer to score. I used to visit Jimmy, a middle-aged Jamaican who had a very smart flat in Mayfair. He also had a pretty blonde girlfriend, who wandered about smelling wonderful while we were conducting business. Jimmy claimed to have been a musician in Edmundo Ros's band in the Fifties, but I wasn't totally convinced, and he'd play cassettes of his compositions, apparently in the hope that I'd like one enough to get the Small Faces to record the song. If you're in a successful band, this happens, and it's always a tricky situation, but especially after you've had a pull on a big old spliff and the song in question is going nowhere slowly. I'd make my excuses and get out of there. Though he never sold hashish, his Ganja was the freshest, direct from Jamaica via Liverpool docks, but one night he gave me a piece of hash as a gift. I think somebody must've palmed him off with it, because it turned out to be a lump of rubber off the heel of a shoe. Nice one. Mind you, we didn't smoke all of it. If I remember correctly, I think we gave the rest of it to Dave and Dennis.

Another bloke I used to score from was John, who lived near Westbourne Grove. He was one of the new breed of dealers, a hippie who played bongos, always a dead giveaway. He seemed to be permanently stoned, and his lips were chapped and blistered from smoking joints down to the tip. Of course, we were pretty well permanently stoned too, but sometimes we'd take time off to play music or sleep.

One evening, a dealer friend of a friend brought Brian Epstein and Graeme Edge, drummer with the Moody Blues, over to the house. We took them down to the dining room in the basement, which we used as our music room, since we didn't take eating very seriously. The dealer took out an orange, cut it up, and offered the segments to us on a plate. We knew we were getting something other than vitamin C, but we had no conception of what we were actually getting into. It was the only time we met Brian, and he seemed pleasant enough. Our feeling was he thought the odds were in his favour that one of us was fair game, being young, single chaps living together, though he would have been mistaken. Everything was okay until I thought the net curtains started to flow down the window like water. Then the wood panelling on the wall began to sway seductively from side to side.

Next, I looked at our upright piano, and as I walked towards it, I saw the keys leaning to the left as I moved my body to the right. Then, when I moved my body to the left, they'd move back again. I couldn't seem to get in line with them and it made me laugh, which was a shock, because it didn't sound like me. Soon, everybody was laughing or contemplating the meaning of life, and conversation had dried up as everybody began to either study their hands, the rope carpet, or the wall. The room seemed to get smaller as we all got more intense, and finally, Brian and Graeme found it had become too strange for them, so they said goodnight and left, taking the geezer who'd turned us on to LSD with them, and leaving us to wander around the house for hours in a state of heightened and giggly consciousness.

After they left, Ronnie, Mick O'Sullivan, and I disappeared off the planet, while Steve, who was having a bad reaction to the acid, went upstairs to his bedroom to pack, as he'd arranged to catch an early train to Manchester to spend a few days with his new girlfriend at her parents' place.

I went upstairs to the sitting room and spent a long time looking closely at one of the Casa Pupo rugs, which was beginning to squirm and swim in front of me. I decided to draw it, and spent what seemed like hours, detailing every stitch, then when I looked in the mirror, I watched, horrified, as my face became liquid, then separated into muscular sections, so I began to draw a series of self-portraits. Everything I saw—the window, the curtains, the wood grain of the table—was so beautiful I had to try and capture them. My jaw kept dropping at the beauty in everything I saw and I'd find myself sighing with ecstasy. As the song would go, it was all too beautiful.

Ronnie was lost in space as well, and when we found ourselves inspecting each other's faces, grinning, and then bursting into uncontrollable laughter, it was as if our hearts were going to explode. We had to get away from each other fast, but we both turned to look anyway, and we found ourselves laughing crazily again, it was so silly. When Ronnie found me again, I'd been spinning in the egg chair for some time, the room rotating slowly around me. He thought it would be a good idea to go for a walk. There was no one else on the street; it was silent except for our footsteps as we walked down Westmoreland Terrace into Lupus Street, and across Grosvenor Road to the Thames Embankment. Across the river, one of Battersea Power Station's four brick chimneys belched out what might have looked like smoke on any other morning, but we were witnessing the birth of the universe. The effects of the acid might have eased off just a little, but not enough for us not to recognize the history of all life written in a puff of smoke above the glistening Thames.

We stood there for a long time, utterly amazed. Eventually, exhausted, we made for home, but the street wasn't silent like before.

As we passed the houses, we could clearly hear the rumbling stomachs of people in their beds, sleeping. We looked at each other in disbelief. This was too much, we couldn't have invented it, yet we couldn't explain it either and we laughed our heads off all the way back to the house. It was an extremely wonderful trip for us, but not for Steve, who stayed in his room with his own devils.

He was not what I'd call a particularly balanced person and he was rarely relaxed, and in the same way that acid can lead you to the heights of illumination and wonder, it can also take you down to the depths of your darkest fears. When Steve finished packing for his trip we could see he was very troubled, so we helped him back to our relative reality by including him in it, and when it came time for him to cab it to the station, Ronnie, Mick, and I went with him, because we felt as if we were in a kind of bubble and needed to stay together.

After paying the cab at Euston Station we walked along the platform to Steve's train in a kind of shock. We couldn't help feeling strange. We were suddenly in the outside world, and as we looked out from the inside of our invisible bubble we'd laugh out loud, not realising how strange we were behaving, and then giggling and mumbling like escaped mental patients. We couldn't put words together, let alone sentences, and we kept sighing and laughing; then I'd hear what I'd just tried to say, stop and laugh again. Boy, we could've been locked up if anyone had understood a word of our mumbling.

We found Steve's compartment and sat in it with him for a while, grinning one minute, laughing out loud the next, and introspective silence all around the next minute. We were concerned for him, because he was losing his nut already, and once left on his own there would be no one to bring him back to earth. He was also going to have to deal with the girlfriend and her parents when he arrived. I don't know why he didn't throw the towel in and come back with us to the house, but he went all the way to Manchester, while we cabbed back to the security of number 22 in our bubble, and carried on raving until we fell asleep, exhausted. It was a big relief when he returned the next day after arguing with her parents and dumping her. He'd only wanted to get laid, not married.

Somehow, the press found out that Brian Epstein had been to our house, and though Arden never mentioned it to us directly, he phoned Brian, warning him to back off, believing he was after our management, when in fact he'd only been socializing with the lads.

CHAPTER SEVEN

"Wakey Wakey, Tea and Cakey!"

After that first night in 1966, we dropped acid more and more, usually at night, so that it would have pretty much worn off by the next day, when we'd have to be relatively coherent again. Somehow, amid all the craziness we even found time to record our first Decca album at IBC.

We'd cut the basic tracks live on one track, then overdub solos and backing vocals on separate tracks, leaving the fourth track for the lead vocals, although Steve often got his vocal live, that's how strong a singer he was. Although "What'Cha Gonna Do About It" and a couple of other songs were already in the can, incredibly, most of the tracks on that album were done while us three hooligans were tripping out of our tiny minds and with Kenney on leapers. If it sounded like a party, it really was.

"E Too D" had developed from a live jam, and though it was misspelled, it was just two chords, E and D, but Steve's fiery guitar thrashing at the beginning still sounds great, and it's a wonder he didn't break more strings, because both he and Ronnie used solid glass plectrums that were as thick as threepenny bits and didn't bend at all. Kenney was way ahead of his time on the drums and played like an old pro at sixteen, and he and Ronnie used to get into a Cubo-Latin groove that was absolutely contagious. Ronnie slapped his beaten-up Harmony bass to make it boom like congas while Kenney ran all over the kit staring wildly into space, leaping out of his head. Old Kenney was one for the blues all right, and I do mean French blues.

"You Need Loving" was another stoned jam that we'd been playing live since I joined the band. It was a nick from the Willie Dixon tune "You Need Love" that Muddy Waters recorded in 1962, and a few years later Led Zeppelin nicked it from us and called it "Whole Lotta Love." I hope someone got paid along the way, though I know we didn't. The instrumental "Own Up Time" was recorded with Ronnie and Steve standing on chairs, and you can hear the screaming and shouting at the beginning. There was nothing worked out, it was just a jam, and I remember worrying at first if I'd be able to play on acid, but once we started recording there was hardly time to think. I just let the acid work, and the album was recorded, mixed, and mastered in three days.

It wasn't original, but someone decided the album would be called *Small Faces* and to use a headshot of us on the cover. So we smoked a doozie and grabbed a cab for Decca House on the Embankment. Here, the photographer and his assistant had already drawn cartoon faces in chalk on a wall up a side road, to be used as a background for the shot. When Steve saw the chalk lying on the ground he couldn't resist drawing what might have been taken for a cigarette in the mouths of several of the faces. Of course, they had a distinctive pinched end to them and we fell about when the record came out and spotted one of the spliffs behind Ronnie's ear. We were dead giveaways when we'd had a smoke, particularly me and Steve, our eyes would close up. "Look at your mince pies!" he'd say. "They're like piss holes in the snow."

One night, we were tripping at the house, listening to "Rain," the B side of The Beatles' "Paperback Writer" and weren't sure what they were singing in the background. We knew it was backwards, and it sounded like "Nyair" and "Ish-nuz" and Steve figured out that if he moved the arm on the turntable across the middle of the record, it would play the record backwards. What a revelation! Of course they were singing "Rain" and "Sunshine."

After we'd heard it backwards and forwards a few times, on a whim, I turned the speed to 33 rpm and, to our amazement, it didn't seem to have slowed down at all. It was beyond reason, I don't understand it, but I suppose our bodies just slowed down with the record. I took it down to 16 rpm, and it didn't seem to sound any different on that speed either. We were buzzing and giggling now, and so Steve put it on at 78 rpm for a laugh, fully expecting it to sound speeded up after 16 rpm, but even that sounded the same, and we fell about laughing hysterically, because we could clearly see the record was spinning like mad.

Ronnie, Steve, and I went to Mick Jagger's flat in Harley House on the Marylebone Road one evening. Mick led us into the bedroom, where Marianne Faithfull was quietly reading a book of poetry in bed, and he and Ronnie left the room to get drinks. Steve and I sat on the bed passing a joint and listening while she read us a poem from the book. It was a beautiful moment and she read well, but it was more memorable for us, because her tits unintentionally popped out of her night-dress a couple of times as she read. It didn't seem to bother her in the slightest and we were delighted. She remembers that evening differently these days and even recalls us setting up our musical equipment and performing, but the truth is there was only one performance and the equipment was all hers.

We visited Marianne at her flat in Chelsea another evening, soon after taking a hit of acid. While talking and listening to sounds, we drank wine and smoked a couple of doozies, then I excused myself and went to the bathroom. As soon as I sat down, I noticed the black and white patterns in the lino floor swirling and swimming, which was the first sign of the acid taking effect. I was so mesmerized that I lost all track of time, but after what felt like only ten minutes I decided to go back to the party.

I unlocked the door, grabbed the handle, pulled, and couldn't get out. The door wouldn't move. I waited for a second, then pulled the handle again, but it still wouldn't budge, so I called out for help. I wasn't loud enough, because the music was louder, but also I didn't really want to draw attention to the fact that I was locked in.

By now I wasn't sure how long I'd been in there. I had lost all sense of reason, and I was starting to sweat. I shouted out louder, but they still didn't hear me, and I was beginning to think I'd have to break down the door when I pushed the handle one last time and it opened easily. All I'd had to do was to push the door instead of pull. Feeling relieved and stupid, I walked back into the room, and when Marianne asked me where I'd been for the last half an hour, I had to admit that, like the three old ladies, I'd been locked in the lavatory.

Mervyn Conn, the promoter, brought an American girl to meet us backstage at one of our gigs, and "Plonk," being the stallion of the group, wasted no time inviting her back to Westmoreland Terrace for a drink. Well, that night she took acid with us, spent the night in Ronnie's room and convinced him that what was lacking in his life was Buddhism. She stayed for some weeks after that and gave him a paper scroll with Chinese symbols on it and explained that it was his soul. She hung it on his bedroom wall, and he would pray to it. I was raised a Roman Catholic. My mother was a practicing Catholic, which meant she never actually made it to mass, but because it was expected of her to raise her children in the faith, my brother and I were forced to go to church every Sunday, rain or shine. We'd walk towards the church, but out of sight of the house, we'd duck down a path by the railway where, depending on the season, we'd watch amateur football or cricket until mass was over. I believe in God and good deeds, but religion gives me a headache.

Acid had definitely changed us and Ronnie maybe more than the rest of us. But where he was looking for enlightenment, his new girlfriend had lumbered him with her religion, and it wasn't sitting comfortably with him, and he became very thoughtful and boring. We'd be smoking a joint, listening to sounds, and he'd sit there, pulling absentmindedly on his sideburn, with the problems of mankind laying heavily over his head like a storm cloud. When the joint would come his way, he'd take a puff and then forget he had it.

"Ronnie, pass the fuckin' joint, will yer?" Steve would shout, with a sideways look at me and Mick O'Sullivan. Steve was Captain Subtle. Ronnie would come back to Earth with a bump.

"Oh, sorry, man." He'd pass you the roach, the burnt bit of cardboard tip, or "groovy cardboard" as we used to call it.

Ronnie had always been a seeker, a spiritual person, but I don't remember him looking for anything other than a good time before acid. Though he had begun to worry us, he snapped out of it as soon as the American bird flew back to her nest, and became his same old self again, one of the lads.

With all the fans going nuts around us, there was less action finding its way backstage than you might imagine. We were never in one place long enough to do as much damage to the girls we might like to, and a good proportion of our fans were much too young anyway. One night in Scarborough an attractive boiler invited us up to her room after a gig where she had the four of us naked and naughty in no time flat. I think she might've been a professional, but this one was on the house and just for fun, and we were in and out and on our way back to London before we knew whether we were coming or going. I never liked going to the clubs much, but sometimes the dancers from ITV's "Ready, Steady, Go!" would be there. We'd hang out at the Speakeasy, the Bag o' Nails, and the Scotch of St. James for drinks, pills, and loud conversation over Stax and Motown while watching the girls bump and grind on the dance floor. We appeared on "Ready, Steady, Go!" many times and Sandy Sarjeant was the best dancer on the show in my opinion. I'd see her at the Scotch quite often. She was a good laugh, and like quite a few of the musicians, I fancied my chances with her. She'd come to the house occasionally, stay the night, and then have to go home in the morning wearing the skimpy number she'd been wearing at the clubs the night before.

Ronnie met his first wife, Sue, on one of our British tours. She was opening the show, singing under the stage name of Genevieve. She wasn't much of a singer, but she was a good looker and a sweet girl. Ronnie really fancied her, but when her manager caught them kissing between the curtains on stage during the show in Cardiff, he told Ronnie to leave her alone or there would be trouble. Ronnie kicked him off the stage and told him to fuck off, which he did, leaving Sue without a manager but with a new boyfriend. She eventually moved out of her flat near Sloane Street and came to stay with Ronnie and us at number 22.

Whatever we were up to or whatever drug we were on, there were always shows to play, and places to be, and late nights were almost always followed by what felt like early morning wakeups from Bill. One of his favourite lines was, "Wakey wakey, tea and cakey," which he'd say while he was driving as well, if he needed to stretch his legs. He could be amusing sometimes. Not often, just sometimes. He could be a cantankerous, devious old bastard and he and I didn't get on from day one. He got the needle to me for some unknown reason and nothing I could say made any difference to him. Perhaps he resented my joining a band that was already famous, or maybe he realized I could see right through him, because he worked for Arden and not the band.

One morning after a gig in Torquay, he introduced us to a friend of his by saying, "This is Steve, Kenney, Plonk...and that's McLagan."

I don't know why he was like that, it was just his way. A grumpy old bastard doesn't need an excuse. He hated most living things and all northerners in particular, which must've been a drag for him because we were always up North, for the punters and the money. A few miles north of London there's a little town called Baldock, and Bill put it on the map for us. Every time we'd go through there on our way to Birmingham, Manchester, and onward, he'd mumble from the front of the car, "Any further north than Baldock, and you're camping out."

We'd wait for him to say it and pull faces at him behind his back. But it wasn't just northerners he hated, I think he detested foreigners even more. There's a restaurant halfway up the Eiffel Tower, and on our first trip to Paris we had a meal there. He was so rude, he not only sent his food back, but he sent the wine back as well. There were other times in restaurants when he was just as rude. If the waiter or waitress brought a plate with only a couple of knobs of butter on it, instead of spreading what was there and then asking for more, he'd say:

"The war's over, you know."

He was such a pain, but we couldn't get rid of him as we didn't employ him. Don Arden did and we just suffered him. We already knew not to say too much in front of him, because he was Don's ears when we were on the road. And maybe Don caught a feeling from us that we weren't pleased with the way he was looking after our affairs, because one afternoon he took us into the Galaxy Entertainments offices, across the hall from where Ron King handled our bookings. He introduced a large, ugly bastard to us as "Mad" Tom. We smiled nervously, then Steve cockily put out his hand.

"Hello, Tom."

Tom grabbed him by the lapels and lifted him off the floor, bringing their eyes close together.

"Mad Tom to you," he said, and lowered him slowly to the floor.

Tom wasn't smiling and neither were we, but we didn't want to see him mad, and then we understood why we'd been introduced.

We got lost once, driving from Manchester to either Burnley, Blackpool, Blackburn, Bury, or Barnsley. They became the same place after a while. We spotted a little urchin of a girl waiting at the bus stop in the driving rain. She had black ratty hair and was soaked to the skin.

"Could you tell me where The Locarno is, my dear?" Ronnie inquired in his most charming, put on "posh" voice. Her disinterested reply was in a broad Mancunian accent.

"I don't know, but it's a bastard long way!"

It said it all for us. It was always a bastard long way.

On a long ride, say up to Glasgow, we would occasionally construct an eighteen-skin joint that would keep us in a sedated mood all the way up the A1. Normally, you'd stick two Rizla rolling papers together and then another on the end to make a three-skinner, but to build an eighteen-skinner you almost needed a degree in engineering, and a will for survival to smoke it! It would never get finished in one go, it was like musical chairs, you'd keep smoking and passing it, hoping it wouldn't come back too soon. But it always did, and if it was a test of grooviness, we all failed every time.

Life on the road was fun, but not without its little scary moments. In August 1966, we toured Britain with Martha and The Vandellas and Lou Christie. To hear Martha Reeves sing "Heatwave" and "Dancing in the Streets" live was an incredible thrill, and we watched them most nights from the side of the stage.

Steve wore a silk scarf on stage one night, and Lou thought he'd look cool in one too, so he bought one and sang his show with it tied round his neck like Steve. But instead of looking cool it only managed to make him look naff. After the Glasgow show we were driving to Whitley Bay near Newcastle for the night, and were in the Jag and away from the stage door within seconds of the last chord of "All or Nothing" dying out. As we got to the end of the narrow street a mob of screaming girls came running after us. This was why we never stayed in the same town as the show.

"Lock your doors!" Bill shouted while he swung a "Reggie," floored it for a few hundred yards and then hung a "Louie" into a dead-end. Nice one Bill! After a quick three-point turn, we came out of the side street, sped round the corner and came face to face with another lot of "divvies" swarming toward us. He was used to these manoeuvres, having driven The Beatles, but apparently so were they. He reversed, pulled into another street, raced to the corner, turned, and there was another lot running towards us.

He was a cool old character, but even he was beginning to worry that we wouldn't get out of the city without getting hurt. Eventually, as we couldn't stop getting cornered, he found his way to the crew hotel with the idea of getting the police to help. There were a few girls hanging around the entrance as we drove up, but he told us not to worry, to unlock the doors and run past them as soon as he pulled up. We jumped out of the car and ran to the large glass doors. But they were locked, a copper standing on the inside with a smirk on his face. The kids were on us like flies on shit. It got very scary very quickly, they were pulling our hair out in chunks and ripping at our clothes. We couldn't get away and the feeling of claustrophobia was building like a fire within me.

The Old Bill didn't realize we weren't fans, we were fan bait, and made no attempt to help us, although I could see our road crew shouting at him to let us in. All of a sudden Ronnie's head got knocked against the plate-glass door and he slid down to the ground at my feet. I tried to reach down to pull him up, but they were screaming so loud and pushing so hard I couldn't get my hand down to him, and then it all went quiet. Everything seemed to be in slow motion as if I was swimming in a thick jelly, and at the same time the horror of being unable to help him gripped me and made me feel like I was drowning.

The next thing I knew I literally saw red and walked through the thick glass door as if I was The Hulk, broken glass flying in all directions. I wasn't scratched, and I'd heard the expression "seeing red" before without knowing what it meant, until that moment. I had completely lost it. The policeman grabbed me and told me I was under arrest. I was hysterical, out of my mind, screaming at him like a madman:

"Leave me alone! Get an ambulance! He's hurt! Why the fuck wouldn't you let us in?"

He had no answer other than to put cuffs on me while the crew did their best to hold back the kids who were swarming all over us. It was one thing on top of another. Bill was trying to get him to let me go, but he wouldn't listen. More police were arriving and someone finally took care of Ronnie, who'd only fainted, as it turned out. The copper finally listened to reason and uncuffed me, but I hadn't had a chance to calm down. I immediately shouted at him:

"You bastard, I ought to kick the shit out of you!"

"That's it!" He said, and arrested me again. This time it was my own fault and it took a lot of pleading by everyone before he finally let me go. We all needed to calm down, especially me, and it took a couple of large brandies before I could. When we eventually drove off to Whitley Bay, I sat in the back of the car completely drained and exhausted. I couldn't speak, I still wasn't sure what had happened to me.

The Rex Hotel in Whitley Bay was a favourite spot for us to stay, get high, or rejuvenate, or all three. It was an old hotel, and we stayed there several times on our way up or coming back down to London from Scotland. The staff appeared to have been there for years and the night porter was a friendly chap, bringing us drinks through the night, but never giving us any bother, even though we'd be raving on dexies, thrashing out new songs on guitars and stinking up the place with hash. Nowadays, most hotels are all the same or similar, and although it was a bit run-down in the mid-to-late Sixties the place had a charm about it. Whitley Bay had seen grander days, it seemed, but The Rex kept up the old standards.

I don't remember eating an evening meal there that often, but when we did, there were two old dears—Mitzi at the piano and Mina on the violin— who'd play genteel classical dribblings while you ate, and now and again they would surprise us by throwing in something from the twentieth century, like "April Love." It was very civilized and relaxing. Outside, the North Sea could be raging but inside you'd be at peace.

But these were rare moments of calm and we always had a tough time getting into and out of halls with the fans. We'd done so many TV shows and were at the height of our fame. Kids came from miles around to see us in the hopes of getting a piece of us, sometimes literally.

One cold, miserable, and rainy afternoon, as Bill was negotiating the back-doubles trying to find the best way into Newcastle City Hall without loss of life or limb, we came upon a phenomenon known only to those who've been there as a nutter. Actually, there were two of them, and she and her mate stopped our car in its tracks by running at us with full force, without any fear, and with the certain conviction that we were going to give them our autographs there and then. They grabbed the bonnet of the Jag, hung on tight, and screamed at us through the windscreen.

"Steeeeeeeeeeeeve, Ronnie, Mac, Kenney!"

They wouldn't let go until Bill promised that if they calmed down, they could come backstage to meet us. Ann and her friend Rita, who wasn't quite as crazy, were sopping wet, out of breath, and full of good intentions when he led them into the dressing room, but they went nuts again immediately. Ann grabbed both me and Steve round the neck, screaming in our ears, "I love yer, I really do!"

She said it over and over to each of us, and we were horrified to realize just how strong she was. She had a grip like a wrestler. Bill tried to get her to calm down, but it was no use, she had to let it all out first. Ann had a loud voice with a thick Geordie accent, and was still screaming at us even as we were signing the books. She was a handful, but she settled down after a while. We'd look out for her after that, and see her at every gig around the country on that tour. She was so loyal to the band and eventually she became a firm friend of ours, not just a fan, and after a year or so, we'd get to a hall and she'd be there waiting for us, on her own by then.

"Hello, boys. Howya?"

"Hello, Ann, come in."

We'd called her "Mad" Ann originally, but she was a really sweet girl once we got to know her. She would take the train down to London occasionally and visit our parents. She'd knock on Mum and Dad's door and tell them how I was doing. I don't know how she got their addresses but Mum and Dad were always pleased to see her, and would invite her in for a cup of tea and a bite to eat. She went back more than once and became a real friend of the family. I saw her years later, when The Faces were playing in nearby Gateshead. She was working as a maid at the hotel we were staying in, and by then she was all grown up and sensible, but still our most loyal fan.

Loyalty can sometimes be painful. A charity football match had been scheduled for a Sunday afternoon at Odsal Stadium, Bradford, between the Television All-Stars, a team of soccer playing celebrities, including our old mate Kenny Lynch, and some Yorkshire sporting personalities. Although none of us was interested in football, we were in the area on a day off, so we were only too pleased to make an appearance. We were to drive round the edge of the pitch at half-time, wave at the fans, sign a few books, and then bugger off. It couldn't have been easier. Except the organizer had seriously underestimated the number of loyal Small Faces fans in the area, because there wasn't enough security for the large crowd.

There was a lot of screaming, pushing, and shoving when we arrived, suggesting not everyone was there to see minor celebrities running around in shorts. Also, because it had been raining, Bill wasn't about to drive the newly washed Jag onto the muddy pitch. The chairman solved that problem by offering to lend us his car. So at half-time, after the sun had come out and the muddied players had walked off the pitch, we climbed into his gleaming Ford Zodiac, Bill behind the wheel, while the announcer squelched over the P.A. in a voice more suited for a boxing match:

"Ladies and Gentlemen, let's give a nice warm welcome to…THEE… SMAAALL…FAAAAACEZZZ!"

As Bill drove towards the touchline to begin our circuit, the kids swarmed onto the pitch from all sides. "Lock your doors!" he barked, then drove to the middle of the pitch looking for an escape route, and although he was used to coping with crowds and especially avoiding them there was no way out. Whichever way he turned the wheel, there were more fans running at us from another direction, squealing, screaming, and slipping in the mud. "Oh, Jesus, here we go!" he said, and almost immediately they were on all sides of us, thumping and banging on the windows with their fists and screaming our names through the glass. I remember Ronnie laughing hysterically as the car's wheels spun wildly in the mud, the girls' bodies pressed against the car, their sweaty, excited faces squashed hard against the windows.

But we weren't going anywhere. We were parked in the middle of a muddy football field, and where the fans hadn't been able to get to us fast enough seconds before, as more and more of them piled in behind, their brief delirious moment turned to horror as they realized they were trapped. It was terrifying for them, and the laughter soon turned to tears, but there was nothing any of us could do, and before long we were starting to panic too. Bill was shouting at them to move back, but they couldn't, and I watched helpless as, squashed flat against the window, one tearful fan got pushed down under the weight of the kids behind her and slid down the window screaming.

The car had sunk deeper into the mud with the kids climbing onto the bonnet and up on the roof, and then, with the sound of crumpling metal the roof started to cave in on us, and we reached up in an attempt to stop it crushing us, at the same time begging them to move back. It was becoming harder to breathe too, partly because we were losing our minds with panic, and partly because we couldn't get the windows open. While I couldn't foresee a happy ending to the drama, the people in the stands hadn't the slightest idea what was really happening on the pitch, and might even have been mildly fascinated, a bit like watching ants on jam. But Kenny Lynch, Harry Fowler, and a few of the other players realized that unless they did something to help, we'd be stuck there all day, and it was only when they ran onto the pitch and saw limping, teary-eyed fans, that they began to understand the seriousness of the situation.

With the help of the police, they pushed through the crowd, pulling and dragging kids away until they got to the car, and I'll never forget the relief that washed over me when Kenny's smiling face appeared between the little girls bawling at us on the other side of the windscreen.

"All right, lads?" he chirped. Noticing the looks on our faces and the caved in roof and bonnet, he could tell that we were far from all right, and he and the others set about helping the bruised and muddied girls up from under the car. Then, after some shoving and heaving, and cheers from us, they pushed the car out of the mud. Bill inched forward, avoiding the kids still standing around, then skidding and sliding, mud flying behind us, we raced off the pitch to the clubhouse, jumped out of the scratched, flattened, and dented Zodiac, and slipped into the womblike leather comfort of our Mark X Jaguar. We sped off, Bill mumbling behind the wheel as we sat in silence, too shocked to speak or even think about rolling a joint.

The short drive north to the Keighley Country Club took no time at all, and it would be a pleasant change from the city hotels we usually stayed in, because it was surrounded by fields and wild country up in the Pennines. The minute Bill parked the car, Steve jumped out, climbed over a low wall, and started running for his life across the field.

Without a word we followed and ran screaming after him for all it was worth, until we were exhausted. We fell over in a heap and lay there laughing and screaming until we were out of breath and any serious thought. Later, after the five of us had got through dinner and a couple of bottles of wine, the manager of the place offered us a brandy in the bar and introduced us to Freddie Truman. He sat and amused us with stories that I've forgotten, but I do remember the advice he gave us that night.

"They asked me if I played cricket for sport or money. I'll tell you what I told them. Fuck sport, take th'money, put it in your bin, and fuck off home. Never mind the other fucker."

He'd hit the nail on the head, of course. We were treating our careers as sport, instead of watching the finances, but we knew precious little about music, and absolutely nothing about money. We may not have got the opportunity to take the money and fuck off home with it, like he suggested, but we never did mind the other fucker!

CHAPTER EIGHT

People in Show Business...

Fans come and go, some are loyal and some get hurt, but it's never a good thing to let them down. Running through the stage door from the car one day I overheard a young girl saying to her friend disappointedly:

"Eeooohh, ain't they little!"

We'd forget that some of the kids only knew us from TV and standing together, there was no way to tell if we were short or tall, and it must have been a shock for some fans to find out we were just a bunch of short, spotty hooligans.

We were playing at an old theatre in Coventry. I went on stage to check my gear before the curtains were drawn and noticed that somebody had set up two microphone stands at the Hammond, where normally I'd only have one. I grabbed one of them with my left hand and the other with my right hand, and as I did, I went into a seizure. It was an electric shock that wouldn't stop. My arms were rigid, stuck straight out in front of me, still grabbing the stands, my fists in a death grip. I could see blue flashes coming from my hands and my outstretched arms and I screamed in pain, but nothing happened. It carried on and on. The situation was irreversible and there was nothing I could do to make it stop. Someone had to help me, it was as simple as that. It seemed to go on for ages without letup, and I knew I was going to die. As soon as I gave up, I saw a brilliant white light at the end of a tunnel. I knew then I was going to be all right, and suddenly felt very calm and serene. At that exact moment I was thrown up in the air like an acrobat, I somersaulted over the organ in front of me and landed hard on my bum among the still unopened curtains. I was in pain, and then, realising that I hadn't finished with the material world after all, I ran off the stage like a whipped dog, hurt and confused.

Ronnie, Kenney, and Steve, watching from across the stage, thought I was just messing about. They'd seen me grab the mic stands, fly over the organ, and disappear all in one smooth movement like an Olympic gymnast. Apparently, I'd grounded two separate systems with thousands of volts going through my heart. I could have died. Well, I did die! But I put on a very lively show that night, I can tell you, and I have to say, it's so good to be alive.

Apart from me that night, Steve was probably the most electric person I'd ever met and definitely the most tiring to be around. It was never boring being with him, and very few could keep up with him day and night, and I know a few who tried. We saw just how electric he was one day as we were driving west out of London on the Great West Road. The road narrowed to two lanes from three where it crosses the railway tracks at Osterley Station. Hopefully, they've widened the road by now, but this was in 1966. Steve was sitting in the front that day, next to Bill, and we were in the fast lane with two cars next to us, as the road climbed up to the bridge. All three cars tried to squeeze into the two lanes and Bill had to steer the car up onto the central divider, perilously close to the cast-iron railings along the middle, and we drove like that for about twenty or thirty yards, until the road widened again. We were all shit-scared, but when Steve saw what was going on, his hair stood on end like a halo and stayed there for a couple of seconds. Kenney, Ronnie, and I screamed with laughter, but he didn't feel it happening and wouldn't believe us at first. He'd had a hair-raising experience and didn't even know it!

Our dressing rooms were a scene of their own. As we smoked hash continually and took so many pills, our faces were constantly breaking out. We'd become spotty wimps with cracked lips, except for Kenney who got a home-cooked meal every once in a long while and didn't stay up as much as us three. Of course we ate in fine hotels, but on the road we'd eat any old crap. In fact, if health was wealth, we were bankrupt. Noticing just how pimply we'd become, Steve had the bright idea of putting red bulbs around the dressing room mirrors to replace the white ones. It was a bit like walking into a whorehouse, but at least our spots weren't so obvious. It didn't bother us that the audience could see our blotchy faces in the bright lights on stage, it was more so that we didn't have to see them ourselves. Then after a while we started using more red lights out front because, being stoned so much, the bright lights had become too harsh for our stonedness.

Occasionally, if we ran out of gear on the road, no matter what time of night we got back to London, one of us would jump in a cab and score, which would generally mean an even later night than usual. The next morning there would be photo sessions and interviews for hours at a time at number 22, because it was the only chance that Tony Brainsby, our publicist, had to fit them in.

One morning, Arden phoned us at the house and told us he'd got us parts in Brigitte Bardot's new film, and the *Daily Mirror* was sending round Jack Bentley to interview us for the paper. I could hardly believe my ears. Brigitte Bloody Bardot! I'd joined the band of my dreams, and now I was going to be in a movie with the French sexpot! I was still thinking about the possibilities when Bentley knocked at the door. He'd wasted no time. Liesel brought up tea and biscuits to the sitting room, and we sat around in a still stoned daze while he asked us what our thoughts were about being in a film with Brigitte. We were thrilled, we said, but none of us had actually seen any of her films, though we all knew how good she looked.

As soon as Bentley left, Ronnie got on the phone to Arden to find out exactly *when* we were going to start filming. He just laughed.

"Whaddaya talkin' about? There's no movie. It was just a way of getting you in the *Daily Mirror,* and it seems to have worked. I couldn't tell you beforehand or you might have blown it."

Though the others had a small part in an even smaller film, *Dateline for Diamonds,* before I joined the band, the closest I got to being in a film was working the Odeon and Gaumont cinema chains on Small Faces' package tours. Unlike the brightly lit ballrooms where we usually played and where the kids stood as close as possible to us, in the cinemas the audience was beyond the orchestra pit and seated in the dark. After a while we began to notice another difference to playing the ballrooms. Many of the young girls in the front rows, believing themselves to be in total darkness, had their hands inside their knickers, playing with themselves while we played. It was as if we were on the other side of a one way mirror and they were in their own bedrooms. They had no idea we could see them masturbating. As the curtains parted each night, the first thing we'd notice was the smell of pussy wafting up at us from the audience as they writhed in their seats.

Though we didn't much mind, it certainly wasn't a turn on, it was bizarre to watch and it was a revelation to realize that to some of our fans we were merely sex objects. Sex objects have a duty to dress well, and as we'd already bought everything that Carnaby Street had to sell, Don Arden thought it was time to upgrade us. It was a problem very few people had, but you couldn't really wear the same jacket on "Ready, Steady, Go!" one week and on "Top of the Pops" the next. Arden took us round to Dougie Millings's shop one afternoon with the idea of him designing suits for us. Dougie was a showbiz tailor and famous for the collarless jackets The Beatles wore when they first made it, and the suits they wore at Shea Stadium.

He had a lot of flannel, if you'll pardon the pun, but he was a character. His son brought out roll after roll of different fabrics and we discussed styles that day, but the best part of it all was going through the racks in the back of his shop, where there were dozens of finished suits, jackets, and shirts waiting to be collected. There were some of Tom Jones's jackets and a couple for Gerry and The Pacemakers, but we flipped when we spotted some of John, Paul, George, and Ringo's uncollected "fab gear" hanging there. While Dougie was taking Kenney's measurements, I slipped into one of John Lennon's jackets. It was pink and it looked pretty fucking cool, but it was too big for me. Ronnie, being a big George Harrison fan, tried one of his on next but that was too big as well. But when I tried one of Ringo's jackets on, I was knocked out to find it fitted me perfectly, and it looked good on me too.

In fact, all of his stuff fitted me well. Thank God for short arses! I wanted that jacket so bad, and naturally Dougie couldn't let me have it, but he made me one just like Ringo's. When he'd finished with us we must have had ten suits each, my favourite being a tan, mohair single-button with a thin, orange stripe that was based on the sharkskin suit that Lee Marvin wore in *The Killers*. It was so cool, and I loved it so much, I wore it even after the hash burns in the front of the jacket became noticeable.

Don Arden had actually started as a singer and an impersonator, but graduated into management after bringing rock 'n' rollers Chuck Berry, Little Richard, and Gene Vincent to Britain for their early tours. He'd use his James Cagney impersonation at the drop of a hat if questions were asked about money. To this day, Chuck Berry demands all of his tour money in cash and in dollars before he sets foot on English soil. It must be a coincidence. Kenney was only sixteen, Steve eighteen, and Ronnie nineteen when Arden found the band, and even though I was twenty when I joined, he encouraged us all to call him Uncle Don. This allowed him to treat us like children, but these children were beginning to have suspicions about him and his handling of their money.

Towards the end of 1966, we realized that wherever the money was going, it wasn't going into our bank accounts, because we didn't have bank accounts, we only had pockets. As we were constantly touring in the North, we could never get to the bottom of it, and there seemed to be nothing we could do. But unknown to us, the Marriotts, Lanes, Jones, and McLagans had got together for a parents meeting while we were out of town, believing someone to do with the band must be getting the money. It took them only a few minutes to realize we were all being shafted, so they made an appointment with Don and walked into his office demanding to know what was going on. He sat them all down and said:

"People in show business spend money." He paused for effect. "And they've spent theirs."

This was when we were earning one thousand pounds a night, every night of the week. Our parents were horrified, and were inclined to believe him because none of us knew anything about finances or contracts, all being minors, and could just about find our way around our instruments, never mind a management or recording contract. As if that wasn't bad enough, he went on to tell them we were all on drugs, which explained how such vast amounts of money had been spent in such a short time. Hashish not being an expensive drug, it suggested something much more serious.

The shit had really hit the fan. Although my mum smoked like a chimney, she'd never got used to me smoking cigarettes, never mind hash, and now she was imagining heroin! All our parents were devastated because it was believable, and Steve's mum, Kay Marriott, told me later that because he'd used the word "drugs," their imaginations ran riot. The red herring worked for a while because they were already suspicious.

We always seemed to be out of our heads when they saw us, and yet they'd rationalized our behaviour. On the other hand, we thought it was only a matter of time before smoking became legal because we didn't consider it to be wrong. Illegal, yes, but not wrong. But though Arden hadn't put it into words, he'd implanted the suggestion in their minds that we were on heroin, and that was the last straw for us. We couldn't trust him anymore. We knew if we were ever going to sort out our finances we'd have to get away from "Uncle Don" first, which also meant leaving Westmoreland Terrace.

After an incredible year together, it was time we had flats of our own, and personally I could hardly wait. Having the smallest bedroom in the house meant clothes, magazines, and anything else I'd collected were in piles in the corners of the room, and as much fun as it had been, we'd done well not to have had any arguments in all that time. Ronnie got a place near Earl's Court Road, Steve moved into a chintzy flat in Williams Mews in Knightsbridge, and I found a two-storey, cheese-wedge-shaped pad in Princes Mews near the Bayswater Road and Hyde Park. Since Bill Corbett was out of the picture because he worked for Arden, we got a new driver. Tony was a lovely guy with a dark blue Daimler limousine, and no attitude. He and the car were perfect. It had foldout seats and blinds on the windows, and was bigger in the back than an Austin Princess, the standard limo of the day. We could fold the seats up and sprawl all over the floor in the back. It was really wicked, like a big den.

Though I hadn't known it when I moved in, I soon discovered there was a Russian Orthodox Church behind my flat, because they rang the bells at all hours, which might have been wonderful for the Hunchback of Notre Dame, but it kept me awake. As if that wasn't all, there were garages the whole length of the Mews, and mechanics worked on cars all day long during the week. With the only windows in the place facing the street, I had to keep the curtains closed all day for a little privacy. After twenty years of Mum's home cooking and a year of Liesel's culinary delights, being suddenly left to my own devices in the kitchen, I was adrift in a sea of pots and pans.

To vary my diet I looked through a recipe book and discovered how to make omelettes. Unfortunately, that's all I managed to cook and for weeks that was pretty much all I had to eat. After a couple of months I found a much better place in Hanover Terrace Mews, Regent's Park. It was a light, airy flat overlooking the park, and after I found a company that delivered cooked meals, life took on a new turn. Steve didn't stay long in one place. He could never keep the noise down. He always played his sounds and guitar at full volume, and when he laughed, he laughed like a drain. He was a very funny bloke who told a joke well, but he'd be the first to laugh, and the loudest, so with that and the sounds it would only be a matter of time before his current landlord had to throw him out. He was the removal company's pinup boy around that time and it was impossible to keep up with his latest phone number.

He liked to have people around him, liggers or otherwise, but he'd rather have bad company than none at all. Mick O'Sullivan lived with him even before Westmoreland Terrace and after Steve was evicted from several flats because of noise problems, he leased a smart town house in Chiswick, where another geezer called Ron appeared on the scene. Ron was very amusing but rather slippery. He found an ancient Bentley for Steve to buy that had no passenger seat in the front. It was like a poor man's limo, but Steve loved it. While Ron drove, Steve lay on the floor in the back, with the seat as a head-rest, a joint in one hand, a drink in the other, and his feet in the front of the car. He thought it was very moody and loved the fact that he couldn't be seen from the outside. Ron drove him around town like that for a few months, and then drove away, never to be seen again.

Mick was very persistent when he wanted something, and Steve was amazed, and often amused at the lengths he'd go to. He told me about the day Mick fancied going for a drink, but as he had no money of his own, he told Steve how they poured a lovely pint of Guinness at the pub down the road and asked him if he'd ever tried it. Steve had never acquired a taste for

Guinness, and told him he thought it was, "Bleedin' 'orrible stuff. I don't know how anybody can drink it. Yuck!" Mick dug his heels in, and went on and on about it, saying how it was lovely when it was just right, that he should just try one pint, that he was sure he'd love it. Steve said, "I've never liked it, and I never will. Fuck off, Mick!"

Then Mick said that he and Ron thought it might do him good to get out of the house. Steve softened finally, and said, "Well, maybe you're right. I fancy a drink. I think I'll have a brandy."

With that, the three of them walked the hundred yards or so to the Mawson Arms, next to Fuller's Brewery, and sat down at a table. Mick still hadn't given up though. He said that Steve didn't know what he was missing. Steve had had enough.

"Oh, all right, okay? Get us a poxy Guinness and leave me alone!"

Mick put his hand out for the cash, Steve handed him a tenner, and he walked to the bar.

"A pint of Guinness and two large brandies, please."

CHAPTER NINE

The Industry of Human Happiness

As we were lost in the financial and legal worlds, we got an accountant and a solicitor to arrange a final meeting with Arden and formally advise him he was no longer our manager. It was easier than we thought. He didn't seem surprised and wasn't particularly unpleasant about it, but we were glad to be leaving his office for the last time.

Though we had to find a new manager and a record deal, more important was to sign with an agent so we could play some gigs to get our hands on some readies. We were skint. The two biggest agents in our field at that time were Arthur Howes and Harold Davison, so we arranged meetings with them on the same day, with the idea of playing one against the other to see who could do the most for us. We considered ourselves to be in a very strong position in England and Europe, as by 1967 The Beatles had quit touring and both The Stones and The Who were concentrating mainly on the States.

Arthur Howes had a reputation in the business for being a gentleman. He was a dapper man, and we shook hands, sat down, and he offered us tea in a very civilized manner. He asked us what he could do for us and we said we wanted to headline our own tours across Europe and the U.K.

"No problem," he said with a smile.

We told him we were looking for new management, a record deal with a large advance, and total artistic control, and he said:

"No problem, I'll help you in any way I can."

We told him we wanted to get to the States, though we hadn't yet had a hit there, and he said:

"No problem, I can introduce you to one of the best agents in the country."

We talked about percentages and he had…no problem taking 10 percent. No problem was basically his attitude. He was a shrewd businessman and he was a nice guy, but we thought that maybe his head was in the clouds.

Next, we popped round the corner to Harold Davison's office in Regent Street, where he and Tito Burns greeted us all smiles and smarmy warmth. The contrast was immediately apparent. They were on us like vultures. Tito led us to his office.

"Come in, come in," he said. "Sit down, sit down."

He repeated himself a lot. We squeezed into his office, and immediately the meeting hit a sticky note when we told them we were looking for a record deal with a major company, large advance, and total artistic control.

"Ooh." With his eyebrows raised and looking shiftily at the wallpaper for help, he said, "We'd have to get you out of your contracts first, before we could make a definite promise. It's not going to be easy." Next, we told them about our hopes of getting on a U.S. tour.

"Ooh, that won't be too easy to set up either because you haven't toured there before, have you?" Headlining European tours was going to be difficult as well, because we hadn't had a record out in some months, and as he explained new acts were coming up all the time. At least we agreed on the percentage. Tito said they'd only take 10 percent, which we found out later was the maximum allowed by law, but he had one provision.

"We take 10 percent of everything," he paused. "Anything you do, recordings, songwriting, or touring, we get 10 percent. In fact, if you take a shit, I want 10 percent of that too." Laughter all round. Well, at least he had a sense of humour. Of course, we couldn't have it all our own way. America would be a tough nut to crack and Europe might be more difficult this time around, and getting out of our recording situation wouldn't be as easy as we'd thought. Of course, we were disappointed but we had to face hard facts.

On the one hand, Arthur was a likable personality, but he appeared to be too agreeable to be realistic. Tito was a bit of a creep, but the agency had The Stones and The Hollies on their books, which suggested they knew what they were doing. If I'd known then that Tito had started out in the business as a singing accordionist, whose hit single was "Bebop Spoken Here," I might have seen him as a loser and had second thoughts. But we decided to sign with the Harold Davison Agency and with Tito as our personal representative. As soon as we did, Arden billed The Harold Davison Agency for twenty thousand pounds, which they passed directly on to us. Now we knew why Arden didn't seem to be bothered about us leaving. We hadn't really left him at all.

Well, they did very little for us, and by signing us they controlled the only major act in competition with The Hollies in Europe. When we finally dropped them later that year, we sent Tito his 10 percent in a sealed box. I hope his secretary didn't open his mail for him.

Arthur, being the true gentleman he was, never held a grudge and eventually got our business anyway. He bought us large cognacs one day when we happened to be on the same flight to Germany. Cheers, Arthur.

As Ronnie was to write later: "I wish that I knew what I know now when I was younger. I wish that I knew what I know now when I was stronger."

Tito put us on the Roy Orbison tour in March 1967. The opening night at the Finsbury Park Astoria was the debut of the Jeff Beck Group, but like ships passing in the night, we didn't see their show, and missed the golden opportunity of meeting Rod Stewart and Ronnie Wood. We heard it was a bit of a shambles because the kids kept screaming for Roy and the Small Faces.

The Big "O" proved to be a lovely man from Wink, Texas, and for all the hardship and sadness in his life he was a very amusing man with a dry wit. He drank us all under the table one night in a little hotel in the north of England. The band that would eventually become the Atlanta Rhythm Section backed him, and the guitarist would tune Roy's guitar each night and hand it to him as he walked into the wings. On the last night of the tour Roy gave the guy his guitar as usual, but he tuned it up two semi-tones. Roy already had a high voice—you only have to try singing along to "In Dreams" or "It's Over" when they next come on the radio to realize how high.

He realized what they'd done as soon as the band began the first number. He couldn't stop the show, but he turned and smiled through his teeth at the band. "You bastards," he said in a whisper and then he sang the show as if nothing had happened. A classy guy.

One of the finest shows I ever saw was the Stax/Volt Revue, which came to Europe in 1967. On March 17, they played the Hammersmith Odeon for one night and the four Small Faces had front-row-centre seats on the balcony. It was a mainly West Indian crowd, and most of them were shouting "Otis! Otis!" all night. The most magical of many magic moments that night was at the very top of the show, when the curtains parted and I saw and heard Booker T. Jones begin playing the chords of "Green Onions." I was in heaven! Then, when Steve Cropper, Al Jackson, and Duck Dunn came in I screamed my head off. In fact, they could've closed the curtains after that number and said goodnight, because it was all I needed to hear. The sound wasn't great early on in the show, it was difficult to hear the organ, and I could tell he was having a hard time hearing it too, but I watched Booker T. like a hawk, and like a real trouper he carried on with a smile.

I remember thinking if I ever got to hear Booker T. and the MG's live, I'd finally hear the Hammond as loud as it is on the records. In the Sixties and Seventies, it was impossible to get the Hammond loud enough to compete with guitars, because it was built for home or church use, not for large halls. But after that show, I felt I could deal with it because the great Booker T. still had that problem and he didn't let it bother him. Nowadays, after spending thousands of dollars on my equipment, I can compete volume-wise with most guitarists. Not all, but most.

It was a fantastic show. The Markeys joined them and added some fancy footwork as well as fine playing, then Eddie Floyd came on and pranced about, singing "Knock on Wood" and Arthur Conley sang "Sweet Soul Music." Sam and Dave really tore the place apart, working the crowd into a frenzy, and finally, when Otis Redding hit the stage, he and the band built the set up into a climax which ended with "Try a Little Tenderness." As great as Otis was, he was no match for two performers at once, and I have to say Sam and Dave owned the stage that night. But Booker T. and the MG's built it from scratch!

One day, Steve and Ronnie played "My Way of Giving" for Mick Jagger, who at the time was producing Chris Farlowe for Andrew Oldham's Immediate Records. Mick thought it would be right up Andrew's street. Immediate was the first independent record label in England, and realizing we were free of Arden and therefore Decca, Andrew was keen to get us on his label as well. It was perfect timing for us to meet him, since he'd done so well for The Stones as their manager. Casually dressed with a stoned grin and tinted shades, he arrived at Ronnie's flat in Spear Mews in a black chauffeur-driven stretched Rolls-Royce. His background was public school, but his accent had more than a hint of San Francisco. Eddie, his chauffeur, was almost as flash as Andrew, and was able to roll the most unsuss, professional joints imaginable. He'd cut a perfectly made tip out of cardboard and roll the joint so slim and straight, it would pass for a cigarette until you lit it. Very impressive.

This being our first meeting with Andrew, Kenney, and I were somewhat reserved with him. I soon noticed that if I asked a question he couldn't answer, he'd slide around it with a stoned smile and pass me the joint, which seemed to set the pattern for all of our meetings in the future. He supplied the pot, Eddie rolled the joints, we all got stoned and didn't ask too many difficult questions. Of course I liked to get stoned, but I would have preferred staying straight until the business was taken care of, so I was on the defensive with him that first day. Steve took it to be a foregone conclusion that we'd sign with his company, his mind having been made up as soon as Andrew agreed to meet us, and to him anybody who smoked dope all day like we did had to be cool.

He was a raver all right, and compared to the older, fat, business-suited managers like Don Arden, Andrew was a breath of fresh air. He and his business partner, Tony Calder, intended shaking up the music industry and making a ton of money while they were at it, and with his flair and imagination we knew he'd present us in a cool way. Also, as the head of a record company, he promised we'd get plenty of studio time to develop our sound and talked excitedly about breaking us in America. But, where Andrew had style and vision, his partner, the prematurely balding disk jockey, Tony Calder, had no flair whatsoever and wasn't looking any further than the pile of contracts he was eagerly waiting for us to sign. His role would be to look after the books and play the part of the bad cop, while Andrew passed joints around.

But we wanted so much to be in at the beginning of this new venture and Andrew's enthusiasm was so catching that some weeks later we went up to their new London offices on the first floor of 63-69 New Oxford Street to sign the contracts. Andrew led us past the reception and outer offices, through double doors to his inner sanctum, which wasn't like any office I'd been in before. It was more like a film set. The lighting was subdued and there were no desks or filing cabinets to be seen. A modern white-marble table and high-backed chairs in the centre of the dark, carpeted room were the only furnishings except for the leather buttoned sofas built into the wood-panelled walls. With his customary conspiratorial grin, Andrew handed each of us a joint and a glass of champagne and sat us down at the table with The Beach Boys' "Good Vibrations" booming out of the hidden speakers. The company's motto was "Happy to Be a Part of the Industry of Human Happiness" and at that moment I really think I was. Feeling stoned and tiddly, we signed the management, recording, songwriting, and publishing contracts with Immediate Records that would make Andrew and Tony millionaires. We'd earn it, they'd collect it. The difficult part would be getting it in our bins and fucking off home with it, as Freddie Truman had once said. To cash in on the Immediate deal, Decca released "Patterns" as a single with the previously released "E Too D" on the B side. It was one of a few finished tracks of ours that Arden had in the vault, but we didn't promote it in any way, knowing we wouldn't get paid, so we were well pleased when it died a death. Finally, with time to spend in the studio and Glyn Johns again behind the board twiddling the knobs, we were able to carry on where we left off and create like never before.

Studio 1 at Olympic Studios in Barnes became our second home and we could go in any time we had something to record, which was often. We cut "Here Comes the Nice" as our first single as soon as we got in there. It was a tip of the hat to Lord Buckley, whose "Here Come Da Nazz" had given us so many laughs at Westmoreland Terrace, but where his monologue was about a hip Christ-like figure, Steve and Ronnie's song was about a Methedrine dealer. Surprisingly, it didn't get banned, although it was blatantly obvious to most people that it was all about speed.

All drug users have code names so they can talk freely on the telephone or in front of strangers, and we were no exception; it became a part of our everyday language. We took leapers and sleepers, uppers and downers, but one of my favourites was "Hayleys" meaning pills. It was Cockney rhyming slang: Hayley Mills; pills. I'm sure she wouldn't be thrilled to hear it, but in the mid-Sixties you'd often hear us shouting across a crowded room, "Got any Hayleys?" We called hash "gear" like The Beatles, "kunsumbru suncumbru," which came from a Charlie Mingus record, "Garcia," for no obvious reason, and "The Nazz" after Lord Buckley, which became "the nice." When we were stoned we were "nice" and Steve would sign autographs with a snigger, "It's nice to be nice." It was his cheeky way of putting one over on people who hadn't a clue what he was talking about. He loved to shout "Nice!" at the top of his voice just to be able to say it out loud, because what he was really saying was "I'm stoned out of my tiny mind, it's totally illegal, and you can't do a fuckin' thing about it!"

The summer of 1967 was a very intense time for us, and we were all over the record shops like the measles. When "Patterns" stiffed, Decca released *From the Beginning,* a hodge-podge of recent and older tracks, mostly unreleased, including a rough version of Booker T. and the MG's instrumental "Plum Nellie," wrongly credited to Marriott/Lane. There were five of our hit singles, including "What'Cha Gonna Do About It" which had already been on the first record. When we were recording "Runaway," the Del Shannon song, Steve thought it would be a laugh to get Arden to sing the introduction in his "Josef Locke" tenor, and he was taking it seriously until Ronnie blew him a raspberry. Then he dropped his pants to turn it into a joke while he sang, but the joke was on him.

Steve bought a selection of Chinese instruments in an antique shop at the back of Shaftesbury Avenue, and on the track of "Yesterday, Today, and Tomorrow" we tried out our new sounds. While Ronnie sang, Steve picked out notes on a stringed curiosity that looked like a miniature banjo, and I came close to passing out blowing horn parts on an old woodwind instrument. All in all, it was a rotten excuse of an album, even though there are some good tracks. Even the cover photograph was taken from the same session as the first record, and you can clearly see another of Steve's chalked spliffs above Ronnie's head. Though again, we did nothing to promote it, the record did reasonably well, rising to Number Seventeen in the charts.

But we were much happier when "Here Comes the Nice" hit Number Twelve the following month. Now we had Olympic booked solid, we could experiment at a time when it was crucial for us to do so. The Beatles, The Beach Boys, and The Stones were all exploring new sounds and developing in the studio, and being with Immediate allowed us the time to join that club, and we set to work recording our first album for our new label. Although Glyn liked to get to bed at a reasonable hour, we'd keep working or playing, whichever was working. He never got stoned so it was difficult for him to see how clever we thought we were being, and we did think we were being clever some of the time, and just not after midnight when he went home. Where IBC was only four-track, Olympic had an eight-track machine, which gave us much more room to manoeuvre. We tried every instrument we could find: harpsichord, Mellotron, bells, Celeste, congas, even a comb and paper—not an instrument you hear much of these days—but now there was space on the tape and the time for us to mess around. I even played bass on Ronnie's beautiful tune "Show Me the Way." On the album's last track, "Eddie's Dreaming," we used the professional services of Georgie Fame's horn section and his conga player Speedy Acquaye. Speedy and trumpeter Eddie "TanTan" Thornton were old stoned mates, but Eddie would drift off, dreaming during a conversation. I remember him trying to get me to eat spinach, which I hated then.

He'd say: "Listen, I've got to tell you, I've got to tell you, it's good for you, listen, listen." He was lovely, but he'd drive you round the bend, which wouldn't have been much of a drive in my case, so Ronnie wrote the song about him. If you listen closely to the track you can actually hear him rabitting on when we brought the faders back up after the playing stopped. You can just make out Ronnie saying, "Fuckin' ay, fellers!," then he laughs and Eddie says excitedly, "This is the one, yeah, yeah." Steve says, "Nice, nice," and then Eddie did what he always did, as if he'd rehearsed it:

"Listen, listen, I got to tell you…" Bless his heart, Eddie was dreaming again.

Though Ronnie was no stranger to singing, with a voice like Steve's in the band it's amazing that Ronnie sang five of the fourteen numbers on that record, and even more amazing, I sang my first solo composition "Up the Wooden Hills to Bedfordshire." The title was what Ronnie's dad used to say to him when he took him up the stairs to bed as a child. Not only did I sing, but I finally broke through the Marriott/Lane songwriting partnership on "Eddie's Dreaming." Apart from instrumentals, which normally would be a four-way split whether Steve and Ronnie wrote a song separately or together, they would put both their names to it. So if I wrote with Ronnie it would be credited as Marriott/Lane/McLagan, whether Steve had anything to do with it or not. It wasn't fair, and I'd compare my situation to George Harrison's, except I never saw a Lennon/McCartney/Harrison composition on any Beatles album. So it could have been worse, and on the good side it just made me work harder to get my songs and ideas across.

It's funny to think that with all the creativity in the air, we couldn't have come up with a better title than *Small Faces,* but it didn't seem to affect the sales. Barely a month after the Decca album came out, our first Immediate attempt blew it right out of the water, when *Small Faces* was released in June 1967.

While Glyn was mixing "Itchycoo Park" (our second Immediate single, released in August 1967) George Chiantz, the tape operator, was sitting in his usual position, leaning back in his chair, his feet up on the control room window ledge. While punching the controls of the tape machine with one hand, he was engrossed in the book he was holding in the other. Glyn arranged the microphones, engineered, edited, and mixed all of our sessions, and the tape operator's lot was to load the spools of tape, and stop, start, and rewind the Ampex eight-track machine. It was pretty unrewarding work, and as an educated fellow, he was underemployed and unashamedly bored. Glyn was searching for a different sound or effect but was at a loss temporarily until George surfaced from his book and suggested an effect called "phasing," utilising another tape machine running at a slightly different speed to the first. Apparently he'd seen it used at a Beatles' session only a few weeks before. It took a few minutes to set up, but Glyn eventually used the effect on Kenney's drum track, and although I believe the song would have been a hit without it, the sound caught everybody's attention and we had another big hit under our belts. We're often wrongly credited with using phasing first, but in fact, the credit should go to Toni Fisher, who used it on her 1959 hit "The Big Hurt" even before The Beatles. "Itchycoo Park" was the follow-up to "Here Comes the Nice," and it shot up to Number Three in the U.K. charts.

Apart from Chris Farlowe and us, Immediate had Billy Nicholls, The Nice, Twice as Much, and P. P. Arnold on its books. P. P. or Pat, as we knew her, had come to England as one of Ike and Tina Turner's Ikettes, and stayed on when Andrew signed her to the label. Sandy Sarjeant was living at Pat's flat near Regent's Park, so she'd pop round from time to time and end up staying the night, and after a while it just made sense for her to move in with me. She was dancing on BBC TV's "Top of the Pops" regularly then, and every other week she'd fly to Bremen, where she was the choreographer and lead dancer of "Beat Club," a popular German TV show that we appeared on frequently.

CHAPTER TEN

The Bubble Bursts

If you'd taken a sharp left after going through the doors at Immediate's offices on any weekday in 1967 and 1968, you'd more than likely have caught Billy Nicholls writing a song in his tiny office. At times like that, it really felt like a family at Immediate, and we backed Billy on the title track of his first album, *Would You Believe,* as well as his playing on Pat's single "(If You Think You're) Groovy," which Ronnie and Steve wrote for her. Andrew organized a short promotional tour for Immediate artists in October 1967, and Small Faces, Pat and Billy, Chris Farlowe, Twice as Much, Andrew, and Eddie the chauffeur schlepped all over Europe doing TV shows, press interviews, and radio-station hype.

We'd be on an afternoon TV show in Holland, between a dog act and a trampolinist, running through "Itchycoo Park" over and over again. The interviews were often a hoot too, if they spoke English, but if they didn't, you could be sure we'd cause a bit of bother. "Bollocks" was the usual word that we assumed nobody on the other side of the English Channel understood. When an elderly Swedish gentleman on national TV says with a straight face:

"What is this…'Itchycoo Park'?"

"Rollocks!" was often Steve's reply. It's not polite, it's not even very funny, but when you're stoned out of your heads, and nobody but the four or five of you in that room understands English, it all becomes a bit of a game. Steve had a way of saying "Fuck off!" so that nobody else would understand, but I could pick it out in a thunderstorm.

In the lobby of a hotel in Helsinki, we were having a drink after appearing on a TV show when somebody suggested that the vase of flowers in the alcove next to the table we were sitting at could easily have a concealed microphone in it. And because we were stoned it became more and more believable as the evening wore on. This was before the Iron Curtain had come down, and with Finland being so close to Russia it didn't take much imagination on our part for us to be convinced we were being bugged. We all had the horrors, and given the choice of catching a midday or a 6:30 A.M. flight the next day we all caught the early flight, running to the plane and carrying our own luggage, for fear of missing it.

We went all over Europe at a relaxed pace, being interviewed on television and radio with Andrew holding court, passing out joints the whole time. We thought we were so cool, walking through the parks passing joints and openly smoking in Amsterdam, but they were all out of their heads, because it was quite legal there.

I saw a side of Andrew I'll never forget in Antwerp. As we were leaving a restaurant, climbing onto a bus, he and Eddie sucker-punched and savagely kicked a reporter who must have done something to upset him, but surely didn't deserve that kind of treatment. It was a brutal and vicious attack that gave Andrew a real charge. It gave me the creeps, and I realized then that maybe he wasn't just the fun-loving, pot-smoking head he pretended to be.

On the last night of the tour we all appeared on a special edition of "Beat Club" in Bremen, where Sandy was the choreographer. Afterwards we had a party at the hotel, where I became jealous and, deciding that if we were married I'd have her all to myself, I proposed to her on our way home at the airport in Berlin. She accepted and I really believed I could control her.

This was 1967, with flower power, beads, bells, caftans, and free love, and I had to go and propose marriage. Not that I was really interested in settling down so much as getting Sandy to settle down. I decided the two of us would take a short holiday in Greece, but before we could leave the country we had to record our next single.

My personal favourite Marriott/Lane song is "Tin Soldier," partly because it's a great song, but mainly because everything came together in that recording. From Steve's count-in at the top, the rich sound Glyn got on each of the instruments, the beautiful lyrics, and everyone's performance, it had all the raw excitement of Small Faces live on stage, even up to Kenney's signature drum fill at the end. He always finished songs live with a long set of fills as if he was signing his name, and this one says: "Kenneth Thomas Jones, damn his hands and rot his bones!"

The only criticism I might have is the snare repeats on the verses, but it's no big deal, and I'm getting used to them now, after thirty years. I played three keyboards on the track, including Olympic's beautiful Steinway grand, my old flat top Wurlitzer electric piano, and a recently bought Hammond M100 that replaced my first L100, which I sold to Ronnie. Ronnie played such a subtle bass, full of melody and right on the money, and that's Pat Arnold with Steve, Ronnie, and myself on the choruses. Steve borrowed my Fender Telecaster for that track, because he wanted to bend the third string above the nut on the intro, and he couldn't do that on his Gretsch. It was always great to play live, but listening to the record is three minutes and twenty seconds of goose bumps for me. Steve's vocal is chilling, and the final build gets me going every time. I can hardly listen to the record without a tear. "Tin Soldier" was a big hit in December 1967, when it got to Number Nine in the U.K. charts.

When it was finally mixed, we smoked and listened to it over and over, which is unusual for me, because no matter how much I like a song, I don't want to hear it too many times. The following morning, November 13, Sandy and I threw some clothes in a bag and made a dash for Heathrow to catch a plane to Athens for a short but well-earned holiday. When I handed my passport in at immigration, the officer looked me up and down a couple of times before he said, "Would you step this way, sir?"

I had no choice but to follow him into an office, where he gave me a body search. He went straight for my nuts, where he found the small piece of hash I had hidden in my underpants.

"What do you call this?"

Cannibal's Raisins, I thought, but replied with a straight face, "Cannabis."

In my imagination, I could hear the cell door shutting with a clang. So much for our holiday in Greece, but worse, there goes my freedom. Sandy didn't even know I had the hash on me, but I must've reeked of it, having spent all the previous night smoking. I notice it on other people these days, and I was pretty stupid to think no one could smell it on me, but I was oblivious to it then, being a heavy cigarette smoker as well as a hash smoker, my sense of smell was up the pictures. They were polite enough, but I couldn't think straight.

I tried to figure out what I would tell Mum and Dad, presuming they didn't hear it from the press first. Eventually, I was formally charged with smuggling, because having shown my passport I was legally outside England when they searched me. Then a local copper took me to West Drayton police station, where I was charged with possession of a controlled substance, not that I possessed it anymore.

The bubble had burst. From a state of elation over completing the record, I now found myself at the hands of the local Old Bill, being questioned about where I'd scored the demon drug, as if I was going to give them the name of a friend. They wouldn't tell me where Sandy was, and I wasn't in the mood to piss around with a lot of fresh-faced coppers, so I told them I wasn't going to say anything until I phoned my manager. Finally, when they realized they were wasting their time, they let me call Andrew who told me to sit tight, not to worry, and that he'd handle everything. After taking my belt and shoe laces in case I might try to make a run for it or felt suicidal, they gave me a cup of tea and a cell to myself. I tried to collect my thoughts, but I was so knackered I drifted into a deep sleep in minutes.

A couple of hours later, Andrew, on a rescue mission and smelling an opportunity to cash in on the free publicity, turned up at the police station wearing his customary shades and a stoned smile. He paid my bail, they gave me my belt and shoelaces back, and I was in the Rolls-Royce puffing on a joint before we left the police station car park. It felt good to be back in the real world, or more to the point out of it, so I sat back and told him every-thing and we set off for The Temple (near London's Law Courts) and a meeting with the Queen's Counsel, Victor Durand.

From the studio to the airport, and the police station to the "olde worlde" oak-panelled chambers of the QC, I felt as if I was caught in a whirlwind. After the short chat, we drove up to Immediate's offices to regroup. The guys were all there, buzzing around me and demanding to know all the details. Steve thought it was a good laugh and, like Andrew, thought it was good for business as long as it wasn't him being nicked, but I wasn't so thrilled. I was emotionally drained and called Mum and Dad to try and explain myself. Of course they'd already had Don Arden convincing them we were drug addicts, so the news wasn't altogether unexpected, but even so Mum took it really hard. It was they who would have to face their neighbours and friends, not me, and they'd been so proud of me. It was going to take time for them to adjust to my new found fame as a "druggie."

After a joint and a drink, Eddie drove us to Gered Mankowitz's studio for a photo shoot. An odd thing to do, but Andrew wanted to capitalize on the situation. In fact, it was a release for me, and I had a much needed laugh giving the camera two big "V" signs.

When I finally got back to the flat in Hanover Terrace Mews I had another nasty shock.

The place was a shambles, as if we'd been burgled. Our belongings and clothes were strewn everywhere, and whoever did it made a professional job of it. The drawers had been emptied out onto the bed and the cupboards emptied onto the floor. Presumably it was an attempt to find more drugs. Pretty silly really, when all they had to do was go into the sitting room, where a fist-sized lump of hash was in a brightly coloured enamel pot on the mantelpiece, in plain view. The Flying Squad never even noticed it. My neighbour told me he had tried to stop them breaking in, thinking they were thieves at first, but they pushed him aside even though it was illegal for them to cross the threshold without a search warrant, as Hanover Terrace was Crown property.

The following week they dropped the smuggling charge, but asked me to go to West Drayton police station before I went to the court in Uxbridge. The local sergeant showed me a coat I recognized as Sandy's, and produced a packet of Rizlas and a piece of hash from one of the pockets, telling me it was evidence found at the flat by the Flying Squad.

"Is this yours?" he asked me.

I understood immediately what was going on. They weren't clever enough to find the hash that was sitting there, so they'd planted some in Sandy's coat to incriminate her as well. Now I was royally pissed off. I looked him straight in the eye and said:

"No it isn't, you bastard!"

It was no way to talk to an officer of the law, and certainly not to a sergeant, but he could tell I was outraged, that I wasn't putting on an act. He thought about it for a moment, and then walked off, so I drove to Uxbridge, where the court was swarming with photographers. When my case was called I pleaded guilty to possession of a controlled substance and was let out on bail for a week. I returned the following week for sentencing, and they fined me the measly sum of fifty pounds, after which I returned to West Drayton nick to collect the stuff that they'd taken from the flat. The copper on duty put Sandy's coat, the packet of Rizlas, the piece of hash, and a knife that I used to roast hash on the counter in front of me, then walked away. I couldn't believe it. He left the hash there, and I could've picked it up. When he came back I pointed to it and said: "It's not mine." He laughed and put it away. I don't think he'd really understood what it was at first. The joke is he probably smoked it himself. Actually, the real joke is that when I handed the coat back to Sandy it all came back to her. She remembered slipping the hash inside the packet of Rizlas and putting it in her pocket some months before. So although the Flying Squad hadn't planted it as I thought, the sergeant at West Drayton had assumed that they had, and believed me when I said it wasn't mine. I don't even smoke the stuff anymore and it's still illegal, but even Bill Clinton has admitted smoking it. The moral to this story is: don't get caught, or if you do get caught, say you didn't inhale!

I knew Dad would be delighted that I was going to marry Sandy, but Mum wasn't keen on me living with her, never mind marrying her. She knew damn well that Sandy's dad was from Trinidad, in the French West Indies, and her mum was white, but she'd tell people Sandy was French because she just couldn't accept black people as equals. Mum thought of herself as a duchess and nothing anybody could do was good enough for her. Sandy laughed it off, but it made my blood boil, and I know it must have hurt her. Because of Mum's attitude I hadn't planned to invite her or Dad to the wedding, but the night before we realized we'd have to and she'd just have to get used to the idea. In fact, once she'd let her into her heart she grew to love Sandy like a daughter.

We were married at Marylebone Registry Office on the morning of January 4, 1968, with Mum and Dad, Sandy's mum and her three sisters to cheer us on. It was such an impulsive move that I never even mentioned it to the guys in the band, and if I remember correctly Dad must've been my best man because there was no one else there. After the short civil ceremony I only had time for a quick kiss before I was off to the BBC in a cab for a "Top of the Pops" recording, where I let Steve, Ronnie, and Kenney in on my good news. They were surprised but seemed pleased enough for us, but the producer of the show, Johnny Stewart, was very irate. He came storming into the dressing room, demanding to know who I thought I was keeping the entire show waiting. At any other time I would have apologized, but that morning I couldn't have cared less; I would've been just as happy to walk out and go home.

"Fuck off, Johnny, aren't you going to congratulate me? I just got married," and I smiled. What could he say? He broke into a grin, shook my hand and wished us well, and then we got on with the television show, swigging champagne in the dressing room between rehearsals. It wasn't much of a wedding day and Sandy wasn't even having as much fun as we were. She couldn't find her keys and couldn't get into the flat after the wedding. As there was no way to get in touch with me at the BBC, she had to get a cab to her mum's place, all dressed up and nowhere to go.

We had no time for a honeymoon because we had to rehearse for our upcoming tour of Australia and New Zealand with The Who and Paul Jones. On the day of the flight, we were just about to board the plane when Jim Watson from the office came rushing into the departure lounge waving contracts at us. Jim was a likable bloke who always had a strained look from all the menial bullshit he handled for Immediate, and when I saw him running I knew something was up.

The flight insurance forms he was holding had to be signed immediately, but Kenney and I smelt a rat when only Steve and Ronnie's signatures were needed. We were a little stoned, and Steve and Ronnie would have signed them but for the fact that the contracts clearly made Andrew Oldham and

Tony Calder the sole beneficiaries if there were a plane crash. Their parents' names weren't mentioned anywhere. It was a sobering moment, to say the least, and it made me wonder if there might be a bomb planted on the plane.

"You can't sign that!" I said, also becoming aware that in Immediate's eyes Kenney and I weren't worth insuring, as we weren't the songwriters of the band. It just went to show the amount of money that was being generated, and the low kind of people we were dealing with. Needless to say, Jim had to return to the office with the unsigned forms still in his briefcase, and with that little boost of confidence so necessary before the longest flight on the planet, we set off for Australia.

CHAPTER ELEVEN
Flight to Hell

This was the flight to hell! The first stop was Frankfurt, and we kept stopping every few hundred yards until we got there. Every hour or so we'd get a meal and a hot towel, or a snack and a cold towel. Then, as we approached Bangkok, the flight attendant said we could get out for forty-five minutes to stretch our legs, and although we'd already done that in Cairo, Bahrain, and Dubai, we were desperate to get some fresh air because it was so hot in the plane. It was 10:30 P.M. local time when they opened the door, but it was hotter outside the plane than inside. Oh well, only another twenty hours to go!

When the plane finally pulled up to the gate at Sydney's Kingsford Smith Airport, it was the morning of January 15, 1968. The Australian authorities have an unusual way of greeting you when you arrive in their country. They walk the entire length of the plane spraying insecticide in your face. But the best was yet to come. As it was our first time in Australia, there was a lot of hype about our visit, and a room had been set aside at the airport for a live TV interview. We sat down in a row on a sofa and our friendly interviewer introduced us, reading our name from a card.

"These are the Small Faces, folks, all the way from jolly old England. Welcome to Australia fellers. This is Steve Marriott over here on the left, Ronnie Lane, Kenney Jones, and Ian McLagan. Ian, isn't it true you're a drug addict?"

"Oh, fuck off!" I said quietly, groaning.

"Leave it out, you cunt!" Steve shouted in his face in disgust, well aware of the effect it would have on the proceedings.

As the cameraman and technicians started packing their gear up, the press conference being over, we had time to reflect that this was not a good start. We hadn't been in the country five minutes and we'd already been sprayed in the face and insulted. I know things have changed a lot since then. For a start most of the gutter press are working for the English or the American tabloids now, but the great Tony Hancock committed suicide Down Under in a fit of depression. They didn't let up on him the whole time he was there.

They could be very persistent. Marianne Faithfull had a go at it while she was there, too. Maybe it has something to do with the climate! We had nothing much to do for a few days but get over the jet lag by lounging around the hotel swimming pool, soaking up the sun until the "'Orrible 'Oo" arrived from the States. The first time out of the hotel, driving to Bondi Beach in a Jeep, we were pulled over by the Sydney Old Bill and ticketed for having "protruding elbows." Things had to get better, because there was a general feeling that you could get arrested for looking at spaghetti!

Before the first show, we had to sort out a technical problem. As "Itchycoo Park" seemed likely to become a big hit, we'd wanted to play it live, but we hadn't yet figured out a way to reproduce the phasing effect on Kenney's drum track that was so important to the sound of the song. The problem was that phasing was a new studio effect, and unlike these days when you can buy a gadget that'll fit into the palm of your hand for a few dollars, there was nothing even remotely like it in any studio then, let alone the music shops.

One day Steve had a brilliant idea while we were sitting around the swimming pool on the hotel roof. As we were constantly trying to talk over the jets that flew over us into Sydney Airport, he suggested we record a few minutes of them on a cassette machine so that we, or I, could push the play button in the drum break, and, "Wallop McKenzie," we'd have our phasing.

It sounded terrible. Although the mono Sony cassette machine was a little gem, the jets never really sounded like anything other than jets recorded on a portable cassette machine, but it was a good laugh all the same. We'd get to the drum break and I'd have to stop playing for a second to start the machine. Of course it didn't always start when I'd want it to, but even when it did, it started and stopped abruptly because I couldn't fade it in or out. On one occasion the tape player fell off the organ onto the stage, which gave the other three a good laugh anyway. I had to have a microphone on a stand pointing towards the speaker on the cassette machine, and the volume had to be just right for it to work or it would feed back. It was a bloody nightmare actually. It wasn't rock and roll, it was fiddling with buttons, like a precursor to the synthesizer age.

Well, soon enough The Who arrived and the fun really began. Pete, Keith, Roger, and John were all in high spirits considering the journey, and they were fired up and ready to start trouble. Roger congratulated me on getting married and ribbed me about leaving the bride so soon, as it was less than a fortnight since the wedding. They'd all known Sandy from "Ready, Steady, Go!" and the London club scene, so there was a little good-natured piss-taking. Keith was in his usual excitable and very affable state, telling me all about his recent exploits, blowing up hotel toilets with cherry bombs across the States. They'd been touring since June, opening for Herman's Hermits, if you could believe that for a bill, and playing to Peter Noone's teeny-bopper fans night after night had given them a great start in America.

It was no stranger than Jimi Hendrix opening for The Monkees, and I regret that we never had a tour offer worth considering.

Someone thought it would be a good idea to take a couple of boats out on a lake. We took along some beers, and eventually it ended up in a water fight with Wiggy, one of The Who's roadies, having his "Irish" knocked off his head. I'd never put two and two together before as to why he was called Wiggy, but that was all behind him now. The lads, on the other hand, had known why he got the name but had never seen him without the thing, and they were screaming with laughter as he dragged it out of the water, dripping like a wet cat. Wiggy just had to see the funny side, but his rug was never the same again, because when it dried out it had shrunk. We saw a lot of his bald head that tour because it got all blistered and burnt with the sun. In fact, he never wore it again and now goes by his real name, John Wolfe, as he's bald and proud.

The first gig was in Sydney in an echoing corrugated-iron shed that had a manually operated revolving stage, and I don't mean someone manually pushing a button. This thing was pushed round by a number of beefy geezers while we were actually playing. Unfortunately for us, whenever they felt like it or got tired, they'd leave it in one place. It was a little spasmodic. They'd start pushing in the middle of a song just when you'd found some little darling to look at in the audience. Steve got pissed off at the guys eventually, so they just left it in one spot, which pissed him off even more. The audience soon picked up on his anger and began squirming in their seats. I was glad when it was all over, and of course the next day the press slagged us off rotten, referring to us as "Bad Tempered Louts!"

When The Who hit the stage I knew we'd missed out by not touring the States. They were even more dynamic than they had been in the old days at the Club Noreik and the Marquee. Arden had put forward an American tour for the Small Faces, but it involved travelling on a bus with no toilet, opening for five bands for months on end and earning very little money. We were doing such great business in Europe that we weren't interested in schlepping around the States for peanuts. As he had no intention of us going somewhere he couldn't control the situation, it was actually a setup, another of his red herrings. But after my bust, U.S. Immigration told Andrew Oldham that I shouldn't bother applying for a visa as I would never be allowed into the country. Of all the places in the world, it was the one country I wanted to visit. Considering "Itchycoo Park" was to be our biggest hit in the States, getting to Number Sixteen in the Billboard charts, it was a bloody shame that Andrew didn't pursue it, since only two years later they relented, allowing me to tour.

The Sydney gig over, an aborigine came to the stage door and gave each of us boomerangs with our names painted on them. It was the nicest welcome we'd had, and we were touched by his gesture as we hadn't seen any native Australians since we'd arrived and wondered where they were.

Sadly, I found out from the crew later that the police beat him up on his way out of the gig, for no reason other than he was black. We noticed that we never heard any black music played in the clubs either, which was a big shock, since we wouldn't have started playing if we hadn't listened to rock 'n' roll and R&B. Luckily, by 1974 the scene had changed considerably, because they'd discovered James Brown, Otis Redding, and Aretha Franklin, and the clubs were rocking with great black music.

As glad as I was to get out of Sydney, the press slagged us everywhere we went. At airports they were on us like hobos on a ham sandwich, chasing us and pushing microphones in our faces.

"You're all drug addicts, right?" they'd shout, and "Hey, you, do you ever wash?" or my favourite, "When are you going home?"

Ah, the newspapers were rotten to us and it was a drag, but it wasn't all bad vibes. At least the audiences were appreciative. We had a lovely moment in Adelaide when we were greeted by a mob of Mods on scooters at the airport. It turned out that they had all moved from England with their parents in the mid-Sixties, taking their Vespas and Lambrettas with them, and they remained Mods in Australia. As we drove to the hotel in an ancient single-decker bus, we were treated to a "scootercade," probably the world's first and last. I had an interesting chat with our new expatriate pals over a couple of schooners of cold Australian beer in the hotel bar, and then they took us to the beach. It was a fantastic welcome and I forgot about the daily slagging off in the press for the whole afternoon.

Never mind the press, there was some underlying aggro between Pete and Steve too. It wasn't that they didn't get on, but I think that Steve was jealous of The Who's success and both being highly strung like racehorses, something had to snap sometime. Steve was always so hyperactive, you'd want to chin him now and then for his own good, but we weren't about to hit him. It was just a thought. But when Pete and Steve got into a scuffle in the hotel corridor in Melbourne, it almost got out of hand. Pete had him in an armlock on the floor, but Steve wouldn't give in and Pete for his part was probably enjoying finally and physically putting him in his place. In the end nobody got really hurt, just some feathers ruffled.

Basically, we got on well and I liked them all, especially Keith, because he was so fucking mad! He liked to drink and would find the funny side of anything quicker than most. He'd hook you in with a conspiratorial "Robert Newton" look, and before you knew it, with a loud cackle from him you'd become part of the scheme. I don't know how they put up with him. I never met anyone like him, he was so much larger than life. He was even larger than Steve.

At long last, having played in Melbourne, we flew to Sydney the next day to connect with our flight to New Zealand and home. Ansett, Australia's internal airline, didn't serve alcohol in those days. It wasn't a problem for any of us, as we were just glad to be leaving Australia. But Paul Jones's backing group were seen passing a beer between them around the cabin. They were silly buggers, because as Australians, they knew the score. When the stewardess saw the bottle, she got her knickers in a twist and had a go at Bob Pridden, The Who's hairy roadie, assuming he was in on it, probably because he resembled a garden gnome. She was a snotty little bitch and Bob, or "Ben Pump" as we liked to call him, told her in no uncertain terms where to get off. Well, one thing led to another and she stormed off in a huff to report all of us bad boys to the chief pilot, who radioed ahead, warning the police to expect trouble.

It was a total farce. When the plane landed in Sydney, we were ordered to stay in our seats until the other passengers got off. Then two policemen marched us all single file across the tarmac, our hands in the air as if we had been arrested, just to take the piss out of them. They took us to the first-class lounge where Paul Jones did his best to calm the situation down. When a waitress came over to ask for our drink orders we fell about, it was so funny, and after a quick one the policemen came back and escorted us to our waiting plane and out of their country.

The New Zealand press heard the exaggerated news reports while we were in the air, so when we touched down in Auckland a crowd of reporters and photographers were waiting for us. Fully expecting a bunch of drunken English arseholes to step off the plane, they were disappointed to find us subdued and tired after the long flight, and after snapping us munching fried chicken at a small reception party, they eventually left us alone. But because the incident had been blown all out of proportion, eight New Zealand policemen were assigned to watch over us, one for each member of the Small Faces and The Who, even though the Aussie band had caused all the bother. We weren't under arrest, but were to be escorted everywhere until we left the country. It was very silly really, but the policemen turned out to be decent blokes and the gig in Auckland passed without incident, except for the boss of the equipment rental company complaining that Roger had smashed a couple of microphones. What did he expect? It was The Who after all...

The next day was Steve's twenty-first birthday, and we flew up to Wellington for the last two nights before going home. It was a hot, dry afternoon when we arrived at the hotel and Keith, Steve, Ronnie, John, Wiggy, and I went straight to the bar after checking in. We met a couple of homesick English merchant sailors there who were Mods before they'd left England a year before. They couldn't believe their luck, meeting their two favourite Mod bands in a gloomy bar near the docks on the other side of the world, and they invited us on a tour of their ship with as much beer as we could drink. They were good lads and were as hungry for English company as we were, but it quickly turned into a version of the cabin scene from the Marx Brothers' *A Night at the Opera* as more and more sailors squeezed into their tiny mess. It was so crowded the bottles of beer had to be passed overhead and the conversation reduced to shouting, with the cigarette smoke as thick as custard. Everything started to go "twiddle twiddle," you know the sound you get when you fiddle with a radio set and the stations are flying past too quickly to be understood. At that point I should have crawled under the table and fallen asleep, but that was when they brought in the bugle! I don't have a clue why, and it's irrelevant now, but someone had to climb Everest, and Keith and John both had to blow that bugle in that cramped little mess.

We had two shows each night in Wellington and the first evening passed peacefully. I have very fond memories of The Who's performance that night because I sat behind John Entwistle's stack of amps for the entire show. They were such a powerful band, but up close they were even more potent and I had the best seat in the house. While Pete's and John's amps beat my eardrums to submission, I screamed with laughter watching Keith's expressions, as he threw his sticks high in the air, and even occasionally caught one.

Being Steve's twenty-first birthday, EMI, our record company, gave him a suite so he could have a party after the show, and supplied a fancy record console, a pile of LPs, and a few bottles of booze to celebrate the event. Our personal policemen were outside his room in the hallway, but when it looked like nothing silly was going to happen some of them went home, leaving two to watch over us.

"Like a drink, officers?" Steve was a little bugger.

"Oh, that's very nice of you. I don't suppose it'll do any harm."

They came in, took their helmets off and sat down. Steve passed them a couple of beers.

"Can I try your helmet on, mate?" He said with a cheeky grin.

"Go ahead." They were feeling more relaxed already and Steve was beginning to enjoy himself. Just then there was a loud knock at the door and Steve opened it. It was Keith and Wiggy.

"Hello, Keith." Was all Steve had time to say.

"Happy birthday, Steve. What's this?"

In one simple movement, he picked up the record player and threw it with a maniacal laugh through the french windows onto the balcony, where it bounced and fell down onto the street below, where another loud bang and a crash told us it had landed in the street. Someone could've been killed.

The "filth" as Wiggy liked to refer to them, were in shock, their jaws on the floor and fists clenched around beer bottles, not knowing how it could've happened in front of them. They were accessories to a crime they were there to prevent. They put their beers down and ran out the door and down the hallway as fast as their legs would carry them. We laughed until we hurt. Then I ran for it too! The next day, the press got hold of the story and tried to make a big deal out of it, but the police were quiet for reasons known only to us and them. The damage was paid for and EMI knew it wasn't Steve's fault, so they brought him another, better stereo player and an even bigger record collection than before, and the hotel staff replaced the broken door and windows.

The second night went as smooth as silk, although the press had slagged Pete off for smashing up his rented amp, and the "scum," as Keith was now calling the police, were dogging his footsteps more than ever. We had planned to get a reasonably early night because of the flight home the next day, and the policemen weren't as eager to come in that night, they skulked down the end of the corridor until Keith arrived.

"Bang! Bang! *Bang!"* The Old Bill, fearing the worst, ran from the scene, not wanting to witness the devastation.

"Keith!" Steve said, opening the door with a smile. "I thought you'd never get here."

"Happy Birthday, dear boy," he said quietly, and picking up the record player, turned and threw it through the newly repaired windows without any effort. That's when I left. I wasn't going to hang around this time. Going through some photographs and memorabilia the other day, I found a chrome hat badge with the letters N, Z, and P intertwined beneath a crown, and surrounded by fern leaves but I can't for the life of me remember how I came to get it.

The next day we left Australia and New Zealand behind us, and after a stop in Fiji and Honolulu, we landed in San Francisco, where a problem was found with the engine. We were told they would put us up at a hotel for the night, then we'd fly out the next day. As I wasn't allowed a visa to get into the States, I was worried that they'd have to put me in a cell for the night, but they never even bothered to look at our passports. The airline people were so apologetic that they rushed us from the plane to the San Francisco Airport Hilton. Finally, I was in the United States of a-fucking-merica! I couldn't believe my luck. When we got to the hotel, Keith came to my room and flicked through all the channels on the TV, without throwing it out of the window. I didn't know which was more incredible. Everybody on TV was so American and the room seemed to be so luxurious, I had to open every drawer and cupboard. Then Keith turned on the radio. There were a zillion stations, gospel, blues, jazz, rock 'n' roll, soul, rhythm and blues, folk, country, Grateful Dead. Oh well, we were in San Francisco, you can't please everybody.

The thing that knocked me out was that the music was on all night, every night, and the TV was all night on some channels too. Back in Blighty, the TV went off the air around 11 P.M. and there were only three channels. As for radio, the BBC Light Programme, Radio Caroline, Radio England, and Radio Luxembourg didn't even come close. I was in heaven and one day, in the words of General Douglas MacArthur, I would return, but the next time it would be legal.

CHAPTER TWELVE

Nut Gone Flakes

As soon as I got back from Australia, Sandy and I had our belated honeymoon at the Trossachs Hotel, next to a lake in the hills above Glasgow. Andrew posted us some acid on blotting paper as a wedding gift, and after a long day tripping and rowing around the lake, Sandy took a bath while I was in the bedroom sketching. After a while I realized I couldn't hear her splashing about anymore, so I called out. When she didn't answer I dropped my sketch pad and ran into the bathroom. She was motionless under the water by the time I got there, but I managed to pull her out and she came to. Through the spluttering and coughing, she told me she'd been dreaming of Thor, the blond-haired God of Thunder, who was carrying her in his arms and soaring up into the heavens. Another second or two and the dream might have been a nightmare, but luckily she was all right. For my part, I was always suspicious of any blond-haired men around her after that.

Though we had some tracks for our next Immediate album *Ogdens' Nut Gone Flake* in the can already, Ronnie, Steve, and me drove to Henley and rented three cabin cruisers and drifted downstream on the Thames. The plan was to work on the new songs together. It was a bit like Jerome K. Jerome's novel, *Three Men in a Boat,* but we took girlfriends, dogs, guitars, and a Sony mono cassette machine as well. Two of the boats were four-berth cruisers, and I had the one that was left over, a seven-berth monster. The Thames is a pretty river, and we gently putt-putted from Henley towards Maidenhead over a period of a week. We'd stop for lunch here, a drink there, and another drink over there. We'd moor the boats at night and Sandy and Sue would take it in turns cooking breakfast in the galley while Steve's girlfriend, Jenny, was putting on her makeup. During the day, we'd jump from boat to boat, roll a doozie, moor the boats and play for a while, recording a taste of an idea and then carrying on down the river. It was very relaxing, and although it was very casual we actually got a lot of work done. "Happiness Stan," "The Hungry Intruder," "The Journey," and "HappyDaysToyTown," which were eventually on side two of the album, were written or developed on that trip.

One beautiful day, when everything had been going so well, the big monster's reverse gear stopped working. As the only way to stop a boat is by using the reverse gear, I now had no way of stopping and I was ahead of the others, coming up to a lock. A large, privately owned, clinker-built vessel was on its way out of the lock and coming straight for us with the owner proudly standing at the pointed end, posing as Horatio Hornblower. Wearing a blue blazer with gold buttons, white slacks, deck shoes, and a captain's hat perched at a nautical angle on his bonce, he looked as if he owned the river. I shouted frantically, waving my arms tried to warn him to get out of the way.

"My reverse gear is broken! I…Can't…Stop!" I shouted.

"Out of my way!" he replied, and turned to look the other way. To him, I was just a yobbo in a rented boat and he wasn't going to have anything more to do with me.

I couldn't smash into the lock—the whole river would close down for days—so I aimed and turned the monster towards his boat, hoping that, with a glancing blow, I'd do less damage to both boats, and it would slow me down enough so I could scrape the thing along the bank and stop. It all happened so fast. Almost immediately, I smashed into him with a crunch of splintering wood that knocked old Hornblower on his arse. The monster ploughed on, forcing his boat into the river wall with a terrible grinding of wood and concrete. He was in shock for a brief moment, then he got up and waving his fist, he shouted at me:

"Scum of the River!"

His boat was wrecked and Steve and Ronnie were laughing their heads off upstream, it was all I could do not to join in.

"I told you," I said.

"You'll pay for this, you see if you don't!"

Ronnie and Steve between them pushed and towed me towards the lock where the lock keeper inspected the engine and applauded me for doing the right thing and told me not to worry about the Admiral who was still cursing me up on the bank.

"They shouldn't allow boats to be rented by inexperienced scum like you!"

"Scum of the River, if you don't mind."

The rental company fixed the reverse that afternoon, and I caught up with the others at a riverside pub. Later the same day, as we were passing a grand house at Maidenhead on the starboard side, I noticed Georgie Fame standing on the lawn. We laughed when he saw us, it was such a coincidence. I proceeded to turn the monster round, waving while I did so. He was still waving when I hit the river wall head-on with a crunch. It's not that I'm a bad driver, but the boat had no turning circle at all, even though the river was quite wide at that point. Luckily, there was hardly any damage except for a couple of broken eggs in the galley and a dent of my ego. Georgie was making a guest spot in a film they were shooting, so we moored and hung out for a while, passed a joint around, and gave him a full account of our adventures.

We spent the better part of a year working on *Ogdens' Nut Gone Flake,* which became our best-known album and a pop classic. The songs on side one included the title track, "Afterglow," "Long Agos and Worlds Apart," "Rene," "Song of a Baker," and "Lazy Sunday." Apart from a couple of days at Pye Studios, and some time at Trident, where we recorded "Rene," all the rest took place at Olympic.

"Rene" was a real Cockney groover and had some of Steve's funniest lines about "the Docker's Delight" whose "ship came in every night." Cutting "Rene" was easy, but we were rocking so hard at the end of the song, I ruptured myself and had to take it easy for a while. Minor health problems aside, we had a great time making that record. We used violinists and cellists from the London Philharmonic Orchestra, including their leader, John McCallum, the actor David McCallum's father. Although we couldn't write the music down for them, they soon translated our ideas into notes on the page that they could understand, and it was a real treat to listen and watch them rehearse and play on our tracks.

It was Steve's idea to get Spike Milligan to write and perform links between the songs on "Happiness Stan," a major epic which took up the whole of side two. This didn't pan out as we had hoped, but someone suggested Stanley Unwin, who was available and an inspired choice. He was "Stan" after all. As soon as he stepped into the control room and spoke, he had us all on the floor laughing our heads off. Steve was screaming with pain, banging the sofa, and begging him to stop. He'd say something that seemed quite normal, but it would end up as mumbo jumbo.

He'd actually started out as a sound engineer at the BBC. One night he and a producer friend had a few drinks at a pub after the show and on the drive home a policeman stopped them. When he asked the producer, who was driving, if he'd been drinking, Stanley interrupted and began waffling the way he does, so that the policeman got quite confused and let them go. The producer was impressed with his patter and told him he thought he had a unique talent, which he should develop into an act, and that was how he got started.

Stanley was an extremely nice person, apart from being so funny, and hung out with us for most of that evening. He sat quietly while we worked on the tracks, listening to the music and occasionally making notes of our conversations. When he came back the next day he was talking more like us than we did.

"How are you, man? What's bin your hang up? Blow your cool, man."

It was brilliant, and it was us, but with a twist, and we were on the floor again. Steve and Ronnie already had an idea of the story so he tried a few variations on the microphone, and developed it until the segues flowed naturally from one track to the next. We were in fits because he never repeated himself, like a jazz soloist.

The tracks on side two eventually included "Happiness Stan," "Rollin' Over," "The Hungry Intruder," "The Journey," "Mad John," and "HappyDaysToyTown." When the work was all done Stanley gave each of us a copy of his book, *Rock-a-Bye Babel and Two Fairly Tales,* which I treasure to this day. He signed mine:

"To Mac, fritty how the keys, orgold, and assisty produce. From Stanley with chuklodes." What a unique individual.

The record was mixed but we still didn't have a title. Ronnie liked the idea of a tobacco tin for the cover, so Andrew got in touch with the people at Ogdens, who even sent their scrapbooks of original tobacco-tin labels to Immediate's office. We were rummaging through them on the table in Andrew's office when Steve noticed a rectangular label for "Ogdens' Nut Brown Flake" and fell about laughing.

"There it is!" he screamed. "Ogdens' Nut GONE Flake!"

We knew it was a winner title and apart from changing that word, very little of the cover needed to be altered other than the shape, which I remember as being Andrew's bright idea, knowing as he did that having the first round album cover would get us extra press. I spotted the "1 lb. Box" label on another Ogdens tin, which was enlarged unaltered for the back cover. My old band mate from The Muleskinners, Pete Brown, painted the trippy picture on the inside sleeve with help from Nick Tweddell, and although neither got any credit at the time, I can only hope they got paid for their work.

For us *Ogdens' Nut Gone Flake* was our greatest achievement, and it became our biggest selling album, going straight to Number One. It joined the ranks of the Decca recordings and the other Immediate recordings for which we were paid absolutely nothing! It would be twenty-six years before Decca agreed to pay us and twenty-eight years before we could convince anyone to start paying the royalties due to us from Immediate Records. Including songwriting and publishing, it has been conservatively estimated that between £10 million and £15 million has been leached from us.

There were a couple of gigs in Ireland in July 1968. We played an outdoor show at a racetrack in Newtownards, County Down, near Belfast, where Steve thought it would be cool to have Sandy dance on stage in front of us. The audience loved her jerking and grinding and, as if it wasn't exciting enough, a section of a low brick wall in front of the stage collapsed when the crowd surged towards us. Luckily, no one was hurt. The following morning we flew to Dublin for a day off and another gig.

I'd told Ronnie all about my summer holidays as a kid in Ireland, and as we were finally in the country he suggested we take a drive so he could meet Gran and Uncle Ned for himself. But my memories of the journey were that it was long and tedious. One of my aunties, whether it was Terry, Maureen, Alice, or Josey, would take me "home" to Mountrath at the beginning of the school holidays, then they'd go back and another aunt would come over for a holiday and take me back at the end of August. We'd catch the 9:45 P.M. boat-train from Euston Station, changing at Crewe in the middle of the night, bound for Holyhead in North Wales.

Terry was the most fun to travel with, she was my favourite, so full of fun. If she found an empty carriage, she'd dump the luggage on the seats, and if anyone asked if the seats were taken, I was to say Mummy and Daddy would be back in a minute. Then she'd pop off to the restaurant car for a bevy or two while I slept in relative luxury and privacy, the carriage to myself, interrupted only by an occasional visit bringing me lemonade and crisps.

There were two ferries that crossed the Irish Sea from Holyhead to Dun Laoghaire at that time, the *Hibernia* and the *Cambria,* and I sailed on both many times. The returning Irish would drink their way home, usually with a song or two, but the journey back to England was often a sad one for those who weren't sure when or if they'd see their homes and families again. In Dun Laoghaire Harbour the boat would be packed with drinking, singing characters. The whistle would blow and half of them would get off. They were only there for a booze-up! Once we got off the boat we'd catch the local train into Westland Row Station, where I had my first taste of cheese and onion crisps, and then the slow train to Kilbricken, and finally a taxi to the house.

If I went with Auntie Maureen, on the other hand, she always took the plane because it was less of an ordeal for her as she was paralyzed down one side from a stroke and used a leg-brace and a walking stick. Consequently, we'd be in Dublin airport on a screaming Vickers Viscount in just over an hour, but then we'd rest for the night at a friend's house in Dublin before setting off on the single-decker bus, which stopped at every little village on the way to Mountrath, where my holiday proper would begin.

With all this past history, it's no surprise I hadn't considered visiting Gran and Ned, and when Ronnie asked me how far it was to Mountrath, I told him.

"Oh, it's a long way from here. It'd take all day."

"Well, how far is it, then?"

"Sixty-one-and-a-half miles," I said without thinking, remembering the sign in the market place that said it was the same distance to Dublin or Limerick, depending if you went east or west. But now, after driving the length and breadth of Britain everyday for three years, sixty-one-and-a-half miles was a piece of piss.

"Come on, we've got plenty of time to get back before the gig, let's get a Joe Baxie,*" said Ronnie. So off we went, him looking forward, and me very excited at the prospect of seeing Gran and Uncle Ned again after some years.

The cab got us in to Mountrath around two o'clock, and as we drew up to the little house on Main Street, it seemed smaller than I remembered.

At five-feet-five-inches tall, I could have touched the upstairs window ledge of Gran's bedroom without stretching. We must've looked out of place in our smart Mod clothes in this little market town of thirteen pubs and a handful of shops in the thick of the country. Thinking it would be more polite, I knocked on the front door, although as a kid I'd always used the kitchen door at the back, and soon enough Gran came to the door. Bent over and dressed all in black, her white hair was plaited and wound round her head framing her face, which was as wrinkled as an apple left on a plate. Her lips and mouth had always reminded me of Tweetie Pie!

"Ian, Ian, how are you?" she howled. "Look at you! Oh, will you look at yourself. Go and fetch Ned, he's over in Kelly's bar."

That was the greeting after all the years. Nothing had changed, Ned was in a bar, and Gran was still asking me to fetch him home like she used to when I was a kid. He was usually to be found in his best friend's, Tom Kelly's, bar across the street.

Whereas Tom had been an All-Ireland hurler in his youth, and the local hero, Ned never did much more than go to the pub. Just before he died in

* Cockney rhyming slang: Joe Baxie-taxi.

1972, he wrote two letters, one to Mum, and inside in a sealed envelope with "For Ian" carefully written on the cover one for me. Mum told me she believed them to be the only letters he'd ever written, she couldn't remember seeing his handwriting during his entire whole life. He poured his heart out to me in the letter.

"I never had my hand up a lady's skirt," he wrote. He added that he'd nearly got into the All-Ireland hurling team like his good pal Tom, but it never happened. It was the saddest thing I ever read. He went on to explain that he thought I was living the life he'd never had, and he was very happy for me. I looked up to him all my life and he thought he didn't have a life. He was a hard working, well-loved man in the town, and nobody had a harsh word to say about him. The fact that he was an alcoholic didn't change that. Sad to say, though I treasured the letter, it went astray when we packed for our move to the States in 1978. I was never able to find it, and as you can imagine I've searched for it many times. But it must be somewhere hidden away because I never lost it. I think I just stashed it for safekeeping and haven't found it yet. Anyway, that's my hope.

"Gran, this is Ronnie," I said, and she cackled with laughter as she looked us both up and down as if we'd just landed from Mars.

"Hello, hello. Will you look at yourselves? Go on now and fetch Ned."

Ronnie was laughing himself now, as we crossed the street. He was tickled. As we walked into the relative darkness of the bar, Ned was the only man there, leaning out of his Wellington boots, elbows on the bar, peering into the middle distance over his half-empty pint of Guinness.

I signalled to Ronnie to slide close up to Ned on his right side and I went round to his left.

"Will you have a drink, Ned?" I said quietly. He came out of his reverie and turned and looked at me.

"Oh, b'the hokey! Ian, how are you? And who's this. Oh, Janie!" He recognized Ronnie and looked from one to the other, not knowing what to say.

"This is Ronnie Lane from the Small Faces," I said proudly. We hadn't seen each other for seven or eight, or maybe even nine years.

"Hello, Ned, nice to meet you," Ronnie said with a laugh.

"Hello, Ned, how the devil are you?" I said, giving him a big hug.

"Oh, Janie!" was all he could say as he grabbed at his lapel and pointed to a faded and tattered colour photograph from a pop magazine of little old me, safety-pinned to the inside of his equally faded and worn jacket. He hadn't known when we'd ever see each other again and I can't imagine how long it had been pinned there. And it wasn't for effect. I realized then how proud he was of me. What a bloke! Ronnie was as amazed as I was and we laughed and drank at the silliness of it all.

After a couple of pints, we went back to the house and Gran entertained us in the front room like real guests, and played the concertina for us. She was a natural, tapping her foot and mumbling as she played. I'd shown Ronnie another world, and we had a blast, and all thanks to him. When it was time to go, she showed me her new concertina and handed me the one she'd had for years, saying in her clipped and abrupt voice:

"Now. This is for you and I don't want to see you again until you can play me a tune on it!"

I saw her one more time in 1970 or 1971, but she died a year or so later, a month short of her ninety-ninth birthday, and I never got to play her the only tune I've ever got out of it, The Marx Brothers' "One Last Sweet Cheerio" from *Room Service*. Now there's a funny thing.

CHAPTER THIRTEEN

A Pot to Piss In

It's quite amazing to think the three of us—me, Ronnie, and Steve—lived together for the whole of 1966. I think it says a lot for the fact that we really did get on pretty well and later on, in 1968, when cash was short, we three and our wives and girlfriends lived together again. We rented half of a large house in the country, near Marlow, the other half being uninhabited.

It was a beautiful wood-floored, two-storey place that was plenty big enough for the six of us and our dogs. They were still working on finishing the M4 motorway when I first drove to the house.

I was driving a Volkswagen Beetle that I bought from Ronnie for fifty pounds. It was my first car, and it was a bit of a joke. The brakes were more of a threat than a promise. There was a thick fog as I drove past Heathrow, and after travelling at walking pace for miles, I opened the side window to find it wasn't fog but grime on the windshield. It was in fact a sunny day. We lived, as I said, quite peacefully together, although there was bound to be more tension with the girls living there as well. Sandy, Ronnie's wife Sue, and Steve's girlfriend Jenny Rylance, got on well enough, but Jenny was one for a late breakfast in bed, followed by her bath, and the application of the makeup. Dressing could take another hour, as she tried on dresses until the perfect one for the day was found. We would've been up for hours by the time she wafted into the large airy sitting room, her hair in ringlets and her eyelashes curled to perfection. She'd perch on the chaise longue in the newest Quorum creation and make plans for the day that was already half gone. She was in her own world.

One morning, Ronnie said, "Sandy's got a lovely bum."

"I beg your bloody pardon," I said.

"Well, I brought you in some tea this morning, and as I walked into the room, all I could see was her bum bouncing in the air. Very nice too!"

Generally, we lived the life of Riley out in the wilds of Buckinghamshire with the countryside stretching in every direction and nobody to bother us.

Our dogs, Shamus, Molly, and Rufus, would occasionally get into trouble with the local farmers because they were known to chase chickens. But that aside, we had as nice a time as was possible without much money, working up songs and playing through the day. Speedy Acquaye came down a couple of times bringing us herb, and one night he set up his congas in the woods. We lit a fire and took the guitars down there and jammed for hours, smoking and laughing at nothing in particular.

Mick Jagger came to visit one afternoon, bringing gifts of two albums. He'd just got back from a States tour and turned us on to the first Blood, Sweat and Tears record, and more importantly, Dr. John's fabulous *Gris-Gris* album, which floored us. "I Walk on Gilded Splinters," with all its voodoo magic, went well with our mood at the time. In fact, whenever I think of that record I'm back in Marlow in 1968.

We cut "Lazy Sunday" which was included on the *Ogdens'* album, while we were living at the Marlow house. It was Steve's song, but it was slower and pretty uninspired when he played it for us at Olympic. It was so slow that when he left the studio for a phone call we started fucking around, taking the piss out of his song. That was a big mistake, because when he walked back in the studio he thought we should take the piss out of it even more.

Bob Pridden, aka "Ben Pump" since the Australian tour, but who was "Plum" to The Who, happened by the studio that day. We added "Roo de doo de doo, roo de doo de di do" to the song because it was one of the funny things he'd sing to keep us all amused in the dark days Down Under. Then the four of us got round one mic and hummed this old chestnut through combs and paper:

"Hitler, he only had one ball. Goering had two but very small. Himmler was somewhat sim'lar, but poor old Goebbels had no balls at all."

We added the line from The Stones' "Satisfaction" and it was complete and we sat back and had a good laugh while we listened. Well, we were pleased enough with what we'd done, but Andrew smelled money and released it as a single without even asking us, and it became a huge hit, getting to Number Two in the charts in April 1968. And here we were, trying to establish ourselves as serious musicians! After the great Tin Soldier," we all felt things were sliding downhill when we had to promote "Lazy Sunday" on TV. Comedy was a part of us, but now we felt as if the joke was on us.

The joke wasn't over. To milk the success of "Itchycoo Park" in the States, Andrew put together an album with three singles including "Here Come the Nice," "Itchycoo Park," and "Tin Soldier." He added some B sides, called it *There Are But Four Small Faces* and released it without our consent or permission. We were pissed off when Decca released *From the Beginning,* but now Immediate was doing it too, the only difference being the records were selling. It wasn't only that they were doing things behind our backs, they were tight fisted as well. As we had more and more hits, and as I was co-writing more songs, I found a Georgian house on a couple of acres in Fyfield, Essex, that I intended to buy. The asking price was only £8,100, and I could have bought it easily if Immediate had advanced me £810 as a deposit. Tony Calder said they couldn't help me because we owed Immediate Records thousands of pounds. It was a bolt from the blue. They said they'd had to pay Harold Davison the money he'd paid Arden to enable us to sign with Immediate, which meant we were still paying Arden without knowing it. There were bills we had to pay from music stores as well. It was very depressing to think that even with our huge record sales, we weren't getting out of debt, and we were expected to live on fifty pounds a week each out of the kitty.

Steve cut the vocal and guitar track for "The Universal" live on a cassette machine in the back garden at Marlow, out of desperation, with his dogs Shamus and Rufus barking in the background. We added drums, trombone, clarinet, guitar, and bass at Olympic. But when it only got to Number Sixteen, and wasn't as big a hit as "Lazy Sunday," it was the last straw for Steve and resulted in his taking a monumental decision that would affect all our lives.

He told me later that the pressure that he'd been feeling to write successful singles was getting to him, and when "The Universal" hadn't been a hit, he'd taken it to heart. Not wanting to take the band down with him, he decided to jump ship and quit the Small Faces. Whether or not that was the reason, it was definitely time for him to move on, and looking back it was all for the best anyway. We just hadn't planned on swimming for shore that soon!

He wanted to get away from the image of the pop group we were stuck with, and that's why he then formed a new band, the heavier Humble Pie. But it's funny how many people love what we did then, just for what it was, "because it wasn't heavy."

Steve annoyed all of us some of the time and some of us all of the time, to paraphrase Winston Churchill. He was hard to live with and so hyperactive that sometimes in the studio he'd suggest an idea, ask you what you thought of it, and then decide it was rubbish, all before you had a chance to say or do anything. The worst of it was you might find yourself in the ridiculous position of defending *his* idea against *him.* It gave you no time to think for yourself and eventually it wore me out. This is not to take away from the fact that he was a brilliant singer, songwriter, and guitarist, but in the area of relationships, he was a total amateur.

When we were recording "Wham Bam, Thank You Ma'am" at Olympic he tried my patience one too many times. I told him to get fucked and walked out. I may even have mentioned that old chestnut, "I'm leaving the group." Whatever, I left the studio feeling better than I had in a month of Sundays. There would be no more aggravation, no more having to deal with his abrasive personality, I was free. I was wrong. One of the roadies suggested I give it more thought, and eventually I realized that it was a bad move, so the next day I went back. Steve was as sweet as a nut and apologized to me. But he didn't have the slightest idea what had caused me to leave, he was oblivious to it, and at the same time seemed genuinely sad that something he'd said or done had upset me.

Then he played me the track of "Wham Bam, Thank You Ma'am" that they'd cut after I left. He was very pleased with himself. He'd got Nicky Hopkins in to play piano on the new track. So the point was well made. He was sorry about anything he did or said, but if I did leave I wasn't to worry, because he could get Nicky any time I walked out. Nice one, Steve. Both versions of the song were released eventually. Nicky's is much better, in my opinion. Let's face it, I loved Nicky, and his playing was second to none, but I don't think he would've lasted long with the Small Faces. You'd need the patience of a saint to last long around Steve.

It was all unravelling so fast, I didn't notice it at the time, but gradually it became less and less fun for us. If playing "Itchycoo Park" live had been difficult, "Lazy Sunday" was a total joke on stage and playing "The Universal" was impossible without a trombone and clarinet. Jesus, we'd almost become a trad band! At least we had "Tin Soldier" and "Rollin' Over" to keep things moving, but the thing that kept it all together in 1968 was constant touring. And if opening for The Who in Australia was a wake-up call in January, touring Britain with Canned Heat in September was the cold shower we all needed.

For a start, Canned Heat never stopped playing. On stage, in the dressing rooms, in the corridor, in the bus, they played constantly because they loved it. Larry Taylor would appear at our dressing room door playing the bass, staring into the middle distance.

You could hardly hear it as it wasn't plugged in to an amp, but he played nonstop. He'd come in, you'd offer him a drink, he'd take a sip, put it down, and play his way down the corridor to his room without saying a word.

The short tour we did with them and Tim Rose was a blast. We all got on so well that when we played Colston Hall in Bristol it was decided we'd have a jam with them, which was unheard of at that time. Bands tended to keep to themselves. After Tim Rose's set, Canned Heat went on and we played next. The audience was having a good time and halfway through our show some geezer got up on the stage and started dancing. He wasn't causing any trouble, he was a fan, but the manager of the place seemed to think there was going to be a riot and decided it had to stop.

He walked out on the stage while we were playing and shoved the young bloke off the stage. I was pissed off, so I stopped playing, ran over and pushed the manager off as well. Before you could say "look out behind you!"

a huge bouncer had run on and shoved me in the back, and down I went too. Steve ran at him and pushed him off and then he was next. We were like dominoes, one after the other we were pushed off the stage and the place was going berserk! Of course, there was no music by this time, just cheering.

Bob "The Bear" Hite was a large fellow, and proved himself to be the man of the hour. He climbed into the audience like a gladiator, picked me up under one arm and Steve under the other, and to wild cheers and applause from the crowd climbed the steps up the side of the stage, us hanging from his big arms like a couple of sacks of potatoes. Once back on stage he turned, smiled at the audience, and let us down. They cheered and roared with laughter. It was a fabulous moment. He'd defused the situation and then we jammed, because no one could stop it now!

In November the same year, we were "special guest stars" on a tour around Britain with The Who, Joe Cocker and The Grease Band, The Crazy World of Arthur Brown, and The Mindbenders. It was a good laugh and hardly anybody got hurt. Musically, it was a treat. I could watch The Who every night, and it was the first chance I'd had to see Joe singing his guts out, arms flailing all over the place. Steve belted it out as usual, giving all of them a run for their money, and I think it was a great tour for the audience, although we got a lot from it too.

The morning after the Glasgow show, Keith offered me and Kenney a lift to the next gig. How could we refuse a drive through the Scottish countryside with him and John Entwistle in Keith's ludicrously lilac Rolls-Royce? While Dougal, his driver, navigated the city streets, Keith mumbled obscenities into the microphone that boomed out of hidden speakers behind the front bumper. Innocent cyclists and pedestrians jumped out of the road, not knowing what the hell had happened, and not being able to see who was in the Roller through the tinted windows.

He collapsed, giggling on the floor, but he was only warming up. He pulled out an inflatable doll, complete with bra, garter belt, and fishnet stockings, blew it up, and stuck the legs out the window. He put his head between its legs and started screaming into the microphone.

"Stoppit! No, Lemmego! Rape!" all in a high-pitched, very convincing feminine voice.

The Saturday shoppers were taken in because as we breezed by, we could see their horrified expressions. Keith squealed with laughter in his Robert Newton's "Long John Silver" voice. We were all laughing, but no one more than Moony. This was such a wheeze he carried on doing it until we stopped at a filling station on the outskirts of the city for petrol. As soon as we got out, two cars screeched to a halt preventing us going anywhere and four thugs in leather jackets jumped on us. They were Glasgow's finest undercover boys, and were not to be messed with, even if they were identically dressed in black turtle necks and leather jackets.

"Where's the girl, you perverted bastard?" the biggest one shouted at John in a thick brogue.

Keith giggled and showed them the doll, an impish grin on his face. They weren't amused.

"Now listen here, we've had several calls about you lot. We've been chasing you for twenty minutes ourselves, but police from here to Newcastle are on the lookout for you. If I were you, I'd put that damn thing in the boot and behave yourselves. Some little old lady almost had a heart attack watching your filthy antics. Now fuck off back to England, the lot of you!"

Steve wasn't happy, and he wasn't getting any happier. He suggested we get Peter Frampton in on lead guitar, so he could concentrate on singing and playing rhythm, but when Pete sat in with us one night, it didn't feel like the Small Faces anymore, as nice a chap as he is and a lovely player to boot. The crunch came at the Alexandra Palace gig on New Year's Eve, when Steve told us Alexis Korner was going to come on at the end of the show for a jam on "Lazy Sunday." Well, Alexis was a lovely bloke but he didn't know our music, and anyway the end of that song is just a lick repeated over and over. Steve was only thinking of himself.

I don't remember much about the show, but that's not unusual. I recall dressing rooms, hotel rooms or conversations far more, but I'll never forget the way Steve walked off the stage, leaving us in limbo. It was as if he'd planned it, marooning his newfound friend Alexis to spend eternity with us in the key of A. When we finally brought the song to a grinding train wreck and walked into the dressing room, I was as angry as I've ever been with him.

He was quite calm, and told us he was going to get a band together with Peter Frampton, and as far as he was concerned the Small Faces were finished. Pete was in the corner of the dressing room like a spare prick at a wedding, and I was devastated. But it was worse for Ronnie, his best friend and writing partner. We looked at each other in silence. There was nothing to say. Happy New Year and fuck you, Steve.

The year 1969 looked grim. By this time, Sandy and I had moved in with her mother Flo, and Pauly and Lindy, her two sisters, in the small council house they shared in Kensal Green.

It was no palace, but I was broke and they were good enough to have us, plus we had nowhere else to go. Ronnie, Kenney, and I talked about staying together if we could, but there was a short tour of Germany and some English gigs left on the books before it would be officially over. We were all skint, and none of us was thrilled about working with Steve, but because we could pocket the cash we agreed to carry on until after the English dates.

After Arden's financial black hole, we'd opened the first ever Small Faces bank account, and as we couldn't trust anyone but ourselves we insisted the cheques required all four of our signatures. When our new accountant brought the cheque book to gigs, explaining how much easier it would be for him if we signed twenty or thirty blank cheques at a time, we didn't bat an eyelid, signing them along with the autograph books and photographs piled up in the dressing room. He disappeared soon after. Later, when we discovered our bank account was empty we learned the difference between an accountant and a chartered accountant. Mind you, I've never met a chartered manager, agent, record company, or publisher either.

As Immediate wouldn't let us have any of our money, insisting we owed them instead of the other way round, I was determined that we'd all have some cash to take home from Germany. So I said I'd hold the purse strings and keep track of the cash like in the old days with The Muleskinners.

Normally, our roadies, Dave Clark and Dave Hodgkinson, would have a float to pay any expenses, and Clarkie would keep the receipts until the end of the tour. But as I didn't trust anyone anymore, I kept account of every penny in a schoolbook so that everyone could see where the money was going. I was a hard bastard to deal with on that tour when it came to money, making Clarkie pay for everything out of his own pocket before I'd repay him.

The tour was fine, and as we knew it was our last go around we put everything into the shows. We had eight gigs in as many nights to play and after four shows in a row we had a day off after the first gig in Hamburg. I paid everyone their week's money in cash, put my little orange schoolbook away, and with wads of German marks bulging in our pockets we headed for the red-light district for a night of nis, nuf, and reeb, or beer, fun, and sin. The Reeperbahn is cordoned off from the rest of the city by high metal walls to prevent youngsters getting in. In 1966, we played our first German gig there at the Star Club, where The Beatles used to play night after night for months on end in the early Sixties.

After a beer in the Top Ten Club, the four of us wandered into a whorehouse where a Russian lady in leather underwear jumped up and down on a bed swinging a whip to try to entice us into bed. Screaming with a mixture of laughter and genuine fear, we ran out of there without looking back. I figured since this was going to be my first time with a whore, she should at least be pretty, and I certainly didn't need any of that pain and suffering nonsense.

We found a place with some decent girls and we split up agreeing to meet in twenty minutes at the Top Ten. After paying the girl, I took my strides off and hung them on a hook on the door while she wasted no time getting down to business. Overriding my objections, she insisted she be on top, and while we were doing the dirty deed, out of the corner of my eye, I saw an arm encased in plaster come round the door.

"Oi!" I said, "What's going on?"

She pretended not to understand, and my new friend forced me down with her elbows, as if this was position number sixty-two from the *Kama*

Sutra. I pushed her out of the way, jumped up, and ran to the door bollock naked. The cash was gone, every hard-earned German mark of it. She was in on it, of course, but there was nothing I could do, I was skint, and I felt stupid. When the lads came out I asked them as calmly as I could if any of their girls had a plaster cast on one arm.

"Yeah, the number I was shaftin' had a cast on her arm. How did you know that?" Steve said. He was more relaxed than I'd seen him in a long while.

"And she left you for a few seconds, right?"

"Yeah, 'ow the 'ell did you know that?"

"Oh, just a lucky guess, I suppose. She stole all my fuckin' cash!"

The only compensation I had was in thinking that some other bloke had shut the door on her arm during a previous attempt. After all my efforts at keeping our money away from the vultures in the music business, I'd been had by the oldest profession in the world. Of course, the chaps had a bloody good laugh at my expense.

The next morning, in case I'd caught a dose as well as lost my dosh, I decided it would be wise to get a shot of penicillin. The hotel directed me to a doctor who spoke very little English, but his nurse said she would translate for him. It was embarrassing, but I explained that as a married man I was concerned that I might have caught VD. He wanted to know if the girl was a prostitute, and when I told him she was, he shook his head and told me not to worry, that they were all checked on a daily basis.

Of course, this was the Sixties, before AIDS had appeared on the scene, but he gave me a jab anyway, for my peace of mind. When I turned to ask the nurse how much I owed him, he spoke English for the first time. "No charge," he said.

The nurse explained that he'd been shot down over England during the war, and as he'd been treated so well by our doctors he didn't think it was right to charge me. I thanked him sincerely and invited her to that night's show as my guest, after which she kindly gave me a good seeing to, knowing I was disease free, if not a considerate chap.

Fortunately, I didn't come out of the German tour totally broke because we did have other gigs, and after paying Arthur Howes his commission, as well as our roadies and solicitor Vic Gersten, we also managed to pay off the money we owed the music shops, and still come out of it with a wad of bills for each of us. I know all this because I still have the orange schoolbook with everything itemized. That's also how I know the last cities Small Faces played in were Birmingham, Coventry, Swansea, Bolton, and Crewe, before the final show in Devizes. The Small Faces saga was over.

After a week or so, Ronnie, Kenney, and I booked a rehearsal room so we could play together, but it was less than stimulating for each of us. We hadn't played without Steve before, and when we did, it seemed pointless and not much fun. Looking back, it might have been better to have brought in a few characters to jam with, because we needed to bounce ideas around, but we didn't think of it at the time. It depressed me, because then it felt like it was really over, and though we said we'd try and stay together if we could, after that rehearsal, I didn't hold out much hope.

As a famous "pop star" I should have been wintering in Gstaad, wherever that is, and summering in the tropics, wherever they are, but as we never actually got to see our money, we were still living at Sandy's mum's council house when Sandy became pregnant. Through a friend, Kenney found us a two-room flat in Finborough Road, Earl's Court for eight pounds a week that needed a little decorating, and still being in shock after Steve's departure fixing it up became the perfect distraction for me. Although I like to draw and paint, I don't have hobbies as such, but I enjoy stripping paint off a door and decorating, because when I'm working like that, the outside world drifts away and problems disappear. I focus on the simpler questions at hand, like what's half of three and seven-sixteenths?

The flat was on the first floor of a Victorian terrace. It was unfurnished with lino floors and chipped paint everywhere, but it had marble fireplaces in the bedroom and the sitting room under many coats of paint. French windows in the narrow kitchen and the sitting room led to a balcony running along the width of the building overlooking the street. It had potential. The bathroom was down a flight of stairs, and the toilet halfway down, so for emergencies in the middle of the night we bought a Victorian potty which we kept under the bed.

The place needed work, and we could just about afford the rent, but I knew I could do it up on the cheap. Although the world seemed to have fallen in on us, there was one bright star on our horizon. Sandy became pregnant. This changed everything, and I began building a nest for our little one, concentrating on what I could change at that moment, in other words, our surroundings.

Kenney was an absolute brick. He'd come over and muck in, stripping paint off the fireplaces and the doors while we threw around ideas about what we might do musically. I laid a new pine floor in the sitting room and found some clean carpet in a dumpster that I laid in the bedroom. A lick of paint here and a lick of paint there and finally our little palace was finished. Every now and then the lights would go out as the meter had a large appetite for two-shilling pieces, which I soon fixed by breaking into it and feeding it the same coins over and over.

Even as Steve and Pete Frampton were getting Humble Pie started, Pete had become a mate, popping in occasionally for a smoke, a glass of wine, and a chat while I carried on working. I think he was lonely, but he helped me cut a demo of "Growing Closer," a song I was working on, and eventually asked me if I'd be interested in joining Humble Pie. They already had Jerry Shirley, the drummer from Apostolic Intervention, a band Steve had produced and a big Kenney fan, and Greg Ridley, the bass player from Spooky Tooth, and it was nice to be asked, but although nothing came of it, they did record "Growing Closer" on their first album, *As Safe As Yesterday Is*, which apart from being a total surprise, I took to be an attempt at peacemaking from Steve and a friendly gesture from Pete.

One evening, Pete was watching me chiselling a piece of wood.

"Mac, my father is a woodwork teacher and he always told me never cut towards you."

I looked up. "Oh yeah? Ouch!" It was too late, I'd cut into the palm of my hand and blood was dripping onto the floor. I learned two lessons that day, never cut towards you and never talk while you're chiselling!

I'd known Keith Moon since December 1965, when all four of us went to his mum and dad's house in Wembley after a Small Faces gig. His mum, Kit, is a lovely woman and she made us corned beef sandwiches and cups of tea, while his dad, Alf, sat quietly in the sitting room. Keith's eldest sister, Linda, got out of bed and came downstairs in her pyjamas to meet Ronnie because she had a crush on him. Keith's wife, Kim, was the prettiest girl I'd ever seen. They hadn't been married long, and their daughter Mandy would only have been a few months old then. I liked Keith because he was a nutter and very amusing. He was larger than life, and very tiring to be around for too long, but an extremely funny, fun-loving bloke to be with, he was everybody's instant friend.

Sandy and I bumped into them in the Charing Cross Road one afternoon after the pubs had shut. We pulled up alongside them in their Rolls-Royce, and as we were directly outside the 142 club, a private drinking club, he suggested we have a drink with them.

He was his usual boisterous self, and Kim seemed especially glad to see us. I never saw the dark side of Keith in those early days, only Kim had to deal with that on a regular basis. But normally he was the best fun you could have. He was unstoppable. Another night the four of us went out for a meal, parking in Soho Square and meeting in Ronnie Scott's Upstairs, the bar above the club. Keith ordered bottle after bottle of champagne, and stacked the glasses in a pyramid, one on top of each other to form a fountain until they fell over and poured champagne and broken glass everywhere. It didn't faze him one bit. He took care of the bill because they knew we were broke, having told Keith and Kim all about Immediate, and how we couldn't get our royalties.

When we got back to where we'd parked in Soho Square, by the strangest stroke of luck, Andrew Oldham's stretched Rolls-Royce was parked next to our Mini Cooper.

"That's his fucking Roller! That's Andrew's!" I shouted drunkenly. Keith stopped in his tracks and became very quiet. He was thinking. He screwed one eye and pierced me with the other, his lips tight and menacing and his head slightly to one side. He had become Robert Newton. Beckoning me with a finger, and only when he had my full attention, he whispered with purpose.

"Let's key the Rollah."

Of course he was right. There was no doubt in my mind, and no turning back.

"Good idea," I said and we scratched the impeccable paintwork through to the metal, up and down both sides several times with my car keys. "That'll teach Andrew, the bastard!" I said, and the girls thought we'd gone mad, but I felt better already and drove off screaming with laughter.

The next day, I was at Immediate's new offices in the Gloucester Place to see Oldham and Calder to try and get them to stop releasing the album of unfinished tracks and live recordings they were calling *In Memorium,* because it sounded as if we were dead. I noticed Andrew's Roller standing at the kerb, and gave it a once over to gloat at our handiwork, but there wasn't a mark on it! It was unscratched, and as he couldn't have had it fixed since last night, I realized with horror I'd done the wrong one. I don't know if there's a statute of limitations on such things, and I can only hope that the owner was an absolute swine who had it coming to him.

On my way down the stairs, who should I bump into but Don Arden on his way up to Calder's office on the top floor. He was both surprised and embarrassed to see me. I hadn't seen him since the day we fired him two years before, since when we'd been trying without any success to get Decca and his company, Contemporary Records, to pay us the huge sums of money they owed us.

"What's cooking?" he asked, a forced smile twitching nervously on his lips. He was sweating, though whether it was from unexpectedly seeing me, or from climbing several flights of stairs, I'm not sure. I leaned in as I passed him and stared into his dead eyes.

"No food!" I said without a smile or irony, and walked on. There have been better returns, but it was quick and accurate and it stopped any further conversation.

One morning, bright and early, hearing the doorbell, I popped my head out over the balcony to see who was there. Being two flights up, it was easier than going to the front door.

There were two suits standing at the front steps, one clutching a handful of papers.

"Hello, can I help you?" I said cheerily.

"Mr. McLagan? Mr. Ian McLagan?" One of them asked.

"Who wants to know?" I replied warily.

"Can I see you for a minute, Mr. McLagan?" He didn't want to tell me his name.

"You're seeing me right now, mate!" I didn't like the smell of this.

"I've got something for you. Could you come down, please?"

I knew it was a writ then. Andrew Oldham had got bailiffs to serve them on us a couple of times before. If they couldn't actually touch you with the writ, the writ was not legally served. We'd had a bailiff try to serve one on us at a gig in Scotland, and we'd ran into the toilet to escape him and told him to "Fuck off!" With that, a burly policeman thumped on the door and told us the law in Scotland was different to England, and you had to accept the writ if a policeman was in attendance. We ripped it to shreds and put the fried chicken we were eating into the envelope and sent it back. I don't know if this is a legal answer, but it satisfied us at the time.

"I've got a pot full of piss I'm going to pour on your heads if you don't fuck off right now!" I said, seeing the scales of justice tilt in my favour for once.

"Now, now, we just want to talk. Just be reasonable. Come down, won't you?"

"Wait there!" I shouted. They turned and began to walk towards the garden gate, a full ten or twelve yards as I ran into the bedroom and dived under the bed for the full piss pot.

"What's happening?" Sandy said sleepily.

"Fucking bailiffs!" I shouted, by way of explanation.

I had no time to discuss the weather. I ran as fast as I could through the sitting room with the full potty and out onto the balcony. They'd made it to the gate but they hadn't really believed me. One was holding the gate open while the other was trying to get past him, they were Laurel and Hardy all of a sudden. I threw the contents in a big arc all along the path and the big splash caught the both of them full on as they tried to manoeuvre their way around the gate. I laughed so loud.

"And don't come back!" I shouted in triumph. They were dripping with pee, and I can't begin to imagine how they got home, but there was no follow up and our relationship with Immediate was finally over, piss on 'em.

Dad, wearing No. 1, British rollerskating champ, 1928.

Gran and Uncle Ned.

Wrapped up like a Christmas present in big snow of 1947 with brother Mike.

Me and brother Mike.

Art school Mac with attitude.

Muleskinners publicity shot, 1964. (© Chippy Carpenter)

Poster of the times. (© Chippy Carpenter)

THE MULESKINNERS
RHYTHM & BLUES

HOU 7353
SOU 2530

Our band's business card with Hubert Sumlin and Howlin' Wolf's autographs.

"Them Muleskinners" award-winning poster designed by Barney Bubbles. (© Chippy Carpenter)

December 1964, the great Howlin' Wolf waving to fan after his gig, his "back door man" in total awe. (© Chippy Carpenter)

First publicity shot. Steve Marriott, Kenney Jones, Ronnie Lane, and Ian McLagan. (© David Wedgbury)

Westmoreland Terrace disc jockey. (© Tony Gale)

Take that, world!
(Photograph by
Gered Mankowitz
© Bowstir Ltd. 1

Steve, Kenney, me, and Ronnie, Ludgate Hill bomb site, November 1965. (© Tony Gale)

Life on the road was taking its toll on some.

Drug charge: Pop star held in cell 50 minutes

Ian Patrick McLagan, 22-year-old organist in the Small Faces pop group, spent 50 minutes in the cells at Uxbridge magistrates' court this morning until his counsel could find an additional surety to stand bail for him.

McLagan, of Andover Terrace Mews, Regent's Park, had previously been granted bail to appear before the magistrates today.

He is accused of attempting to export dangerous drugs and of possessing dangerous drugs.

His original bail was £500 on his own recognisances and one surety of £500.

But when police in court today asked for a further remand and did not object to bail the chairman of the magistrates, Mrs. Gertrude Fisher, ordered two sureties of £500 each and his own in £500.

Mr. David Miller, for McLagan, said only one surety was immediately available. He understood from discussions with the police that one surety would be sufficient.

Mrs. Fisher replied: "The police do not arrange bail. We the magistrates have decided there should be two sureties."

McLagan, his dark hair at shoulder length and wearing a black suit and yellow shirt, was led to the cells below the court until the second surety appeared.

Detective J. McLeod told the court McLagan was arrested at Heathrow Airport on November 13. It was alleged he had a quantity of cannabis resin—a dangerous drug—in his possession.

Asking for a remand until next Wednesday he said this would afford time for the substance to be analysed.

There was no objection to bail. McLagan arrived at the court in a white Jaguar saloon car. There were six teenage girls waiting to see him. One of them, 15-year-old Yvonne Stalwood, a factory worker from Slough, rushed up to him screaming. She threw her arms around him.

After McLagan was released, he was driven away in the Jaguar.

IAN McLAGAN in Uxbridge today.

English newspaper report of drug bust.

The author at 20. (© Tony Gale)

"Mad" Ann, arguably our most loyal fan, a[nd] me. (© Doug McLauchlan, private collectio[n]

Ronnie and me with Gran at home in Mountrath, County Laois, Ireland, 1968.

Ronnie Lane, Ronnie Wood, Rod Stewart, me, and Kenney Jones. "Good boys...When they're asleep..."
Hard Corps wake-up call, Ann Arbor, 1970. (© The Tom Wright Collection, the Center for American
History, The University of Texas at Austin)

Me, Woody, and Rod before the show. "Who's paranoid?" 1972.
(© The Tom Wright Collection)

Ronnie Wood sh
Mac the first ste
1972. (© The To
Wright Collectio

"Live" shot of me. (© The Tom Wright Collection)

McLagan and Lane conspiring on stage.
(© The Tom Wright Collection)

Kenney Jones drinks as Ian McLagan keeps a watchful eye on Rod Stewart groping Ronnie Wood,
while Ronnie Lane puffs on a Golden Virginia.

Out in the cold. First U.S. gig, Boston Tea Party, March 1970.

Wrist job, 1974. (© The Tom Wright Collection)

Me in a tuxedo, Hollywood Bowl, 1972.
(© The Tom Wright Collection)

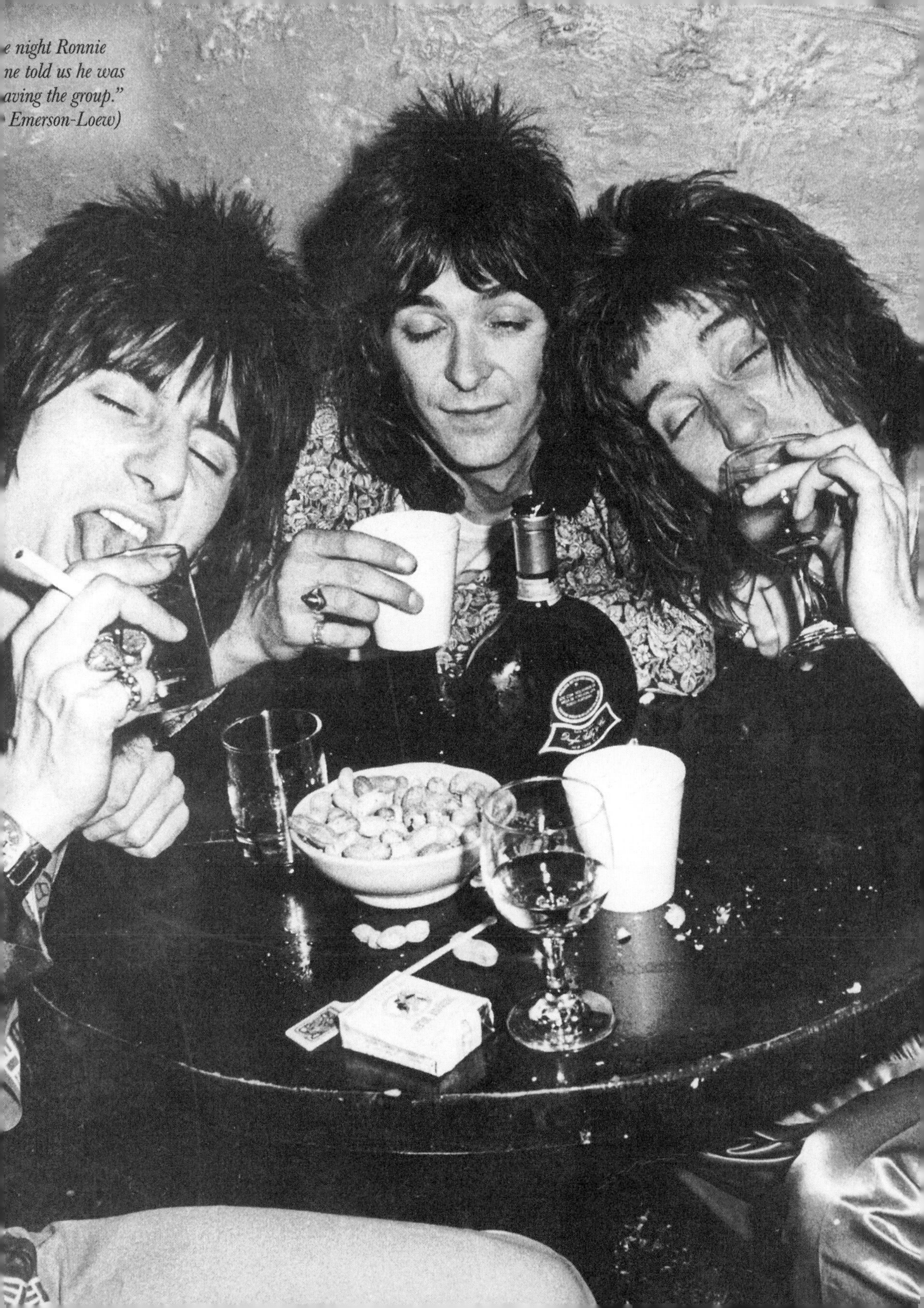

e night Ronnie
ne told us he was
aving the group."
Emerson-Loew)

PART TWO
1969–1975

CHAPTER FOURTEEN

Meet the Faces

I first met Ronnie Wood at Steve's "Lazy Sunday" house in Chiswick in 1968, and the fact that Steve introduced us was typical, because he always had his finger on the pulse. Woody was a happy drinker and smoker, and an amusing and generally all-around good chap with pinprick, piercing brown eyes and the jet black straight hair of an Apache brave. He came across as an old friend that I hadn't seen for a long while. As Ronnie Lane was aware of his personality and potential, he hadn't wasted any time and they had already started working up a few songs with the idea of forming a band, so I kept in touch with developments.

They'd meet at Ronnie and Sue's little flat on Elsham Road, Shepherd's Bush, and I'd pop round and noodle on Ronnie's flat-top Wurlitzer electric piano while they picked the bones out of some chords on acoustic guitars. Although Woody had been earning decent dosh in the States with the Jeff Beck Group, he'd had enough of playing bass and wanted to get back to playing guitar again, this time as one of the band instead of as a sideman. Originally, the intention was for them to form a band with other musicians, but when it came down to it, me and Kenney were always lingering hopefully in the middle distance, and it soon became obvious that we were the guys they were looking for.

Ronnie had mentioned to Stu that we were looking for a place to rehearse and, bless his heart, Stu said we could use The Stones' rehearsal studio in Bermondsey on the promise that we'd pay for it when, or if, we got a record deal.

"You might as well use the room, they never go down there. It's a bloody waste of space, if you ask me," he said, his chin to the wind. It was exactly what the doctor ordered, and although it was only a cellar below a flag-makers warehouse, it was everything to us. He'd had it painted and carpeted, and had a C3 Hammond with a Leslie, assorted guitar amps, and a drum kit already set up. We hadn't really planned anything, but we needed to jam to let the ideas flow and the songs develop. Woody couldn't say no then, anymore than he can now, and he'd invite other guitarists down, as if we were interested in any of them, and then Mickey Waller would turn up sometimes, which left Kenney twiddling his thumbs for a while. It was a right old shambles most nights, but then this was the beginning of one of the most shambolic outfits in the history of rock and roll. However, when the four of us played together it began to take shape and sound right.

We were only missing one item in this musical bean feast—the lead vocalist. Woody hadn't endured the experience we'd had of the lead vocalist leaving the band to form a supergroup, and Ronnie Lane and I were particularly shy of getting involved with a front man again. It was not as if we could have a band without one, but we thought we could take care of the singing ourselves. It might've been pretty good, and we might've got a record deal, and pigs might fly, but luckily for us Woody brought Rod Stewart, his band mate from the Beck group, down to Bermondsey to have a crafty listen while we piddled about. He didn't sing, though. He just sat in the small room next to the main studio, listening with a beady ear, while we thumped, plinked, twanged, and bashed for a couple of hours, and he'd still be there if it wasn't for Kenney dragging him into the studio. He was actually quite shy, and a bit reserved at first, but pretty soon he started to wail, and before you could say, "Gimme the cash," we had the start of a rocking little band.

"Ladies and Gentlemen, in the blue corner, The Faces."

Although I have to go on record as being against Rod in the beginning, in fairness to both of us, it was to do with my experiences with Steve and nothing to do with my feelings about Rod himself. Rehearsals took on a new momentum after he joined. We got rid of everybody else and concentrated on working up the new songs, and at the same time a pattern of behaviour evolved that continues to this day, called Going to the Pub. During the Small Faces era, we hardly ever went out in public for fear of being recognized and getting screamed at. It sounds silly now, but by the late Sixties things had calmed down considerably, and it was a real pleasure to just go to the pub with your pals. Of course, pubs have been around for donkeys years, and "pub rock" hadn't been invented then, but when I first heard that term I felt like we'd been cheated, as if no one had ever seen The Faces perform live, or for that matter, heard any of our records.

Oh we were the boys for a drink all right, and that's no error. A more convivial bunch you're unlikely to meet! As soon as we'd finish rehearsing we'd dive into the King's Arms, fifty yards up the road, for a quick one or two in the saloon bar, where we quickly became regulars. We must've stuck out like sore thumbs, but one day on his way back from the toilet, Ronnie overheard the landlord telling some of the locals about us in the public bar.

"Oh, they're nice boys. All shorts!"

This had nothing to do with our size, because let's face it, we weren't all short anymore since Woody and Rod had joined the band. He meant that we drank spirits like brandy and Coke, or vodka and tonic, which being more expensive than pints of beer, made us appear a better class of customer. That and the fact that we drank so much.

One day, when I walked in the door at Bermondsey, Stu ushered me into his office on the ground floor and played me the *Original Delaney and Bonnie* album that had just been released. There were photographs of the musicians on the back cover, and it was the first time I had knowingly heard Jim Keltner, Carl Radle, Bobby Keys, Jim Price, and Bobby Whitlock, and Delaney and Bonnie's soulful singing. But what seemed exceptional to me was Leon Russell's piano playing on "The Ghetto." He soared! Stu played "The Ghetto" over and over for me, and I was amazed at how the piano on the end section built like a skyscraper, layer after layer, up and up. It just got more and more exciting. Stu turned me on to this new gem, and then he told me a revealing story about Nicky Hopkins, our mutual pal, and Rod and Woody's mate in the Beck group.

"That bloody Nicky," he said with a scornful look. "I played it for him the other day, and that's what I hate about him. I only played it once and he went straight to the piano and played the whole thing, note for note. It really pisses me off!"

It was funny because he was serious, but I understood his frustration, as neither of us could compete with Nicky as a piano player. Our talents are our own, but we couldn't just play something that brilliant after hearing it for the first time. He really was annoyingly, incredibly talented.

We three Small Faces went to the Lyceum in September 1969 to watch the last London show Jeff Beck played with Rod, Woody, Nicky, and Tony Newman on drums. It was a great band and a fantastic night, and though Rod didn't command the stage with Beck the way he would later with us, I could hardly take my eyes off him. He was so flash! But Nicky really blew my mind that night. Hunched over the piano on the side of the stage, not even looking at his hands, his fingers were all over the place and yet his face showed no emotion, as if he was looking through the Exchange and Mart! He made it look so easy, but he had no ego, and neither did Stu.

Stu was a very special person. Although The Stones, bless 'em, let us use their room in the beginning, it was Stu who actually made the arrangements. The Faces would always be grateful to him for that. But there was more to Stu than met the eye. He helped several bands when they were starting up, Led Zeppelin being just one example. He was a very unhip person, who wore golf shirts, and rarely, if ever, dressed up. He'd stand there, trouser pockets bulging with screwdrivers, wallets, and God knows what else. He had a unique stance with one leg out to the side, arse bulging, one hand on his hip, the other hanging limply from the wrist, and his large chin jutting out to seaward like a sailor waiting for a ship home.

"Cuh! That bloody Marianne," he'd mutter dismissively, peering into the middle distance, his eyes shut, and in his usual stance. We never knew what she'd done or said to piss him off, but that wasn't the point; he just liked being able to say what he thought.

Stu had been The Rolling Stones' piano player, but when Andrew Oldham took over from Giorgio Gomelsky as their manager, he was thinking more of their image than their musical worth, so he eased Stu out of the band because he wasn't sexy enough. He stopped being a paid member of the group, but stayed on as their road manager and friend. He played the piano live and in the studio with them whenever it took his fancy and whenever he was asked, which was often. The Stones had the pick of the pianists, but when they played down-home blues, Stu had the attitude money couldn't buy and managers couldn't understand. He was as content on the golf course as he was in the studio. He had a straightforward, down-to-earth quality I liked. There was no bullshit with him, and everybody who knew him well impersonated him at some time or another. Keith does a very good Stu as do Mick, Charlie, and Woody. But above all, he was a "feel" piano player, a self-taught boogie-woogie man without an ego, who would talk about pianists for as long as you'd care to listen.

We shared a love of the boogie-woogie players, Meade Lux Lewis, Albert Ammons, and Pete Johnson, and he gave me a 78 rpm record of "Honky Tonk Train Blues," which I'll treasure forever. We agreed wholeheartedly about the blues players like Big Maceo, Otis Spann, Roosevelt Sykes, Johnny Johnson, Sunnyland Slim, and Memphis Slim, but he had a blind spot when it came to Jerry Lee Lewis. He told me he never liked his playing, but I think it was more of a snob thing. When rock 'n' roll came in he was already playing boogie woogie and his feeling was that Jerry Lee fucked about too much to be taken seriously, as if it wasn't proper playing.

Stu was a one-off. There will never be another bloke who can say the things he did, and who got to play with the best band in the land anytime he wanted to, as it suited him. He was generous with his time and loved the music even more than golf! Bless his heart, it gave out in 1985, fifty years too soon.

Although we were rehearsing regularly, we had no gigs, whereas Woody's brother Art had gigs, but no band. He'd had a fine band in the early Sixties by the name of The Artwoods, which included Jon Lord, Derek Griffiths, and Keef Hartley, but by 1969 he'd given up the music business and was back working as a graphic designer. When they asked him to play at a Cambridge University Ball, he asked us if we'd do it with him, but we didn't have too many songs rehearsed so Woody brought in Kim Gardner from Creation to play with us. So with two bass players, two singers, and a rented van, we set off for Cambridge under the assumed name of Quiet Melon.

They treated you well at university gigs in those days. You were given a full roast dinner served with silver cutlery in a dining hall, and bottles of champagne, pitchers of ale, and lashings of strawberries and cream. Just what you need before a show.

We played all the old chestnuts that night: "Hoochie Coochie Man," "Mojo Working," and "Kansas City," and generally had a good old piss-up. Rod sang a couple, Art took over for a few, and there was abuse from the side of the stage from whoever wasn't playing at the time. At the end of our set, the bloke handed us £250 in cash. P.P. Arnold was supposed to headline, but she never turned up, so we played the same songs again for another £250 and none of the University wallahs noticed the difference. We cut some tracks for Art under the name of Quiet Melon at Philips, with Ronnie turning up late for the session and wearing cycle clips because he'd had to cycle all the way from Twickenham on his bike, as he didn't have the bus fare. The company wasn't impressed enough with our performance to actually release it, but Art finally got them to put the tracks on the market in 1996.

We played a few more shows as Quiet Melon, trying songs out and making mistakes, but what we really needed was a new name and a manager to guide us to worldwide fame and fortune. For a time it looked as if one of the better known managers was going to scoop us up. We'd heard that Allen Klein was interested in having a chat, so with caps in hands we went to meet him at his Mayfair flat. We were already aware that he'd handled Sam Cooke, The Beatles, and The Rolling Stones, so he was obviously someone we couldn't ignore and wouldn't upset for anything. As soon as his pretty assistant went out of the room to get drinks for us, he started making what I thought was idle chatter, talking about Herman's Hermits.

Without any thought for my own future in show business I said something along the lines of:

"They're a bit Mickey Mouse, aren't they?"

He glowered, turning on me. "Whaddaya mean? What's wrong with Micky Most? He happens to be a very good friend of mine!"

"No, no," I protested. "Mickey Mouse. You know, Minnie's boyfriend."

He hadn't the faintest idea what I was talking about, and he didn't make eye contact with me after that. Before long the meeting was over, and the door shut firmly behind us on the way out. We decided to look closer to home for a manager, and preferably one with a sense of humour.

The Speakeasy was a late night boozer near London's Oxford Circus, frequented by celebrities, roadies, pop stars, would-be pop stars, pop stars' wives, girlfriends, bits of skirt, managers, would-be managers, whores, and drug dealers, who in turn were all looking for each other over a drink, a steak sandwich, and a loud band.

I used to hang out there occasionally and never met anyone interesting, and it was on just such a night that Kenney met Billy Gaff. He was short and podgy, with very little hair, a worried expression, and a bit of a shifty eye, as if he was running from something or someone. That should have put Kenney off, but it didn't. Billy was working for Robert Stigwood and he had very little money or experience, but after a short conversation with Kenney, Billy convinced him he could get us out of our contracts with Immediate and get a fat advance from a new record company without too much effort. It all sounded too good to be true, but as we were loaded down with debt and couldn't see Rod and Woody for the thieves, we thought we might as well let the dog see the rabbit.

We had a meeting at a lawyer's office where he sorted through the many contracts that were keeping us poor, and Billy impressed me. Though he was small-time he came over as someone we might eventually trust. This was a new one on me! To cut a long story short, we took him on at a low five percent and he got us a deal with Warner Brothers Records and Publishing.

The Small Faces were four characters out for music and fun, and The Faces were five characters with the same attitude, no question. However, there was a basic difference between Steve and Rod. Steve needed to feel you were agreeing with him or he couldn't function, being a very insecure person on many levels. But I never felt Rod needed us in that way. He was cocksure. Both of them were excellent lead vocalists. They were also very aware of their personal power, even if they didn't know it on an intellectual level. Rod was up there to put it about and so was Steve. They were both intuitive, natural talents.

The singer is a strange commodity for several reasons. He doesn't always play an instrument, or play one well enough for it to matter. Rod plays a mean banjo, but who cares? Mick Jagger plays a harp and can handle a guitar and keyboards, but once again it's not important compared to his singing and performing. Most band members I know ridicule the singer because the voice is not an instrument like a guitar or drums. There's no such thing as a vocal roadie and there's nothing to set up or prepare. I mean, anybody can shout. It's a snob thing, but we musicians use that power over them to outweigh the power they have over all of us—the power of communication from the heart. No amount of "from the gut" guitar playing quite compares with making a statement with words and melody. Of course, the truth is they can take all the piss-taking we dish out because they don't really care about us, they're not even listening to us, they're looking at themselves in the mirror! Bloody singers!

Rod was always a dapper fellow, and a bit of a Jack the Lad with the girls. The first time I saw him at Eel Pie Island back in 1963, he was wearing a three-button suit, with the bottom one undone, of course. He wore a shirt with a long, pointed collar, a fiercely knotted tie, high-heeled boots, the whole bit, not to mention his back-combed hair and the longest nose this side of a Gerald Scarfe sketch. He was hard to miss. I noticed him even before he got on stage because he stood out in a crowd of art students and wannabe beatniks.

He was Rod the Mod, and I was Mac the art student. I wore the unofficial uniform of all underpaid, beer-swilling art students at the time, a pair of Levis and a brown corduroy jacket, the elbows covered with leather patches so the beer slops on the bar wouldn't do any permanent damage to the material. Rod, on the other hand, always dressed smartly, even in those early days, but then he was always on the razzle. Rod generally got what he wanted. He'd already signed a solo contract with Mercury Records, the main condition being that they'd give him a brand new Marcos, which in 1969 was one of the sportiest, most affordable, yet moody-looking sports cars around. He wanted to drive it home from the airport, so when he returned from the last Beck tour his bright yellow knob-on-wheels was waiting for him at the kerb when he walked onto the street.

Rod could be very silly. He liked saying the word "thin" and he'd pronounce it thinly as well. He decided to call his first solo album *Thin,* but Mercury thought *The Rod Stewart Album* was a much better idea. If you look at the front cover, you can see that Rod won it on a technicality, because the word "thin" is printed very, very small in the bottom left corner. He got Woody and me to play on the record, and I'm on most of the tracks. Although Lou Reizner is credited with producing the album, he did very little other than arrive in one of several antique Rolls-Royces he owned, and smile a lot in the control room. He was a nice guy, but Rod was already honing his craft and making all the important decisions. His next effort, *Gasoline Alley* (Mercury), released in September 1970, was credited as being co-produced with Lou as well, but I think he parked the Roller at home for those sessions.

With Woody, Martin Quittenton, and Mickey Waller, and me on occasional tracks here and there, the band Rod assembled for the record would change very little over his next five solo albums, though Pete Sears handled more of the keyboards on the later recordings. Woody almost always played bass on the basic tracks and then overdubbed lead or slide guitars, and in fact it was he who showed me Nicky's tricky piano riff from The Stones' "Street Fighting Man" that I used at the end of that song. The first album was done very quickly, because Rod learned early on that if you spend too much time, and therefore money in the studio, it takes longer to recoup your royalties, and in that way he's even more Scottish than his parents, who were actually born there.

CHAPTER FIFTEEN
"Hmneigh!"

When The Faces walked through the door of Warner Brothers' new London offices, Ronnie, Kenney, and I had a sense of déjà vu, as it had moved into what had been Immediate Records a mere six months before. Ian Ralfini, the English head of the company, welcomed us into Andrew's old inner sanctum, and after handshakes and a drink, we signed new contracts for the second time in the same place. With cash in hand and money in the bank, we couldn't wait to join Rod in the sports car brigade, so we each went out and bought convertibles.

Ronnie Lane, not being much of a driver but a discerning kind of chap nonetheless, bought a silver Mercedes 190SL. Woody bought a red 1959 Jaguar XK150, as befitted a West Drayton gentleman. It was a beautiful monster that had no syncro-mesh, so when changing gears you had to double de-clutch, quite an awkward manoeuvre even for a racing driver, but Woody handled it somehow. Kenney got himself a white MGA and I bought a British racing green Triumph TR6.

I loved that car, but for all the speed, it was a pain to drive in traffic because of a heavy clutch that was set too high. My heel would be off the floor and my leg would start shaking and shuddering when I'd find myself edging along in the rush hour, as I often did. But the engine had a beautiful deep purr to it, like a speedboat, and with overdrive in second, third, and fourth gears, I had seven gears to play with. I could actually play tunes with the engine revs if I'd had enough to drink, slipping it in and out of overdrive and gears. Of course, I don't recommend this as a thing to do while driving, only to say that I could and did. But then whistling would probably have been safer than slinging it into first gear at fifty miles per hour just to get the right note!

We must've been a sight turning up for rehearsals at Bermondsey Street. A flash of yellow, red, green, white, and silver, and a lot of vroomm, vroomm at the side of the road. Mind you, the street was usually deserted, but we were dead flash and cocky with it. One evening, after the usual two or three brandy and gingers at the King's Arms following rehearsals, Rod pulled up alongside my TR6, turned his nose up at my auto, and revved his rude yellow beast.

"That fuckin' thing can't beat mine."

Well, I can tell you, I'm not a man to back down, so I stuck my tongue out, jerked forward, and stopped. He was in first already and sped forward for a split second and then we were away! Luckily, it was a one-way street, but it was narrow, and some eighty yards ahead it narrowed even more. The road became one lane as it turned into a long, arched brick tunnel under the railway. Brands Hatch nothing, this was a chicken run, and it was a straight dash to the tunnel, neither of us giving way. We must've been fucking mad! As we got to the arch I just managed to pull ahead and scraped his wheel arch, screaming into the tunnel ahead of him. He was really pissed off because he hated to come second, and we could have killed ourselves, because neither of us would give in.

Rod could be a sarcastic bastard at times. He'd pull a twisted grimace behind a victim's back and make a derisory sound like "Hmneigh" usually not heard or understood by the poor sucker, so that everybody would be in on the joke except the person being laughed at.

The hardest part was not to crack up while this was going on, and we all got to be quite good at it, but he and Woody were the guv'nors. It could be slightly amusing and brief, or incredibly loud and cutting, producing belly laughs, or it could be cruel. It became as private a thing to The Faces as Cockney rhyming slang was to the Small Faces. It was a very inside thing, and the funniest jokes were almost never understood by the people being laughed at. Anybody was fair game for the quick, piss-taking, sideways glance. Even among members of the band, no one was above being had.

We threw our first album together at DeLane Lea Studios in Soho. *First Step* was just that; we pointed our toes at the water and jumped in. Strange to think that even with Rod's vocal talents in the band, we put two instrumentals and a long slide guitar solo on our first recording. "Flying" and "Pineapple and the Monkey" still sound good to me, but generally it's a record with no direction, just a lot of side roads disappearing into the distance. *First Step* (Warner Bros.) was released in March 1970 and got to Number Forty-five in the U.K. album charts and 119 in the States, but the single "Flying" failed to chart.

Our next album, *Long Player,* came out in March 1971 and got to Number Twenty-nine in the U.S. Later on, of course, Rod had a big solo single with "Maggie May" in October 1971, which launched him as a superstar. But The Faces had a string of hits too, including "I'm Losing You," in December 1971 and "Stay with Me" in March 1972. However much fun we had together, there would always be an underlying conflict between the twin careers of band and lead singer that would eventually result in the break-up of the band. But back in 1970 we still had a lot of recording, gigging, and partying to do!

Rod's mate, Ewan, came to the studio one day. He was a sports car dealer and full of flannel, but a good laugh and a perfect victim. When Rod asked him if he'd like to play tambourine with us while we cut "Three-Button Hand-Me-Down," he jumped at the chance to be immortalized on vinyl. He'd never been in a studio in his life, so he knew nothing about recording. Rod explained that to ensure good separation from the instruments, particularly the drums, he'd have to play in the corridor, outside the studio, and he was fine with that. He'd have played in the street, naked, if we'd asked him. Our engineer, Martin Birch, was in on it, so he placed the microphone and stand at the far end of the corridor, gave him a set of headphones so he could hear what we were doing, then we played the song a couple of times, while he adjusted the balance.

"Can you hear yourself all right?"

"Yes, loud and clear," Ewan shouted eagerly. This was his big chance to be on a record, and it was a bloody shame really, since he had absolutely no sense of rhythm and his microphone wasn't even plugged in. We cut the track, and walked out of the studio to see Ewan banging away and sweating like a real musician. Rod held back a smile.

"Nice one, Ewan, come and 'ave a listen," he said kindly.

Rod whispered in Martin's ear to turn the track up really loud, and we listened back watching Ewan's reactions as he listened out for the tambourine that wasn't there. He was so thrilled to be in the studio he didn't notice our snorting and elbow-jabbing. Rod was overly enthusiastic, egging him on and nudging me behind his back.

"It's really good, Ewan!"

"Really, was it all right?"

"Yeah, you sound pretty good. Can you hear it all right?" The playback level was so loud, he couldn't tell what was going on.

"Yes. Is it okay, really?"

A sideways glance from Rod to the rest of us.

"It's really useless, Ewan!" he said and slapped him hard across the back of the head.

Ronnie and Sue were living in a spacious ground-floor flat in Cambridge Road, Twickenham, near Richmond Bridge, and Mike McInnerney, the designer of The Who's *Tommy* album cover, lived nearby with his wife Kate in a rambling, ramshackle, overgrown garden flat next to the Thames. Mike was a congenial character who had painted a sky scene with clouds and birds all over the ceiling and walls of Ronnie and Sue's octagonal sun room, so when it came time to think of an album cover we naturally went to him for ideas. Woody had a guitar tutor *First Step* that suggested a title and we gathered at Mike and Kate's place for a photo session soon afterwards.

The sitting room had beaded shawls hung across the windows, and Kate made a bowl of punch and handed out glasses made from jam jars, which she put on a low table in front of us while we sat on a low settee being photographed. We sipped at the punch as the photographer, Martin Cook, snapped with his camera. Then, getting a little tiddly, we went out into the garden where the inside sleeve shot was taken. We were all supposed to be miming our instruments with Rod in singing mode, but Ronnie had his hands in his pockets as Woody tried to explain what we were all doing.

We all got very drunk that afternoon. The music was loud, the excitement was high, the drink was strong, and the next thing you know we were all dancing around the sitting room, shouting at the tops of our voices! We ended up jumping up and down on the low table, hanging from the chandelier above us and smashing the table to pieces, all the time laughing our crazed heads off, Mike and Kate included. There was broken glass and splintered wood everywhere, but what Kate didn't tell us until later was that she'd poured a whole bottle of wood alcohol into the punch to give it an extra kick. It was rocket fuel! The silly cow could have killed the lot of us.

The Faces' first real gig was at a U.S. Air Force base in Cambridge in December 1969. It was a complete shambles and we all got very drunk in the dressing room after the show. That's not to say we went on stage sober, but we had to celebrate somehow and I recall an accident happening to a double bass that was standing up against the wall when we came off stage, and was in a thousand little pieces when we left the gig.

We began to notice that accidents would sometimes occur with Rod and Woody in the band, but with one gig under our belts, The Faces were born.

On January 9, 1970, just after midnight, high above the traffic speeding around Hyde Park Corner, Sandy gave birth to Lee McLagan, our son and my heir. He cried, and we cried too. His birth was one of the most beautiful and moving experiences I've ever witnessed. I was so moved I wrote a poem about it, my first ever, but its gone where all the odd socks go, wherever that is. Sandy was tired and torn but otherwise fine, and after a while I left her and little Lee to sleep. Meanwhile, I celebrated the night away with Woody and Krissie at their flat above Lower Sloane Street, where champagne, cannabis, and my new drug of choice, cocaine, were consumed in great quantities to "wet the baby's head." It was a joyous time, with the newly born Lee, the new record deal, and money coming in. What could go wrong? Life was bloody perfect, and it could only get better!

After a few British shows we flew to Sweden and Denmark for a week of gigs and a laugh a minute. There was no letup on the humour, and when we drove up to the OK Motor Hotel Motel, we knew we were staying somewhere special. We didn't want to sleep, preferring to booze it up and play the wall radio in my dingy hotel room. Eventually, the night porter shouted up the stairs:

"You must go to sleep!"

With that, we were in darkness and the radio went silent. He'd pulled the plug on us. Well, we couldn't, and now we wouldn't go to sleep. The window, high in the wall of the room, led out to a gently inclined roof and, as it was a mild moonlit night, we climbed out onto it and carried on partying until we got bored.

It was around 3 A.M. when I went to bed but I was woken up at six when the night porter switched the power back on. The lights came on automatically, and the radio blared at me from the wall. I was wide awake when the swine from downstairs shouted up at us:

"You must wake up!"

The Faces' first tour of the Americas began at the Varsity Arena in Toronto, where we opened for the MC5 and a bunch of other name bands and did quite well, thank you. Even though I don't remember anything about it, I've been told by more than a few punters who were there that night that we killed the lot of them.

Whether that's true or not, the following day we flew into Boston to play at the Boston Tea Party to start our U.S. tour proper. Apart from the twelve hours I spent at the San Francisco Airport Hilton on the way back from Australia in 1968, this was my first time legally in the States, and I was very excited as I had reason to believe it might never happen. After all, the U.S. Embassy had told me in no uncertain terms that because of my bust in 1967 I would never be allowed in. Some departments of the U.S. Government had an unbending attitude towards past petty crimes, it seems, and yet they changed their collective minds in March 1970, allowing me in for a couple of months, with one additional border crossing during that time. I could work, but I couldn't take a holiday. But as it happens, being in the States was like a holiday for me anyway.

This was to be the pattern for me for the next eight years. Our American agent would petition for me to tour, asking for as many other entries as possible, in case a gig came up in Vancouver or Toronto. In fact, the only Faces gig I didn't play was one in Toronto, where Billy Gaff volunteered the information about my bust to the Canadian Immigration people at the airport and asked if there would be any objection to my entering the country. He might as well have told him I was a child rapist, and did they need a babysitter? The officer led me to a room where they searched me, stripped me, and searched me again, presumably for concealed weapons. I was told to get dressed after which they escorted me to a plane bound for New York. They were even less forgiving than the U.S. authorities.

God Bless John Lennon for sorting the whole mess out. As a direct result of his winning his legal battle against the U.S. Government over his right to remain in the U.S. I was granted a visa to enter the States at any time. My visa states, and I quote word for word:

Previous ineligibility under section 212(A)(23) removed. No longer ineligible since previous finding covered by Lennon precident (sic)

Forget the atrocious spelling–it spells freedom to me.

John is the only Beatle I never met. In the summer of 1967 The Stones were in Studio 1 at Olympic recording "We Love You," Mick and Keith's answer in song to their recent bust by the Drugs Squad. John and Paul came by to show their solidarity and sing harmonies on the song. I was lost in space in Studio 2, working on a piano part, when I felt a presence in front of me and, looking up, I saw John Lennon's face peering at me round the open door. Our eyes met for a split second, I looked down, did a double take but he was gone. Sadly, I never came close to meeting him again. God Bless you, John.

We flew into Boston's Logan Airport on March 26, 1970, with three nights ahead of us at the Boston Tea Party. It was cold and windy, and the three smaller Faces hadn't realized how cold it could be in the North East. Rod and Woody must have had an inkling because they wore winter coats.

Of course, we should have had a group argument at that point, but group arguments were as far away as London. The wind was howling through that day, as we waited for long minutes outside in the street for someone to open the door. When we finally got in, Lee Michaels and Barry "Frosty" Smith, his drummer, were checking their sound, and what a sound it was. Lee was the leader of a two-man band that was the headlining act. He had a stripped down Hammond and what sounded like a million Leslie cabinets! The sound was clean, but it was enormous. The building was literally shaking.

A football appeared out of nowhere, and before you could say Stanley Matthews, it was the War of Independence! Lee, Frosty, and crew, a bunch of colonials against The Faces and crew, the British gentry. We were reminded that we were in Boston where we'd lost once before, and they weren't playing soccer, they were fighting the war all over again. The game spread all over the empty warehouse with a fair amount of kicking and shouting and occasionally we kicked the ball too, but a show of blood ended the proceedings. We admitted defeat and let them have America for the second time, though we swore to return.

I'd had no luck trying to get my B3 anywhere near as loud as Woody's amp and as I now knew it could be done, I ran upstairs to the dressing room and cornered Pete Buckland, our head roadie.

"How come my B3 isn't as loud as that?" I whined.

He patiently explained that whereas Lee only had drums to compete with, I had guitar and bass volume levels to overcome. Also, my Hammond was like a Model T Ford next to his GT40! I'd just have to save up some dosh and upgrade my gear, bit by bit.

Then, during our sound check, I discovered my B3 wasn't in tune with the other guys, because of electrical problems to do with voltage and cycles. It meant that I had to play in the key of F while Woody and Ronnie were playing in E. It was a royal pain, but by the second night Pete sorted it all out for me. As we walked into the dressing room, Woody introduced me to the DJ, J. J. Jackson, and Charlie Daniels, the Master Blaster. Charlie had been introducing the acts at the Tea Party for ages, and Rod and Woody knew them both from the Beck group days. Charlie was a very handsome, stylish black man. Tall and slim, he could pull a babe without any visible effort. He always wore a bandanna tied tightly round his head and it was years before I realized he was bald. I just thought it was a cool look. He brought us on stage each night at the club and we liked having him around so much he eventually came on tour with us.

After the show, the dressing room was packed with girls and the heady combination of patchouli oil and pot smoke. All of Boston's beauties were out in force to meet and greet the latest English band to hit town, but Rod and Woody already had a following. The American groupies were much more up front about sex than the English girls. They were ready to party and they let you know it.

A crowd of them came back to the hotel and gave us all a seeing-to over the next few nights. It was trousers off and away we went, and though we were sharing rooms on the first tour, some girls didn't seem to mind what they did in front of strangers. It was unbelievable. Sometimes you'd have to persuade nicely, but generally there was no foreplay, though it was all very innocent and friendly. I was in seventh heaven. Finally, I was in the States and loving all things American, especially the girls.

CHAPTER SIXTEEN

Made in Detroit

We played a gig in Virginia, one in Wheaton, Maryland, and then flew to Detroit, where we checked into the Cadillac Hilton, which was a bit of a dump. It was fantastic to actually be in the city where Marvin Gaye, The Temptations, Smokey Robinson and the Miracles, the Four Tops, Stevie Wonder, and Gladys Knight and The Pips all recorded at Hitsville USA, Motown's studio. Looking around from the window of the hotel, I got some idea how such great music came out of there. The place reminded me a little of Glasgow. We went to the Eastown Theatre early for a sound check, but as I had a problem with my equipment, I hung around while it was fixed and couldn't find the rest of the lads when it was ready. Some bright spark told me they'd just walked out the front door, so I went to follow them, stepped out onto the street, and the door slammed behind me.

I was in front of a line of people waiting for tickets for the night's show. I turned to go back, but there was no handle on the door, so I couldn't get in. The kids were checking me out to see if I was in the band, and being a little unsure of my bearings, I wandered off up the street with the hope of catching the chaps getting into a cab round the corner.

It was bloody cold and I was still wearing the same thin leather jacket I'd been wearing in Boston when I almost froze. With horror, I come to the realisation that I didn't have any cash or even a hotel key, and all I knew was that it was called the Cadillac something. I found out later there were three Cadillac hotels in Detroit, not to mention a Lincoln and probably a Ford and a Chevrolet too!

I was lost, cold, broke, foreign, and after hailing several empty cabs without success and looking around for a familiar face, I became aware that I was the only white man in the neighbourhood. Panic started to set in at this point. You have to realize that this was my first week in America and I'd seen the black areas only on news broadcasts. I'd heard about Detroit, New York, and Chicago, and I began to feel extremely alien in these surroundings. I had no idea which direction to walk. I hadn't paid any attention to street signs as we drove in, and I only remembered it was on a freeway. I could have been going completely the wrong way.

I walked for a while, hoping to turn a street corner and spot a cab or something familiar, and I saw four black guys walking straight towards me, side by side, taking up the entire sidewalk.

My heart was pounding with the possibilities of the situation, so I made no eye contact and stepped into the road when they drew level.

"Hey man, are you in the band?" I heard a voice say. I turned my head and looked at four of the friendliest, most open faces you could ever hope to see. What a relief!

"Yes!" I shouted, a little too loud. "Do you need tickets? Do you wanna come to the show?"

"Hey, that'd be cool man. Where you from man, England?"

I told them, yes, and they wrote down their names while I told them what had happened to me.

"Oh man, hey, you wanna cab, here." The guy stepped off the sidewalk, raised his hand, and a cab pulled up to the kerb out of nowhere.

"Where you goin'?" the cabbie asked.

"Well, it's a hotel called the Cadillac something, but I forget which one and my money's at the hotel."

"Hop in, we'll find it easy enough." It was as simple as that. I thanked each of the fellers, told them the tickets would be on the door, and away we went. It just goes to show it doesn't pay to believe in stereotypes and to always keep book matches or a hotel key on you at all times!

We played a blinder that night, opening for Savoy Brown, and we left the stage with the crowd wanting more.

The first time I saw Sly and the Family Stone was the first time they played in London. The show at the Lyceum ballroom was rescheduled after their first appearance got cancelled. When they finally played, it was a magnificent show of just over an hour. Sly finished with "I Want to Take You Higher," repeating the chorus over and over. Abruptly they stopped the song and left the stage with the audience and me going crazy, hollering and screaming. I was up at the bar on the balcony, and it felt as if it was going to collapse with the people jumping up and down. We waited for a good five minutes before they came back on. Greg Errico brought it in.

"WackaWackaWackaWacka, WackaWackaWackaWacka, Higher, I wanna take you higher..."

We knew immediately we were only getting more of the same, and it was fine, as long as they didn't stop too soon. They played for at least ten minutes, Sly hollering, screaming, and dancing. But when they finished, that was it, they were not going to come back on. It was a final statement.

I've never understood encores, they're so fake. I don't know why a band can't play what they came to play, and then get off the stage. That's all, thank you, and goodnight!

In America, The Faces, like the automobiles, were made in Detroit. In England, John Peel played our record when nobody else would, and had us on his show live and drunk and continued to play our record. But in America, the kids from Detroit were the fuel that ignited us. Life was tough in Detroit, and they had the same attitude we had. They really *needed* to rock and roll. They were loyal too, they'd keep coming back and bringing their friends, who in turn brought their friends.

Between the beginning of April and the end of May 1970, we played two nights at the Eastown, two nights at the Palladium in Birmingham, on the outskirts of Detroit, three more nights at the Eastown, and a show at Michigan State University, eighty miles away. Eight shows in as many weeks! We were becoming the local heroes and the girls kept coming back for more.

We were staying at Holiday Inns then, as they were usually clean and dependable but ultimately extremely boring and soul-destroying homes from home. The monotony got to everybody after a time. It was not possible to walk into the identical room in twenty different cities without wanting to hurt it, just a little. If anything was built to be destroyed, it was the two-storey, motel model Holiday Inn. They were often built next to freeways, which meant there was generally no life close by, no bars or anything other than the freeway to look at. This had its advantages though, because when fans came back to the hotel to party, there was less chance of disturbing other residents—with all the traffic droning past outside. Not that it stopped us from disturbing other guests.

The Party, which is what the fans called it, started in the bar if it was still open, then continued into the pool area, if there was one, then carried on in any or all of our rooms and the corridor. Some kids would follow us for a few days at a time before they got tired and went home to mum and dad, but for us it went on every night for months on end. Even debauchery has a limit! I'd get back to the hotel sometimes and just flop on the bed, waking up at 6 A.M. knowing exactly where I was, but having no idea where *that* was and still drunk from the night before last! When we'd go back to a town after a month, the girls would be waiting, refreshed, dressed to impress, and ready to rock and roll.

My first time in New York and the streets are alive. Whatever people say about the city, it's never enough. It absolutely amazes me. I'd live there if it wasn't for the crime, the cost of living, and the pollution. I couldn't believe my eyes and ears that first time. You'd see housewives, Hassidic Jews, drunks asleep on the sidewalk, beggars and businessmen, hustlers and pimps, prostitutes and policemen, cab drivers with an opinion and hotel clerks with an attitude.

It was all there and it was all in your face and I loved it. We stayed at a few different hotels in New York during the Seventies. Some were more expensive, like The Plaza, the Sherry Netherland, and The Pierre, but in the early days of 1970 and 1971 we stayed at the cheaper dives like The Gorham and Loews Midtown Motor Inn. Loews is gone now, but I have fond memories of that place. It was on Eighth Avenue between 47th and 48th, and it was drab before I knew quite how drab New York could be. There were many naughty goings on in those early Faces years, even though three of us were married, but you'd never have guessed it if you'd seen us then.

As Rod has put it, "The Faces would shag anything with a pulse." There's some truth to this, but the girls who hung around with us were no slouches in the pulse department! There was a different gang in each of the major cities hanging around with us, not just looking to get into bed, but being with the band. They had their favourites, though they didn't appear to mind very much who they were with, and eventually most of them got a good seeing to. One way or another, we rarely let a customer go home unsatisfied!

Sandy called from home one morning while I was asleep, and one of the New York girls picked up the phone before I could get to it. Naturally, she was upset, and it wasn't easy to talk my way out of that one, but luckily she didn't wake up the other two girls in the other bed because that would've been harder to explain. In fact, it was quite innocent, they all fell asleep in my room and nothing at all happened, but I wasn't making any effort to behave myself in those days anyway, it didn't come natural.

As you entered the lobby at Loews Midtown, between the elevators on the rear wall, there was a grandiose plaster copy of a Greek statue of a naked person. We'd joke about it and sometimes we couldn't resist the temptation and it would end up in Billy Gaff's room or in a broom closet on a different floor to ours. That was the first rule of damaging hotel property. Never do it on your own floor.

We were staying at Loews when we played a couple of nights at the Fillmore East, New York, with Black Sabbath opening for us in 1971. But if you think that's a match made in hell, how about The Staple Singers, Black Sabbath, Tiny Tim, Muhammad Ali, and The Faces all staying in this one crummy hotel at the same time? One morning, the elevator doors opened and Muhammad Ali and his wife were standing there. I was struck dumb, they were both so beautiful, and I wasn't sure who had the nicest skin out of the two of them. As a boxer, you'd imagine he'd be scarred, but he really was a beautiful man. I wish I could've said something to him or got his autograph, but I just couldn't speak, I was so awestruck. I just stood next to him, looking into the middle distance, perspiring quietly. I've been over it many times in my mind since, and if I ever get to bump into him again I'm going to at least say "How are you, Champ?" But I was speechless in his presence. He was in town to fight Oscar Bonavena, at the start of his comeback trail after the World Boxing Association stole his title from him because he refused to be inducted into the U.S. army. From a distance, I stood and watched him being interviewed for TV in the lobby, but I couldn't say hello up close.

One afternoon, as I walked along the corridor from my room, one of the members of Black Sabbath came out of his room ahead of me and walked on toward the elevator. As he passed a band mate's open door, a voice from the room called out in a thick Birmingham accent: "Whereyugoin', man?"

The answer came back quick as a flash. "I'mgoinout." Ah, the cut and thrust of polished conversation!

Most mornings when we stayed at Loews Midtown, we had breakfast at a little place across the street, the Olympic Restaurant, that was owned and operated by a Greek family. The sign outside was broken for about a year and it was actually the "Olymp," but we called it the "Orange-a-juice" because the second you walked in the guy at the front would ask you what you wanted to order.

I'd say, "Orange juice, please."

"Orange-a-juice!" He'd shout down the narrow restaurant to the back, where another guy was nearer the fridge.

"Orange-a-juice!" The second guy would repeat it and bring the freshly squeezed juice, handing it to the first guy who'd hand it to me. Everybody got into the act. The food was good, it was inexpensive, and they were fast getting your order. You'd have juice, two eggs, toast, and coffee for under two dollars. As we'd be in there every morning whenever we were in New York, you'd get to see the whole family over a period of time. They kept pretty much to themselves. It was touching to see one of the waiters standing outside on his day off, leaning against the window in his best suit. All dressed up and nowhere to go.

I took Kim there in 1992 after telling her about it many times and things had changed very little in twenty years. The prices were higher, but not much, the service was still good, and they'd fixed the sign. When I drove past there in May 1996 after playing Madison Square Garden with Rod, I was pleased to see they'd got the place next door as well, so it seemed business at the "Orange-a-juice" was good.

The second time we played Detroit, I woke up to a deafening pounding on the door. It was insistent, as if there was some absolutely important reason to get out of bed immediately, or some rude, inconsiderate bastard had broken the unwritten code of ethics. If he didn't want an argument or a screaming match, why would anybody knock on my motel room door at any time before 2 P.M.? I looked at my watch. It was 9 A.M.! This was war!

"FUCK OFF!" I yelled from the bed.

"Hey, man!" Bangbang, Bangbangbang! "Hey, Mac, wake up, okay? Open the door, man!"

It was an unfamiliar voice or voices, but they had to be suicidal, whoever they were. I jumped out of bed in a rage and opened the door to find two strangers, one with an Afro the size of a hedge. The other was all sweaty, with an intense look on his face. They were standing there as if we were old friends.

"Whatthefuckdoyouwant, andwhothefuckareyouanyway?" They weren't fazed.

"Hey, man," the intense one said. "I'm Tom Wright and this is The Chuch. Okay, here's the deal. We've got a rented limo with a driver, a gram of coke, some pot, a bottle of Cold Duck, and a six pack of beer on ice. I'm a fantastic photographer, we're gonna take you to a location out in the Arboretum, you can get fucked up, I'm gonna get some really cool pictures of the band, then we'll bring you back to the motel, we'll go off and develop the pictures, and we'll bring back the prints this afternoon before you leave, okay?"

He had a very twangy, whiny voice like Jack Nicholson, and he didn't take a breath the whole time he spoke. He must've been a car salesman or a preacher in another life. It was a real pleasure when he stopped talking. I was in a daze.

"What the fuck are you talking about?" They explained that all the other guys knew about it, that I should have been told, and that they were all getting ready at that moment, and I was the last one to be woken up because they'd heard I don't like to be woken up too early. Yada Yada Yada Yada! Amphetamines are real conversation killers.

Of course, nobody knew anything about it. It was a con, but it worked. We were all hoodwinked into a photo session we hadn't planned with complete strangers at a location miles from the motel on a day off. This was our first meeting with members of the Hard Corps. There were more of them, but these two would be enough to deal with right now. However, everything Tom said came true. The drugs and booze were in the limo and they did take us to the Arboretum in Ann Arbor, which is a very beautiful park, and he did take some very fine photographs.

We found out much later that Tom Wright was Pete Townshend's best mate at Ealing Art School, but he got busted for pot, and being American was deported. But before he left London he gave Pete his collection of rare blues records, which can't have done any harm to the listening ears of one already so aware. His photographs were so good, he became our tour photographer and toured with us for months on end, developing pictures in his hotel bathroom every night after the show, and generally just giving it 150 percent of his energy all the time. That was Hard Corps.

The Chuch, or Royden Walter Magee III, which is his real name, helped out and became our equipment roadie, touring with us until The Faces broke up in 1975, and continuing on with Woody and The Stones to this day. That was Hard Corps.

We came back to New York to play two nights at the Action House on Long Island at the end of April. After those gigs we had five glorious days off before we went back to Detroit and the Eastown again. That Sunday was hot and humid on the streets of New York, and you could feel the tension building. People were impatient and angry. Spring had suddenly turned into summer overnight and no one seemed happy. By chance, Billy Nicholls, our old pal from the Immediate days, called up out of the blue to say he was staying at Andrew Oldham's house in Connecticut, and he asked us if we'd like to come for a visit. It was always good to see our old mate Billy, but even more so after a month of hotels, bars, airports, and dressing rooms.

Ronnie and I were dead keen to get out of the city, so I left directions for the others to come out later and drove the rented station wagon. The bloody thing was swaying all over the pot-holed Hudson Parkway while Ronnie checked the map and twiddled the knobs on the radio looking for a decent station. He caught a song halfway through that sounded so soulful we had to turn it up to deafening to get the full effect. When the song ended I said, "That's the sort of record Paul McCartney should be making." But I was too clever for my own good, because minutes later the DJ told us it was his new single, "Maybe I'm Amazed," from his first solo album.

Billy showed us around the house that we'd bought for Andrew, and then we drove into the nearest town to buy Paul's album and a ton of groceries and booze, all on Andrew's tab, of course. Back at the house after a nosh and a drink, we lit a joint and put our feet up to listen to the record properly, with a glass of fine cognac. When the lads arrived we set up a couple of amps next to the piano and worked out the chords. We played it at the next gig and eventually cut it for a B side and again live for our second album, *Long Player*. Rod used to bring out an orange box for Ronnie to stand on for a cheap laugh when they sang that song together. Everybody tore the arse out of Andrew's phone bill, and it was great to be able to phone home and have a decent conversation without having to worry about the cost or feeling bad about Andrew having to pay. But then, we figured we'd paid for it already.

It's amazing we didn't burn his beautiful house down or at the very least wreck it or throw the piano in the lake, but we just got very wrecked and decided to haunt Ronnie. We waited until he went to bed, and after he'd nodded off we cut some holes in some bedsheets and crept into his bedroom in the dark. We started moaning quietly at first, so he didn't wake up with a start, and then got louder and louder until he screamed with horror. He really thought he'd seen a ghost, or five ghosts, and we chased him all round the house and grounds and then fell about in a sweating heap, laughing. Okay, so we ripped up some sheets and ran up Andrew's phone bill, but it's no comparison to the royalties we never received. Maybe we *should* have burnt it to the ground.

CHAPTER SEVENTEEN

On the Razzle

I was very comfortable with The Faces. It never occurred to me that we wouldn't be popular or that we would be big, for that matter. It just felt right. I didn't smell money, I smelled fun, and we had lots of it. It was as if young America was waiting to be entertained. Apart from spectacular bands like The Stones, The Who, and Sly and the Family Stone, stage presence generally meant the occasional reefer or bottle of Cold Duck passed up from the audience! Bands at that time ignored the paying public, boring them with endless guitar solos and, even worse, bass and drum solos. It was heads down and let's get back in the dressing room.

Though Rod had been an incredibly shy singer—he was known to hide behind the amps for whole songs when he and Woody were with Jeff Beck—now he really blossomed as a performer. In those early tours the girls discovered a big-nosed, spiky-haired geezer, prancing suggestively and rolling on the floor, with a pink feather boa round his neck, cross-dressing for the girls and out dressing all of the boys. He was a vamp and he was camp and he was comfortable with it. Woody was the guy's guy, with a cigarette stuck in his mouth or between the fingers of his right fist, eyes blinking continually with concentration as he worried the guitar, sang, and camped it up with Rod. Ronnie, puffing like a blowfish, ambled backwards and forwards across the stage in his characteristic "Ronnie Lane Shuffle," laying down the solid and melodic bass lines that were the foundation to all of our songs, and singing so sweetly. Kenney kept us all together, whacking his kit mercilessly with a fixed stare. Often he'd be concentrating so hard he'd lock onto my eyes, although he wouldn't actually see me at all, and I'd blow him a kiss and wait for his reaction. His eyes would clear suddenly as he realized what he'd seen, and he'd get a bad taste in his mouth and look away in disgust. Ugh! I alternated between annoying Kenney, sliding up and down the Hammond, hammering the Steinway, sipping a drink, and lighting another Pall Mall. We were happy boys, happy. These were the days and this was the life!

Though I was married and had a baby boy, I was as promiscuous on the road as I'd always been as a single bloke and nothing was going to change that. Being away from home for months at a time with pretty girls hanging around just waiting to jump into bed was too much temptation for this one weak man. When I was at home with Sandy things were different, because I never fucked around on my own turf, but when I was on the road I was on the razzle.

We seemed to be in the right place at the right time. Some of the girls followed us from gig to gig, and we got to know some of them so well, they became almost like family. Generally, all it would take was a wink in the direction of a pretty face and she'd be waiting for you backstage. We were innocents abroad, and it was all in the spirit of exploration.

One night after a gig, I took a pretty blonde number back to my room, and we'd just got down to business when there was a knock at the door. She said it was probably her friend, and I thought, Dammit, there's always an ugly sister. But I opened the door to a beautiful black girl with a very pretty smile. I said hello, she giggled, undressed, and climbed onto the bed with her friend. Goodnight.

Things would usually get out of hand anytime one of the roadies found a pair of boilers who liked to be noticed and didn't object to getting naked in front of the band and crew.

This became known as "surgery," and we would all squeeze into one room where the girls would get undressed, ready for the operation. Someone even went to the lengths of carrying a surgical mask and stethoscope. It was all very funny, with lots of stupid comments and general mayhem, falling over, laughter, and probing with household objects. No one ever got hurt, and it had very little to do with sex, although the girls invariably got all worked up. At that point we'd leave them to do or be done by whoever was willing, but never by anyone in the band, because by that time we'd have hurried to the bar for a quick one before they closed.

We concentrated on the East Coast and the Midwest on that first tour, but the first gigs we played in California in May 1970 were four nights at the legendary Fillmore West in San Francisco. Bill Graham presented some of the best shows The Faces ever played in America. He was a master showman and light years ahead of everybody else, in my opinion. He understood what putting on a show was all about and saw to it that the audience, the hall staff, the band, and crew had as good a time as possible. Compared with a Bill Graham show, most others paled, and his legacy lives on at his venues in San Francisco to this day. I had the privilege of working with him on all The Faces tours from 1970 to 1975, The Rolling Stones tours of 1978 and 1981, a ton of Bonnie Raitt gigs over four years, the 1984 European Bob Dylan tour, as well as numerous David Lindley, Ronnie Wood, and my own Bump Band gigs.

Bill introduced himself to us in our dressing room before the first night at the Fillmore West.

"Well," he said. "The place is packed to the rafters, your stage is set, your crew have been fed, there's beer in the cooler, and I know you've got plenty of dope. All you have to do is get out there and have a good time." He made it that simple. He put it together, and you had nothing to do but have fun.

Bill promoted The Stones' American tour in 1981 and his company, Winterland, also had the concession for the swag, so he brought the programmes into the dressing room for the guys to okay at the start of the tour. Keith Richards pointed out that although the programme gave special thanks to Stu and me, there were no photographs of us, and he thought there should be. We weren't really bothered about that, but I added that if there were to be any changes made, my name had been misspelled, as MACLAGEN, instead of McLAGAN. Bill said he'd fix it, and sure enough, the next day a photographer came and snapped the two of us during the show. A couple of days later he brought the new programmes in and proudly opened the inside back page and showed us our photographs.

"Thanks, Bill," I said. "I hate to mention it, but my name is still wrong."

"What? I don't believe it." He jumped up, grabbed the book, scanned it, and apologized again.

"Right, that's it. Hold that thought. I'll be back!"

Two days later he came into the dressing room at the Brendan Byrne Arena in New Jersey, dragging a large cardboard box.

"Check it out," he said, and sat on his knees in front of me, opening the newest programme at our page. Everything was fine and I thanked him.

"Thank God for that," he said. "These are for you." He opened the box, which held a gross of black T-shirts with "McLagan McLagan McLagan McLagan McLagan" down the front in white. I was blown away. It was his way of writing a hundred lines and making sure everyone knew how to spell my name as well. What a bloke! I dished them out to band and crew alike, and Keith and Woody wore them on stage that night. The next day, Bill turned up with a box of shirts, which read "Stu's Boogie," for Stu. I still get my name spelled wrong all the time, but Bill couldn't have done more to get it sorted out, God Bless him.

Us newer boys to American touring could hardly believe the size of the country and how many places there were to play. We still had another swing along the East Coast before we went back to regular-sized gigs in the British Isles. A couple of months later we were back on the treadmill in the States again, followed by a short European tour, culminating in Germany, at the Love and Peace Festival on Fehmarn Island. It was a godforsaken, windy place in the Baltic Sea, but Canned Heat, Sly and the Family Stone, The Faces, and a lot of other acts had come from around the world to play or, in Sly's case, to collect his cash and leave.

There was a force-ten gale blowing straight towards the stage, and people in tents were huddled in front of bonfires to keep warm. When we finally went on about midnight, wearing scarves and overcoats, we had to lean into the wind to stop falling over.

Love and Peace in Germany 1970 was quite different from the American version in 1967, because somebody shot the promoter, burned his trailer to the ground, and stole all the cash.

We toured the States for the third time the next month, playing the same old places, Detroit, New York, Philadelphia, Chicago, and Boston, but we were moving up the ladder fast. When we played the Eastown the first time, we opened for Savoy Brown. Only a few months later they opened for us at the same venue. We were also getting more and more opening slots in arenas, which gave us a chance to be seen and to take the crowd with us.

Although Rod's solo album was starting to sell more than The Faces' *First Step,* both Mercury and Warner Brothers were promoting us hard. Early in 1971, we found ourselves in Miami, where we stayed at the Newport Resort Motel on Miami Beach. It was cheap and they had a great nightclub downstairs that booked quality acts like Ray Charles, Ike and Tina Turner, The Temptations, Jerry Lee Lewis, and Gene Vincent. It was a family vacation hotel and a rock and rollers place too. When the sun had gone down and the other guests had finally put their kids to bed, you could sit there, your whole body tingling from sunburn, and sink a few bevvies while watching a great show, if a good act was playing there at the time. One night The Coasters played, but there was no way of telling if there were any original Coasters on the stage, though they were billed as The Original Coasters. I saw Roy Head perform there one time, and I mean perform. He had a heavy, round-bottomed microphone stand like Joe Tex used, and he had all of his moves down. It was the same stuff that Prince does today. Roy's big hit was "Treat Her Right" and he rocked the joint righteously.

Probably the worst night Jimmy Rodgers ever had in his whole career was the night The Faces went to see him at the Newport Resort. He was a pop singer from the Fifties whose big hit was "Honeycomb." We had nowhere else to go, so we sat at the bar in the back and watched him go through a few tunes before Rod had a bright idea. We moved to a table and he pulled us in close.

"Okay, when he finishes the next song let's give him a standing ovation like he's never had before." Rod could be really wicked.

The next two songs were met by tumultuous applause from our table and it had the effect of getting the rest of the audience clapping too. And although there weren't many people there they really got into it, as if his fan club were in town for a convention. By the third song we were pissing ourselves laughing, clapping and whistling, with Woody shouting out:

"Author, Author!"

"Right," Rod said. "Do nothing after the next number, total silence, and see what happens."

Of course, Jimmy was having an unexpected career high that night. He couldn't believe his luck and was probably considering asking for a raise after the show. Unfortunately, this was the moment he decided to sing his biggest hit, "Honeycomb." When he finished the song, we carried on talking as if nothing had happened. The three or four other tables that had been getting pretty rowdy along with us hadn't really been listening, so now the clapping dwindled as soon as they realized they were on their own.

Almost total bloody silence broken only by the clinking of glasses over our smothered laughter. It was a horrible thing to do and it'll all come back to haunt us, but then we were horrible, especially Rod.

Maybe the Japanese audiences are every band's payment for that night because, although they really seem to enjoy a show and will applaud and scream, as soon as it's over, they stop. It can be very unnerving. Just ask Jimmy Rodgers.

Detroit had taken us to their hearts, and the fourteenth time we played there was as headliners at Cobo Hall. This was officially the big time and two new riders had been added to our American promoters contracts. The first said that they were to supply a nine-foot Steinway grand piano and for it to be tuned once when it was placed on the stage in the afternoon and again when it was put into position ready for use. The second rider basically said that if the piano supplied wasn't a nine-foot Steinway, then any damage that might occur to it would be the responsibility of the promoter. Then I went out and bought an axe!

The first time I got to use the axe was that first night at Cobo Hall. Our crowds in Detroit were probably the best in the country and they deserved the best, so when I checked the piano in the afternoon I was pissed off. Whatever it was, it wasn't a Steinway, and I figured Bob Bugaris, the promoter, knew better than that. Towards the end of the last song, "Twistin' the Night Away," I asked Chuch for the axe and hacked the keyboard to pieces with a flourish! Bits of ivory and wood were flying everywhere, and I had a grand old time.

The next time we played Cobo, Bob Bugaris said nothing about the smashed piano, and I figured he had learned his lesson, but I couldn't believe what I saw when I got up on the stage that afternoon. The piano was a Steinmeg. I thought it was a joke at first; I'd never heard of it, and I decided it was a cheap copy of a Steinway. Well, all the other promoters had managed to get a decent piano, and if they were having trouble finding one, Pete or Chuch would call

Steinway in New York and they'd locate one easily. It wasn't that much of a problem. He was the only promoter who was being difficult.

That night David Ruffin of The Temptations and his wife came backstage before the show. He was tall and slim, smartly dressed, and wore a pair of huge square shades and he was a gentleman. Rod was extremely nervous meeting him for the first time because he was such a fan, but David relaxed him when he said he'd genuinely liked our version of The Temps' "Losing You." Rod had often mentioned him as being one of his favourite singers in interviews and when he asked David if he'd sit in with us, he readily agreed. Detroit's young things were dressed to impress and ready to rock just as we hit the stage. I think we played a blinding show, but I forgot David was coming out for the encore and just before the end of "Twistin' the Night Away," I attacked the piano like a man possessed.

I was still playing chopsticks when the song ended and Rod introduced David Ruffin! The crowd went crazy as he, his wife, and a couple of friends walked onto the stage, and as they passed in front of me dropped their coats into the open piano. Now, not only had I hacked the keyboard to bits, but I'd become the hat-check girl! I had to laugh, it was too ridiculous, and in the frenzy of the moment no one noticed that I wasn't playing. David and Rod sang so sweet together, the crowd loved it. Motown's own and their adopted son.

I found out years later that a Steinmeg is in fact a very old Steinway, so I had butchered a perfectly good piano for nothing, even though Bob had kept to the contract and paid for the damage, believing me to be right. By another quirk of fate, the Steinway people decided to make me a Steinway Artist soon afterwards, which is a hell of an honour if you consider that all Steinway Artists up until then were classical pianists like Vladimir Ashkenazy, Daniel Barenboim, Arturo Rubenstein, and the like, and there were certainly no rockers in that list—until little me.

It was a mob scene at the Ponchartrain Hotel, across the road from Cobo. Even though we ran from the stage to the limo, and it sped the fifty yards to the back entrance of the hotel, by the time we got to the elevator there were kids everywhere. The days had already passed when we could have a small gathering at the hotel. Now there were thousands who wanted to party. We ran through a fire exit and up to the next floor, pushed the button, and twenty kids came out of every elevator door. It was lunacy, and by the time I walked up the sixteen flights to my room I was knackered.

After a quick splash, a big line, and another to keep my balance, a large slug of Bourbon and ginger was the order of the day. Now I could face a look outside to see what there was on the menu. Opening the door a crack showed me the corridor was packed with girls and geezers chatting excitedly and waiting for the big party, but also, sitting cross-legged on the floor outside Rod's room, there was the great David Ruffin. I closed the door and called Rod on the phone.

"Did you know David Ruffin's outside your room?"

"Yeah, I know."

"Well, what are you going to do? You can't just leave him there."

"I dunno. I'm getting changed. I'll let him in, in a minute."

He never did. He stayed in his room the whole night. Although he'd meant every word when he told interviewers how much he loved David's singing, he just couldn't pluck up the courage to invite him in for a friendly chat. I don't really understand it, especially as David was such an easy person to get on with. It wasn't his problem.

You'd meet all types on the road, and not just after gigs. There was a sports convention at the Stouffers Hotel, on the banks of the Mississippi River in St. Louis, and while we were eating breakfast a salesman introduced himself to us. Steve said he was a fan of the band but had missed the show because of the convention. He was a clean-cut, smartly dressed bloke with a trim moustache, and he said if there was any football gear we wanted, he'd give it to us.

He was quite genuine and gave us a soccer ball and some shirts and shorts and promised to catch up with us and see the show next time. We all liked to kick a ball around, especially Rod, so we got into the habit of kicking it about in car parks and on private airfields while we waited for the limos to turn up.

He appeared in some other city, though I don't remember where. All I remember was that I didn't recognize him straight away because he'd changed quite a lot. He wasn't as clean-cut as he had been in St. Louis. Now he was wearing jeans and a T-shirt, but he was the same affable kind of bloke he'd been in St. Louis. He'd loved the show and gave us a bag of some very fine pot before he left.

It was in Atlanta on the next swing through the South that he rang me in my room.

"Hey, Mac, can I come up and see you? I've got a gift for you."

"Sure," I said. When I opened the door I didn't recognize him. This was a long-haired hippie in a fringed suede jacket, Indian shirt, and a feather hanging off one ear. He had changed completely. He wasn't clean-cut anymore, but it was still good to see him. He was a really nice character and not a problem, plus he always seemed to have gifts. This time it was a couple of extra strong reefers and a bag full of MDA in pills. He came back after the gig and hung with us and then he was off again. MDA was like acid but without the visuals. It was a very physical drug, and the football got a good kicking for the next few days, and we'd find ourselves running about all day long and not get tired.

The last time I saw him was a complete shock. We were playing at the Boston Garden, and he walked into the dressing room with long, greasy hair, a full beard, and covered in tattoos. He wore black leather pants and vest, Indian bracelets, and rings on every finger. He was a fucking Hell's Angel! He was still the nicest of guys, nothing seemed to have changed except the look. This time he gave me an eighth ounce of coke and a couple of reefers and then he was gone. I never saw him again, but I often wonder if he was with the FBI or the CIA. I may never know, but I know he was a fan.

Billy Gaff was a mess, I mean physically. He always looked as if he'd just escaped from the hands of terrorists or narrowly survived a train crash, or both. The eternally worried look on his face suggested he knew the end of the world was nigh, but had been told to keep it to himself. Though he wasn't a particularly ugly man, there was something about him that made you want to torture him. I don't expect managing The Faces helped his state of mind, but it was hard to resist slapping him over the head just the same, and it became a sport, like trashing hotel rooms.

If he travelled with us in the car, invariably, when the boredom set in, Billy would end up with trash all over him. His hair was having trouble enough covering his scalp, but it was the kind of hair-"don't" that was hard to resist messing with. To his credit he took most of it with a pinch of salt, except when the crew would strip him and throw him in the hotel corridor, spitting venom in front of a crowd of young fans. It was often his room we'd wreck because we knew it would be paid for and anyway it was his room and not ours.

He was our manager and we were a bunch of idiots, and he accepted that. He brought American Talent International in as our agents for the first tour of the States and Ira Blacker as our representative with them. Unfortunately, we'd never signed a contract with the agency, just for each tour, and we were only paying them 10 percent instead of the 15 percent they wanted.

We hadn't signed a contract with Billy Gaff either, for that matter, but the senior partner at ATI, Jeff Franklin, urged Ira to get us to sign, so that the firm could boast we were on their books. We had no desire to leave the agency, we were pleased enough with them, but we figured if it ain't broke why fix it? Ira kept on Billy about it, so in the end Billy told him he'd have to discuss it with us. A meeting was set up at ATI's New York headquarters and we were ushered into Ira's office.

Ira was a large man getting larger and younger than any of us. He was also a nervous man. To give an example, one time he travelled with us in our limo back to New York from the Spectrum in Philadelphia. A joint was going the rounds and when I handed it to him he didn't even puff on it. He threw it out the window! I was really annoyed.

"What the fuck did you do that for, you fat fuck?" was my term of endearment.

"You'll get busted, there are police everywhere!"

What an idiot. Possession of a joint was a misdemeanour in New York, like a traffic ticket, and you'd have to get caught first. He was much too tense.

Anyway, we sat down and he immediately offered us a drink. Although we're known to enjoy a drink or two or three, it was much too early. We could tell he was nervous, because he poured himself a Scotch and water, took a slug, and began bullshitting.

"See here, guys, we've worked together long enough for you to know this agency has done right by you since you've been with us, and I want you to know nobody, I mean nobody, pays as little as you do for our services. All I'm asking is that you give me a contract with your signatures on it that gives me some strength in this agency." Ronnie got up and went to his desk as we mumbled to each other.

"Ira, I think what you're saying is very fair, but it's the others, they're dead set against it."

Ira suddenly saw a ray of hope in the situation. Rod pointed out the silliest looking modern lamp hanging behind Ira's head that had metal arms dangling off of it that held little boxes of light. It was bizarre, but he probably never saw it and possibly didn't even have anything to do with buying this objet d'art. He was drinking and we were all sober. It was Kenney's turn.

"I think it's a good idea, but what do we get out of it?" Game, set, and match to Jones. Woody was next. He sidled up to Ira's desk, jumped up and sat on it, and it started to topple. He quickly jumped off.

"Ira, I'm not against it on principle. In fact, I'm for it. But, whatever it is, I'm against it! Ha ha!" With that Groucho line he ran back to his seat laughing maniacally. Everyone was laughing now except Ira. It was getting very silly.

"Have a drink fellers, okay?" Ira was desperate now. He hardly ever drank, and we never drank Scotch. The man should've done his homework. Vodka, brandy, white wine, maybe. Maybe he should have scored some pot. Ha bloody ha. It was my turn.

"I'll sign anything, anywhere!" He looked hopeful for a second, but then realized I was talking to Woody. It was Rod's turn.

"Ira, you stupid person, I think it's time to sign a contract or something of that type of nature. Eeeeaaaaayyy!" Rod summed it up for all of us by rearranging his desk and pushing his modernistic lamp into disarray. The meeting was over. Ira was drunk, we never did sign papers, and we never paid them more than 10 percent. All the years watching Marx Brothers' movies finally paid off.

CHAPTER EIGHTEEN
"Cool Your Act!"

One of the Faces' finest hours was on the night of August 25, 1972, when we played the Hollywood Bowl. For a laugh I rented an old-fashioned penguin suit like the ones Groucho Marx used to wear and later bought it from the rental company at no small cost. The audience brought picnic baskets and bottles of wine and the smell of pot wafted up onto the stage. The tux came with all the trimmings, white tie, waistcoat, braces, cuff links, and collar studs. I wore white basketball boots instead of evening shoes, but the pièce de resistance was the white carnation in my lapel into which I poured copious amounts of the finest Colombian coke. I could pull the carnation to my nostril, do a hefty line in plain view of the audience, and no one suspected. No one except Ronnie and Woody, who knew I'd done it and kept sliding over to the piano for a sniff while I played.

The next day we flew to Las Vegas for a stadium show and drove into town afterwards for a gamble and a look at the place. As soon as we pulled onto the Strip we saw the neon sign above The Hilton advertising Elvis Presley and B. B. King. The King was in the main room and B. B. was downstairs, and as we'd all seen B. B. at the Whisky in L.A. the year before we decided that this was our night to catch Elvis live. We were shown to a table at the back of the room. The curtains opened immediately, and the band went into the opening number. James Burton on guitar, Glen D. Hardin on piano, Jerry Scheff on bass, Ronnie Tutt on drums, and The Sweet Inspirations including Cissy Houston singing backing vocals. This was the cream of the crop, and I'd never seen any of these legends live before.

Soon enough, the man himself came out on the stage. Now this wasn't fat Elvis nor was it the 1956, before-he-joined-the-army Elvis. This was the "Live in Las Vegas," with the wraparound shades, white bejewelled, bell-bottomed pantsuits, Lonsdale belt, ridiculous high collars and karate kicks Elvis. It was a very schlock show, but he was very good anyway and what else could it have been in Las Vegas? This was what he did every night of the week. While he was singing, he'd lean over the front of the stage and middle-aged ladies with big hair would run up to the stage and grab the brightly coloured silk scarves from round his neck. His rhythm guitarist's main job, it seemed, was to keep him supplied with scarves. After half a dozen songs he went into a rock 'n' roll medley and finally the show started to rock. "Blue Suede Shoes" got everybody going. We jumped up whistling and screaming.

Out of nowhere, a slimeball appeared at the table, pulled his jacket behind his holster so we could see the gun. In a low voice he said:

"Cool your act, or out you go."

We were horrified. This was Elvis, after all.

"He's the King of rock 'n' roll, man!" I shouted. He wasn't having that.

"I told you once." He said quietly, but with force.

Shit, we couldn't believe it. If you couldn't scream at an Elvis gig, where could you? It didn't make sense! It was ridiculous. We sat down, he left, and Elvis sang a few more ballads and everything settled down again. After a few more songs, he ran across the stage and went into another rocking medley and without thinking we were all up on our feet, screaming. This was the king of rock 'n' roll and we were rocking! Before we knew it, the man with the attitude was back.

"I told you to cool your act, or out you go, and I meant it. Godammit!" We sat down without a word. This was like being back at school, except when I was at school the teachers weren't armed. If Elvis knew he'd have been pissed off, I know he would. Long live rock 'n' roll. Everywhere except Las Vegas.

Belgium is another place that doesn't seem to know what rock 'n' roll is all about. Is it just me, or is Belgium really boring? Of course, it's all to do with first impressions. The first time I was in Sheffield with The Muleskinners, we had a rotten time, and if I'd never gone back and seen a different side of the place I'd probably still be slagging it off. But I don't remember ever having a really great time in Belgium, although I will say this: when it comes to what we know as french fries, the Belgian fries that you get from street vendors are unbeatable. I realize that "nice fries" is not much to say about a whole country. It's a bit like the Glaswegian opening line, "nice tooth." Or the words you least want to hear from a stranger in a public toilet, "nice cock."

The Faces played the Bilzen Jazz Festival in Belgium a couple of times, though I'm not sure what we were doing on the bill in the first place, not being much of a jazz band. But we did our bit in the muck and bullets of a typical muddy festival and then ran from the stage. We had a charter plane waiting to take us back to Blighty, and because the airport closed quite early we jumped into a couple of cabs and sped off. Rod and Kenney in one, and Ronnie, Woody, and I in the other. We were all drunk or getting there and Ronnie was in the front of the cab, swigging and offering around a bottle of Mateus Rose to anybody who wanted some. There were no takers. After a while Ronnie said he'd have to stop for a pee, and as we were out in the country the cab driver pulled over on the side of the road and gestured for Ronnie to get out. He opened the door, stepped out into the dark, and disappeared into a ditch with a shout.

"Argghh...Fuck!"

There was silence, then he groaned and stood up in the muddy ditch.

"Oh fuck!" He said again wobbling. He'd fallen sideways and was covered in mud.

We helped him climb out of the ditch, then he started to pee, trying unsuccessfully not to pee on himself. Woody shouted out the window as we laughed with disgust: "You cunt, Ronnie. You're drunk, you cunt!"

Ronnie could only laugh as he climbed back into his seat. He seemed even drunker than before and his mohair suit was muddy all down one side where he'd fallen. We drove on for a minute, and then Ronnie leaned over and stuck his tongue in the driver's hairy ear. The poor fucker screamed and almost went off the road.

"Bleu, blah, bleuh!"–or something like it–he shouted at Ronnie in Belgian, shaking his fist at him. He was annoyed but he wasn't sure what Ronnie might do next. Ronnie was in fits and so were we. It was so disgusting but it was funny. He laughed, hiccoughed, and then we knew what was coming next.

He was going to throw up. Oh my God. He slid across to the window just in time and had managed to wind it halfway down before the liquid laugh hit the Belgian night and sprayed all down the door and the back window, which luckily was shut. He wasn't feeling very good now, and the cab driver was horrified. We made it to the airport and home without any other incidents, but to this day I cannot think of drinking Mateus Rose or Lancers, another of Ronnie's tipples. If I ever sniff that aroma, it takes me back to that cab and the smell of Ronnie puking.

After a long night in Atlanta's underground bars, we woke up very groggy and were late getting to the airport. We had to fly to Boston to play a gig on the Common for the Mayor the next afternoon, but we missed our flight and only barely caught the next one. Since we were playing for his Royal Hugeness the Mayor, special transportation arrangements were laid on to get us through the rush hour traffic as fast as possible. They supplied two police cars with two of Boston's finest to drive us. It was an extremely humid summer's day, and we were a little sweaty and still stoned as we stepped through the arrivals door of Logan Airport and were confronted by two coppers waiting at kerbside.

We were intimidated by the police at first, because we were holding, but they seemed friendly enough. Woody and I got in the back and found we were locked in, there were no door handles, and there was a rusty spring sticking out of the front seat and the car stunk of pee and old cigarette smoke. Ronnie got in the front next to the cop.

"We'll get you there, don't you worry about a thing," he said. He screamed into the traffic at the speed of sound, lurching all over the road and passing cars on both sides. He shouted through a bullhorn every now and then, yelling at other cars to: "Get the fuck outta da way!" We were feeling more than a little uneasy, and Ronnie's face had turned a shade of green. He turned to us in the back and said, without thinking.

"I feel like a bag of shit."

The copper, not realising Ronnie meant that he felt terrible, came to our assistance immediately.

"Hey, you want some shit? I can get you anything you want. You want some heroin or coke, some speed? Don't get it from the street, boys, I can get you the best."

Needless to say, we didn't take him up on his offer, kind as it was.

We were booked to play a festival at the Pocono Raceway in the Poconos Mountains near Allentown, Pennsylvania, in July 1972, and soon after we landed in the small helicopter, a thick fog came in and threatened to close it down. It was so thick you could hardly see the hundred thousand people sitting out there in the dark, and they probably wouldn't have been able to see us either. The fog wasn't the only reason the show was in doubt. Backstage, among the trailers converted into dressing rooms, there was the usual argy bargy going on between band managers, the stand-up comedians of the business.

"My band's bigger than yours, so we're going on last."

"No, you're not. My band's huge! We've gotta close the show or I'll break their legs, etc., etc."

I'm making the dialogue up, but I can guarantee it's not much more adult than that. Managers often have inflated egos when it comes to their boys and would think nothing of invading Poland if they could get away with it. That night though, the argument wasn't about who should go on last but who could get on quickest. Emerson, Lake and Palmer were supposed to be the headliner that night, but for once they wanted to play first so they could get out of there early, because the fog was getting too thick for helicopters to fly. They knew that whoever went on last would probably be stuck there for many hours, because the helicopters wouldn't fly in thick fog and the one narrow road down the mountain, which was the only other way in and out, was bound to be jammed after the show.

ELP's manager, Dee Anthony, had a little chat with Billy Gaff, which developed into a face-to-face screaming match. Billy wasn't the strong, forceful type, he was more the "I'll piss in my pants if you don't stop threatening me" type. We had a problem.

Now, to allow a quick turnover between bands, they'd built an extra-wide stage so two bands could be set up at the same time, and our equipment was already in place on the left-hand side. But when we climbed the stairs to the stage, ready to start, we found that ELP's crew had hurriedly set up their gear in readiness. Just as we were about to walk on, ELP started playing. There was nothing we could do about it, we'd come second, and a bad second. But they wouldn't get away scot-free.

We wandered on in front of them as they began their first instrumental and hung around looking bored, which wasn't difficult for me because I personally have never been a fan. They may be clever, and they may have been popular, and Keith Emerson may be a showman, but as a musical experience they were about as interesting as a slab of concrete. Finishing my drink with a flourish, I left the stage to a small ripple from the crowd. There was nothing to do but let them carry on with their seemingly hard work.

The fog had come in thicker by the time they finally stopped playing, but even after the lighting guys took all the coloured gels off the lights, we could hardly see past the first ten or fifteen rows. With the stage bathed in very bright, white light, we gave a show worthy of the occasion, and when we finished the fog had cleared enough for us to run to the huge military helicopter. Rattling and shuddering, it lifted off ever so slowly and noisily took us out of the mountains and back to safety.

One way or another, these were glorious days of first-class, worldwide travel, cheap drugs, and free love. Nothing could go wrong—or could it? Sandy, Lee, and I had moved into a large, double-fronted Edwardian house on a quiet street in Kingston. Though it had been converted into two flats, we were restoring it back to a single home again. The work never seemed to stop nor did the touring. As the Clontarf Cowboy, Phil Donnelly, once said under his breath as a pretty girl passed him in the street:

"Gimme some pussy. I know you've got some on you."

The trouble was that there was so much temptation it was impossible to say no, and I never considered it for a minute. We were touring all the time, and pretty girls would be lined up along the hotel corridor after gigs. Sandy was none too pleased about it, of course, but she found her own solution and an easy way out when we had a flaming row one day at the house, which ended when I threw a plate across the room. She drove off and took Lee with her. I figured she'd come back and we'd talk, I'd apologize, and we'd get on with our lives, but she never came back. Nobody, including her mother and sisters, would tell me where she was, and she never called me. Of course, I deserved it, but I deserved to see my son, Lee, too.

It was some years before I discovered she'd been having a fling of her own and good luck to her, but she'd used the excuse of the argument to leave me and move in with her new boyfriend. All I knew at the time was that they were gone.

I went back on tour without finding out where they were, and though several girls tried to help me through it, I sunk into a severe depression. It was a problem I couldn't solve until I knew how they were. I had a sustained, piercing headache that wouldn't go away. I was playing badly, drinking far too much, and doing too much blow in an effort to forget my troubles. I slept rarely, but when I did, I'd wake up to the headache always waiting for me. Eventually the other guys took the bull by the horns and got a doctor in to see me. He recognized the symptoms immediately.

"You're depressed. You need to relax." And he gave me a prescription for Valium. What a twerp! Well, the headaches went away almost immediately, but I became a walking zombie, comatose twenty-four hours a day. I shouldn't have been drinking at all because the interaction of alcohol and Valium is very dangerous, but he didn't tell me that, and I didn't know. I was even more of a total mess. While I was in this downward spiral, Charlie Daniels started calling me "Fantastic" as a gee up, really, because I didn't feel at all fantastic. But it didn't do me any harm to feel good about myself in a period when I was miserable and had lost my way.

As soon as I got back to England, I put the still unfinished house in Kingston on the market and found a place in Sheen adjoining Richmond Park that had no bad memories attached. It was a three-storey Victorian mansion with six bedrooms on Fife Road that was at least six times too big for me. But I could afford it, so I bought it. The blueprints showed that one room had been extended into a billiard room, so I bought an antique billiard table and had it installed. Apart from that, I decided there would be no alter-ations whatsoever. I had learned, like Pavlov's dog, that renovation equalled isolation, and because Sandy left while the house in Kingston was being remodelled, I intended to leave the house exactly as it was, even though it sorely needed a lick of paint in places.

Although it was tough not having Lee around, I finally got over Sandy by this time, and realizing that nothing was going to change the situation I would go and visit Lee when I felt strong enough to deal with it. The new boyfriend was a sanctimonious piece of work. His advice, unasked for, was to come over more often. He had no idea how painful it was to leave Lee there each time, but this was the way it was going to be, so I kept in touch through letters and the odd postcard to ensure he knew I still existed while I carried on with my life.

We were promoting "Maggie May" on "Top of the Pops" one week and Gladys Knight and The Pips were on the same show. Woody had given me a copy of her *Nitty Gritty* album in 1969 and I'd been a fan of hers ever since. One of the standout tracks on that record, "Didn't You Know You'd Have To Cry Some-time," had floored me, as much for the vocal performance and the amazing James Jamerson bass part, as for the sheer beauty of the song. So I bought everything of hers I could find after that. I watched her from across the studio, as she sang "Help Me Make It Through the Night," her current hit, and though I'd wanted to meet her, I had such a crush on her that I was too embarrassed to say anything. I managed to say hello to her brother Bubba as he passed me in the corridor, but I didn't have the nerve to say, "Where's your sister? She's very shaggable." I had a feeling that wouldn't go down very well with him.

"Help Me Make It Through the Night" touched a nerve with me, and I'd been playing her version of this Kris Kristofferson song since it came out. After Sandy had left, I'd become a bit of a wild man, shagging any girl I could get my hands on for a bit of a cuddle or some company. I just wanted to get through the night and I needed some help, simple as that. Of course, everybody in the band knew I had a crush on Gladys, and Shirley Arnold, our secretary, wasn't going to let me leave the studio without meeting her, so she took me aside in a friendly way and said, "Look, Mac, I know you're dying to meet her and I know you'll regret it if you miss this opportunity. Let's just go and say hello to her."

Okay. It sounded reasonable. "Thanks, Shirley," I said, and we walked up the corridor to her dressing room.

"Go on, knock on the door." I did, but so gently there was no way she could have heard. Shirley wasn't going to waste all day.

"Bang, bang, bang!" She walloped the door and walked off. There was no going back now. The door opened and Gladys pretty face appeared.

"Hi," she said with a smile.

"Er, hello Gladys, I'm er…I'm Ian McLagan of The Faces, and I'm a big fan of yours." I felt like a complete idiot, but the worst was over. Now she could only slam the door in my face.

"Well, it's nice to meet you. Come on in." She opened the door wide and I did as I was told.

"I've got all your records, er, er…" It was useless. I couldn't remember one title, and my mouth had dried up. My legs had turned to jelly. She, on the other hand, was so charming and understanding.

She seemed genuinely pleased to meet me and she could tell I wasn't faking it. She could tell I was a fan, and eventually I calmed down enough to have a really nice little chat with her. I'm still a fan and I've seen her perform on several occasions, though I've never spoken to her since, but she is a very genuine lady with great class. A true star.

Around the time Sandy left me, Ronnie took a holiday in Ireland with Mike McKinnerny's wife Kate, which caused a few raised eyebrows in the band. It was very strange, and when Ronnie returned from Ireland he told Sue he was going to move in with Kate, which devastated Sue. I was still getting over Sandy, but I made a clumsy pass at Sue one night at The Wick, Woody's house on Richmond Hill. We were meant for each other. By that I mean we'd both been dumped and were both feeling bloody miserable, no ingredients for romance. I was desperate for love, but it took me a little while to figure out that we could only be friends, and in the end neither of us got too hurt.

Actually, that's not strictly true. I followed her to Toronto on a whim, where she was staying with friends. She and a friend picked me up at the airport and because of all the downers and coke I'd been taking I was a mess. When I got out, I shut my right thumb in the rear door of the station wagon as her friend pulled away. I managed to get him to stop, opened the door with my other hand, but my thumb was crushed and the nail was hanging off. I went up the steps to the house and shut the door on another finger! What a fuck-up. I eventually let Sue get on with her life while I went back home with neither her nor the thumbnail.

The one good thing to come out of that trip was that we both learned to ski. We rented a car, bought some cognac and beers at the government liquor store, and drove up the mountain for a couple of nights of fun at a ski resort not far from Toronto. We both desperately needed to have some fun and it had to be right now! As neither of us had ever skied before, we had to rent the gear and get on those slopes as soon as possible before we chickened out. I seemed to be in a big hurry in those days, always chasing the perfect high, and although I was stoned, coked, drunk, and sedated on a daily basis I could never seem to get high enough. After cutting a hole in one of the gloves for my extremely painful thumb, and buttoning and zipping up a whole mountain of outerwear, we set off for the learner slopes, where the first thing they taught us was the snow plough. This is where you point your skis together in the shape of a "V" to form a kind of emergency brake. After about an hour of snow ploughing, we were ready to get on with it, but they wouldn't let us on the ski lift without a signed ticket to prove we'd had the proper instruction, which would've meant many more hours of practicing.

We just didn't have the time! We knew one way or another we were going to do it, so after a couple of swift brandies, we trudged up the mountain through the virgin snow, carrying our skis while everybody else soared above us on the lift. We got some odd looks but nobody stopped us, and it was only when we finally got to the top and sat down for a rest that we began to realize what we'd got ourselves into. The start was much steeper than we'd imagined it would be and very icy, so as we watched ten- and twelve-year-olds jump off the lift, turn, and drop out of sight over the rim, I almost lost my breakfast.

This was not going to be easy. We couldn't turn back and have a bunch of kids, experienced skiers though they might be, laughing at us, so after a moment of calm we eased our skis over the icy rim and picking up speed immediately, we plummeted down the mountain. We were out of our depth and out of our heads.

"Fucking HELL!" and "EEEEEEK!" was all we managed to scream as we raced down the mountain. For the record, the snow plough only works if you're doing about ten miles per hour and we must've been going at least fifty miles per hour, avoiding trees and other skiers by sheer luck. It was a straight shot all the way down to the hotel, which got bigger and nearer every second, but after a short while the slope eased up and our confidence grew and then we began to start enjoying the experience. The brush with death was almost over.

We skied over to the lodge, looking as professional as we could, unhooked our skis, walked shakily into the bar, and ordered the first of many large brandies to calm our nerves. We were lucky not to have broken our necks, but having done it, I know I'll never ski again.

CHAPTER NINETEEN

"I'm Leaving the Group"

I'm leaving the group" was one of the group sayings that we used whenever there wasn't enough ice in the drink, or the eggs were too runny. It was a standing joke. But when Ronnie used those very words on my birthday, May 12, 1973, to tell me he was quitting the band, I didn't find it at all amusing. It was just as we were going on stage in Roanoke. Only half believing him and not knowing what else to say, I dismissed him with the other standard group saying:

"Bollocks, you cunt!"

He gripped my arm tightly, came up uncomfortably close, and let me know he was deadly serious.

"Fuck off, you cunt!" he said angrily. I couldn't believe he was serious. I still thought he'd come round, but I left it at that and got on stage.

Ronnie had been going through big changes since living with Kate. He dressed like the farmer he aspired to be. She was a hippie, a stranger to the soap dish, and since living with her, Ronnie had become much scruffier. During the previous jaunt around Britain he hadn't travelled with us at all, preferring instead to drive the two of them in his Land Rover, and when we did see him she was always around and always in the way. On the next short American tour, he didn't travel with us all the time, preferring to get about in a rented Winnebago, so we hardly saw him then either. He was either oblivious or just bloody minded. I was never sure which. But it was impossible to talk to him on that tour, and he became more and more distant as it went on. She had his ear bent the whole time, telling him he didn't need Rod, that he should fire Rod so he'd be the lead singer in the group, which was exactly what he told me before he came out with the dreaded group saying.

It was bloody tragic. I had been close to Ronnie for a long time and felt he was deserting me as much as the band. There had been a subtle balance, like in a marriage, that could never be the same without him. Rod naturally put all his best songs on his own albums, so when it was time for a Faces record, he wasn't really interested. Nothing was going to change that, but Ronnie couldn't take it any longer. His mistake was in asking me to leave the band with him. He wanted to take the power away from Rod but by leaving the band he gave it all to him, and the balance was off. If he had stayed and fought the war, we might've made another great album, but as it was we only cut a couple of singles after that, and never made another album. I missed Ronnie's beautiful melodies, songs that only Ronnie could bring to the band.

Things took a nastier turn on stage that night, when he came over to the piano and swore at me in the middle of a song. I ran after him, kicked him up the arse, and chased him off the stage. I'm not proud of it, but he asked for it. I loved Ronnie, always have, always will. It was a bloody shame he left, because he had so many beautiful songs to write and record and there is no reason why they couldn't have been on a Faces record.

That night after the show, Woody, Kenney, Rod, and I had a group meeting in the bar of the hotel, but this was different from the normal booze-up. Ronnie's leaving had begun to sink in and it was made easier only because he was behaving so badly. He was angry on stage like I'd never seen him before, and conversation between the two of us was now impossible. He had let me down badly and I was going to miss him, but in his eyes it was the other way round, I'd let him down. I think he really thought I'd leave and start another band with him, but as far as I was concerned we already had the band I wanted to be in, but he didn't want to be a part of it anymore.

The four of us sat at a small table in the bar sipping cocktails, munching on peanuts, and throwing peanut shells on the floor and at each other. We drank and talked and threw peanuts and laughed for a moment, then we talked and drank and became quite morose.

We all felt let down, but I blamed Kate as a Yoko Ono for our times, as much as Ronnie. Of course, we'd get another bass player, but who could fill his shoes? No fucker, that's who. It still makes me angry to think about it, and Ronnie admitted to me as recently as 1992 that he regretted leaving the band and said that he should never have actually used those words "I'm leaving the group" unless it was a joke. After he left us, Ronnie set about forming his own group, Slim Chance, and took them on a circus-style tour of the U.K., playing a different town each night under a Big Top. It was a great idea, but it lost a lot of money.

After some serious thought, we agreed to see if Andy Fraser from Free would be interested in playing with us. We were all fans of the band and Rod played their first two albums to death on the road. You could always hear Paul Rodgers' voice wailing from his room. I remember walking into the Civic Hall in Dunstable before a gig and "All Right Now" was blasting out of the P.A. It was the first time I'd heard it and I thought it was Steve's voice.

I didn't think we could top that, and naturally I wanted The Faces to do better than Humble Pie. We called Simon Kirke to get Andy's number and called him the very next day, but as he didn't seem to be very interested, Simon suggested Tetsu Yamauchi, a bass player they'd met while they were touring Japan. In fact, theyd made an album as Rodgers, Kirke, Kossoff, and Yamauchi, but nothing much was happening, so we arranged to get together with him.

God Bless him, nobody could speak any Japanese and his English was pretty much restricted to a shout of Teachers. It wasn't a call for more education, it was a shout for more intoxication! His problem was he believed all he'd read about our boozing. Though we all liked a drink, we'd pace ourselves, being professional drinkers like Dean Martin. Tetsu never understood that and Rod swears he saw his breakfast tray being delivered one morning with a bottle of Teachers on it. Yikes! Well, his playing was fine when he was relatively sober, but that was relatively rare. It's easy to look back and see events with a sharper eye, but things definitely went downhill after Ronnie left and Tetsu joined, and it wasn't so much Tetsu's fault, because Ronnie's were huge boots to fill.

Ever since we'd formed the band, getting Rod in the studio for a Faces session had been difficult enough, but when we started *Ooh La La* it was worse. We worked for two weeks at Olympic before he even walked in the door and then he complained that some songs were in the wrong key for him. So we recorded them again and waited a week for him to come back. We cut the track for "Ooh La La" three times before he eventually passed on it, leaving it for Woody to sing.

Glyn Johns held it all together, squeezing performances out of Rod and urging him on, without which we wouldn't have got the album finished at all. Rod has always been mean with his money, but he was even meaner with his time.

Ooh La La (Warner Bros.) was released in April 1973, went to Number One in the U.K., and was a Top Thirty hit in the States. In my opinion, it ranks second to *A Nod's As Good As a Wink (to a Blind Horse)* (1971) among the four studio albums we made.

There are classic rockers, "Silicone Grown," "Borstal Boys," and "My Fault." There's "If I'm on the Late Side,"and "Flags and Banners," both Stewart/Lane collaborations, "Cindy Incidentally," "Glad and Sorry," an absolute gem from Ronnie Lane and Ronnie Wood, "Ooh La La," which speaks for itself, and "Just Another Honky," another great number. The instrumental in 5/4 time, "Fly in the Ointment" was a total throwaway and was only put on the album to piss Rod off, and it seemed to have worked. The week the album came out, he did all he could to scuttle it, and told anyone who would listen how useless it was. The press may have printed it, but the punters didn't believe him, and it hit the charts anyway. But he never gave it a chance and I don't think he's ever really given it a listen.

But now, without Ronnie and his songs, it was impossible to get Rod into the studio. He'd sold millions of records with the help of The Faces constantly touring and promoting them, but I wonder how many he would have sold without us as his backing group. We did record a couple of singles, "Pool Hall Richard" and "You Can Make Me Dance," but the recording career of the band was over, and there would be no more albums with or without Ronnie Lane.

CHAPTER TWENTY

Kim

As a single man again, after a long period of self-hate, I was beginning to get back in action and on the pull whenever I could, although it involved spending a lot of time in dark and noisy nightclubs. There was a crowd of us that would meet at Tramp, which included Woody, Rod, Keith Richards, Keith Moon, usually with his wife Kim, plus friends, drivers, liggers, potential strays, and the ever-present drug dealers. It was an annoyingly loud disco, but it served its purpose. It was somewhere to watch the girls, have a drink, watch Omar Sharif watching the girls, do some blow under the table, and take a pretty face home to bed. No one wanted to go to sleep, and when Tramp finally closed we'd pop into Keith's house in Cheyne Walk for a nightcap, or Moony would invariably invite us to their place in Chertsey, where the party would keep going into the next day. Keith Moon was everybody's friend, and Kim was simply the best host, and very attractive with it.

Tara, their unusual modern concoction of a house, was surrounded by trees and grassy slopes and looked as if several tents had been joined together, painted white, and then frozen. It didn't strike me as much of a home, or a place for children. It was more like an airport lounge! The vast sitting room had sliding glass walls, floor to ceiling on two sides, and a sunken area you could sit in around the fireplace, which was in the centre of the room.

The bar's walls were covered with huge paintings of Thor, Spiderman, and The Hulk, and there was a jukebox filled with the Moons' favourite singles: The Beach Boys, Jan and Dean, and Dion and The Belmonts for Keith, and The Beatles, Paul McCartney, The Faces, and Rod Stewart for Kim. Keith was so jealous of Rod, he'd even eject "Maggie May" in front of me if Kim played the record.

For toys, Keith had a lavender Rolls-Royce for everyday use and another one for more prestigious occasions, as well as an AC Cobra, a Ferrari, a Mercedes, a Chrysler hot rod, a hovercraft, and a milk float decorated with wallpaper. Keith couldn't drive and never had a driver's license, and proved it to the world when he drove his Rolls into the pond at the end of the drive. Also living in this bizarre hive of activity was their six-year-old daughter, Mandy, Kim's seven-year-old brother, Dermot, and Kim's mum, Joan, who was a character in her own right. Joan had moved in with them when she split up with Kim's dad, Bill Kerrigan. Dermot was in school with Mandy, and Joan had been acting as a sort of secretary for Keith, though it wasn't an Oscar-winning performance, because she did little more than pour drinks for everyone while I was there.

The day after spending most of the night at their place, I flew them both to a festival in Frankfurt where The Faces were playing. It was one of those gigs where Sly and the Family Stone were supposed to play, but didn't. I caught sight of Sly walking past my open hotel room door dressed for the gig and ready to play but apparently, after collecting his money, he kept on walking. I suppose it was a case of gain-stopped play. We flew back the next day and went straight to Tara.

One afternoon, Keith decided to go to Ringo's house wearing the full uniform and regalia of Adolf Hitler, leather boots, jodhpurs, moustache, and all, so I was recruited to chauffeur him. He was in fine form and ordered me to stop at an antique shop in Chertsey, where he pranced about haggling over the price of something he had no intention of buying in a German accent, just to be noticed. It was quite scary how easily he would transform himself into a Nazi, and most people would pretend it just wasn't happening and leave him well alone. It was all a giggle, but he could get testy sometimes, and that's when I was dealing with Der Fuehrer, and not Moony.

Kim, on the other hand, was always easy to be around. She's unbearably pretty, with a lovely nature and always interesting to talk to; she listened too. At the same time, she had a charming "lost quality" about her, as if she was in her own world, like a child. Not a bad thing when you consider Keith's schizophrenic nature. One night I ran into her at The Wick, Woody's house above the River Thames in Richmond. She'd escaped from Keith for a few hours and was just visiting, and I spent several hours with her that got me thinking about her in a new way.

She appeared to be adrift and seemed to be pleased to be away from him. I must've had a crush on her always, but I never fully realized it until later on. Apart from anything, she was Keith's wife, and although I was a single chap, I wasn't looking for romance. I'd been there, done that, and wasn't going to do it again any time soon.

I was at Tara one night when Keith disappeared into his bedroom early, and in a bad mood. My date dozed off and Kim and I were left alone to enjoy each other's company, drinking and talking through the night. We had a spot of breakfast and went to their local, the Golden Grove, for a drink. It was only a hundred yards away at the end of their drive, but I drove the BMW anyway. Keith joined us for a drink later, then he went to a session, leaving Kim and I alone. The pub closed and we served ourselves, as Kim was almost family there, and when I went to pay for drinks she tore my ten-pound note in two, giving me back one of the halves and keeping one for herself. It was a flirtation without forethought, because my date was fast asleep in a guest bedroom back at the house. I offered Kim a lift back to the house, but she'd cycled to the pub, so she rode and I drove.

Their Graceland-style, wrought-iron gates were shut, and Kim was astride her bike attempting to open them for me when I jumped out of the car to offer my help. She was wearing a fluffy, white angora top and jeans, and she looked so sweet I put my arms around her and kissed her without thinking. It knocked her off her bike and we both fell over laughing. I hadn't intended to kiss her, and now everything had changed between us. This had taken our friendship out of the bounds of just being friendly. Even though I knew she wasn't happy with Keith and I was single or, at least, separated, she wasn't. The silence lasted for a long second or two while I tried to comprehend what had just happened. She smiled and broke the ice.

"Would you like another drink?"

There was no turning back, but there was very little going forward either. Kim had left him before, which was the reason she'd been so pleased to see Sandy and me when we bumped into them in the Charing Cross Road. He'd just picked her up at the station after months of separation, and she wasn't sure if she was doing the right thing. So although she'd had every intention of leaving him long before I appeared on the scene, she was waiting for the right moment, more than the right man.

I learned later that he'd broken her nose three times and there had been other injuries to her back and head. There were many sides to Keith. Whether he was schizophrenic or not, I don't know, but he certainly had severe mood swings. Her leaving was long overdue because he wasn't going to change and things weren't getting any better.

I still got on well with both of them, because it was still relatively innocent between Kim and me, and they were my guests when The Faces performed at the Reading Festival in August 1973. We went to Tara afterwards, where Lionel Bart, wearing a pair of old dungarees and a mass of body hair, was holding court. The party carried on all night as usual, with Woody, Tetsu, and a host of others. The following day, a distinguished military-type came up and asked me the question I couldn't easily answer.

"What are you doing here?"

"I'm Keith's friend." I said, wondering who this moustachioed, military person could be. In my heart I knew exactly what I was doing there, but I could hardly say I was waiting for a good moment to steal Keith's wife. Kim came to the rescue.

"Daddy, have you met Mac? He's one of The Faces."

Bill Kerrigan was a Captain in the British Army, a rubber planter, and all-round Colonial type who couldn't have been less impressed if she'd said I had rabies.

"Pleased to meet you," he mumbled. He wasn't pleased to meet me. A tall, dashing, handsome man with a terribly British, upturned moustache, he could have been David Niven's or Cary Grant's understudy. He was larger than life and as suspicious as only a father with such a beautiful daughter could be. Keith was scared of him because Bill had overturned a table on him once, and Keith never felt totally secure around him ever again.

One afternoon, Kim agreed to meet me in Richmond for a drink. It was only a few miles away from my house in Sheen, and it was a brave step forward. We arranged to meet outside the Imperial, a pub I used to frequent in my art school days, but as I pulled up I spotted her in a phone box calling to cancel the date. Lucky I got there when I did, and after a reassuring hug I convinced her to come back to the house for a drink, and we spent a magic afternoon, chatting and drinking. She was very shy, and it seemed as if she might run off at any moment; she was like a frightened fawn. Neither one of us liked meeting behind Keith's back, but she was so unhappy with him, and I wanted her so much and he obviously didn't. She needed time to sort herself out, and she and Mandy needed to get their own place and start a life of their own away from Keith.

It would take time, and as I was about to begin another tour of the States, it would give us both time to think it over. While I was having a final fling in the States, Kim left Keith for good. Spiriting Mandy and Dermot away in a taxi while Keith was asleep, she took them by train to her Dad's house in Verwood, near Bournemouth. Then, knowing how volatile Keith was and how persistent the newspapers would be, she moved in with Molly and Bob, friends of Joan's who lived in Egham.

They were an older, childless couple whom Keith had never even heard of, and they took her in and protected her as if she was their own. While the press searched high and low for her, she stayed hidden. Oblivious to all this drama, I called Keith from Tucson, Arizona, and when Joan told me Keith was out, I asked her to put Kim on. That's when I found out she'd left and taken the children with her. Joan had been sworn to secrecy, but she gave me Molly's number.

Molly answered, but said there was no one there by the name of Kim, and perhaps I had the wrong number. After I explained who I was and that I was calling from the States, she told me she'd be back in a few hours and to call back then. I was thrilled and went off to the gig exhilarated.

Because of past damage and room wrecking, The Faces had been banned from all Holiday Inns, but in some cities there was nowhere else to stay, and as they didn't know us from other bands, we'd check in as Fleetwood Mac and they wouldn't bat an eyelid. After the Tucson show, the bar was packed with kids, and the party overflowed into the grounds and pool area, where a model train circled the motel. The party continued for some time after the bar shut, no one was in any hurry to leave, and then somebody tried to get the train started. We climbed on it and then it fell over with a crunch. The derailment was an accident, but vandalism nonetheless, and I decided it was time for bed, running before there was anymore trouble.

When I got back to my room, all I could think about was Kim, so I called the number again. Molly answered and passed the phone to Kim. She seemed glad to hear from me, and it was so good to hear her voice. I was dying to see her, so I drunkenly asked her to come to Los Angeles to get away from England, and she agreed. I said I'd get Charlie Fernandez, our tour manager, to organize everything, as I knew he'd keep it to himself. I rang off and went to sleep a very happy man.

I woke up too soon, to a deafening rattling and rumbling that seemed to come from the inside of my head. I was lying on the bed, fully clothed, and I was still drunk. The windows were rattling and shaking and there was a persistent banging. I didn't know what was happening.

"BangBangBangBang!"

I shouted from the bed, "Go away, or you're dead!"

"BangBang! BANGBANGBANG!" Whoever it was, they would have to die. My head was pounding.

"Open up immediately or I'm gonna break the door down! This is the Sheriff!"

I jumped up, found the door and opened it, and there in the blistering Arizona sunshine was the Sheriff, his rifle aimed straight at me. Above him was a helicopter. I'd forgotten all about the derailment.

"Were you one of the group that derailed the train?"

"What train? I've been asleep, officer."

"Get back in your room and stay there!"

"Yessir!" Blimey, that was easy. What was I going to say–"Yes, I derailed the train"? They never found the culprits, but my money's on Fleetwood Mac.

That day we flew to Phoenix. I was on a cloud, though I told no one why. I called Dad as soon as I got to my room, and after the usual chitchat, he said:

"Here, did you know that Keith Moon and his wife Kim have split up? It's in all the papers."

Mum and Dad were always up on the news, and though Dad didn't know Keith personally, he knew he was a friend of mine.

"Actually, Dad, that's why I called. I've been seeing her." There was a short silence.

"Are you happy?"

"Yeah, very happy. She's a wonderful girl."

"Well good. I bet she is. Listen, er...don't mention anything to your mother just yet, she still hasn't got over you and Sandy splitting up, okay?"

Dad would eventually break it to Mum in the right way. He was a very cool character. At the age of twenty, he was the speed skating Champion of Great Britain. Shortly afterwards he retired. He was a modest man and wasn't one to dwell in the past, which made him more a champion in my eyes. You'd never know about his glorious past except for some silver cups, a champagne bucket, and a silver cigarette box on the sideboard in the dining room. My brother and I would never have known he had any medals if we hadn't found them tucked away in two shoe boxes at the back of his wardrobe. He'd never shown them to us kids.

One day, around the time of the derailment, he was making a pot of tea for himself and Mum, as he did every morning. Carrying two cups and saucers, a newspaper under his arm, and whistling, he climbed the stairs. After more than forty years off the ice, he made a racing turn near the top where the stairs curve. That's a side step where you cross your right foot over your left.

The next move is to lift your left skate, or in this case your left slipper, out from behind the other one. But in a cascade of hot tea, he tripped and tumbled down the stairs, landing in a heap by the front door. Mum heard the noise and his muffled groans, jumped out of bed, and ran downstairs after him.

"Mac! Mac!" she said. "Darling, let me help you up."

Lying on his back, covered in hot tea and broken crockery, bruised and sore all over, he said:

"No, leave me where I am. I can't fall any further."

I couldn't have been more excited. A few days after the Tucson derailment, we booked into the Beverly Wilshire Hotel in Los Angeles. As we would be there for ten days, we had two-storey suites on the sixth and seventh floors of the new building in the back of the hotel. I expected Kim to have checked in at the Beverly Hills Hotel and called as soon as I got to my room, but there was no Kerrigan, Moon, or even McLagan registered. My heart sank, thinking maybe she'd changed her mind, so I called Molly to find out what flight she was booked on. They passed the phone to Kim.

"Hello. Yes, I'm sorry. I got to the airport too late and missed my flight. I'm coming tomorrow, okay?" She was in a state and quite disorganized. I was surprised she'd even made it to the airport.

"Yeah, of course. Are you all right?"

"Well, the press have been hounding me, the papers are full of the news about me and Keith splitting up, and they won't leave me alone."

I told her it was all the more reason to get over as quickly as she could and reminded her not to check into the Wilshire, because I didn't want the guys to see her in case they'd mention it to the girls, and then the whole world would know. I could hardly sleep, but I called Molly and Bob the next day, and yes she'd got on a plane. They didn't know which flight or airline, but she was definitely on her way. I called the Beverly Hills, the Hilton, and a couple of other hotels without any luck, and then I had an idea. I got an outside line and called the number of the Beverly Wilshire.

"Kim Kerrigan's room, please." It was a long shot. The telephone rang.

"Hello?"

"Kim! Where are you?"

"I'm on the seventh floor."

"Jesus! Are you in the old building or the new part?"

"It's old, I think."

"Look out your window." As I opened the curtain I saw Kim's lovely face opposite me, as she opened the shutters of her window.

"Shut the window quick!" Christ, this wasn't going to be easy. If anybody else in the band had been looking, they would've seen her.

"Don't go anywhere, I'm coming straight over." I picked up my key and walked out the door. There was a familiar face standing by the elevator. Harvey was a journalist who'd been touring with us, working on a story about the band.

"Hey, Mac, where are you off to?" I had to think quick.

"I'm going to see an old mate at the Beverly Hills Hotel. Are you going out?"

"Yeah, we can share a cab. I'll drop you off. It's on my way." There was no way to avoid him. We got in a cab and drove off into the balmy-scented smog of Los Angeles, headed for the Beverly Hills Hotel, where she should've been staying if she'd followed the plan. On the way, we stopped at a traffic light alongside Richard Pryor in a Mercedes, an attractive blonde sitting next to him. He must have felt me looking at him, because he turned and shot me his "trademark" wide-eyed, guilty look over his shoulder, then he drove off. I understood the look well enough.

At the hotel, I got out, thanked Harvey for the ride, apologized for not having any cash on me, and waved him good riddance. I grabbed the valet parker's arm and asked him to follow me into the hotel. I explained as simply as possible that I was trying to dodge the geezer in the cab, that I needed to get back to the Beverly Wilshire Hotel, and that I had no money. He was a diamond. In a matter of minutes we were back at the Wilshire in someone else's gleaming Cadillac. I got out at the front door of the hotel, thanked him, and walked to the elevator as casually as I could. I pressed the button and the doors opened.

"Good evening, Mr. McLagan. You're in the wrong building, you know." I couldn't believe it. The elevator operator had been working on our side of the building the day before, and he was only being helpful, but I thought I might never get to see Kim.

"Yes, I thought I'd check out the rest of the hotel, thanks." It was a lousy excuse. I wasn't used to all this cloak-and-dagger stuff. Finally, a very jet-lagged and confused Kim opened her door.

"Where have you been?" She was a sight for sore eyes, and I slipped inside and shut the door quickly, kissed her, and knocked off her glasses. She poured me a drink as we told each other all our news.

The first thing I had to do was to get her to another hotel before anybody saw her. Charlie booked her a suite at the Century Plaza in Century City and moved Kim and her luggage in while we were doing press interviews the next day. Los Angeles was our hub; we'd fly off to Las Vegas, Santa Barbara, and San Diego, do the show, then fly back that night. When the limo dropped us off at the hotel, I'd pretend to be knackered.

"Ain't you coming out, Mac?" Woody asked.

"No, I'm really tired. I'll see you later." I'd open the door to my room on the sixth floor.

"See you tomorrow." I'd shut the door, run upstairs to the seventh floor, shoot along the corridor to the elevator, and jump in a cab to the Century Plaza. It was exciting, and we both enjoyed the thrill of it, but it was more than that, I really wanted her, and I was getting the same feeling from her. Kim used to say I reminded her of a thief in the night, because I used to wear a dark blue leather jacket and matching pants and carry a leather bag. I'd creep over there every night like a burglar and then, the next afternoon, I'd slide back to the Wilshire ready for the gig as if nothing happened. Charlie was our cupid, and he fielded any questions that were asked by saying I was just very tired.

Ronnie Wood was the only one in the band who sussed it, but even he didn't know exactly what was going on. He just guessed that I was up to something, because he thought it weird me not being in the thick of things, especially in L.A.

Kim and I had a very romantic and magical few days, and then she flew back to sort her life out, and I had a couple more gigs to do before I flew back for a British tour that would continue until Christmas.

CHAPTER TWENTY-ONE

Dark Side of the Moon

K im's divorce settlement gave her very little in the way of money. All she really wanted was to get away from Keith and live her own life. Although he still loved her and had hopes of getting back with her, it wasn't on the cards. Although he tried several times to force himself on her, even after the divorce, it was all over. Kim was given a small cash payment, and she and Mandy moved into a rented house in Twickenham. The house at Fife Road was far too big for one person, and I tried unsuccessfully to get them to move in with me, but for the moment Kim needed her independence.

I'd spend the night at Twickenham, or they'd stay with me in Sheen, but Mandy had to be in school in Twickenham anyway, so one way or another we'd always end up there in the morning.

One evening, when Kim was at the house, Keith called asking to speak to her. I told him she wasn't there, but he knew it was a lie because he was at the kitchen door a moment later.

He had to have been watching the house and hiding somewhere very close. Kim quickly ran upstairs, then I let him in. He was on his best behaviour, but not the jolly Keith I was familiar with. He suggested we go for a drink and a chat, and as I didn't want him in the house, I agreed and took him to The Plough, a hundred yards from the front gate. Keith had asked us not to embarrass him by going out together socially, and as annoying as it was, we'd respected his wishes and kept ourselves pretty hidden. Over a brandy, I asked him to leave Kim alone, and reminded him that we'd done what he wanted, and now it was his turn to respect what Kim wanted. There was a pause as he screwed his eyes like Robert Newton.

"Kim is my wife, Mac. I love her and I need to see her." He could act the part of a villain, but it was just an act, even though I knew he had friends in low places. But I believed him when he said he really loved her, and also that he thought Kim would go back with him, though I knew she never would. I asked him not to come to the house again. When I got back, I ran upstairs to let her know he'd gone, but she was in a state. Apparently, seconds after we'd left for the pub, somebody came in and searched the house from top to bottom, banging doors and opening cupboards and closets. She'd hidden inside a closet in a guest bedroom at the back of the house, and after a few minutes the person left. Keith's appearance at the house was a setup, of course, and though I can't imagine what he was looking for, or what he intended doing, I think it was more for the terror value. Keith could be a sneaky bastard.

Financially, things were going well for me. Apart from the house in Fife Road, I still had the house in Kingston, and I was buying Mum and Dad's house for them. I had a brand new BMW 3.0 CSI, and a mint 1932 Ford hot rod in the garage. I needed just one thing, and that was for Kim and Mandy to move in and make the house a home, but Kim still wasn't ready to make that commitment.

When I'd bump into him in the clubs, Keith would be as charming as ever, but on December 30, 1973, he phoned Kim at Twickenham to wish her a happy birthday. She thanked him, and then he added, "By the way, the next time you see Mac, his fingers will be broken." Word soon got around that he'd paid a local thug two hundred pounds to break my hands.

I'd met this character in the Small Faces days, so I knew what I was dealing with. He'd taken over Bill Corbett's gig when he was off sick once. He was a geezer about bother, a tough pretty boy who punched brick walls with his bare fists to impress younger toughs. He was not to be trusted or fucked with. While we were playing a gig in Hassocks, near Brighton, one night in 1966, Bill had returned unexpectedly early from his sick bed. Some words were exchanged between the two of them, and then Bill looked him hard in the eye.

"You'll come second, and a bad second at that," he said.

There was a short, tense moment, and then Bill knocked the much younger man down a flight of stairs. It was straight out of the movies, and he was knocked out cold. Bill had apparently caught him stealing some of our readies, which was unforgivable, since he considered that to be his job. When the young punk came to, he scampered off without a word, and that was the last we saw of him.

When Pete Townshend got wind of Keith's arrangement with the geezer, he called Kim to warn me, and then paid him another two hundred pounds to leave me alone. That's only one of the reasons Kim and I call him Uncle Pete. Well, for a week or two I carried an iron bar on the floor of the BMW just in case Keith had paid him a little extra, but Keith must have eventually forgotten about it, because nothing ever happened.

In early 1974, Kenney and I returned to New Zealand and Australia, when The Faces took the longest plane flight possible from England to the world Down Under. We flew to Los Angeles first, where Charlie Fernandez informed us we had another fifteen hours of flying to go. Someone at the office in London had told us it was going to be ten hours, but that was just to get us on the plane. To soften the blow, he led us to the first-class lounge and brought Mickey Hayes along for a drink. Mickey was a lovely chap with a red beard, like a ginger Father Christmas, and he'd been our baggage guy for some time but wouldn't be coming to Australia this time around. He had a ready laugh, and we drank until we ached. We got on the plane fully loaded and he left to drive home. He got about a mile down the road before the police picked him up and threw him in jail for the night, poor bugger.

As long as the flight was, it wasn't as long as the trip in 1968, and this time round the press wasn't quite so annoying and the audiences were much more into the music. The promoter rented me a joke of a piano in Auckland, so it got the axe treatment at the end of the show. Then we flew to Hong Kong for the first rock 'n' roll show they'd seen in years, if not ever. We played in a football stadium surrounded by tall buildings, the balconies full of people rocking in the cheap seats. Woody and I had asked a suspicious-looking character who was showing us around if there was any coke to be found.

"No problem, man," he said, and came back with some dirty powder in a bindle, which turned out to be heroin. We passed.

The highlight of this swing through the Pacific region was our arrival in Japan where we got an unexpected Beatles welcome. The kids at the airport were holding large banners that said "Faces," "Rod and the Faces," and even "Tetsu and the Faces" on another. It was so funny, he'd just joined and already he was the leader of the group. Warner/Pioneer, the Japanese record company, held a press conference for us before we even got to the hotel, where we sat at one end of a vast room at a long table behind ridiculously large vases of flowers. The journalists could hardly see us but, speaking into the microphones set up for them, they politely asked us loads of questions, the answers to which they already seemed to know. Then we were introduced to the ritual of smashing open barrels of sake amid much laughter and shouting. Sake splashed everywhere and we all got soaked. I liked the Japanese. They enjoyed a good booze-up and a laugh.

We checked into the Tokyo Hilton, and I wasn't in the room five minutes when there was a knock at the door. The two young girls standing there wanted to welcome me to Japan and unpack my bags for me. There was a lot of giggling, but it was such a nice gesture, and they got on with it while I sat and watched. Once they'd put all my clothes away, they ran a bath for me and then they left; they were just doing their bit to make me feel welcome. It was all so friendly. We played at the Budokan in Tokyo, where Tetsu introduced each song and each member of the group to the audience. They listened politely and then applauded. Then they'd stop for the introduction, and then wait for the next song. It was really strange for us; there was no whistling or impolite behaviour at all. We had to supply that.

We were kicking a football in the hotel corridor after the last show when an American tourist came out of his room to complain about the noise. It was a fair comment to make, but one of us said something like, "Get lost, you shithead," and he got angry for some reason. He ran into his room and we continued booting the ball about, but then he came back, wielding a wooden shoe tree. He came thrashing at me with this thing and caught me on the cheek, drawing blood. Rod and Woody disappeared into their rooms, but Tetsu wasn't going to take that and he went all Japanese, beating the living crap out of him. I found out later that Tetsu is a black belt at Kendo, which, as far as I know, is all about hitting people with a stick and getting away with it.

The Far East and Down Under tours were behind us, and as Rod was unwilling to record as The Faces, Woody took matters into his own hands and got his basement studio at The Wick organized so he could start his first record, *I've Got My Own Album to Do*.

I cut some demos there while the room was getting ready, and Woody co-wrote and recorded two songs with Mick Jagger that sounded so good they were eventually released. Kenney played drums on "It's Only Rock 'n' Roll," which, after overdubbing Keith's guitar in place of Woody's, Mick put on The Stones' album of the same name, which hit Number One in the States. Not bad for a home recording. The other track, "I Can Feel the Fire," was track one on Woody's record.

Woody called Sly Stone's drummer, Andy Newmark, for the sessions and was hoping to get Willie Weeks on bass. I was floored. We used to listen to Donny Hathaway's live album all the time, and on "The Ghetto" Willie played a blinding solo. When he introduced him, we'd always thought Donny had said, "On bass, Willie Wheatstraw." But it was, "On bass, Willie Weeks, y'all." We were English, what did we know?

Ronnie Wood thought nothing of it, but I had trouble sleeping the night before the first session. As it turns out, the best musicians are often the most generous and the most forgiving, and the most fun to play with because they have nothing to prove. This was to be the case. As the sessions went on, Mick Taylor came and played and George Harrison co-wrote and played on "Far East Man." Paul and Linda McCartney came over to my house one night out of the blue, bringing their young guitarist, Jimmy McCullough, with them. While Paul was offering Andy Newmark a job with his band, Wings, Jimmy was trying it on with Kim. Skulduggery everywhere you looked.

Apart from the rhythm section of Andy, Willie, and myself, Woody then brought in Keith Richards, who added "Sure the One You Need" and "Act Together" to the list of songs, and played on everything. Keith was in great form, and was just what was needed to keep things buzzing, and he moved into the guest house at the bottom of the garden that had once been Ronnie Lane's for the duration of the recording.

I've Got My Own Album to Do was a comment on Rod's attitude towards recording with The Faces. He always had his own album to do, but now Ron had one too. Gary Kelgren, co-owner of the Record Plant in San Francisco and Los Angeles, was co-producing, but he was higher than we were most of the time. He'd brought what he called "penguin dust" from America, also known as MDA, which our old friend Steve the salesman had first shown us. The atmosphere got very wild some nights as a result.

The sessions went long most nights, continuing to the next afternoon sometimes, and even going straight through to the next night once or twice. It was a very sunny spring, and I'd get back and Kim would pop by for a Pimm's No. 1 before I flaked out in the hammock in the back garden among the apple blossom. It was idyllic.

When my work was over, Kim, Mandy, and I flew to Mombasa Beach on the Indian Ocean for two weeks of rest and relaxation, where eventually, after a year of trying, I finally convinced Kim they should move in with me. I didn't think Keith would try anything silly at my house, so we enrolled Mandy into the school around the corner, and we became a family. Life was good, it was very, very good. It was almost perfect, except for one thing. Keith never gave up. Even after we'd been living together for some months there would be phone calls at all hours of the day and night. If Kim answered, it would almost always be him, and if I answered, there'd be silence at the other end. He'd do it twenty or thirty times a day. Sometimes there'd be a silence, I'd hang up and pick it up twenty minutes later, and he'd still be connected. Eventually, I'd pick up the phone in the morning, and if it was working, I'd leave it off the hook and put a towel around the ear piece to mute the alarm sound.

Kim developed a nasty case of conjunctivitis, which erupted anytime she heard his voice, so she stopped answering the phone for a while. But that was no good if I wanted to speak to her, so we developed a code. I'd let it ring three times, hang up, and then call again. This worked for a while, then somehow he figured it out too. Back when she was still living with Keith, her period would start as soon as he returned from a tour. Her body was saying what she couldn't, and though he wasn't making life at all easy, it had been worse, and it would eventually get easier.

CHAPTER TWENTY-TWO

Fort Ike

In July, Woody, Keith, Andy, Willie, and me played a couple of nights at the Kilburn State Theatre to promote Woody's record, with Rod joining in the festivities on a couple of numbers. It was videoed and recorded, but never shown, more's the shame. The Faces toured Europe nonstop from August to Christmas, and I didn't feel well on Christmas Day. But I started to feel better around 5 A.M. on Boxing Day and thought it would be fun to go for a joyride in the BMW. Kim made up a pint of Pimms in a pewter jug and we set off turning left and right alternately, to see where it took us. What a useless idea! We passed the house twice before I decided the plan wasn't working, and when we ended up on the M4 going west, I suggested we call it a day.

We got caught in traffic on the Cromwell Road, and when I zoomed away from the lights, a police car followed. As soon as I was out of his sight over a humpbacked bridge, I put my foot down and took a sharp left and right, but they chased me and pulled me over.

I hadn't drunk very much, and was speaking quite lucidly, until the copper asked me what my number plate was. I was trying to say MGN 13L, but I couldn't get my teeth round it, and said "EmnZheeELn ThurzheemEln." Soon after that, by no coincidence, my license was taken away for a year.

In February, we began a short tour of the States, and by the end of March we were in Los Angeles, jamming and hanging out with Bobby Womack at the Record Plant after our gigs. They were Jim Keltner's sessions, which had been going on for months, and many famous musicians were hanging around. We played two nights at The Forum and were warming up in the tuning room, Kenney banging on anything that got in his way, even if it was your collarbone, when Mick Jagger came in, all smiles. Bobby Womack turned up as well, which meant that all the singers who had recorded "It's All Over Now" were together in one room. Bobby wrote it with his sister Shirley, and his group, The Valentinos, recorded it in 1964. It was already on its way up the charts when The Stones covered it, their record overtaking Bobby's, becoming a much bigger hit. Years later, Rod covered it on *Gasoline Alley* and it was a hit again. Hopefully, though there's no guarantee in this business, Bobby made a pile out of the songwriting from all three versions.

After the show, Mick asked us if we'd be interested in meeting Ike Turner at his recording studio, and we jumped at the chance. I'd loved Ike and Tina Turner since "Everything's Gonna Work Out Fine," and we used to play our version of "Too Much Woman (for a Hen-Pecked Man)" regularly on stage. Mick reminded me that Ike wasn't just a songwriter and bandleader, but he was a fantastic pianist too. He played piano on Jackie Brenston's "Rocket 88," the record that's often said to have started rock 'n' roll. We piled into a limo and arrived at a place where a sign read "Bolik Sound." I thought, Bollocks? He must be nuts. Surely somebody, sometime must've told him what a bollock was. I should've asked him what Bolik meant, but there was no time for that.

Inglewood isn't the kind of neighbourhood that you'd want to hang around in the street for any length of time, but we had no choice. The video cameras watched our every move as we stood there, looking nervously about. Finally, the door opened to a long corridor straight ahead with security gates at either end and armed guards to ensure we didn't steal anything on the way. This was Fort Ike! Luckily, Mick was our passport into the inner sanctum, and before too long, word got through that he'd arrived and we were allowed to enter the corridor. At the other end, we waited for clearance again before we were shown through to the kitchen area, where Ike was smooth-talking a couple of beauties, Tina not among them. Mick said hello and introduced us to Ike, who was charming in person, and who took us on a tour of the complex. First, we went to his private office, where he sat down at his antique desk and pointed to a large silver ornament in the shape of a crab.

"First things first," he said, and lifted back the hinged shell to reveal a huge pile of Peruvian flake. We were impressed. He pulled a silver chain from round his neck and showed us the double-headed, silver snake that hung from it. The snake heads were hollow, like spoons, and he scooped up the blow in them, stuck them up his hooter, and snorted two huge nosefuls.

"Aaah!" He waited for a moment, savouring it, and then offered the snake heads to each of us in turn. Mick mentioned the "Rocket 88" record, and he jumped up from the desk and rolled out an upright piano from the wall, like a Murphy bed, and played some rocking piano. He was brilliant.

"Come on, let me show you around." We followed him down the corridor to the guest bedroom suite. It was very ornate, with a four-poster bed and plush carpets and velvet drapes and a TV screen set high into the wall. He turned on the TV and showed us a short grainy video. "If you get tired, you can stay here, we've got plenty of room."

There was a minute video camera above the bed, and suddenly I understood it all. Ike and Tina had an album with a gatefold cover that showed a grainy photograph of Tina on a four-poster bed on the inside sleeve. This was the same bed! My skin crawled. I decided I wasn't staying the night, whatever happened. "Here's the den, and the whatever, blah, blah blah…" I wasn't listening anymore, I'd lost interest.

"That's the control room," he said, pointing through the door at some people sitting in the darkness, who didn't apparently warrant being introduced.

"And this is the studio." With that, Tina made her entrance, not looking very pleased with Ike.

"Hi, guys." She gave us a fleeting smile. She didn't seem to fit in with Ike's setup. She was very gracious to us, but she didn't look comfortable, she was already on her way out the door. Ike took us down some steps, showed me the piano, and showed Kenney the drums. Then Ronnie was handed a guitar, Tetsu a bass, and we began to play. Bit by bit Ike would stop and lead the informal affair, but as time went on, he got more and more serious. He'd interrupt to tell one of us what he wanted. He sat down at the piano and said, "Play this, okay?" It was very little fun from then on. He disappeared into the control room and barked orders every now and then. He was recording one of his tunes, using us as his band. I was looking around for some blow, but there was none to be found. We were trapped. Mick was nowhere in sight either. I think he saw what was developing and skedaddled back to the safety of the hotel. It was a total drag; we didn't get out of there until 8 A.M.

There was a record turnout for us at San Bernardino's Swing Auditorium, and a party was thrown for us at the Greenhouse Room after the last night in Los Angeles.

The place quickly filled up with luminaries and liggers but, to everyone's surprise, one of the first people to arrive was Bob Dylan. The thought of actually meeting him had never occurred to me, and I flashed on Nick Tweddell, from The Muleskinners, who had turned me on to Bob's first record.

There was a room to the right of the door where we could sit and talk, and Bobby Womack and I were hanging there waiting for something to happen. Finally, he'd had enough.

"Come on, let's go and meet Bob Dylan."

"Oh, you can't," I said. "He's probably surrounded with wankers all bothering him at this moment." Bobby was not to be put off.

"Hey, I want to meet the man, not the wankers, okay?" I couldn't disagree with that, so we left the security of the room and joined the party. Sure enough, he was where the mob of people was, sitting at a table in the middle of it all. We couldn't see him, but we knew he was there, and I followed Bobby as he waded among the bodies. He had his back to us. Bobby walked up and at the opportune moment put out his hand.

"Bob, I'm Bobby Womack and I love your music, and I just wanted to say hello."

"Hi, howya doin'?" Bob said, trying to make eye contact over his shoulder.

"Hello, Bob, I'm Ian McLagan." He could hardly see us, as we were behind him, but as Bobby said afterwards, "This wasn't to do with him meeting me. I wanted to meet him, and I did." I thought that said a lot about Bobby, a man of great talent putting his ego aside to meet a hero.

Just then, Led Zeppelin's manager Peter Grant grabbed Richard Fernandez' cowboy hat off his head at the jam-packed bar. Being a gentleman, Richard was rooted to the spot, amazed at this show of ignorance, and Grant, as an overweight English bully, had no intentions of giving the hat back. I saw this happening and as soon as Grant turned his back I pulled it off his head and slipped it back to Richard, while looking the picture of innocence. Grant could afford to buy a million hats. He walked over to where Bob Dylan sat at his table, pushing people aside as he walked.

"Hello, Bob. I'm Peter Grant. I manage Led Zeppelin."

There was a short, tense silence. Bob said, "I don't come to you with my problems."

After the party, we went to the Record Plant yet again. That night, Billy Preston, one of my all-time idols, was there. I had all his solo records, from 1964's *The Most Exciting Organ Ever,* which featured "Billy's Bag," a fantastic track. He'd worked with Mahalia Jackson, Sam Cooke, Little Richard, and Ray Charles, and is probably one of the most talented and generous players in the world.

I watched over his shoulder as he adjusted the drawbars while he played, something I hadn't thought of doing until I saw him in action. He made the organ sing, and then he suggested I sit in and play piano. He's so brilliant that I would normally be intimidated, but he's such a sweet person, he made me want to play, and I forgot my nervousness. I'll treasure that moment forever.

We flew to Seattle the next day and checked into the Edgewater Inn, a very popular hotel with bands at that time and probably still because of its location. Being on the waterfront, all the rooms at the back face Elliot Bay, a part of Puget Sound. The rooms are above the water, and they even rent fishing rods and bait in the gift shop, so you can fish out of your window. Once, I left a rod hanging out the window overnight and in the morning it was gone. The fish are very big in Seattle.

After the gig, I invited everyone to my room for a party. First, I rang Charlie Fernandez to remember to bring lots of booze back from the gig; then I set up my sound system, and unpacked all my bags. I'd been on the road for a while and had to be sure there were no spliffs inside my socks or bindles of coke in my washing bag before I went through customs the next day. I had a toot and decided to separate the blow into packets, so I could hide one or two in the room in case we ran out later.

Well, we had the party of parties. Everybody came, and everybody got stoned and drunk. Somebody invited a couple of hookers, and they put on a show for us, as I recall. The place was rocking, we had the big fun, and there were empty bottles all over the place, ashtrays full and my suitcases open and clothes all over the bed and the floor. It was a mess, but I had a plan. As it was 6 A.M. already, I ordered breakfast so I could eat it before I went to bed, eliminating one more chore when I woke up, and then I wouldn't be hungry either. It was foolproof. When the breakfast arrived, I decided I'd eat it in bed to save the time it would take to clear the bottles and ashtrays off the table. Yes, it couldn't fail.

I woke up to the phone ringing, and Charlie pounding on the door with all his might. "Mac, wake the fuck up!" Bang!Bang!Bang!Bang!

"Hold on!" I said, and picked up the phone.

"Will you be checking out today, Mr. McLagan?" A voice asked me.

"Yes!" I barked and put the receiver down.

I looked around. I was wet. No, I was sticky. I had the mother and father of a headache and I literally had breakfast in bed. Coffee, milk and sugar, eggs, bacon, and orange juice all over me and the bed, and the plates and tray on the floor. I jumped out of the bed onto a coffee slick and fell on my arse.

BANGBANGBANGBANGBANG!

I ran to the door and opened it. Charlie was standing there looking very worried in the corridor.

"We…You're late," he said calmly. He was a gentleman.

"I'll be there. I'll get the bags. I'm running," I said and slammed the door.

"Do you need any help?" he shouted through the door.

"No. Just give me a minute."

I had to collect my thoughts, but I couldn't think with all the crap in the way. I had to clear the decks.

"Rrrrring, Rrrrrrring!" I grabbed the phone.

"No!" I screamed, pulled the phone out of the wall, and threw it out the open window into Elliot Bay. Splash! Phone books, splish, splash. The bottles had to go. Splash! Clink! Splash! All of them out the window. The chairs were next, the sheets and blankets, and all that was left of the breakfast, including the tray and plates. Anything that wasn't mine had to go. I grabbed a bag and threw some clothes in, checked under the bed, closed that case, threw it towards the door. I was in a sweat. Damn that coffee table! Out you go. SSSplash!

BangBang!

"Go a-fucking-way!" I hollered. I wasn't worth knowing at a time like that. I took a minute to try and remember what I'd done with all the blow. Jesus, we'd be flying into Vancouver in an hour. There was some behind a picture on the wall; I got that out and snorted up a noseful. Oh, and I'd put some in my toilet bag. Found that, did a quick line. Checked my pockets. "Aarrgh!" A plastic bag with about two or three grams in it. What should I do? Dump it? I didn't think so. I'd decide on the way to the airport.

I opened the door and Charlie ran in, grabbed the bags, and passed them to the waiting porter. A quick look around. The room looked very uncluttered, not tidy, but apart from the bed and the chest of drawers, there wasn't much of anything left in it.

There was a man in a suit, casually leaning against the corridor wall opposite my door.

He seemed to be smiling.

"Good morning!" I snarled.

"Good morning to you," he said pleasantly as I walked up the corridor to the waiting limo. Charlie told me later he was the hotel manager, and he'd been standing there the whole time I was packing and found the whole episode very amusing. What a character. I was surprised to receive a letter from him later, in which he apologized for billing me eighteen dollars for the telephone, but he had to because the phone company had charged him. What a lovely bloke. Also, he said he looked forward to my next visit, and that I'd be welcome anytime. It just goes to show you never can tell.

CHAPTER TWENTY-THREE

Thank You and Goodnight

On April 1, only a couple of weeks after coming back from the States, Rod moved to Los Angeles, and the following week, Woody, Andy, Willie, Bobby Womack, and I began recording Woody's second record, *Now Look,* at the Wick. Keith Harwood engineered, and I was given co-production credit with Woody and Bobby, which really only meant that I was there most of the time and played on everything. The day after we started, though, I took a day off to celebrate Kim's divorce from Keith, in the hope that finally he'd leave her and Mandy alone. It had been a long time coming, and we took her friend, Penny Wilson, to an Italian restaurant in the Fulham Road, where the three of us spent four hours eating and drinking ourselves into a stupor.

We recorded solos and vocals on Woody's record at a little studio among fields full of cows near Amsterdam, then did more overdubbing at Olympic in London, and finally mixed it at Electric Lady Studios in New York. Keith Harwood was a lovely bloke with a winning personality who had brilliant ideas, like putting reverse echo on Woody's pedal steel so it appeared to come in out of nowhere. Phil Lynott got Keith to engineer Thin Lizzy's album, *Fighting,* after we got back from New York, and he brought me in to play on their record. He'd come over to the house when he wasn't working and help me organize my home studio, because I really hadn't the faintest idea what I was doing with all those leads, switches, and buttons. He simplified my whole system and wouldn't take a penny for it. It's so tragic that his daughter was born only a few months before he died in a motorcycle crash in 1976. He was so young, the "up and comer" of the time, and worked on both The Stones' *Black And Blue* and *Love You Live* albums. Mick Jagger called me from the States when he heard about his death, because he and Woody were very upset and knew that I would be too. When The Stones' *Love You Live* was released in 1977, they dedicated it to his memory with the words: "Those Whom the Gods Love Grow Young."

He's sorely missed by everyone who knew him.

After finishing mixing *Now Look,* Ronnie took a cab ride to Montauk, Long Island, where he started rehearsing for his summer job with The Stones. When the tour finished at the beginning of August he had just enough time to catch a flight to Miami, where we were to rehearse for The Faces' second American tour of the year. Meanwhile, Rod hadn't been lazy; he'd recorded *Atlantic Crossing,* his first album without me and Ronnie. Strangely, on the flight to England in March, Rod talked about making his next record in America and asked me if there were any musicians I could recommend for him to use. I suggested Booker T. and the MG's if he really wanted to make a great record with a great band, and he did use them. He went down to Muscle Shoals with Tom Dowd and had the one and only Steve Cropper play Ronnie Wood riffs.

The rented house we stayed at in Miami, 461 Ocean Boulevard, was the house Eric Clapton made famous with his album of the same name. It was on the beach, and it was wonderful to be able to dip in the ocean whenever I felt like it, which was often. A couple of girls ran the house, cooking and cleaning for us, so all we had to think about was the upcoming tour. Rod had given the show plenty of thought and threw us all a curve when he told us he wanted to get Jesse Ed Davis in to play rhythm guitar behind Woody. He thought that as Woody had just toured with Keith Richards playing rhythm guitar, he might not be able to handle it alone anymore, even though he'd played rhythm and lead with us for years. It was unnecessary, and it made Woody look like he wasn't capable. There was a lot of tension in the house and we hadn't even started rehearsing, but there was worse to come.

Rod wanted to use strings on stage. Woody and I were totally against it, because it wouldn't be rock 'n' roll anymore, it wouldn't be The Faces, it would be crap. But he was adamant. He seemed determined to turn The Faces into a lounge act. He brought in Jimmy Horowitz, a pianist and arranger, and an old friend of Billy Gaff's. He would rehearse the different musicians in each city on the day of the show and conduct them on a riser at the back of the stage. These would be musicians who didn't give a fuck about the music, just the paycheck, and we'd never see them again. Rod had bought his ticket to Las Vegas, but I wasn't going with him.

Jesse Ed was a different story. A Native American, he was a brilliant guitarist, and a character, and I warmed to him immediately. I knew his guitar playing from Taj Mahal's first two incredible albums and, later on, his slide guitar on John Lennon's version of "Stand by Me." But having met him, I discovered a gentle man who had a sly, rascally side that particularly appealed to Ronnie and me. One night, when we were in Arizona, another Indian and his wife came back to the hotel after the show and presented Jesse with an eagle feather. This was a great honour, and as even owning an eagle feather is illegal, Jesse took it from him with humility. The guy's comment was, "It's good to know one of our people has a steady job."

It was a very touching moment for everybody, but Jesse saw the funny side, and he just grinned. There were a few of us in his room that night, getting high and listening to sounds, but after a while I realized that Jesse and the guy's wife had slipped into the bathroom. Some time later, Jesse came out of the bathroom looking flushed, followed by the missing squaw. We couldn't believe it. He'd shagged her! We were expecting a fight, but the couple left the room without any bad feelings. Jesse explained in his easy, gentle way that he'd fancied her and because the guy was so proud of him, there would be no problem. He laughed his rich, deep laugh. He may have been an Indian, but he understood the white man's ways as well as anyone.

Jaws had just hit the theatres in Miami, and although Jesse had seen it in Los Angeles the previous week, he went with us to see it again one afternoon. It was just what we needed to release the tension that had built up since we arrived in Miami. Jesse waited for the scene where the shark jumps out of the ocean and bites the fishing boat in half. When the moment came, I jumped out of my seat, Kenney screamed, and Tetsu said, "Aghhh!" which means "Aghhh!" in any language-and Jesse laughed his head off. I jumped in the ocean as soon as we got back to the house. Tetsu went in too, but Kenney wouldn't. I had to, or I'd never have gone in again, but Kenney swore he'd never swim in the ocean again. Tetsu swam far out to the reef, as if nothing had happened, and got us all worried because he was a long way out and was in for a long time, splashing about and defying nature. Later that day, some poor geezer had his leg bitten off by a shark only a mile up the coast from the house. That was it for Kenney.

"Fuck that, I'm never getting in a bath again!" And at the time he meant it.

Ronnie and I had a talk about the situation with Rod and the strings, and he called Bobby Womack in Los Angeles, reasoning that if Rod could bring in an extra guitarist and an orchestra leader, we could get an extra singer! Bobby said he'd join us in a couple of days, which meant Ronnie, Jesse, Bobby, Tetsu, and I would have our own party every night.

The strings were useless. Admittedly, the technology hadn't yet been developed where they could be amplified and heard clearly above a band like ours, but they sounded tinny and out of tune when you could hear them.

Jimmy Horowitz looked absolutely ridiculous, waving his arms about in a penguin suit, and the strings were only used on four or five songs anyway. Rod loved them, but they were still useless. Each of the players had a small pickup attached to his instrument, and some of them weren't too pleased about having an electric gizmo clipped to their delicate fiddles. One night one of the violinists unclipped his unit, which caused them all to go off.

After I heard that, I made sure each night a few of the string players understood that they could unplug them if they didn't like the sound. This was war!

After ten days of gigs, I couldn't wait to get to Los Angeles, where Kim, Mandy, and Dermot would be waiting for me at the Century Plaza. Charlie had organized flowers in the suite as a welcome gesture, but he'd gone overboard. The suite was full of them. When I got in from Oklahoma City, at about 1 A.M., I could tell which rooms were ours, because Kim had put MAC stickers, which she'd had printed specially in London, on our doors. Mandy and Dermot were so excited to be there, and we stayed up half the night talking about the trip to Hawaii later that week.

The most important and biggest gig The Faces ever played in or around Los Angeles was on August 30, 1975. We were paid $250,000, which I believe was our biggest payday, and it should have been a fantastic success. Anaheim

Stadium was packed with punters and Fleetwood Mac played a great set–but there was one important thing missing that afternoon–our equipment. Since the gig in Oklahoma City on the 28th, the truck had broken down somewhere on its way to L.A. The repair crew had fixed it, but it broke down again the next day and never made it to Anaheim. As we waited for good news of our gear in the air-conditioned trailers backstage, Mick Fleetwood flailed and Stevie Nicks twirled in the summer sunshine. Warner Brothers' heads, Joe Smith and Mo Ostin, were waiting with us, and when Joe asked me what the latest news was, I told him, "I've got my Mo and Joe working, but it just ain't working for me." There was a small nervous laugh, and then we went back to chewing our nails.

We eventually went on late, using all rented equipment, and played a short, shabby show to a restless crowd. Everything–amps, guitars, piano, drums, drumsticks, picks–was rented, even microphone stands. The only item of our gear on stage that day was a brand-new Hammond organ I'd had streamlined by Keyboard Products in L.A. The show should have been a blinder, but it turned out to be a bleeder! At the end, we decided to take it out on the equipment and wrecked the lot, and it seemed like a good idea until Woody climbed on my new Hammond and started jumping up and down on it as I played. He didn't realize it was mine and only got down when I screamed at him to get off. Luckily, it wasn't damaged at all. But our reputation was. What should have been The Faces' finest hour turned out to be forty-five minutes of total embarrassment!

We spent four days in Hawaii, staying at the Kahala Hilton on Oahu. We had two gigs at the HIC Arena, and the rest of the time was ours. All the girls were there, including Rod's glamorous new Swedish girlfriend, Britt Eckland, Woody's girlfriend Krissie, and Kenney's wife Jan, as well as Jesse Ed's wife Patty. Because Kim and the children were with me, I splashed out in a grandiose suite with ocean views all round. I was very much in love, and it was a relaxing, wonderful time.

Mandy and Dermot were only seven and eight years old then, making sand castles on the beach, while Kim and I dipped in the pool, sipped a drink, and slipped into a balmy sleep. It was perfect.

Ronnie, Jesse Ed, and I were sitting on the beach, chatting, when Jesse fell silent.

"See that guy over there?" He was pointing to a short man in a suit walking by the pool, fifty yards away. "That's Jeff Wald, the singer Helen Reddy's husband and manager."

I asked him how he knew him.

"I know him from L.A. I did a session for him once and couldn't get my money out of him until I threatened to sue. He's a real cheap asshole."

"I'm glad I don't know him."

We watched him walk over to Rod and Britt's suite. The door opened, then it closed, and he walked back into the hotel. Rod came running down to the beach, very excited.

"Here, you'll never guess what. Helen Reddy's husband just swore at Britt. There was a knock on the door, she opened it, and he told her to get the fuck out of his room!"

"You're kidding," I said.

"Apparently, they've double-booked our room, and it's the one he always stays in. He's a regular, and he's demanding we get out. He's kicking up a right stink!"

Rod and Britt decided to go back to L.A. He said, "D'you wanna give us a hand wrecking the room before he moves in?"

"Yuss!" I replied. My speciality was always the bathroom. I could get truly creative around a tap and a toilet seat!

"Let's go." Ronnie and Jesse were in too.

We ran to the room and got to work immediately, throwing bedsheets everywhere. I put a couple of bath towels down the toilet, flushed it, turned the sink taps full on, and then as soon as the toilet was ready, flushed it again and again till it was overflowing. I did it one more time, and the sink was overflowing by then. It was only water but it was everywhere; the carpets would be soaked.

I think it was Woody who unscrewed the mouthpiece of the telephone, then took out the microphone and screwed it back up. It's a subtle touch.

When they tried to call the operator to complain, they wouldn't be heard and the operator would hang up. Rod arranged the bed somehow so it would collapse as soon as someone sat on it. Then we ran back to the beach and waited for the sparks to fly.

A short time later, we saw Wald walking towards the room and the bell captain carrying his bags. Then after a minute, he walked angrily back to the hotel lobby. Ron Perfitt, our baggage roadie came over, wondering what the fuss was about, so we told him what had gone on. I was still wearing swimming trunks but I was dying to find out what was happening, so Ron and I ran into the lobby to see. Wald was shouting at the receptionist and demanding that we all be thrown out of the hotel. The poor man was trying to get him another room, but Wald was throwing his weight around and shouting so much, the manager took him down the hall to his office.

A small throng of people had gathered, because they were as fascinated at his display of rudeness as we were, so we merged with them and followed them along the hall. The hotel manager's door opened and out came Wald, the manager behind him.

"It's just not good enough!" he shouted. Then he saw me.

"He's one of them!" he screamed, and threw himself at me, his fists flying. I stopped him before he could do any harm, got him by his hair with my left hand, and grabbed him by the throat with my right. It took him by surprise, but he wasn't having any of that; he was still struggling. So I forced him backwards over the arm of a sofa to hold him down and in the struggle knocked his head on a large painting, dislodging it. To add insult to injury, the heavy frame fell on his head with a clatter and a groan, and a guffaw from me. If he wasn't mad before, now he was really upset! I held him there as best as I could, but the manager had disappeared. I shouted to Ron, "Call the police! He's going fucking crazy!" I didn't know how long I could hold him there.

A security guard appeared and ordered me to let him go, thinking I must have started the scuffle.

"No fuckin' way!" I said. "He's a nutter. Grab his arms or I'm not letting him go!"

"Let him go!" the guard barked. He thought he knew better, so I did as I was told and let Wald up. Quick as a flash, he went for me again. He raged and lunged at me with both hands. I managed to push him off me and finally, the guard restrained him. Wald was screaming at the top of his voice.

"Get the police, godammit!" Then he turned to me. "I'm gonna have your arms broken, you fuck! You'll never get off the island alive!"

This was not good. Even if he was only saying it, I had to assume he might actually do it or, at the very least, assume he could have somebody do it for him. He obviously knew people on the island. He was a regular after all. They took him away, and I went back to the beach to tell Kim what I'd been doing with myself all that time. Of course, Dermot and Mandy thought the whole thing was a big adventure, and it just added to the fun of the holiday for them, but Kim and I agreed that before the police arrived I'd better flush what drugs I had down the toilet, in case things turned even nastier. So we went back to the room and waited for Hawaii Five-O to arrive.

The policeman was a friendly bloke who explained that Wald had accused me of assault. He knew nothing about me calling for the police. It was all news to him. I told him my side of the story, and more importantly I told him about Wald's threats, and he confided in me that Wald had got into trouble in Hawaii before and that they knew he was a person with a violent temper. The policeman knew I wasn't making it up.

"Okay, I don't want you or your family to worry about a thing. If you see him at the pool today or tomorrow, you don't have to avoid him because we'll be watching. If he makes any approach, we'll be on him like a ton of bricks. I don't think he'll bother you anymore." He got up to go. "Have a nice stay and come back soon. Aloha." The rest of the stay was wonderful. Wald was nowhere to be seen. I just wish the policeman had said, "Book him, Danno!"

With Kim, Mandy, and Dermot back in Blighty, the tour was soon back to normal, and almost exactly a year after the derailment, as it had become known, we flew into Tucson again and were horrified to find we were booked in the same motel. I believe we were the "Grateful Dead" by then, lucky to be alive and lucky to be allowed a room. It was the night before the show, and we had no chemicals at all, so we went to the bar in a very subdued mood. Some genius suggested a cheap way to get drunk, and we were in! We took a shot glass each, and a twelve-ounce can of beer, filled the shot glass with beer, and looking at a watch waited for the second hand to get to twelve. Then we downed the tiny drink, refilled the glass and waited for sixty seconds before we did it again. A minute later, we all drank it down and refilled the glass. This next minute was definitely shorter, and the next, shorter still.

By the end of one can of beer, a couple of chaps had already dropped out, and they'd only had twelve ounces of beer, but the one ounce every minute gets you drunk faster than you would normally, and we got rolling drunk that night on a couple of cans.

These were moments of high hilarity, but life on the road was becoming an "us and them" situation. Ron Perfitt, our trusty baggage handler and sharp wit, composed a band memo chronicling the previous days' events, which quickly became a very pointed and bitchy newssheet, as we travelled across country. One I remember was "The Pittsburgh Perspirer," but there were others for different cities, which he'd print whenever he had the time. He'd use snapshots, slanderous handdrawn cartoons, and editorials with snide comments aimed at Billy Gaff, Rod, Pete Buckland, and our agents, who became known collectively as the "Bullshit Brigade," because they were full of it.

Pete got lumped into the Brigade because he worked more and more with Billy and Rod, who had distanced himself from the rest of us. Kenney, not being one of the drug users, was quite content to hang with Rod too. The Brigade started checking into separate hotels after a while, so me, Ronnie, Tetsu, Jesse, and Bobby were left alone to continue our partying and drugging without interference. It wasn't a good situation, and looking back I did nothing to ease the mood. In fact, I aggravated it. I was feeling bloody-minded towards Rod because he didn't care about the band, increasingly violent towards Billy Gaff because he only cared about Rod, and generally pissed off with Kenney because he couldn't see how Rod and Billy were fucking up The Faces. The

Brigade wasn't too popular with the crew either, and it bugged me that the crew cared so much for us, while the management didn't give a fuck.

One morning, after staying up all night, Chuch suggested I go with him to the gig and watch the crew set up. It's strange to think that after all the years of performing I'd never seen the crew do the biggest part of their work before, and it was an eye-opener. Usually, I'd get to the gig a half hour before the show, pour a drink, play for an hour or so, and then run to the limos, but that day I gained a new respect for them and all they do to put the show together. Mike Grassley was our rigger on that tour, and I followed him up the bleachers and the stairs to the catwalk, somewhere between eighty and 120 feet above the floor, depending on the hall, way up near the rafters. I was worn out after a short climb, and although he was carrying a long rope around his shoulders, he carried on relentlessly. He climbed up onto the I-beam and inched his way along, then lowered the rope to the floor, where his partner attached a wire to it. Then he hauled up the rope again and a chain was attached to the wire. These chains weigh 120 pounds or more, which is my weight, and once he'd pulled up the chain he locked it in place around the I-beam. Then he did it twenty or thirty more times.

It's incredible to think how strong they are and how they worked without any safety net. The whole lighting rig and the huge speakers were hung from dozens of these chains, and they had to be hung in exact positions for tension and balance.

I finally made it up to the relative safety of the catwalk and watched him work from there, thankful that I didn't have to go out there with him. I don't have a head for heights and I was relieved when I was back on the stage again.

While Pete set up the P.A. and Chuch set up the amps, Jeff Sova, the piano tuner, was single-handedly responsible for transporting, setting up, and tuning the Steinway grand piano that we took with us. He was ready to tune it and asked me if I wanted to watch him while he did. I was interested enough in the subtle intricacies of the action of the Steinway piano to see how he went about his work. I took a step to the left to give him some room to work, but hadn't noticed the piano was right on the edge of the left side of the stage. I dropped like a stone, hitting the concrete floor with a crunch! I'd landed face down with my right wrist and my head taking the impact, and I was in pain. I couldn't move and I could hardly breathe because I was winded.

As I'd taken the step to the left, Jeff had turned to his right to pick up a wrench, and when he turned back I'd disappeared. He looked around, couldn't see me and thought I'd changed my mind and wandered off. Bloody pop stars! I'd have been lying there on the floor still if it wasn't for Mike Grassley, who saw me fall and shouted for help from high up above the stage. It's ironic that after being eighty feet up on a catwalk without an incident, I'd fallen seven feet and done my wrist in!

Finally, someone heard him above the noise, and helped me up. My wrist hurt like hell, and I couldn't think of playing on it. There was no one at the gig who could get me to a doctor, the crew had plenty to do, and Richard Fernandez, our tour manager, and the guys weren't due to fly in to town for some hours. I sat in the dressing room, put some ice on my wrist, took a couple of hits and tried not to worry.

When Richard arrived, he bundled me off to the hospital and they found it wasn't sprained, only strained. The doctor gave me a shot of morphine to ease the pain and I felt very wonderful and very relaxed immediately. The pain had gone, and I was in another world. I was drifting downstream without a care in the world. His advice for me was to lay down with an icepack on my wrist until the next day and then use heat. That was easy for him to say, but I had a gig to do.

That night I played the loosest and greasiest I've ever played, although, as I couldn't feel my wrist, I might have done more harm to it. But thankfully it was all right, and after the gig Pete brought a pretty girl to my room who gave me a blow job because she said she felt sorry for me.

My wrist was hurting again the next day, so before we left town I got another fix of morphine at the hospital and down I went again, feeling no pain, just loaded! The next weeks were a blur of numbness and in each city we went to, the doctors would prescribe milder and milder drugs for one or two days at a time. I'd been hoping for more morphine, but they knew what was happening even if I didn't; it's quite incredible how quickly the body gets to need the drug. Eventually, I was put on Percodan and then Darvon, but I loved it all too much. It took a month or so before I finally picked myself up from falling down and got off all those prescription downers and back to my normal drug habits.

The last gig was on November 1, 1975, at the Minneapolis Labor Temple. The tour had not been a happy one, and The Faces were based on having a real good time together, so it was destroying our souls not being the rocking band we'd been in the glory days with Ronnie Lane. Rod's solo success had eclipsed The Faces, and as we weren't a recording band anymore we could only exist as his backing group, playing his hits and the odd Faces songs on Rod Stewart and The Faces tours. Added to all that, Billy Gaff was representing Rod more than the band, and as we were now being officially advertised as "Rod Stewart and The Faces" I fired Billy as my manager.

Meanwhile, Rod knew that The Rolling Stones were courting Woody, but I trusted them, and assumed it was flattering enough for Woody that he'd make a chunk of change on their tour, come back to The Faces, and carry on like before. But although Woody was saying nothing, he'd gone as far as he could with Rod and saw clearly that The Stones were a recording and touring band who really wanted him. I can't really fault Billy Gaff for pushing Rod. He was having the hits after all, with or without The Faces, but he wouldn't have had such huge hits without being able to tour constantly behind us. Rod would use The Faces for as long as he could.

Woody went to Munich to record with The Stones in December, he and every other guitarist in the free world, except Mick Taylor, who'd left them "because they couldn't afford me," as he told me with a wry smile in 1984. Keith's first choice, ironically, had been Steve Marriott, but that didn't work out, possibly because there would have been one too many singers in the band, and Steve certainly wouldn't have sat in the background. Woody really wanted to be a Rolling Stone, but who wouldn't? They were my favourite group too. He still wasn't saying he'd joined, so I didn't ask him, figuring he'd tell me when the time was right. Wrong.

I opened the *Daily Mirror* over a cup of tea one morning and read the headline, "Faces Break Up." My heart sank. It was a quote from Rod, and my first thought was how dare he say we'd broken up, when all he was really saying was that he was leaving the group. He should have called to prepare Kenney and me, but he didn't consider our feelings at all. Reading it in the morning paper over breakfast was a big blow.

Rod's ego was bruised because The Stones had borrowed Woody, and so he'd been quick to get the scoop, to be one up, to get his picture in the papers first, because that meant everything to him. It was, "Pull the ladder up, I'm all right, grab the headline, and fuck 'em all, save one." The Bullshit Brigade had got the last word. Merry Christmas, Rod.

Kim, 1978.
(© Eric Sway

Dad, Kim, me, Mum, and Joan, Kim's mum. (© David Sprecher)

Kim and I on our wedding day, October 9, 1978.
(© David Sprecher)

Me and Woody. (Photograph by Henry Diltz)

Muddy Waters, Willie Dixon, daughter Shirley Dixon, Keith Richards, Woody, me, unknown, and Charlie Watts backstage at Soldier's Field, July 8, 1978.

The New Barbarians: me, Woody, Bobby Keys, Zigaboo Modeliste, Keith, and Stanley Clarke strike a backstage pose, 1979. (Photograph by Henry Diltz)

Recording "Truly," Shangri-La, 1979. (Photograph by Henry Diltz)

Keith's always loved my singing! (Photograph by Henry Diltz)

Keith, Woody, Mick, and me in Toronto for Stones/Barbarians all-nighter.

Bonnie and the Bump Band during the recording of her album, Green Light, *1981. Ray Ohara, Johnny Lee Schell, Ricky Fataar, and Bonnie Raitt. (© John Livesay)*

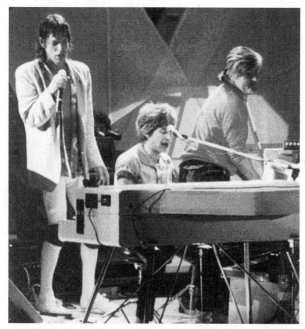

Mick Jagger introducing me and Stu, 1981. (© Ed Finnell)

Me with cigarette.

hat key are we in?
hotograph
Henry Diltz)

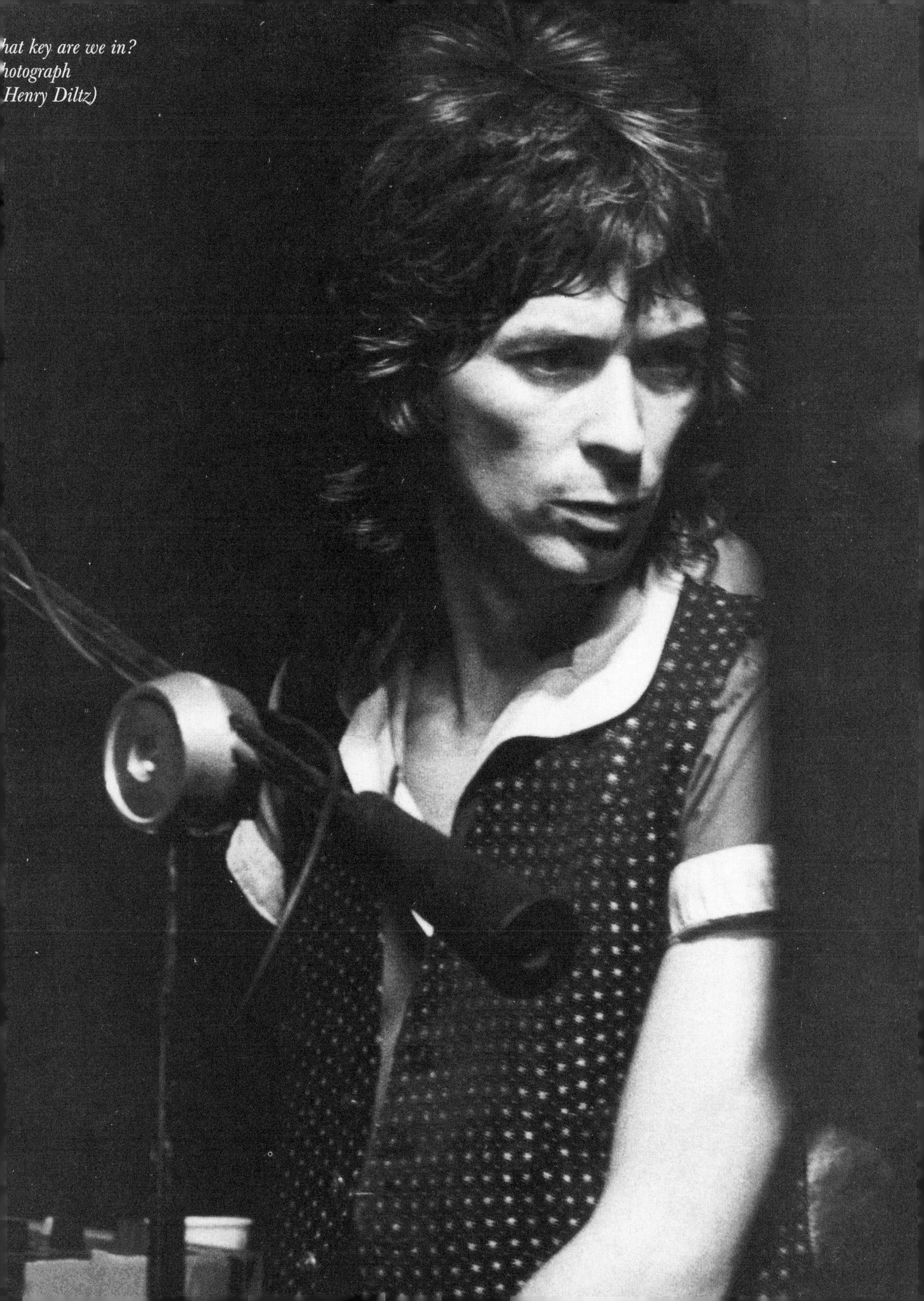

*Me, Charlie, Mick, Bill Graham, Keith, and Ronnie before show at Kemper Arena, December 1981.
(Michael Halsband, 1999 N.Y.C.)*

*Rule one: if you're going to be photographed with someone famous,
get on his right side so that the credit line reads: Ian McLagan and Charlie Watts,
and not the other way round! (Michael Halsband, 1999 N.Y.C.)*

Me, Kenny, Ronnie, and Ronnie, Wembley, 1986.

Ronnie Lane and me mug it up prior to his 1990 tour of Japan.
(Photograph by Cindy Light)

"Scrappy" Jud Newcomb and me of The Bump Band,
Hole in the Wall, Austin, Texas, 1995. (© Todd V. Wolfson)

Kenny, me, Ronnie, and Rod before final Faces romp in Dublin, 1995. (© Julie Cowan)

n and Mac, home
the range, 1997.
Todd V. Wolfson)

PART THREE
1975–1998

Has-Beens in Harmony

In 1976, things looked decidedly dismal, but I didn't sit on my arse and moan about it. The Faces planned to make a record without Rod, and Warner Brothers showed enthusiasm at first. But as Chuch was preparing to leave for France to check out studios for the project, Derek Taylor invited Kenney and me to Warner Brothers' West End office for a little chat with him and Mo Ostin.

Derek, who had only recently become the head of the English Warner's, had worked closely with The Beatles for years and was a gentleman. That's not to say Mo wasn't a gentleman, but he didn't waste words. He said the company wasn't interested in The Faces going back into the studio, as Woody was joining The Stones, which was about to be announced officially in the press. I didn't want to believe it, but was horrified when he suggested Kenney and I think about forming a group with Steve Marriott. We looked at each other in disbelief, and I told him it was the last thing I wanted to do, and left the office in a black mood. Without our record company behind us, we were fucked.

Woody had said nothing, but the day after our meeting with Mo and Derek, he flew to Nassau to record with The Stones. It was over, and I was devastated, but I had to find work immediately to pay the mortgages, especially the one on Mum and Dad's house. We still hadn't had accounts for the last tour and there would be other unfinished Faces business to deal with, but first and foremost, I had to round up my equipment. Apart from my B3 and two Leslies, after checking around, I discovered the rest of my English gear had been shipped to the States at some time since November, and my American gear had mysteriously disappeared. Billy Gaff wouldn't return any of my calls and surprisingly, Pete Buckland, the head roadie, didn't know where the gear had been taken. Chuch was with Woody in the Bahamas, and the other roadies and the people at Ampeg didn't know where it was stored either. The brand new B3 that I'd bought the previous August, two Leslie cabinets, four complete sets of Ampeg SVT heads and cabinets, as well as a

Hohner Clavinet and several Wurlitzer electric pianos, were hidden away somewhere in the States, and no one seemed to know where they were. I had no record company, and now I had no equipment. I was fucked again.

As if my luck was going to change, that's when Tony Calder rang Kenney out of the blue, and assuring him he was no longer working with Andrew Oldham or Immediate, he told him he was now with NEMS. By the strangest of coincidences, that company had recently bought up the entire Immediate catalogue and rereleased "Itchycoo Park." He wanted us to get back together to make a promotional video, promising to pay us one thousand pounds each if we would do the video. Billy Nicholls remembers how we used to call Calder "the Mekon" behind his back in the Immediate days.

The Mekon was an evil little green alien with a large bald head in the Dan Dare comic strip, which appeared in the British children's magazine, *The Eagle*. He couldn't walk, but he got around in a miniature spaceship. Okay, Calder wasn't an evil, green alien, but he was balding.

I had no desire to re-form The Small Faces. The thought of even being in a band with Steve made me tense up, and though they'd been great days, I didn't want to live them over again. David Endoven from EG Management had other ideas though and called a meeting to discuss them with us. Less than a week after Mo had suggested Kenney and I get together with Steve, here we were in the same room with him and with Ronnie too!

It was a bit like a scene from a Western. None of us wanted to be the first to loosen up and smile. That didn't last long though, and once the tension eased, we agreed in principle that if we were to play one live show and film and record it, we could make a ton of money and walk away without any commitments to each other afterwards. In the magic words of Freddie Truman, "Take th' money, put it in your bin, and fuck off home. Never mind the other fucker." David added that if we went into the studio and cut some new tracks, we could repackage some of the old recordings, make a deal with Tony Calder, and make even more money.

Well, we were greedy bastards. Not that greedy, but we recorded videos for "Itchycoo Park" and "Lazy Sunday" later that very day and surprisingly enjoyed each other's company in the process. Though "Romany" Ron and "Scruffy" Steve looked like they'd seen better days, we had a good laugh anyway. As a direct result of the video shoot, "Itchycoo Park" (Immediate) became a hit for the second time, getting to Number Nine in the U.K. charts in December 1975. But at the end of this little business venture, the Mekon reneged on the deal, and we never got paid–again! (You may wonder how four seemingly alert young men could be taken in a second time, but you obviously haven't had to deal with the little green, balding men in business suits that we have.)

One good thing came out of the videos, though it wasn't money. I drove down to Steve's Tudor cottage in the country soon afterwards and wrote some songs with him. He was living with his wife, Pam, and their baby boy, Toby, in tiny Beehive Cottage in Moreton, Essex, which he and Ronnie had bought together back in the Immediate days when they'd been given a small advance from their publishing. As it turned out, it would be all they'd ever get from them, but they didn't find that out for some time. We played together most of the night, developing ideas and songs in what had once been Ronnie and Sue's converted garage, which Steve had made into a studio. I played him some of my ideas and he played me some of his, and a couple of new songs just fell out of the night sky.

I was hungry and looking, as Steve would often say, so when Ronnie rang and asked me if I'd play a couple of TV shows and a gig at Norwich University with him and his band, Slim Chance, I readily agreed and surprised myself by having an absolute ball. He was in great spirits too, and the band rocked and I enjoyed playing his new songs as much, if not more, than the old Small Faces and Faces tunes.

Ronnie and Woody called me in to Olympic to play on a couple of tracks with Pete Townshend on the film music for *Mahoney's Last Stand,* starring Alexis Kanner and Sam Waterston. Ronnie called soon after and invited Kenney and me to go down to the country for a chat and a play, and as we were still "hungry and looking'"and had all the time in the world, Kenney took the wheel and we spent an unhurried sunny afternoon driving west as far as the Welsh border.

Ronnie seemed as keen to see us as we were to see him. His whole life had changed since The Faces. There had been three albums released including *Anymore for Anymore, Ronnie Lane,* and *One for the Road,* as well as a couple of hit singles. He had a large spread with an old farmhouse and outbuildings set amongst rolling hills way out in the country. Though he was born in the East End, he really looked the part of the farmer now, or more like the gypsy. He was unshaven with sideboards, he wore an earring, and with the kerchief round his neck, the waistcoat, and heavy boots, he could've passed for Romany Ron, and Kate, who'd always had that gypsy look, was looking rougher than the last time I'd seen her.

When Ronnie took us into the kitchen for a cup of tea, Kenney and I shot a horrified glance at each other because there was filth everywhere. There was nowhere to sit down, and the table was piled high with days of dirty plates. There were grubby clothes hanging all over the place, and you could hardly see out of the filthy windows. Kenney looked at me and winced. It was a bloody shame; they didn't have to live like that. He wasn't broke and it wasn't clean. I was horrified for the kids. I've lived in the country, so I know what dirt is, but you don't have to live in it, and I thought it was just unhealthy.

Kate handed us tea in chipped and unwashed cups and Kenney gave me another look. I wasn't going to drink the tea, so after a respectful time I asked Ronnie if he had a beer, thinking that I could drink it from the bottle.

"I don't think we've got any, Mac. D'you wanna go down the pub?"

"Sounds good to me!" I said, rubbing my hands. I only wanted to get out of this depressing kitchen, but a pint or two of local bitter would wash the journey away better than anything.

Outside, he showed us all the vehicles that were parked in a field behind what were once the cowsheds. He had his Land Rover, some trailers, and several gypsy caravans in perfect nick, plus the beautiful Airstream trailer that he'd shipped from the States and converted into a recording studio. It had LMS painted on the side, which was a joke on the London, Midland, and Scottish Railway, but actually stood for Lane's Mobile Studio.

We piled into Kenney's Volvo and drove to Ronnie's local, The Jolly Bastard. It was bustling with farmers, sheep shaggers, and Ronnie's piano player, Charlie Hart. A lovely character, he could play all kinds of other instruments too, and we had a good laugh for a while. But Ronnie got stroppily drunk very quickly and suggested we form a band, calling it Ronnie Lane and the Small Faces. Well, the conversation between us went steadily downhill from there, because he wasn't listening anymore. Charlie was embarrassed too. Ronnie didn't seem to be breathing the same air as the rest of us. We went back to the farm later, and although we did play with Charlie for a little while, the point of it all was gone.

Kenney and I stayed at a pub in Shrewsbury that night, and after a drink with Ronnie the next day we decided we'd found out all we needed to know and set off for home, dejected. It was a pretty sad and strange couple of days, but on the drive back we started getting giggly. Now at least we knew it wasn't going to work, and although it was a bloody shame, we weren't going to dwell on it. Kenney was in a silly mood and started fucking about with the gear stick, doing a kind of "Jacques Tati" at the steering wheel, purposely throwing the motor out of gear and revving the engine wildly. He made me laugh until the tears rolled down my face. At one point, he even took his hands off the steering wheel and jumped in the back of the car! It was so crazy and dangerous, we were both in fits of uncontrollable laughter. Now normally, Kenney is as good a driver as anyone on the road, or better, but when he did it again and again, it got to be really painful. My sides ached so much from laughing. We stopped for a meal and a couple of large brandies to calm us down and get over the big disappointment we shared about Ronnie's behaviour. It's funny to think I'd been with Kenney for eleven years up until then. We couldn't keep wives that long!

Ronnie may have thought we'd be content being his backing band, but Steve was dead serious about us all getting back together as Small Faces and it was he who finally turned Ronnie around. Joe Brown and his lovely wife Vicky were mates of Steve's and happened to have their own studio, Grange Sound, in the back garden of their house in Chigwell, so we jumped at the opportunity of a weekend of fun together. I went down to see Steve again the night before we went to Joe's house, and it turned out to be very productive.

I'd never met Joe before, but I knew him well from the "Oh Boy" TV pop show of the late Fifties that had launched Cliff Richard as a star.

Joe had spiky blond hair back then, and I told him Rod should pay him a royalty for his hairstyle. Joe Brown and his Bruvvers were a class act. During my first time on stage, Johnny Eaton and I played his hit song "Picture of You" as a duet at an amateur show. With all the good feelings that were flowing, it was impossible to imagine how the night would end. Ronnie was the fly in the ointment. As Steve and I had written a couple of songs together, it put Ronnie's nose out of joint, because he realized the Marriott/Lane glory days were over, as there was nothing creative happening between them. I'd finally got my foot in the door after all those years of their song-writing partnership. I was flattered that Steve wanted to write with me and surprised at how easy it was.

Steve and I had been doing vast amounts of charlie and after working through the night, we took a break at lunchtime for a drink at Joe and Vicky's local. We'd been having a jolly time in the pub garden, the sun was out, and Steve and Joe were telling jokes, one after the other, when all of a sudden Ronnie got pissed off and started talking about going home. He'd never been much of a drinker—not that it had ever stopped him from drinking to excess—but that afternoon he got nastily drunk. The dark mood passed, but when we were back in the studio and began singing background vocals, Ronnie threw down his headset suddenly, saying it was "all a load of old bollocks," and made for the door. It had all turned to rat so quickly, we were floored. We tried talking to him, but he wouldn't listen and sulked, and said he'd had enough and wanted to go. Then he became abusive and in the end Steve and I chased him out of the control room and up the driveway, screaming at him. It was horrible and it should never have happened, and after he'd gone we were all a little tearful. Joe, Vicky, and John Wright, our engineer, did what they could to console the three of us, but after a lot of talk Steve offered to call a bass player he knew. We all thought what we were doing was worthwhile and that we should continue. Rick

Wills came down later that day and sat in with us. He was an old mate of Steve's, with an easygoing personality, and he was a fine bass player.

Kenney and I found him good to play with, and before we knew it we were a band again, so we set about recording an album that would eventually be called *Playmates*. It was produced by a certain "Kemastri," which was our names crammed together–Kenney, Mac, Steve, and Rick.

John Wright was a great engineer but a funny old bastard. He had a handlebar moustache and a twitch, and Steve couldn't resist taking the mickey out of him, twitching while he talked to him. It would take a while before he'd realize what he was doing, and then he'd tell him to piss off. He knew sound, but he was very set in his ways and drove an old Rover 90 that he was constantly repairing between takes. He came round to the house once, but when Kim sent out for curry, he wouldn't touch it. "How can you eat that rust?" he said, disgusted. So Kim had to cook him a fry-up instead. While John was mixing tracks, we sat in Joe and Vicky's sitting room drinking and puffing on what Joe referred to as a jazz Woodbine.

Steve was bored waiting around and went upstairs to their bathroom to shave off the walrus moustache he'd had since Humble Pie days. I was glad because it made him look older than his years, but when he came back down, we fell about laughing because he'd only shaved off one side of it and he looked very strange. He wanted to see how long it would take Johnny Wright to notice the difference, so we all went down the garden to the studio. John was preoccupied listening to the finer points of a bass drum track when we walked in and he didn't notice anything. But then Steve had also covered the shaved side of his upper lip with his hand.

"Whaddaya think, John?" John hadn't the foggiest idea what was going on and thought Steve was genuinely asking about the mix. Steve leaned on the desk next to him, changed hands, showing him a clean upper lip and asked him again. John sensed something was up, but carried on, darting his eyes at each of us in turn. After changing hands several times and moving around the room, Steve stood in front of the desk, took his hand away, and looked John straight in the eyes.

"Well?" Steve asked. John saw nothing.

"Well, what?" He was getting angry now.

Steve told him to turn the tape off, which he did, and he was silent for a second and then he finally twigged.

"You bastards! I knew something was going on. You bunch of fuckin' bastards! I thought you were listening to the sound, you fuckin' bastards! Oh, I'll get even with you for that, Marriott!"

The album finished, we started rehearsing at a place on Lots Road, off Cheyne Walk. The rot was already starting to set in for me. Playing some of the old songs was fun. "Tin Soldier," 'What'Cha Gonna Do About It" and "All or Nothing" were great live. But some, like "Itchycoo Park," had been a problem from the beginning for me, mainly because of the chorus. I didn't find that was "all too beautiful" and I really disliked having to play the tune. The whole music scene had changed, with punk bands starting up, and that hippie feeling didn't sit right with me. It was bad enough doing "Lazy Sunday" but "Itchycoo Park" was something else. Even when Ronnie asked me to tour Japan with him in 1990, I told him I'd do it on one condition, that we wouldn't play that song. He wasn't at all happy about it, and though we did run through it in Austin a couple of times before we flew to Japan, I dug my heels in and wouldn't play it on stage.

But the music wasn't the only problem. Thanks to Joe and Vicky's generosity, and as the album was already in the can, we agreed to pay them back when the deal was done. But it was only when we had a firm offer from Ahmet Ertegun of Atlantic that we discovered Steve wasn't free to sign anything.

He was still tied to A&M Records and his manager, Dee Anthony. I hadn't realized how much he needed Kenney and me until that moment. Without us he was fucked! So before any of us could dip in the pile, Steve's old partners got their hands dirty first, and after bailing Steve out of his contracts, there wasn't much left to get excited about. Later, when we started touring, he horrified us all by spitting on the crowd, as if he was in a punk band. Here we were trying to build up a following, and he's spitting at the punters who've paid good money to see us! I have to laugh at it now, but if he'd flobbed one in my direction, I would've chinned the bastard.

His voice wasn't doing it for me either. Where he'd been so soulful and ahead of his time for a white boy in the Sixties, by the middle Seventies he'd become so flash and vocally gymnastic, it wasn't as good on the ears. Where I'd seen the possibility of a new band playing new songs, the reality was that we'd become a tired revival band, and not the fiery outfit we'd been ten years before. In the words of a song that Steve and I wrote at the time, but which we never recorded: "We're has-beens in harmony, double-parked on the highway of life." It was his line, and it was funny then, but much too close to home now.

CHAPTER TWENTY-FIVE

Heart Attack

We toured England and Germany, leaving a trail of wreckage and phlegm, and were sitting in an Edinburgh hotel bar after a gig with comedian Billy Connolly and his manager. He'd just done a gig too, and we sat around drinking and laughing at his stories until our sides ached. They split when the bar closed, and as we had adjoining rooms Steve and I went upstairs for a nightcap. I poured the drinks while Steve broke out some more blow, rolled up a Scottish five-pound note, and made two of them disappear. He was still laughing at Billy's wild stories.

"What a funny cunt! He's mad as a fuckin' hatter!"

I did the rest of the blow, took a sip of my drink and turned just in time to see the glass slip from his fingers and smash on the carpet below. He was slumped in the armchair, and for a second I thought he might be messing around, but he was silent and wasn't moving. I jumped across the bed and shook him, but there was no reaction. I felt his chest for a heartbeat. Nothing!

Jesus fuckin' Christ! I was stunned for a second, then I hit him in the chest as hard as I thought was right. Nothing. I hit him again much harder, but there was still no response.

"Steve, Steve, you can't fuckin' die, you bastard!" I didn't know what to do, and then I thought of the kiss of life. I put my mouth to his and forced air into him. Almost immediately, he came round and looked at me very suspiciously. He tried to pull away from me.

"'Ere, what the fuck are you doin'?" He looked at me as if I was a total stranger.

"Steve, you just died on me! You're heart wasn't even beating!"

"I'm fuckin' sittin' 'ere wiv a poxy drink in me hand, and the next minute you're bleedin' kissin' me. What the fuck's goin' on, you cunt?"

Before I could answer him he'd slumped into the chair again. Fighting back the tears, I got on the phone as quickly as possible and called Dave, our roadie, and tried punching Steve in the chest again, but still without success. I kept thumping and shaking him, and then he came round again.

"Steve, you're havin' a heart attack, or something. I've got to keep you awake or you're gonna peg out on me again!" He seemed to come to, but wasn't all there yet. Suddenly, Dave was pounding at the door. I let him and Dennis in. Steve was still awake and I told them what had happened, but then he went out again. Dave felt his heart, grabbed his arm, and said calmly, "Help me get him on the floor. Dennis, ring for an ambulance. Hurry!" Dave slammed him on the chest a few times, and he came round again, and finally seemed to be coming back to life.

"What the fuck's happening, man?" Dave explained that he was having some sort of an attack, that an ambulance was on its way, and that everything was going to be all right. He seemed to be reassured.

"Hello, Mac. You all right?" He was obviously doing a little better.

The medics were at the door soon enough, and after checking him out they said that although he seemed to be okay, they'd have to take him to the hospital for a proper checkup because that was their procedure. They also had to notify the police in case it was drug-related. Steve slipped me his blow and I put it in my pocket, but before I could flush it down the toilet or do anything with it, the room was full of large Scottish policemen looking for drugs. They were a rude bunch and knew it. What were we doing in Edinburgh? What band were we, how many of us were there, were we on drugs?

There's something about large, fresh-faced, clean-shaven, sober policemen in the early hours that puts the fear of Christ into small, unshaven, drunk, and coked-out musicians at the end of a long night. They woke everybody up, including the crew, and searched all the rooms except Steve's and mine. They found some pot in somebody's pocket and took him away, then they turned over Steve's room as I watched through the partly open adjoining door. When they'd finished in there they went out into the corridor and came back round to my door.

Quick as a flash, I threw Steve's packet of coke into his room and shut the door quietly. It was like a farce, but luckily they never sussed it, or things might have turned really ugly. After searching my room, they let us take Steve to the hospital, as he was very pale and still needed to be checked out.

We learned as a consequence of the unfortunate evening in Edinburgh that Steve had experienced several of these heart tremors or palpitations before. I don't know what was wrong with his heart, but I do know he was the most highly strung person I've ever met. As anyone who's done drugs with him could tell you, he was a heart attack waiting to happen.

Mick Ronson was producing the Rich Kids at a small home studio in Mortlake, near London, and wanting to add keyboards on a track. So he called me. As it was only a mile away from the house, I drove over there that afternoon. Midge Ure, Steve New, and Rusty Egan were all good characters, but meeting Glen Matlock, the ex-bass player of the Sex Pistols, was like bumping into an old mate after a long time. I was flattered to be asked to play on such a young band's record, and Mick was great to work with. Glen told me the Sex Pistols listened to the Small Faces records a lot, and I thought how strange it was that I'd never read about any punk band citing their influences in the papers, except one night I heard Johnny Rotten talking lovingly on the radio about his collection of reggae records.

Before the Sex Pistols ever walked into a studio, I spotted Johnny Rotten walking along the Cromwell Road, and something about him made him stand out. Maybe it was the cocky swagger. He was certainly a larger-than-life character. It was like seeing Rod Stewart that first time at Eel Pie Island, when he too stuck out a mile.

Towards the end of 1977, we recorded the instantly forgettable re-formed Small Faces' second album, which I prophetically entitled *78 in the Shade*. We cut most of the tracks in Steve's studio at Beehive Cottage, using a mobile unit parked in his driveway, and Shel Talmy, who'd produced all The Who's classic early sides, like "I Can't Explain" and "My Generation," and The Kinks' classic, "You Really Got Me," was our producer. Steve and he didn't see eye-to-eye about hardly anything and though Shel did what he could with our album, when the songs aren't there, there's nothing anyone can do to fix it. He did get us into a studio in town, where we cut Bobby Womack's "Looking for a Love" and Chuck Berry's "Don't You Lie to Me," and though they turned out quite well, the situation between him and Steve never improved.

Chuch came over to Fife Road one night when we'd taken a few days off from Shel's continuing torture. The Stones were in the process of recording *Some Girls* in Paris and Chuch was in town for twenty-four hours to buy strings and drumsticks. We had a silly evening that became an even sillier night after he said he needed a haircut. I've cut my own hair for years, so I offered to give him a complimentary ear lowering. When I first met "The Chuch" in 1970, he had an afro that would have made Billy Preston's wigmaker very proud. But by 1977, it had all but faded away on top, and although the sides were still bushy, it looked like a hairy doughnut. All that was about to change for good. He said he wanted it really short and gave me free rein to make some mistakes while I was doing it. Kim, he, and I were drinking and chemically inspiring ourselves while we listened to the jukebox blaring in the hall, as his crinkly hair began to hit the floor in clumps. I trimmed as we talked and laughed, but when he looked at his watch it was later than he realized, and he said he'd have to leave soon. It was morning and I was almost finished, so I showed him the mirror. It looked good, but it was much shorter than he had wanted it, and there were scissor marks all over his head. But I thought it was a good cut, and I think he liked it, though it was a little unusual. He finished his drink and went straight to the airport.

That night, he called me from the studio in Paris.

"Hey, Mac, howyadoin'? Hey, Charlie said hello. He looked at my head and figured I'd been busted and spent the night in jail." He laughed, and I told him that I'd be willing to cut Charlie's hair any time. He passed the phone to Woody.

"Hey Mac, why don't you come over and have a play with us?" I didn't need asking twice and jumped on the first available flight to Orly Airport. Pathé Marconi is an old established studio originally designed for recording large orchestras, and Woody was just inside the huge studio door, a smile on his face, as I walked in. He showed me around the room, took me over to the grand piano and handed me a straw. Laying out two lines on the piano lid, he shouted across the room:

"Hey, Keith, look who I've got here."

"Oh, it's HIM!" Keith gave a gap-toothed grimace. "Oh, I see Woody's taken care of you, then?" He laughed as I wiped the residue from my nose, then led me into the control room. Stu appeared, all chin and pockets, and an easy smile.

"Hello, stranger. How's things?" I told him everything was fine and asked him how they were doing.

"Oh, pretty good, you know. If these buggers would only get on with it, tsk!" No one could ever get a swelled head around Stu. The salt of the earth, he always had his feet on the ground.

Mick, Bill, and Charlie were listening back to "Shattered," one of their new tracks. To my ears it was fresher than anything they'd done in a long time. It was raw and almost punk. Chris Kimsey, their engineer, said hello and Mick gave me a toothy smile and a hug. I waved to Charlie and Bill.

"What have we got here?" Charlie asked nobody in particular, turning his nose up, and pointing at me.

Eventually, Keith picked up his Telecaster and started to play. Charlie followed, and then Woody and Bill. I sat down at the Hammond and noodled along with them. It felt good to be playing with them. No, it felt great, and it made me want to play. Simon Kirke was over behind Charlie, smacking the congas, and Stu sat down at the piano, and then it dawned on me. Years after seeing them for the first time at the Station Hotel, Richmond, here I was playing with my favourite band.

Mick stood in the middle of the floor at the microphone singing and howling, and I'd forgotten how good his harp playing was. We went through several tunes, a couple I knew from somewhere, and another that sounded somewhat familiar, and then it was all new from then on in. Every now and then there'd be a break to sip a drink, or in the case of Keith, Woody, and me, to pass the joint and do another line of coke, then Keith would start it up again. The music seemed to build up to its own climax, he and Woody bouncing off each other, practicing what Keith calls "the ancient art of weaving."

Studio time is quite different from Greenwich Mean Time. When you're locked in a room with no windows, time has no value, but when you're getting high and playing music as well, it takes on another dimension. Bill and Stu never took a pill or a potion in their lives, and somebody's got to be straight, though I'm not altogether sure why.

We took a break for a bite to eat at an African restaurant later that night, and then went back to the hotel. I threw my bag in the room, and caught up with Charlie and Woody in Keith's room. Keith was keen to play me some of the tracks they already had on tape. He put on "Claudine." The whole band was in classic form, but Mick's live vocal floored me. At the end of the song, he asks the question, "Am I in my right mind to be locked up with these people?" My answer would be "Yes!" It was my favourite band playing at their peak, and although it was never released, Keith gave me a cassette copy that night which I treasure to this day.

When Keith put on "When the Whip Comes Down," I told him I'd been working with the Rich Kids and how Glen Matlock had become a pal. He was very interested in the punk scene although, like me, he didn't know too much about them, since the punk bands had alienated themselves from older groups like The Stones, The Who, and The Faces. I figured some of the young geezers had to be listening to something. Nobody lives in a vacuum.

He played me their version of The Temptations' "Just My Imagination." "We need an organ on that one, Mac, whaddaya think?" It wouldn't be difficult. It was going to be a cinch. Then he played several different takes of "Shattered," and Woody interrupted, "Here, Keith, let me play Mac that other take, man."

"Shut up, Woody. It's my room and it's my tape machine, okay?" Keith laughed as he said it, and it was a joke at Woody's expense, but there was more than a grain of seriousness about it too. They're like brothers, but Keith, being the oldest, is the bully. And though their relationship is strong, Woody usually knows how far he can push it, but Keith *always* knows, and doesn't mind telling him. When you're in Keith's room, Keith works the tape machine, and that's that.

Charlie wasn't saying much, but was constantly amused by the shit that Keith put Woody through. He shrugged a sleepy, resigned smile, knowing nothing would faze Woody, as he's very resilient. What a bunch of characters. Keith went into the bathroom while Woody laid out another line on the glass tabletop. I'd been drinking all day, and on into the night, but the blow was working against the alcohol, giving me the false sense of security I was used to. I was just high enough.

When Keith came out of the bathroom I noticed immediately how refreshed he looked. Innocently, I asked him, "Blimey, you look good. Have you just had a shave and a shower?" His heavily lined face broke into an evil grin.

"That's what a syringe full of heroin will do for you, Mac." And he laughed.

"He's fuckin' terrible!" Charlie said, and shook his head with a resigned grimace, knowing the pleasure Keith got out of shocking people. I was horrified for a second, but then I thought, that's his buzz, not mine. He never offered heroin to me, ever, in all the time I was around him, but if he had a joint, a drink, or some blow, what's his was yours. He wasn't going to turn anyone on to something they weren't already using. Later that night, he jabbed a needle straight through his jeans into his bum, and left it there, the syringe sticking out as he walked around the room, laughing loudly.

The next day, we got down to some serious work, and after I played an organ pad on "Just My Imagination," Keith started to run down "Miss You," a song they'd worked on before with Billy Preston. Mick wanted a Wurlitzer electric piano on it, and knowing that was my instrument, I quickly worked out a simple part to play. I've used "Wurlys" for years, it's almost become a trademark sound for me. I played one on "Tin Soldier" and "Stay with Me" and I still get requests to play, like the one from Buddy Guy's producer, John Porter, for "Feels Like Rain" in 1992.

Keith kicked the band in gear with Charlie playing tight with him and, though the song was rehearsed, Mick changed the bridge slightly, and then we kept playing it over and over. The Stones are notorious for recording dozens of "takes" of a song, and Keith listens for each player's peaks and valleys, even if it takes hours or days, before he feels everyone peaking at the same time. Eventually, Mick said he wanted to hear it back, and we took a break to listen objectively in the control room. Bill suggested I listen more to what he was doing, and leave more space. He was right, I was tripping over myself at times, following what he was playing too closely. We played it again and got it soon after that, and even though we put it down on tape a few more times, it was already in the can.

To actually be cutting a track live with The Stones was a great feeling and a rush. It's a lot different to overdubbing, where you slot into what's already there. You can contribute to the whole thing, reacting and interacting as you play. *Some Girls* went platinum, and "Miss You" became their biggest hit single up until then, with several re-mixes being released, and I'm very proud I was on it. It's always a surprise when any track I've played on comes on the radio. I get a tingle for a second until I remember it's me I'm listening to.

As I had to go back to London the next day to carry on recording at Steve's studio with Shel, I had to catch a flight that evening. I asked Woody if there were any readies handy for the two long days of recording, and he went off to ask Mick, who came over to the piano with a pained expression on his face.

"I've only got a few francs. Is that all right?" he said in his best Cockney accent. Disappointed, I said, "Whatever you can afford Mick." And he handed me 120 francs.

"It's all I've got at the moment, but I'll make it up to you, don't you worry." I said goodbye, jumped into a cab for the airport and home. Never mind the dosh, I was buzzing!

Years later, during their 1981 American tour, I told Woody that I'd never been paid, or even got a gold record for my work on that album.

He called The Stones' office that day. They sent me a gold record for "Miss You" and a platinum one for *Some Girls,* which made up for it. Sadly, when I needed cash badly in the mid-Eighties, I had no choice but to sell them both, as well as The Faces' only gold record for *A Nod's As Good As a Wink*. I've received others since, and hopefully there'll be more to come, but they're unlikely to be as precious as those great records.

CHAPTER TWENTY-SIX

Lawyers, Guns, and Money

When I'd bought the house on Fife Road, Sheen, in 1972, the market was at an all time high, and as I couldn't afford the mortgage payments by 1977 I'd had to sell. Pink Floyd's Roger Waters bought the house and made out like a bandit, but I lost a lot of money on the deal, because by then the market was at its lowest for years. It was just rotten luck, but we found a Georgian gem on West Hill, in Wandsworth, that we fell in love with immediately. As the owner led us up the stairs from the front hall, I grabbed Kim's bum, because she's got a lovely bum, but also to let her know I thought this was the place. She turned round, flashed a quick smile, and whispered, "Yes!"

This was Kim's, Mandy's, and my first house together, which made it even more special. There were three floors with a basement, and although the rooms were small, it was a very cozy home. A high-walled, traditional English garden in the back gave us privacy and quiet even though we were on the main road, and there was nothing but Young's pubs as far as your legs would carry you! It was to be a very happy house, although we only lived there for a year. In fact, Woody brought his pretty new girlfriend Jo to the house one evening, and when it got late, they stayed the night, with the result, nine months later, that their first baby, Leah, was born.

Small Faces began rehearsing in Camden Town for yet another English and German tour early in 1978, and one rainy night as I was driving down Kingsway on my way home to Wandsworth, I heard an incredible band on the radio. Although I'd had a couple of drinks, it sounded like Stuart Henry was playing a reggae record on his Radio Luxembourg show, and though I didn't know exactly what it was, I liked the sound. Unfortunately, the radio signal was so weak and kept drifting in and out so much I had to pull over to listen. But when I stopped there was nothing but static, and though I reversed a few yards it was still no good. By the time I drove off it had finished. It was very frustrating.

The next night, I was at about the same place on Kingsway when the song came on again. This time I heard it from the beginning, and found it was "Roxanne" by The Police, and what I thought was reggae was actually a strange and winning mixture of reggae and rock 'n' roll. I went out and bought the single and album the next day and played them to death.

Some weeks later, I saw a picture of them in the music papers. They looked like punks, and when I read that they were playing in London I was interested enough to find out what they were like live. They were supposed to open for another band at the Nashville Rooms and what is now the Three Kings on the Cromwell Road. When we got there, we discovered the main band had pulled out, but The Police would play as scheduled. I went to the bar to order a drink. A bloke in a parachute suit with dyed-blond hair was leaning on the bar with his back to me. I whispered to Kim, "That's got to be him, the singer, wotsisname." He turned and looked in my direction. I said:

"You're Sting, aren't you?"

"Yes, and you're Ian McLagan."

I was pleasantly surprised he knew who I was. That sort of thing didn't happen very often. I told him how much I loved "Roxanne" and another short bloke, also with dyed-blond hair, eased his way along the bar towards us.

"Hello, Mac."

"Andy?" I was surprised to see Zoot Money's Big Roll Band guitarist, Andy Summers, who I hadn't seen for some years. "How the hell are you? What are you up to these days?"

"I'm with this lot," he said, pointing to Sting and Stewart Copeland, who was also across the bar.

I'd known Andy from gigs and motorway cafes since 1965, and that was pretty amazing, but it was nothing compared to the show. When the three of them hit the stage they played such a dynamic set, that even though the room was half empty, they rocked the place, Sting bopping all over the stage while he sang and played, and Andy's guitar lines cutting through Stewart's offbeat reggae feel. We knew then they were going to be enormous, they were so original.

People often say they know exactly where they were when John Kennedy got shot. Well, I don't remember where I was then, but I know exactly where I was when I first heard Muddy Waters, Thelonious Monk, The Beatles, The Stones, Booker T. and the MG's, and The Police!

As far as Small Faces was concerned, *78 in the Shade* was exactly where our album stayed. The record hit the charts with a strange silence, and it stayed in the shade even while we toured to promote it. My heart wasn't in it anymore, and eventually I stopped answering the phone to Steve.

But when Glen Matlock called and asked me to tour England with the Rich Kids, I jumped at the chance, and had a good time on stage again. Steve New was only eighteen years old and had already given up heroin and booze! What a bunch. They were very intense and played hard, which I liked, and Glen touched me when he asked me to join the band after the very first gig. We swapped shirts like football captains and then drank hard like musicians. They were great fun to be around. It was partly their youth, and partly because they were so hungry to play, and through them, I got to meet characters in the punk scene that might never have crossed my path, like Mick Jones of The Clash, Billy Idol, and Rat Scabies, a hell of a drummer.

The phone at the house on West Hill rang late one night. Woody was on the other end calling from Woodstock, in upstate New York, where The Stones were rehearsing for their upcoming American tour, and after the usual "owsyerfather" passed the phone to Keith.

"How's it going, Mac?"

"Lovely, thanks. How's everything with you?" Something was up.

"Great. Listen, we're lacking a keyboard player, do you fancy coming on tour with us?"

"You're kidding?" My favourite band is asking me to tour with them? The band I used to watch every Sunday night back in Richmond. "Yeah, fuckin' right, I do!" I replied without a second's hesitation. This was my dream coming true. I left two days later on the sixth day of the sixth month at six o'clock, flight three, gate three, seat three, and all this to someone who believes three is his lucky number!

They'd wanted a flavour of reggae in the show, and as Stu wasn't into it, they got Bernard "Touter" Harvey, Peter Tosh's keyboard player, to sit in with them. He's a great player, especially for reggae, but when it came to rock 'n' roll, he just didn't have the chops. Of course, I couldn't play reggae at all, but the guys had figured it would be easier to get me to learn how to skank if they needed it than the other way round, and Charlie, Keith, and Woody were ready to spend whatever time it took to teach me.

They'd been rehearsing for some weeks at Bearsville Studios, and equipment was spread out all over the huge room, and characters hanging around everywhere, some I knew from tours with other bands, and some I didn't. I'd met Bobby Keys once before, but he introduced himself in typical Texan fashion, "How y'all doin', Mac?" Then Woody appeared.

"Mac, how are ya? Want a drink? How was the flight? How's Kim? Do ya wanna line?" Nothing changes. I was in a daze, but it was nice to be back in the fold, a lovely feeling of camaraderie.

"Ma-a-c!" Keith's dark face appeared round a doorway with a wink and a smile. "Mac, old chap, everything okay? What can I do you for?" He grinned, and suddenly he was a friendly barman, and as I was gasping for a drink, he wasted no time ordering Chuch to get me one. I spotted Stu coming round the door jamb, chin first.

"Hi, everything all right? Do you want to check out the keyboard setup while there's a minute of relative peace and bloody quiet from these pests? How was your flight, okay?"

Mick came over then, grinning and shaking my hand, seemingly quite pleased to see me, followed by Charlie, who pointed a finger at me, and with a derisory voice, asked Mick, "What's he doing here?" The sneer giving way to a smile of welcome. "Okay? Trip all right? Kim all right?"

"Yes, yes, and yes," I said.

Very soon we started to play, and even playing recognizable songs, so I began scribbling notes. I had to learn fifty songs before we got on stage, and probably only needed twenty. But they all had to be ready for Mick and Keith to choose a set. It was all very confusing, and before the night was over

I had sheets of garbled notes I couldn't understand. It was hell for leather, and the last one to the bar buys the drinks!

Touter was still there at the studio, which made me feel a little awkward, but it's possible he hadn't been told in case it didn't work out with me. We played, I reckon, about twelve hours with short breaks. It was fun playing "Honky Tonk Women," "Brown Sugar," and all the other songs I'd loved over the years. This time I was inside the songs, not only listening but playing along, and it felt good. It was a surprise and a blow to my ego, when I realized just how many songs they had and how little of them I actually knew. My brain was overloaded with music, and I was overtired, to the point where I started to unlearn things. Keith eventually called it a night and I was shown a room with a bed. I got in it and slept like a log for about six hours.

Jim Callahan woke me up. JC, as everybody knows him, is the head of security, and the dryest man on the planet. A very gentle, large man who could do damage without breaking into a sweat, he told me in his calm Cockney voice that I'd be late if I didn't get a move on. I asked him if I'd overslept.

"No, but we've got a flight to catch."

"Flight! Where to?"

"Lakeland, Florida, for the start of the tour." I was beginning to wake up.

"When's the first gig, then?" Panic.

"Tomorrow, didn't you know? I should've thought someone would've mentioned it." Chuch had said something about a few days of rehearsals, the swine.

"You'll go in tonight when it's quiet, about 2 A.M., and have a run through. You'll be all right. You're not worried are you?"

"No," I lied. I was more than worried. I wasn't at all confident, but I just had to roll with it and change up into extremely high gear. Somehow, you do. It's amazing how much you can learn if you have to, and how well you can bluff when the need arises. I had no time to think. I just had to get on with it.

The other thing I had to deal with was the deal itself, the money I was to be paid for the tour. It had to be sorted out, and Pete Rudge, who'd set up the tour, began to badger me to give him a price. I told him I'd think about it and discuss it with him at the sound check later. Thank God he was off my back for a while, because I couldn't concentrate on anything but the music.

Normally, it would be a manager's job to discuss money, and as Pete represented The Stones, somebody should've been representing me, so I could leave all the business outside the dressing room. But as I had no manager and didn't have the faintest idea how much to ask for, I was stuck for an answer. If I asked for too high a figure, they might get someone else in, although it was a little late in the day for that, and if I asked for too little, then that's exactly what I'd get. Somewhere in the middle there's a price everybody could be pleased with, but I had no way to figure it out.

Freddie Sessler, an old pal of Keith's who always hangs around with The Stones, offered to help by telling me what Billy Preston earned for the last tour. He suggested I ask for a little more than that, so that when Rudge came back with a lower figure, which he was bound to do, we could settle for a sum everyone could be happy with.

After we checked into the hotel in Lakeland, I had a few minutes to unpack and think. It was something I hadn't had a chance to do in twenty-four hours, and I thought of calling Kim, but it was too late in London by then. Anyway, I said I'd go up to Keith's room as soon as I'd unpacked my bags. Chuch had brought the Wurlitzer and a couple of amps and guitars over to the hotel and set them up in Keith's suite, and Charlie walked in as Keith was setting his stereo up. He had a Nakamichi rig, which was state of the art then, and there were cords and cables running everywhere.

He loved to play cassettes loud, and he played reggae extra bassy so that it boomed, because as he told me, in his best rasta voice:

"That's how they play it down in Trenchtown, Mon."

I'd never got into reggae when I first heard it in London. It didn't hit me because I couldn't understand it. Desmond Dekker seemed to be soulless and silly to me. I didn't get into him until much later on, mainly because I couldn't understand what he was singing about. But there was no denying Bob Marley's talent when I heard his voice, and maybe that was part of his magic. He had a universal appeal. It was like it didn't matter he was playing reggae at all, his personality came through the music.

Keith played me more radical things, like "Innocent People Cry" by Gregory Isaacs, "In a Dis a Time" by The Itals, "Mama Liza" by Jacob "Killer" Miller, and a load of other stuff designed to get inside my head and heart. It was all so new and it took a while to appreciate the depth of this new music, but all I had to do at the moment was to pick up on the rhythms and get comfortable with them. Charlie loved the drumming and was a great help explaining the technical side of the way they played the bass drum and snare drum kind of ass-backwards.

"It's backwards rock 'n' roll, basically, if you think about it." I was amazed. Keith showed me how the left and right hand bounce off each other on the keyboards, called skanking, which is the groove that pulls and pushes the beat, or as Keith puts it:

"Like a lion walking in the jungle. Padding from side to side, real slow."

Keith, Woody, and I played and Mick would listen until I'd get the groove, and then he'd start singing too, and we'd go over and over it until it felt natural. Then Keith would put on another cassette and away we'd go again with everybody sitting around jamming. I'd just graduated to rock 'n' roll university, and I was getting the best help on the rudiments that money couldn't buy. I played along to the tapes until it all begun to feel like second nature, and at about 3 A.M. we drove to the arena for a sound check.

The stage was already set, so we went over songs for an hour or so, the only interruption being Pete Rudge leaning over my amp and asking me whether I was ready to talk turkey yet. We got that out of the way quickly, when I told him the price I'd worked out. He said, "You're fucking joking! Who do you think you are, Billy Preston?" thus proving the art of conversation isn't dead, it's just sick. There was no comeback to that, other than bollocks, so I said, "Bollocks!"

He laughed and went off to discuss the minutes of our little meeting with Mick, I presume, though I wasn't taking much notice, because I had work to do. Now it was all in their hands. When he came back he explained with a straight face that as it was not a big grossing tour, they couldn't afford my price. He actually expected me to believe that, though I made no comment. When he told me what their offer was, I said I understood, but it wasn't enough, especially considering I'd flown in at the last moment. He said he'd come back to me, and when he did come back with a slightly higher figure, we shook hands, and with that out of the way, heaved a sigh of relief and allowed myself a private giggle. Considering that I'd been unemployed two days before, and wondering what the hell I was going to do with myself, and now here I was with my favourite band, in semi-tropical Florida, and being well paid for it. They say it's tough at the top, well, it's rough on the side and even worse down below. Things were looking pretty good.

Freddie Sessler was a rare case. A podgy, middle-aged Jewish man, he lived to get fucked and fucked up, and he always had the best quality drugs on hand. Whatever you wanted, he could get you high or low, but money never changed hands, because the drugs weren't for sale. He wasn't a dealer. He was a generous man. Mainly though, he loved the attention he got from being around The Stones, particularly Keith. Sometimes Mick would get pissed off with him, because he was the eternal raver, and he would get in a state sometimes, but he never sold drugs, he enjoyed using them too much himself, and also, no one could ever accuse him of dealing.

He appeared to be wealthy, but he earned his money by wholesale selling of office knick-knacks like monogrammed pencils, personalized matchbooks, and other assorted items of a very boring nature. Maybe this would account for his huge drug use and his need to be seen with The Stones. It came to his attention that there were doctors in New York who didn't have medical practices, and there were times when even he ran out of drugs. So he combined business with pleasure by setting up a poor and therefore thankful doctor in his own practice, renting office space, and supplying the furniture himself. Then, any time he wanted Seconals, Tuanols, Mandrax, or even 100 percent pure pharmaceutical cocaine, which was unobtainable on the street, he got his own personal doctor to write a script for him. Now he could get any prescription drug he wanted legally, and he would turn up at gigs with sealed one-ounce bottles of Merck pharmaceutical coke and invite you to break the seal and help yourself. Oh yes, we were always delighted to see Freddie's smiling face come around that dressing room door.

Hanging out with Keith became the general rule for me. We'd get back to the hotel after a gig, and if I wasn't in his room after a short while, I'd get a call wanting to know when I would be there.

Keith's room was the party room because he liked people around him, and he liked to listen to music and get nicely toasted. It was my nonstop rock 'n' roll university. We'd listen, and play, and talk for hours about the music. It was an ongoing education to me, and there was something to learn from each of The Stones. They had forgotten more about the music they loved than most people ever learn. Bill Wyman had an amazing collection of early rock 'n' roll, blues, and folk-blues recordings, and he could answer most questions I'd ask without having to look it up. Charlie's first love is jazz and he could fill you in on that subject, or point you in the right direction. Mick and Keith knew about the blues, rock 'n' roll, rhythm and blues, country, and country blues, and Stu knew his boogie-woogie better than anyone. Woody had two older brothers, Art and Ted, who played him Duke Ellington, Count Basie, and Louis Armstrong when he was growing up, as well as turning him onto the blues. So being around them all was like having the British Museum of Popular Music reference library at your fingertips. They were all well-rounded listeners. Well, maybe not Stu. He was more of a purist; with him there were sharply defined lines that could never be crossed. He had no time for country and western music and wasn't a particular fan of Elvis or the hill-billy sound, but apart from him, all ears were open, and mine too. I was exactly where I wanted to be with exactly the right people.

We were at a hotel in Myrtle Beach, South Carolina, in late June and Keith, Woody, Charlie, and I had spent another night playing reggae in Keith's suite. As we were right on the beach and it looked like a beautiful morning, I suggested a swim, and Charlie said he'd have a look outside with me. I changed into my swimming trunks, expecting him to do the same, but he stepped onto the beach sporting the three-piece suit, shirt, tie, shoes, and socks he'd worn all night. We had the beach to ourselves, and the Atlantic Ocean lured me in immediately. When I came out of the water, he was sitting in a deck chair in the bright sunshine, sweating profusely. He'd taken his shoes and socks off and rolled his trousers up, but was still wearing the suit. I asked him if he was going in for a swim, and he looked at me as if I was mad.

"You must be jokin'," he laughed. Before long he took his jacket and waist-coat off, hung the jacket on the chair, loosened his tie, took off his shirt and hung it over the jacket, then he put his waistcoat back on and tightened his tie up again. Charlie was on the beach. A gentleman always maintains his cool, and he never completely undresses.

Some nights Charlie and I would drift from room to room, scouring the corridors until we heard music. We'd invite ourselves in, stay for a while, have a drink and a laugh, then move on to the next room. It was like Harpo and Chico's travelling chess game that they played onboard ship in *Monkey Business*.

Whatever was going on around us was incidental, and after a while, when we got bored, we'd wander off, find another room where there was music, and gate-crash the party.

In July, we played at Soldier's Field in Chicago, but I don't remember anything about the gig. The highlight of the evening was meeting Muddy Waters and Willie Dixon backstage. The photograph was taken after the show, and we all went to a club on the south side with Willie and his daughter, and I watched transfixed from the side of the stage, as Pinetop Perkins tinkled the ivories, Willie sang, and Keith and Woody played guitar.

We'd played twenty shows, but I still hadn't signed a contract for the tour, not because I was unhappy with the terms of it, I simply hadn't seen a copy. Mick may not have known this, but when we arrived in Dallas he called me to his suite. Jane Rose, Mick and Keith's assistant, had a copy of the contract in her hand, and Mick wanted to know why I hadn't signed it, and what the problem was, and I told him I hadn't even seen a copy.

"Well, here it is, sign it at the bottom. This has taken too long already." He was either in a grumpy mood, or it was all an act. I think it was bullshit, and as Howlin' Wolf said once, "There's only one thing worse than bullshit, and that's crab shit, because the crabs get deep down into the bullshit, and that's where they shit!"

Jane handed me the papers, and after looking at them briefly I said I'd sign it after my lawyer had looked it over. Mick wasn't pleased, as he had apparently assumed I'd sign it without even reading it. I was insulted, and he was angry, and like a petulant child, he pouted and said:

"Oh, you're not going to be like Billy, and hold us to ransom, are you?"

This was the second time I'd been compared to Billy Preston, but neither had anything to do with music. Freddie Sessler explained later that The Stones had finished the 1975 tour before Billy Preston had signed a contract, so when the live album, *Love You Live,* came out with him on every track, he was in a position to bargain and eventually got a percentage of it. Mick was really pissed off with me, and though he and Jane bitched about it, I wouldn't sign it, and instead, sent it to Barry Rothman, who was Woody's lawyer in Los Angeles.

When we arrived in Los Angeles three days later, Barry came to my room at the Westwood Marquis, where I made it crystal clear that because of what had happened with Billy, all I wanted to do was understand it, sign it, and get on with the tour, because things were getting too tense between me and Mick, and I had no wish to aggravate matters. Rothman said he thought there might be a way to get royalties out of it, but I told him straight to his face, "No! Read it, explain what it says, get it back to me, and I'll sign it!"

He said he would, but I didn't hear from him again until we got to Oakland Coliseum on July 26, which was the final gig of the tour, and also Mick's thirty-fifth birthday. Joe Rascoff, The Stones' accountant, Barry, and I had a meeting in a trailer backstage. Barry began talking about them giving me the right to, at some time in the future, without prejudice, discussing the possibility of a percentage, should any footage or recordings be made, licensed or used in any form whatsoever, blah blah blah...

I was dumbfounded. He hadn't listened to a word I'd said. He was on his own agenda, and I was really pissed off! He'd be sending me a bill for this crap too. It was really annoying. I had no choice now. I'd already lost face, but I turned to Joe and asked him if he had the original contract with him. He said he did, and I told him I'd sign it there and then. Apologizing for the bullshit, I signed the same contract that Mick had asked me to in Dallas. Rothman still hadn't explained it to me, but I poured myself a drink, wished Mick a happy birthday, and went on and played the final show of the tour.

After that show in Oakland, Keith asked me if I'd stay on for a short break in Los Angeles, because they wanted to record at RCA Studios while the band was still hot from the road. Keith, Woody, and Jo had rented a house owned by one of the Getty family, just above Sunset Boulevard on the "Strip," so Chuch came over to the Westwood Marquis to help me move out of the hotel and into their place. It was more like a movie set than a home. Perched above the heart of Hollywood, the main room of the house had a large swimming pool at one end surrounded by trees and plants with a footbridge across it and an electric sliding roof above. There was a massive fireplace in the centre of the room, a pool table to one side, and a huge projection TV on the other. There were sofas in front of the fireplace, a dining table to one side, and a wall of glass doors giving a perfect view of smoggy Hollywood. My new home, at least for now.

CHAPTER TWENTY-SEVEN

Ratchet Man

Keith Richards had a thing for deadly weapons, and he always carried a couple of Jamaican "ratchet" knives with him. A crudely made flick knife with a wooden handle and a steel blade, it's got a steel key ring attached to one end of a brass plate that encases the handle. You slide your index finger into the ring and pull it back, at the same time putting pressure on the side of the plate with your thumb and middle finger, which loosens the blade. As you flick the blade open, you let go of the ring and the ratchet action locks it open. You need a supple wrist action and coordination to get it open, and it wouldn't be hard to lose a finger as you put the blade away. Whichever end of it you are at, it's a very dangerous knife. Especially once Keith had filed the mechanism down. Then the blade release worked so smoothly, it almost slipped out without help. He'd pull both of these lethal weapons on you at the same time, drawing them from the hip like Jimmy Cliff did in the film *The Harder They Come*. He could have been deadly, but never was.

With Keith it was more what he might do than what he actually did, though I did see him punch some fool in the jaw as we were walking out of Club 54 in New York just for bothering him. After several nights spent practicing with one of his knives, and after I'd proved to him that I could not only handle a ratchet but treat it with respect, he gave one of them to me, which I treasured until the night his went missing. It didn't seem fair for me to have one when he didn't, so I gave it back to him.

Keith had a similar fascination for guns. Although he kept them hidden from view, as a foreigner, not to mention a drug offender, he couldn't legally own or carry a gun. And yet in those days there was always a .38 special in a holster, wrapped in a coloured neckerchief and tucked into a crease of the sofa beside him, where it was within easy reach. And it wasn't for show. It was always loaded. Considering he was stoned most of the time, it's amazing that he never killed or wounded anyone, and on the three tours I did with him, I only saw him fire a gun once.

I cooked a traditional English-style breakfast for all of us one sunny after-noon, and because I was the chef of the moment I was the last to sit down to eat. I've always been a slow eater anyway, and Keith was impatiently waiting to have a line, and had laid out blow on the table and passed the straw around until it was my turn.

"Come on, have some coke…"

"I haven't finished my breakfast yet," I said, and with that he emptied the bottle over my beautifully prepared and only half-eaten eggs and bacon. What a swine, I'd gone to great lengths to cook for everyone there, and I'd been really enjoying my breakfast, but you couldn't stay pissed off long with Keith. He laughed so hard I had to see the funny side, and anyway I was just as eager to get high as he was, and my appetite soon disappeared.

One evening, Mick came to the house in a very agreeable mood. It was business as usual, Bobby Keys was chatting with Keith and Woody over by the settee, and George Dekker's "Time Hard" was booming loud and bassy on the stereo with the chorus, "Everyday, things are getting worse," repeating over and over. Mick opened a bottle of beer and asked if I fancied a game of pool. Mick rarely turned his charm on me, but when he did I was keen to listen, because he could be extremely entertaining, and you never knew, you might learn something.

We potted balls for a while, and then he suggested we change the rules. It didn't make any difference to me as long as they were the same for both of us, and it was only in fun, so we got another couple of beers and began to play. He got quite drunk, quite soon, and because he kept changing the rules, it became harder to follow. He turned to me very seriously for a moment and said:

"Well, how much do you want for these sessions coming up?" His eyes were all over the place and he was wobbling, hanging on to the cue.

"$15,000," I said quietly. There was silence for a moment as he cued-up the next shot, then he looked round at me squinting.

"$50,000? I'm not payin' you anymore than $20,000, and that's final."

Now I could've taken advantage, but I had a price worked out. I figured that $1,000 a day wasn't too much to ask, but $15,000 was a better number than $14,000. Plus, as I knew from past experience, we'd go all night for nights on end if things were going well, so there was no limit on the time, only the money.

"No, Mick. $15,000. Fifteen." I stressed it.

"Oh, yeah, okay, fine." He laughed and we shook hands on it, but by then his interest in the game had dwindled, and he called a cab and left.

Earl McGrath ran Rolling Stones Records then, and he came up to the house the next afternoon, all smiles and congeniality. "Mac, we have to sort your money out for these sessions." I told him I'd discussed it with Mick the previous night and that we'd agreed on $15,000 for the two weeks.

"Mick remembers nothing," he said. "And I know he won't pay you anymore than $14,000."

"Earl," I said. "It's a reasonable price, especially since he already offered me $20,000, and I turned him down." There was some moaning about the fact that $15,000 didn't divide equally into fourteen days, but I didn't give way, and he left with a smile saying he'd draw up the contract and get back to me.

The next day Jane Rose came to the house and handed me a pile of papers. "Mac, sign this, okay?" she said as if butter wouldn't melt in her mouth.

"Let me read it," I said.

"Trust me, you don't have to read it. Just sign it. It's a standard contract." And with that, she dismissed me and walked off.

"Trust me" and "Just sign it" are two phrases that should never be used in the same sentence, and what the hell is a "standard contract" anyway? I smelled a rat, and when I read it, the contract was for $14,000. So after all the bullshit, and with all their money, they were trying it on for $71.42 a day, just a dollar chasing a dime. Well, I dug my heels in, and the contract had to be rewritten, which probably cost them more money than I was asking. The sessions went into the third week eventually, but I never discussed business or played pool with Mick again.

I started thinking about the money that I was piling up in the States. What with the tour money I already had in the bank, and the recording money I was just about to earn, I had a small nest egg which I couldn't have earned in England. I wondered what Kim and Mandy would think about us moving to America. There was hardly any work at home, where everyone still seemed to be blinded by the punk scene, and as Woody and Jo had already bought a house in Mandeville Canyon, and he would be starting his third album soon, I figured I might as well be where the music was happening. Luckily, Kim was as keen as I was to make the big move. The only problem she could see was Keith, because although he showed no interest in keeping in touch with Mandy, if he'd wanted to be bloody-minded, he could stop us taking her out of the country. Kim decided she would talk to him soon, then we could make plans for our future.

RCA Studios on Sunset Boulevard in Hollywood was where Elvis cut *G. I. Blues* in 1960. This was all lost on Stephen Stills, though, who was doing his best to gate-crash The Stones' session before it had properly begun. Even after JC had told him to fuck off, he'd set himself up in the toilet outside the main room, thinking that even The Stones would have to take a pee eventually. Keith found a door that led into an alley, so he avoided the confrontation by peeing against the outside wall whenever he felt the urge. Stills was so desperate to come in and jam, he wrote Keith a poem and slipped it under the studio door, but Keith just spat on it and threw it in the trash. As the studio was block-booked for two weeks, all the equipment was set up and left in place, with Chuch's private office made of flight cases and baffles in a corner of the vast room, so he could tune guitars in peace. Stu had set up Charlie's drums in the middle of the room facing the control room window, with Keith and Woody's amps on either side. Bill's amp was on the left, and the grand piano, Wurlitzer electric piano, and Hammond organ were all together on his right, near the control room window.

Most days, Jim Keltner sat behind Charlie as he played, peering over his glasses, watching everything like a wise owl. He and Charlie were old pals, and it showed the respect they had for each other, and the friendship they have. Stu would play or hang out, depending on the song, but mostly he'd be there waiting for the right moment, or for the track to come together. Bill and he were not night people, so it was especially tough on them.

The session might start at 6 P.M. or 8 P.M. and it could be midnight before things got really rolling. Between takes, Stu would nod off, his head resting on his forearms on the lid of the piano, but as soon as Keith started playing, he'd yawn, ease back on the stool, and tickle the ivories as if there had been no break at all. Charlie was more resigned to whatever the hours were. He'd hang in until the last note, giving a resigned "Stu" face across the studio with a smile, as if to say, "Bloody guitarists, they don't know when to stop."

Mick was resilient, but he'd only go so far. He'd see the session flagging and wouldn't waste any time hanging around. He had to think of his voice. And that's not to say he wouldn't go all night, but it would have to be good enough to warrant him staying. As for me, as long as there was music and chemicals, I was in for the long haul, and anyway someone had to keep Keith and Woody company. We cut a lot of material over the time we were in there, but none of the recordings were used to my knowledge. Most of the songs were in pretty basic shape at that time, but "Where The Boys All Go" and "Summer Romance" were eventually re-recorded for the *Emotional Rescue* album. My feeling is that Keith just wanted to keep the tour rolling a little longer.

Woody's new manager, Jason Cooper, and I talked in general terms about him getting me a record deal, and I was excited about the prospect until Keith heard about it, and warned me to stay clear. He didn't trust any manager, but especially one who had carved Woody such a great deal out of The Stones as he had. One day, we were sunning ourselves on the deck, when Keith announced that he'd be my manager. Putting on a joke pair of shades that had a knob and bollocks for a false nose, he said, "When I'm wearing the knob and bollocks, I'm your manager, and you've got to listen to meee!"

One afternoon after breakfast at the Getty Hotel, Keith brought out a stash of Iranian opium and, after poking around, found an ice pick in the kitchen drawer. He cut off a chunk of the opium, cooked it on the gas ring, and inhaled the smoke through the cardboard tube of a toilet roll and passed it on. Woody, Bobby, and I took turns and then while he was having a last hit, Keith let the ice pick slip from his fingers and it dropped and stuck in his bare foot. I saw it land. It must've gone in about half an inch. There was a short silence followed by a scream, and then he pulled it out. It could have been a lot worse than it was, but because the ice pick was red hot it cauterized the wound immediately, and when a dose of painkillers started to take effect, we drove to the studio.

Keith had a pretty song he wanted to do that day called "I'll Let You Know," and though he was limping and feeling more and more pain, we cut a good track with him, Charlie, Woody on bass, and me on the Wurly.

Woody overdubbed a pedal steel on it and I added a B3, but as the day wore on his foot got very sore and swollen, so Keith took a couple of serious painkillers. When it came time to sing a guide vocal, he sat on the high chair in front of the control room window with the microphone set up in front of him and fell fast asleep. It was a crying shame. He'd been singing the words all day, but when he woke up he couldn't remember them at all. It's still a lovely track, very poignant. It turned up a few years ago on a bootleg cassette, and it sounded really fine, but it's a shame we'll never hear the melody or the vocal he had planned.

Smoking opium was a new phase for me, and I really liked it. One afternoon, I asked Keith if he had any left. He said, "Yeah, but we're taking a break from it. You're getting to like it too much." He could see the sparkle I had in my eye for it, and he knew I was liking the stuff too much to continue. While he ain't no saint, he ain't the devil either.

CHAPTER TWENTY-EIGHT
Premonition

While I was spending days and nights at RCA in Los Angeles, Kim was working in the beauty salon at Harrods in Knightsbridge. One night she had a vivid dream that she'd bumped into Keith Moon in an art gallery in Africa, and the next moment she was back home, and Ray Cole, my roadie, rang her and told her that Keith was dead. She told him it wasn't possible, as she'd just seen him. When she woke up she was in a terrible state, and the dream bothered her all morning. She told it to her friend Penny, who tried to cheer her up by saying that although it was terrible, if it was to happen, at least she wouldn't have to worry about getting Keith's permission to take Mandy to the States. A week later, on September 7, 1978, just as in the dream, Ray Cole telephoned her and told her that Keith had died during the night. She was devastated and horrified that her premonition had come true. Apparently, he'd been taking a prescription drug to help him stop drinking, but he took too many of the pills and carried on drinking, which caused a fatal reaction.

When I heard the news a few hours later, I called her immediately in case she'd heard it from someone else. But by then it was too late, the press had already camped out on our doorstep. She was effectively trapped in the house. She cried, and though she wasn't surprised that it had finally happened, the shock of the news, and the dream still fresh in her mind, had left her feeling very low. I don't think she'd ever stopped loving Keith. They'd been childhood sweethearts after all, but she couldn't live with him. He was impossible. I realized then I'd been in Los Angeles far too long. I'd been drifting downstream and I needed to get back home to Kim and Mandy.

The recording sessions had already wound down, so I packed my bags, had a last drink with Woody, Jo, and Keith, and hopped on a plane to London early the next day.

As the cab pulled up across the busy street from the house on West Hill, I was struck by a very attractive blonde wearing a black corduroy number, scurrying down the street towards a waiting cab.

It was Kim, of course. I asked my cabbie to hang on while I ran after her. "Kim, wait!" I shouted, but she thought I was another journalist with a deadline, so she ran even faster. "It's me! Kim, hold on. It's Mac!"

As she climbed into the cab, she turned her head and saw it was me, smiled and let out a sigh of relief. I ran up and gave her a rib-crunching hug, and we kissed again and again. This was what she needed, and it was the welcome home I needed too, but she was exhausted, poor love. She looked as if she hadn't had a good sleep in weeks. Apart from grieving over Keith, she'd had a bad case of measles while I'd been away and as a result had lost ten pounds in a week. All that and having to deal with the pesky reporters as well, it was a wonder she looked as good as she did. As she was already late for Keith's funeral, I told her I'd catch up with her afterwards, if she'd call me and tell me where I had to go.

It was the only wake I'd ever been to and it was a real celebration, which was as it should have been, being Keith's. His mum, Kit, was kissed, hugged, and cuddled by everyone there, and in spite of her grief was able to have a good laugh sharing her memories of Keith as a little boy. His sisters, Linda and Leslie, were tearful too, but after a glass or two they loosened up, and we all had a laugh between sobs. Pete Townshend, Roger Daltrey, and John Entwistle, the surviving Who members, mingled and commiserated with Kit, while I said hello to their ex-manager Kit Lambert, who I hadn't seen for ages. I'd first met him when The Muleskinners opened for The Who at the Club Noreik back in 1964, when as we talked, I realized he was slowly rotating around me, even as I tried to turn and face him. I think he was trying to look at my bum! There was no other explanation for it, unless he had one leg shorter than the other. But this time we chatted without spinning. I spotted Charlie and Bill in a huddle in the bar. As I approached them Charlie screwed his face into a mocking sneer, pointing his finger at me.

"Who invited you?"

"Blimey, what are you doing here?" Bill said sarcastically. "I thought you were still in the studio with Keith and Woody!" He knew how hard it was for me to drag myself away. It was a good mix of family and friends. Every now and then there'd be a roar of laughter as somebody remembered something outrageous Keith said or did. I think he would have liked it, except maybe for the fact nothing got broken, no one took their clothes off, and no one had half as much to drink or half as much fun as he, had he been there. God Bless him, there'll never be another Keith Moon.

I loved Kim more than anybody or anything in the world, but from 1973 to 1978 we never used the "L" word when describing our feelings to each other. We'd both been let down before, so from very early on when she told me she couldn't conceive of "falling in love" or being "in love," I didn't argue. I just avoided the word, hoping that over time she'd change her mind. We never mentioned the "M" word either, but that was fine with me. Marriage was definitely not on the cards; I'd sooner chew razor blades.

Having decided to move to the States, and to Los Angeles in particular, Keith's management had asked Kim if we'd like to move into Keith's beach house in Malibu, as it would eventually become Mandy's property, once Keith's estate was sorted out. Since it was sitting there empty, and we had nowhere to stay until we found a place of our own, we quickly agreed. It couldn't have been more convenient. The only possible stumbling block was that we didn't have visas or Green Cards, although I was told that as a musician with "special talents," I could get a Green Card without too much fuss. Kim and Mandy's situation might cause problems, but Jason Cooper had the solution in mind.

"You and Kim are so great together," he said. "Why don't you get married? You know you're gonna stay together anyway, and then she'll automatically get her Green Card by being your wife. It's simple. Come on, there's really nothing else you can do. What's she gonna say? No?"

With that in mind, and with my fingers crossed, I proposed marriage. Not in the more accepted, romantic way of kneeling and telling her I loved her, but by offering her a Green Card. Luckily for me, she said "yes" and by the time we actually got married, we could admit that we had loved each other all along. Well, it was about time. I had to fly to New York to play three songs on the NBC-TV show "Saturday Night Live" with The Stones on October 7, so we set the date for October 9, the following Monday. Perfect! We stayed at The Plaza on Central Park and rehearsed all week, sometimes going into the very early hours. It wasn't that we needed to rehearse, but the show's top stars John Belushi, Dan Aykroyd, and Bill Murray liked to party, and nobody wanted to be the first to call it a night. John and Dan took us to the bar they'd just bought, and we spent the whole night in there. Dan even rode his Harley straight through the doors and parked it in the middle of the bar. It was a great week, all in all, and it was even quite a laugh doing the show. But it was very exhausting work, raving every night. Beds were seen, but rarely used.

There was a Beatles sketch in the show, and while Bill Murray had a good "Liverpool" accent going for him, his "John Lennon" needed a bit of fine tuning, and before I knew it I was helping him with my Lennon impersonation. By showtime, Mick had almost sung himself hoarse, so we played "Beast of Burden" a couple of keys lower, in D. But his voice was still rough. The show went out live, of course, and it was a bit ragged, but it's been replayed many times, so someone likes it.

There's a great moment where Mick put his tongue in Woody's mouth during "Shattered." Yeugh! But that's good live television and that's one of the reasons people want to see Mick perform. The next afternoon, Charlie, Bill, Stu, and I flew home on the Concorde and in great style, and drank to our happy days ahead.

CHAPTER TWENTY-NINE

The New Barbarians

It was Monday, October 9, 1978, and back in London, the house on West Hill was humming with activity. Penny was helping Kim with her hair and her dress upstairs, as Mandy was organizing buttonholes. I was standing in the kitchen in a daze and in the way. I was trying to get a spot of breakfast inside me, but the crazy week in New York was catching up on me. Wandsworth is famous for two things, the prison from which Ronald Biggs, the Great Train Robber, escaped and Young's brewery, not to mention the wonderful pubs that are all over the town.

As we weren't on the run from the law, the chaps went for a quiet couple of pints at The Star, and let the girls get on with the preparations. The civil ceremony at Wandsworth Town Hall was short and to the point. After a lot of kissing, cuddling, and smiling for the press, we drove to Froggies, our favourite French restaurant, for the reception, where the owner Jean-Michel, a good friend, had prepared his upstairs suite for the afternoon. The restaurant was also a favourite of Jacques Tati's, and we had an ongoing deal that any time Jacques came into the restaurant, Michel would call me so I could observe him from a distance. Sadly, the famous French movie star and director of *Monsieur Hulot* fame died soon after, so I never had that pleasure. We began at three o'clock when the restaurant closed, and Michel said as long as we were out of there by six o'clock, when his evening customers would start to arrive, everything would be fine. He'd prepared a piano-shaped sugar cake specially for the occasion, and what an occasion!

My mum and dad, and Joan, Kim's mum, were there, and Bill, Kim's dad, sent us a telegram from Zimbabwe, as he couldn't leave the tea estate at that time of year. Dermot couldn't make it because the headmaster of his boarding school in Bournemouth wouldn't let him out for the day, but Stu and his wife Cynthia, DJ Annie Nightingale, an old friend, and Dave Sprecher, my pal and solicitor, came. Dave took great pictures of the whole shebang. It was how I'd imagine a typical French wedding reception would be, not just because of the fabulous food, champagne, and wines, but because it all got very silly, very quickly. I'd made several cassettes with a mixture of soul, blues, rock 'n' roll, and reggae, and one cassette ended with a short sketch by Peter Cook and Dudley Moore's "Derek and Clive," which was on the deck when Mum asked me if she could have the first dance.

"I'd love to, my darling," I said, forgetting the tape would end with "Hello, Colin," a one-sided phone conversation. The short piece ends with Dudley saying something like, "Yeah, see you. Ta ta…" He hangs up the phone and then says quietly, "…cunt."

Mum's face dropped. She stopped dancing and then, deciding she couldn't possibly have heard it, carried on as if nothing had happened. It was quite a small room, and with just a smattering of friends and relations. As the champagne flowed, so did the conversation. Dad was flirting with Penny and Bubbles, while Mum was chatting to Joan. After I'd finished eating, I went downstairs to the gent's for a line of coke, and came back upstairs and handed the packet to Kim so she could have a celebratory snort. I asked Ray Cole to mash it up for her, so they went down together. It must've looked very odd when, some minutes later, my dad opened the gent's toilet door and Ray and his new daughter-in-law came out together. Nothing was said, but I can't help wondering what he thought.

Mum and Dad weren't drinkers and Mum was too excited to eat very much. The glass of champagne must have gone straight to her head, because she dozed off in a chair by the table as the conversation and the music flowed. When she woke up, she threw up! She didn't run for the bathroom, she just turned and retched behind the table next to her chair. I was amazed, and there were a few sniggers from us younger chaps, but I cleaned it up, and we carried on regardless. Again, it hadn't happened. It was a great do, good food, wine, drugs, vomit, and a good laugh, an unusual cocktail. In the end, we were having such a good time and got so blitzed we didn't leave until 1 A.M., but by then Michel wasn't bothered either.

That night, back at the house, Kim and I had the mother and father of an argument. I don't remember what it was about now, but everything between

Mr. and Mrs. Mac was fine again in the morning. There was no time to relax or think anyway, because we had to pack everything and sell the house, which went quickly, as it was a bargain. A month later, with all our belongings packed and long gone, we closed the door behind us, and took a cab to Heathrow Airport, where we stayed for our last night in Blighty, and where Stu came to see us off with a very civilized couple of bottles of Beaujolais.

The next morning, I had a swine of a hangover and a sinking feeling about moving to Los Angeles. When The Faces had first played there, I found the place depressing, because everything looked so perfect—on the surface—and the record company people were as manicured as the Beverly Hills lawns. But I got over it, and my bad mood subsided quickly, as Kim and Mandy's excitement rubbed off on me. We raised a glass of champagne as we climbed above the clouds over Hounslow. We were bound for new adventures in the New World.

The immigration officer at LAX looked at me oddly when I explained that the reason we'd brought the large aluminum trunk full of bedding was because there wouldn't be any at the house we were renting. I could hardly tell him we were emigrating, that our two dogs would be arriving in a few days, and that we didn't have work permits or Green Cards. He let us in anyway, and John Wolfe's familiar face and bald head was waiting for us in the baggage terminal. He gave us the keys to the house, and another set of keys to a rented station wagon for the drive from the airport. I wasn't expecting to drive, and Kim and I had spent most of the flight trying to drink Pan-Am out of alcoholic beverages.

John led the way, and Kim, Mandy, the luggage, and I followed in the wagon. He must have been late for a date, because he drove unreasonably fast along the twisty Pacific Coast Highway in the dark and Mandy kept sliding cross the front seat as Kim desperately held on to the aluminum trunk drifting around in the back. I had to try and keep up with him, but I was having the devil of a time driving on the wrong side of the road and was more than a little drunk. We arrived at the house that had once been Keith Moon's home, unloaded the luggage, and drove to the only restaurant close by for a bite to eat, where the three of us dozed off before our meals arrived. The next day, I woke up to the sound of waves hitting the beach and sunshine streaming through the shutters; it seemed like Paradise compared to England.

The house on Broad Beach had been constructed on the side of a cliff and looked like it had been built upside down. The garage was on the ground floor and the front door was accessed by a flight of steps down to one side, which led down even more steps into the two-storey living room. The main bedrooms were below that, and at high tide the waves of the Pacific Ocean lapped at the supporting concrete pillars. This strange building was designed by someone with a sense of humour, or someone whose idea of fun was to have raw sewage occasionally fill the bathtubs. And no matter how hard we tried, in the eighteen months we lived there we never managed to completely rid the place of fleas. Some Paradise!

There was a pool table in the garage and an upright piano in the corner, which was terribly out of tune, but had a lovely feel. I learned later it had once belonged to Richard Manuel of The Band. Fifteen years and five moves after the big move to Malibu, so much dust had built up inside the piano that clouds formed every time I played. I'd taken the lid and front panels off and put a vacuum cleaner nozzle down inside, when I heard something rattling. I felt around and pulled out a glass vial half full of a white powdery substance. I thought I knew what I'd found. Though I'd stopped doing cocaine some years before, I didn't think about it too long, in case I weakened, so I flushed it down the toilet.

It was unlikely to have been Keith Moon's because he wasn't one to stash drugs away. I remember Woody giving him a gram of coke one day, as he was getting ready to go and tape a radio show. Keith laughed, opened the packet, and rubbed it all over his face, snorting like a pig and screaming with mirth. No, it was unlikely to have been Keith's. I had to presume it belonged to Richard Manuel. I can imagine him spending a night with Keith and hiding it before he went home, thinking it would be waiting for him when he came back. Sadly, Richard's gone too now, but whenever I play one of those Band songs on that piano, I think of him and wonder.

Our neighbours on both sides were nice people, although Steve McQueen wasn't the most welcoming person in the world, and since Keith's short stay at the house had been so traumatic for him, he wasn't in any hurry to meet another British musician. Keith would be near the top of a list of neighbours in your worst nightmare, along with Atilla the Hun, Saddam Hussein, and Adolf Hitler. Apparently, Keith rode a motorcycle through the adjoining fence into his yard once, reenacting Steve's stunt in *The Great Escape,* and on other occasions, he wandered in, naked, drunk, and uninvited. As a result, if we ever saw Steve in the street, he'd throw a careful smile at Kim as she drove by, but would squint at me as if I was Keith's reincarnation. He died of cancer within a year of our arrival, and sadly I never got the chance to say to him, "Hello, Steve, I'm Mac. I loved *Bullit*. It was a brilliant film. Fancy a drink?"

Thanks a lot, Keith.

The day after we arrived, Woody called me to play on his third solo album, *Gimme Some Neck,* and I was more than happy to get straight to work. He'd cut all the tracks previously, and all I had to do was overdub pianos and organs at Cherokee Studios. Nothing changes with Woody, which is how it should be with a good friend. As I popped my head round the door, I heard: "Aaaaaaaye, Mac!" Then, "Hey, Geoff, play Mac that last track. Wait 'til you here this one. How's Kim, all right? And Mandy? 'Ere, fancy some of this? What would you like to drink?" I was straight in the deep end, and here we'd go again.

As I say, nothing changes with Woody. By the time the album was ready to be released, he and Keith were looking for an excuse to play live, but as there was no Stones tour in the offing they put a touring band together for fun and profit. Neil Young showed some interest and even suggested The Barbarians as the name for the group, which they had to change to The New Barbarians when we found there was already a band with that name. Neil got tired sitting around waiting for them to get it organized, so he bailed out. Then Boz Scaggs came and sat in for a day, which was fun, but he didn't hang around either. Apart from Bobby Keys and me, they roped in Zigaboo Modeliste from The

Meters on drums and Stanley Clarke on the bass. It seemed like an unlikely mix for a rock 'n' roll band, but as it turned out, it worked very well.

I'd been working on some new songs and Jason Cooper said he would represent me as well as Woody if I was really serious about wanting to make a record. He was a jovial, ginger-bearded giant of a man, an ex-footballer who liked to be called "Moke." I liked him and believed in him, but was especially excited when he said if things went well he could get me a record deal by the end of the tour.

We rehearsed in Keith and Woody's usual shambolic fashion. I'd meet them at Woody's house in Mandeville Canyon. After tasting a new cocktail or a beer Woody had just discovered, and Keith playing me a blues gem he'd found, we'd make our way to the rehearsal studio. Hours after the arranged start time, we'd arrive, chat, do a couple of lines, laugh, play, smoke a joint, sip a drink, do another line, and play another song until Keith had had enough or we'd run out of blow, which was late or never. Days became nights, and after some weeks we flew to Toronto in a hired BAC 1-11 for the first gig.

Keith had been busted in Toronto early in 1977 for possession of heroin, and in October 1978 the court sentenced him to play two shows for charity, which meant the opening gig of The New Barbarians tour was actually punishment! They'd hoped The Stones would perform, and even though they weren't touring at that time they agreed to put in an appearance, so it quickly became the most sought-after ticket around town, especially as they weren't supposed to be on sale in the first place.

When we flew in from L.A. on April 22, 1979, the customs people in Toronto were really easy on us, as if none of us had any previous convictions. But there was nothing to worry about, as Keith wasn't carrying any drugs. They were already waiting for him at the hotel. When Mick, Charlie, and Bill arrived from England, they picked on Bill, of all people, and went through him like a dose of salts. They frisked the only person in the whole outfit who'd never taken a drug in his life.

The concert was a benefit for the blind and took place about thirty miles outside of Toronto, in Oshawa. Poor Bill wasn't having a great day. Somebody bumped into him backstage, and without looking or thinking, he said, "Why don't you watch where you're going. What are you, blind or something?" He was. Backstage, the atmosphere was very light considering The Stones were un-rehearsed and The New Barbarians had never done a gig before. John Belushi was hanging out and getting high, and it was a blur of laughter and conversa-tion which felt like the start of a new term at school, because everyone was catching up on the latest news and gossip. In time, there was nothing left to do but play. The hall was packed to the rafters, and Belushi whipped the crowd into a frenzy as he introduced us to the audience, one by one. Then he shouted, "Come on up here!...Keith Richards and Ron Wood!...Lead singers!...The New Barbarians!...GO NUTS!"

And they did. Woody and Keith brought in "Sweet Little Rock 'n' Roller" and we rocked. After our set, Zig and Stanley left the stage, while Stu and Chuch moved the amps around and rearranged the drums. Belushi introduced Charlie, Bill, and Mick, and the crowd went nuts all over again. It was a very loose, bluesy show, and Mick and Keith even played "Prodigal Son" as a duet.

When the show was over we took a break, and then played both shows over again. Everybody was knackered at the end of the day, especially Keith, Woody, Bobby, and me, because we'd played four shows in one night. It was more like The Star Club, Hamburg, 1963, than Oshawa 1979.

It was a charity gig so there was no payment, but we were given a specially printed red T-shirt as a memento. But we got a shock the next day when Keith's immigration lawyer handed Woody and me a bill for $25,000 for arranging our visas for the trip. This was a journey we wouldn't have had to make if we hadn't wanted to support Keith, and the lawyer seriously expected us to pay up.

Ted Newman-Jones is a guitar maker from Austin who I know through Keith because he always catches up with The Stones' tours as they travel through Texas. I was celebrating my thirty-fourth birthday that day in Houston with a bottle of Jack Daniels, and we were drinking and chatting, while I was applying black shoe dye to a pair of shoes on the floor. My drink and the bottle of dye were both in front of me, and I'd sip, then dip the applicator in the bottle, paint some more, and then have another sip. I was too busy nattering to concentrate on what I was doing. I picked up the bottle of dye, put it to my lips, took a healthy swig and saw Ted looking at me in horror. "Jesus, Mac! Don't drink it!"

I realized what I'd done and ran to the bathroom as fast as my legs would carry me, spitting it all out before I swallowed. Thank God Ted was there! Mind you, if he hadn't been there I probably wouldn't have been so distracted. But he did save my life. Thanks, Ted.

When we got to Chicago, my new manager, "Moke," took me to Mercury Records' office to meet Bob Sherwood, then president of the company. Moke knew him from CBS, but this was my first meeting, and I was knocked out to find he was a music fan, a rarity in some record company offices, and I liked him straight off the bat. The deal was pretty much set up, but he wanted to meet me and hear a couple of finished tunes. Moke convinced him to front me the studio costs so I could record a couple of songs, and it didn't hurt for him to know that Woody would play on them too.

But I couldn't hang around waiting for the money to come through, because I wanted to get The New Barbarians on a track before the tour finished. I'd heard a reggae song called "Truly" on the radio before I left London that blew my mind. "Truly" was by The Cimarons and I found the song on a green vinyl album in a record store in Wandsworth. It was a very simple tune with a loping, reggae groove to it, which was right up Keith's street too. He and Woody had liked it when I first played it for them, and as we'd all been saying it was a shame the tour was almost over I thought this might be a way for us to get to play a little more and for me to get a track out of it for my record at the same time.

I was cautious about asking Keith to do it, because he rarely recorded with anybody other than The Stones, and I dreaded him saying "no." But Bobby urged me to ask him because he thought he might go for it, and when I finally plucked up the courage, I was surprised by his enthusiasm. After he was aboard, Woody, Stanley, and Zig quickly said yes, too. Harold Grennell, my other next door neighbour on Broad Beach, happened to be part owner of a studio at Zuma Beach called Shangri-La, and he'd told me he'd give me a deal on his studio if I ever wanted to record locally. I was half set on using Cherokee for the record, but I went to have a look at the place with Rob Fraboni, who was one of his partners, and the house engineer and producer. The studio was fine, but more important to me the Steinway grand piano they had was bright and clangy, with a fast action. It had also been owned by Richard Manuel at one time. We had a two-day break in L.A. coming up, so I handed them one thousand dollars in cash and booked the studio for a whole day and a night to be sure I could finish the song. I was beginning to get a little dizzy, as it was the first time I'd ever booked a studio.

The New Barbarian's sound engineer, Buford T. Jones, offered to engineer the session, and Chuch, Gary Schultz, and Johnny Starbucks, our crew, set up the equipment and organized the booze. Keith and Woody surprised me by arriving early. They were rested, rehearsed, and ready to go, God Bless 'em. Zigaboo was late, which was a problem because I'd figured it might take a couple of hours to get a drum sound, but Woody jumped at the chance of playing drums. If Zig hadn't turned up we'd still have had a decent track, because Woody can play a fair old reggae groove.

Chuch, Gary, and Johnny found some gold-lamé, Parliament Funkadelic-style band uniforms in a back room, and set the tone of the session by wearing them all day. Everyone was feeling good and relaxed, but in case it got too loose, Keith said, "Come on, Mac, crack that whip. Tell us what to do, it's your session. You're the boss."

He was right. He knew I wasn't used to taking command, and was letting me know it was down to me to start, or it would just develop into a stoned jam. Zig arrived apologizing, and Woody got out from behind the drums, plugged his guitar in, and before you knew it we were cutting. We only ran it through for a couple of minutes before we were ready for a take. I took the intro on the piano and then everybody fell in after that. After we'd played the song through, we grooved on at the end, and eventually the headphones went dead when the tape ran out. Twelve minutes long, the basic track was done in the first take! I was over the moon with excitement, and the track sounded as good in the control room as it did in the studio.

Keith bubbling on guitar, Woody jabbing and sliding, Stanley swooping up and down the neck of the bass, Zig putting fills in the most unexpected places, and me thumping away like a good'un…It was lots of fun, and I could have listened to the playback all night.

But we still had a lot of work to do. Keith put another guitar on, and then he and I sang the harmonies on the choruses. Bobby and his brother Daryll, also on tenor, overdubbed their parts and honked all the way home. We tried to get decent takes of a couple of other tunes, but when they didn't fall into place like "Truly," we called it a night.

A few days after the tour was finished, Keith invited all the band members, wives, and girlfriends to a dinner in Beverly Hills. He had his own plan to hatch. After we'd eaten, he asked if any of us wanted to jam, and naturally we were all keen. The crafty bugger had booked the main studio at RCA on Sunset, and we went in for the rest of the night and cut four tracks, one for each member of the band except me, because I already had my track. Lowell George walked in off the street in an old boiler suit looking sadly overweight. But he played beautiful slide guitar, as Zig sang a soulful version of The Stones' "Fingerprint File."

The New Barbarians tour had been fun. Some people who saw us thought it was a bit of a shambles, and others have said they saw a fantastic show. The only problem we had was in Milwaukee, where word got around that Mick Jagger or Bob Dylan would be appearing. They weren't scheduled to appear, and we knew nothing about it until the audience got restless and some idiots began throwing chairs and causing damage. We were ordered to return and play another gig, but Keith wouldn't do it. He figured either Moke or the promoter had leaked the information to increase ticket sales, so he was happy to let them sort it out. The following year, when Woody took me and another band to Milwaukee to pay for the damage, it would be fair to say the New Barbarians tour began and ended by repaying debts to society.

CHAPTER THIRTY

The First One's Free

Now that The New Barbarians' 1979 tour was over and Moke had got Bob Sherwood from Mercury to cough up some dosh for studio time, I set about putting a band together. I'd always loved Jim Keltner's playing on John Lennon's records, and I'd met him a few times when I'd been with The Stones in L.A. I invited him over to the house and played him a tape I'd made up of tracks that had unusual drum patterns or interesting drum sounds or feels. He liked them and suggested Paul Stallworth play bass. Though I didn't know Jim well, I trusted his judgment on picking the right bass player.

Woody had recently bought one of Plas Johnson's old tenor saxes in a pawn shop, and Bobby had been showing him the basics. He practiced every day and was an incredibly quick learner. So, with Jim and Paul as the rhythm section, Woody on guitar, me on keyboards, the horn section of Steve Madaio from Stevie Wonder's band on trumpet, and Bobby Keys and Woody on tenor saxes, we were all set. Geoff Workman, who'd worked on *Gimme Some Neck,* engineered, and Woody and Bobby's friend, Seymour Cassel, the actor, came along for the ride.

We went into the studio at the back of Cherokee, and cut two of my songs; one of them; "Somebody," actually made it to the record.

Bobby surprised us all when he brought out a bag of coke the size of a "Big Mac" that some Colombian dealers had given him. But this wasn't cocaine hydrochloride. You couldn't snort it. This was base cocaine. As it wouldn't dissolve in water, you had to smoke it. It was the first time for all of us, and we smoked and played, and then smoked all night. We cut the tracks, overdubbed organ, horns, lead vocals, and background vocals, and mixed it. Then Seymour took Woody, Bobby, Jim, and I back to his house above the Hyatt House on Sunset, where we carried on smoking until we ran out of blow.

The house had been Lennie Bruce's in the Fifties, and it had great views over the smog covered hell of Hollywood, though none of us noticed because we were all waiting for our turn at the pipe, and that's how it was that night, and for nights to come. There was little conversation anymore, and what conversation we had was mainly about the pipe. The Colombian dealers had known exactly what they were doing, as the first one was free. We partied for a couple of days before we ran out the first time, and then sent out for pipes, acetylene torches, test tubes, baking soda and a lot more cocaine.

A gram wouldn't last five minutes this way, and at roughly eighty to a hundred dollars a gram then, you realize why there was a big push by the dealers to get everyone onto the pipe. Even the process of cooking it was addictive, and I truly believe we all got addicted that night at Cherokee. It took some of us a long time to get away from the drug. I think it's far worse than heroin, because you can get high on heroin, but with base, you never get high enough.

The evening started out as my first solo recording session and Woody's debut on the saxophone, and it ended up as the beginning of an addiction to the pipe which lasted for more than a year for me and a little longer for Woody. It was the cause of the only argument I ever had with him in almost thirty years of friendship. We couldn't see how bad it was then. It was just an incredible new buzz.

The good news was that, thanks to Moke, Mercury saw the potential in me, liked "Somebody," and gave me a budget of $100,000 to make the record, and another $100,000 as an advance. Unfortunately, because of my new addiction, this influx of cash couldn't have come at a worse time.

Bobby said he had a hit song for me and turned up at the house one day in a pair of cut-offs, cowboy boots, and a Stetson. He was wearing a serape and carrying a bottle of tequila and a cassette tape. We had a couple of shots and listened to "Little Troublemaker," the song that Johnny Lee Schell, his Texan friend, had written.

Johnny sang and played guitar on the demo tape, and it was really rocking. It had a classic sax solo on it, courtesy of Bobby, and I was knocked out. Now all I needed were a dozen other winners, and I'd be home free. There were several songs of mine in varying stages of development that I needed help with, and when Bobby brought Johnny Lee over to the house the next afternoon, I'd met my new partner in crime.

Johnny had actually recorded at Norman Petty at his studio in Clovis, New Mexico, where Buddy Holly and The Crickets had made all their classic records. We arranged some of my songs and wrote one together, and soon afterwards started rehearsals at the Beach Boys' studio in Santa Monica. When Jim Keltner arrived, he wanted to know where the piano was, but I told him I'd written the songs on guitar, so I'd be playing guitar instead. "Man, you've gotta play piano, that's your instrument, come on now." I hadn't even bothered to set up a keyboard, and I knew he was right, but it was a pain having to relearn the songs and work out parts on piano, so I could sing while I played. Jim wasn't finished with me. When we got to Cherokee, he insisted I set up the grand piano next to the drums, which was an unusual request as the drums are so much louder than the piano. Normally, you'd try and separate them as much as possible, but Geoff and his assistant, John Weaver, managed to cover the piano in blankets and put baffles around it in such a way that hardly any drums could be heard through the piano mics. Jim understood that what was more important than perfect sound was for us to have eye contact. We cut all the tracks that way after that, and it worked extremely well.

Johnny and Paul were as heavily into the base pipe as I was, and we'd light up as soon as we arrived, carry on all day, and sometimes all night. If health was wealth, I was bankrupt. In fact, I was way overdrawn. But in spite of all the drug taking, I still managed to write some decent songs, seven of which made it to the record. I was creative in spite of the drugs.

Ringo was living in Los Angeles during those naughty times, and I'd bump into him occasionally in dimly lit rooms on Lookout Mountain Avenue, off Laurel Canyon. We called it "dealer's row" for obvious reasons. He'd recorded a version of "Tonight" on his album *Bad Boy* in 1978, a song I'd co-written, and when he asked me how the record was coming along, I said it would be improved by his presence on a track. The gentleman that he is, he came the next day, and played on "Hold On"; and it was a very special thrill for me to rock out with him. I was wearing a pair of shoes he particularly liked one night, and when he tried them on they fit him perfectly. It wasn't that surprising, as his Dougie Millings jacket had fitted me so well all those years ago, so I gave them to him and drove home wearing socks. A month or so later, a parcel arrived from the south of France. It was a pair of beautiful white shoes from Ringo, a perfect fit from a perfect gent.

Woody hadn't been involved in the sessions, but he popped in when we'd finished most of the mixes. It was an opportunity to play him my version of his beautiful song, "Mystifies Me." I hadn't told him we'd even recorded it, so it was a thrill for me to watch his reaction as Geoff cranked up the speakers and he listened to it for the first time.

Johnny's song was such a stand out rocker, I named the album *Troublemaker* after it and Mercury Records sent me on a promotion tour of the major cities around the country with my assistant and pal, Tom Yuill. We visited radio stations and distributorships, I was interviewed, I thanked DJs and reviewers for spreading the word, we were wined and dined by everyone we met. It all must have helped, because on release it sold between 65,000 to 70,000 copies, which wasn't too shabby for a beginner, and *Troublemaker* even made it to Number 125 in the charts.

When it came out in England, the company ruined the design of the album cover and blew what credibility I had by printing a lightning flash in the top right hand corner of the front cover that warned, "Beware! There Are Some Heavyweight Musicians Playing on This Album." I didn't even know about it for some months, but when I found out I was really disappointed with the company and called them to complain. They told me they'd change it, but the damage was already done. If ever a record company wanted to make an artist look stupid, this was as good a way as any. It wasn't as if I'd assembled a supergroup. I'd just cut one song with The New Barbarians and Ringo had played on another, but it looked as if I'd said: "Forget me, look at all the famous people I know!"

Woody's fourth album, *1234,* was recorded at his Mandeville Canyon home in 1980, and Andy Johns, Glyn's younger brother, had the unenviable task of producing it out of a garage and a bathroom. Every day I'd arrive, Woody would grab me, and motion for me to follow him into the bathroom, where we'd have a hit from the pipe before we did anything. After another one, we'd go out to the garage where the equipment was set up, and Charlie Watts and Nicky Hopkins were waiting to play. It was such a waste of great talent, but we'd only run through a number a couple of times before Woody would nudge me with a wink, and we'd disappear into the bathroom for more of the same. I'm not proud of it, and I'm not ashamed either, because that's who I was then. I make no apologies for it now, because I was hopelessly addicted, and I don't lecture anyone about drugs. My generation's parents had to suffer two World Wars, alcohol, tobacco, and British B films. We had to cope with the Atom bomb, rock 'n' roll, and every drug known to science. Worse still, the kids of today have to fight a war on the very streets where they live and drugs are cheaper, stronger, and more readily available.

I'd completely lost the thread in Los Angeles, and because of my craziness, Kim flew off to England for a break. She'd had enough of me and, as I was too preoccupied with the pipe and all the paraphernalia that came with it, I'm embarrassed to say I didn't even miss her for a couple of weeks. When I finally surfaced, I found out where she was and pleaded with her to come back. She had left me, and I hadn't noticed. After apologies, promises to shape up and a lot of begging from me, she said she would come back. It was time for me to put the drugs behind me. It would be a lot harder than I'd thought, but for a time at least, I started working on our marriage again and writing new songs.

Our neighbour, Harold, brought Rob Fraboni, his partner in Shangri-La, to the house one night, and he and I talked about plans for my next record. I was surprised at how much Rob knew about my background, but he was a huge Stones fan. The night we'd cut "Truly," he'd crept about in the background, and after we'd left, he'd even mixed a dub of the full twelve minutes of the song because he had his own ideas about the way it should have been mixed, the crafty bastard. We talked at great length about music and sounds, and I discovered he'd worked with The Band and Bob Dylan, among others. After all the sessions at Cherokee for *Gimme Some Neck* and *Troublemaker,* I was dreading the thirty-five mile drives into town, and I warmed to the idea of using a studio that was no more than a mile away and also possessed a superb Steinway.

I told him Johnny Lee would definitely play guitar on the record, and he suggested I meet Ricky Fataar, a South African drummer who'd recorded and toured with The Beach Boys. He set up a session so we could find out how we played together. Ricky was a lovely "feel" drummer, and I liked him as a person too. He had a natural good vibe about him and Johnny. He and I worked really well together. When Rob Fraboni brought Ray Ohara, a top Japanese session player to the house one day, we knew he was the bass player we'd been looking for and the songs began to shape up as soon as we started playing with him.

Finally, I was in a band again. It dawned on me that I hadn't been in one since the revised version of the Small Faces had drifted apart three years before. Ever since 1963 and The Cherokees, I'd been in one band or another, because that's what I did. I played with The Rolling Stones too, which had been a great thrill, but I wasn't actually *in* the band. That fact hit me like a ton of bricks when I was rehearsing with The Stones for "Saturday Night Live" in 1978. A photographer had been taking pictures while we played, and between songs he asked for a group shot. I stopped myself just in time from joining them in the lineup. Because I'd been playing and living with them for months on end, and they'd always made me feel like I was one of the lads, I had reacted like a member of the group. I sat back down with the sobering realization that there was a fine, but clear line between being in the band and being a sideman. In this situation I was definitely a sideman.

I'd thrown the pipe and all the paraphernalia away, but we still got high. Rob was a coke snob; he always had special brands hidden away. He'd lay out a taste of Colombian and then offer you some Peruvian flake he'd stashed from a year ago. He had wine stashed in the same way. I just wanted to get high, but Rob was a crafty fucker. He worked out a plan so that we wouldn't run out of drugs during the sessions. As one of the partners of the studio, he could inflate the amount of studio time that he told the record company we used. That way, we'd have a coke allowance built into the deal. I shouldn't have listened. As I wasn't watching the clock and never saw a time sheet, I never found out how much he billed them.

Shangri-La is long gone as a studio, but I understand the house was originally built for Hopalong Cassidy. Elvis Presley reportedly owned it for a while, and it had been a whorehouse before The Band bought it and turned it into a studio, which was where Martin Scorcese filmed the interview sequences in *The Last Waltz.* One way or another, the place had character, and it attracted characters. Tim Kramer was the house engineer when I first worked there and he was an absolute gem. He was very short, very Jewish, and very funny, and he was a master with the knobs. When I first met him I didn't think I'd get on with him, because he was as hyperactive as Steve Marriott and just as loud. But he was as quick to laugh at himself as anybody else, and we laughed at him a lot. He would laugh himself into a heap on the floor trying to get to the punch line of a joke. I had a lot of good times making that record, and I think we made a very fine album, but one night I was having trouble singing one of the songs I'd written called "So Lucky."

As Ringo told me while we were cutting "Hold On" during the *Troublemaker* sessions: "I go into the vocal booth sounding like Stevie Wonder, but when I come out to listen, it's always just me."

Well, I was having a similar problem and my voice was hoarse from straining to get the notes. Ricky "Mon" (as we called Ricky after his natural reggae feel) suggested I try again the next day. It wasn't going to sound any better until my throat was rested. So we called it a night and I went home.

Kim woke up in the middle of the night with a start. I was sitting up in bed singing the verse of "So Lucky" at the top of what was left of my voice. I don't remember it because I was fast asleep, but after a chorus, I turned over as if nothing had happened and carried on sleeping.

Mike Doud, who had been my art director for *Troublemaker,* discussed album titles, but he'd already turned down my first choice, *Studio Tan.* By a strange coincidence, Frank Zappa had just put out a record with the same name. My second choice was *Bump in the Night,* which comes from an old Cornish prayer:

> *From ghoulies and ghosties and long-leggety beasties and things that go bump in the night, may the good Lord preserve us.*

He liked the title, and with that settled, The Bump Band became the obvious choice for a group name, which appealed to everybody. Mike brought Gary Panter down to the studio with selections of his artwork for me to look through. Gary had published several comic books, and although his work was very violent, his twisted sense of humour came through and I liked a lot of his ideas. Tim Kramer told him the story about me singing in my sleep; Gary liked that image, and took some Polaroids that night. He came back a week later with two paintings. The main painting shows me in bed, in a cold sweat, with musical notes piercing the wall and scaring me as I clutch at the bedsheets. He painted a rear view of the same scene for the back cover, and when I asked him what the yellow flash was in the bottom left corner, he told me that was my blond-haired Kim.

Some time later, Tim came to the house while Kim and I were watching television in bed. He didn't knock, he just came running into the room and jumped on the bed between us. He surprised us, but he frightened our dog, Springer, who took a bite out of him. He screamed in pain and ran out the door, but on his way out of the room, he shouted over his shoulder, "Gary was wrong!" Tim noticed, in the seconds before Springer's teeth had clamped down on his bum, that Gary had painted Kim on the wrong side of the bed. What an observant, funny chap.

As I'd written all the songs for *Bump in the Night* on guitar and wasn't feeling too confident about my keyboard playing as a result, I played rhythm guitar on all the basic tracks, except "So Lucky." Of course if my pal Jim Keltner had been there, he would have insisted on me playing keyboards again, but he wasn't, and Rob didn't push it either. Woody came in one day to play bass and lead guitar on a song we co-wrote called "Little Girl" that became the only single off the album.

Bump in the Night as an album release was doomed from the start. Although it got universally good reviews, Moke became very ill and had to be hospitalized. The record company lost interest after that, and because the project had gone over budget, I even had to hand over some of my publishing money to keep the sessions rolling. It's probably a collector's item these days, because Mercury Records can't claim to have released the record—it just escaped! I was disillusioned with the whole business, but I've often found that when one door closes, another one opens.

As luck would have it, during those sessions, a friend of Rob's, Mark Aglietti, introduced me to Reneé Geyer, a singer from Australia.

She was looking for a band to cut two sides for a single and asked The Bump Band to back her on the record. She's an amazingly soulful vocalist and we cut a decent track on it, and eventually cut an album with her, of which I'm very, very proud. She managed to involve everyone in the songwriting and liked "So Lucky" so much, we recut it for her, but with more intensity. She called her album *So Lucky* after my song, and though it didn't do anything much in the States, the Australian gold record hangs proudly on my wall to this day. So if you haven't heard her sing yet, remember you heard Reneé Geyer's name here first!

We were cutting a track one night when Bonnie Raitt came over to check out the studio. She watched us through the control room window, and after we'd got a decent take Rob introduced us to her. She was great fun and seemed to like us as a band as much as the studio, which was what Rob had secretly hoped. She already had a band, though they didn't always play on her records, and she wanted to cut some tracks with us and see how we worked together. I guess she was looking to change her band. I'd always loved her recording of "I'm Blowing Away," so I was thrilled when, a few days later, we took a break from *Bump in the Night* and spent a couple of days working with her until we got a couple of tracks that she was pleased with. And as a result she decided to use the Bumps on her new album.

Soon after my record was finished, I took The Bump Band on a short tour of Los Angeles. Actually, it wasn't a tour so much as one gig at Perkin's Palace in Pasadena, where Reneé sat in with us, and another the following night at the Lone Star Cafe, a Texan joint on the corner of Sunset Boulevard and Pacific Coast Highway. The comedian and film star, Robin Williams, was a good friend of Ricky Fataar's, and luckily for me he came to the gig that night, because he got up on stage and jammed with the rest of the band while I changed a broken string on my guitar. It was the first time I'd ever played live under my own name, and I'd had such a good time that now I'd got my feet wet I wanted to swim in the ocean.

CHAPTER THIRTY-ONE

The Adventures
of Super Mac

My old compadre Bobby Keys and I had often talked about going to Lubbock together, as a pilgrimage, and we decided the best way to do it would be to tour around Texas. He mentioned it again while he was playing on my record in 1980, and as there was some spare time before we started on Bonnie's record, we decided to give it a try. Johnny's friend Mike Speed wanted to be a manager. Using Bobby's and my name, he booked us a short tour of Texas that would take us through Albuquerque to Amarillo, Austin, Dallas, and best of all Lubbock, both Bobby's and Buddy Holly's birthplace, where I intended to visit Holly's grave. We played at Soap Creek near Austin, opening for The Fabulous Thunderbirds, and Jimmie Vaughan gave me chills when he told me Hank Williams had played on that very stage. We played at Steamboat on Sixth Street in Austin too, and Al Kooper sat in with us, jamming on guitar to Stones' songs all night.

We played two nights at a club in Dallas, where the people were incredibly friendly, particularly the bartenders, and they told us they'd come to Lubbock on their day off for a drink. Bobby, Johnny, and I spent the morning looking for Buddy Holly's grave at the cemetery, but we never found it, so we went for ribs and beer at Stubb's Barbecue instead. The sign on the wall said, "There will be no bad talk or loud talk in this place," but the jukebox was full of Jimmy Reed, Muddy Waters, and Howlin' Wolf singles from the Fifties and Sixties, and it was loud and nasty. We went to Fat Dawg's that night to check out the club, as we were going to play there the next night. The Dallas bartenders met us there, and as the night wore on we began to slug shots. I had no idea what I was drinking, but it worked very quickly, and everything began to swim around me. I watched a barman toss an empty Jack Daniels' bottle over his shoulder into a garbage bin behind the counter, and I thought I could do that too. I climbed over the bar and threw several bottles over my head, some of which landed on the floor with a loud crash and splash. At least one popped and burst on the pool tables that were in mid-game, sending broken glass and liquor in every direction.

It was decided that we should leave at that point and Dave Fantini, our roadie, carried me out, or that's what I've been told. My next clear memory was looking over the balcony of the motel and seeing a red pickup below me that looked strangely appealing. I haven't any idea why, but I had an overwhelming desire to jump over the balcony and land on the roof of the pickup. Let's just say I felt invincible. Mercifully, I was fast asleep before I hit the roof, bounced onto the fender, and landed in a heap on the ground nearby. If I'd been awake I would have broken both my legs at least. Horrified, Dave ran over, helped me up, and carried me to my door, but I wanted another go at it. He threw me onto the bed, and knowing I would be in a lot of pain when I woke up he threw buckets of ice on my legs and left me to sleep it off.

I woke up on the day of the gig. I couldn't move my legs, I was wet, freezing cold, and in agony. I couldn't stand up and had to be carried to the bathroom for a pee. I couldn't put any weight on my legs at all, so Bobby carried me on his back to the camper, and then we drove to Joe Ely's house, where I sat in his hot tub for over an hour hoping the pain would ease up. It didn't, but during the course of the day I found I could walk slowly and Dave got me a cane so I could walk to the stage. Sitting at the piano was no problem, but playing guitar was more difficult until I moved the mic stand next to the piano, so I could lean on it while I sang and played. All in all, the show wasn't bad, and although I was in agony, at least the band had a good laugh out of it every time I tried to move.

When I came off stage I discovered my new manager had flown back to Los Angeles with what money there was from the other gigs, and then Fat Dawg's presented me with a $900 bar bill! I never thought touring could be so painful. I'd only wanted to see Buddy Holly's grave, not dig my own!

Bonnie introduced me to NRBQ during the making of her album and I'll always be grateful to her for that, as they are one of the greatest bands around. The name stands for New Rhythm and Blues Quartet. She loved them so much and we covered two of their tunes, "Me and the Boys" and the title track of her record, *Green Light*. After we'd got the basic tracks done, I took a day off while Johnny tracked more guitars and Kim and I went out for a curry and a few beers. I rang the studio from the Java Bar in Santa Monica, and Johnny answered. "Hey, Keith Richards called, and he wants you to call him back, pronto!" He'd left me a number in Worcester, Massachusetts, and so, much excited, I rang it from the bar. I knew they were about to start a tour, and when Keith came to the phone, after the usual bollocks, he asked me where the fuck I was, and when was I going to start rehearsing with them. I laughed, and told him I was finishing Bonnie's record, and told him I'd be back in touch within twenty-four hours, after I'd talked to Bonnie. Hoo-fuckin'-ray!

I sauntered back into the dimly lit bar, sat down next to Kim, and called the barman over. "A round of drinks on me!" I said, just loud enough for the few people in the bar to hear. Kim looked at me quizzically and then I told her the good news. We celebrated that night in grand style. Bonnie was surprisingly understanding about me leaving her while the recording was still going on, but she knew it wasn't something I could, or should, turn down. I promised to check every track for possible keyboard overdubs before I left. For the next two nights Rob, Tim, and I concentrated on getting all my work finished, and not just on her record, for there were keyboards I still had to play on Reneé's album as well. We had recently moved from Keith's Broad Beach house to a single-storey ranch style house on Point Dume, a few miles away, and when I got home the second night around 4 A.M. I was worn out and brain dead.

There was no time for sleep because it was only a few hours before I had to leave for the airport, so we jumped into bed for a quick kiss and a cuddle. Just as we climaxed, so did the earth beneath us!

It was a 5.2 earthquake and the ground shook, shuddered, and shivered violently. A Victorian gilt-framed print of a painting called "The Sweethearts" hung on the wall above the bed until that moment, when it came crashing down on top of us. We were out of bed, in each other's arms, covered in broken glass and shouting for Mandy all at once. Luckily, there was no serious damage, but it was a hell of a wake-up call! You never really get used to them, because you never know when it's going to happen, or how severe it's going to be, and it can be deceiving. The ones that rock aren't always as bad as the ones that roll, and that's when you realize just how fluid rock can be. It's bloody frightening.

The Stones had rented Longview Farm, a studio complex surrounded by country. With nothing but trees, rolling hills, and Rolling Stones everywhere you looked, it couldn't be faulted. Nothing changes with those boys, and hugs and snide remarks filled the air in equal measure as I said hello to one and all. Then Chuch showed me to my bedroom and took me past the poolroom to the studio, which was a huge barn with exposed wooden beams and a stage the whole width of the far end. The gear was already buzzing in readiness. A B3 and a Yamaha electric grand sat next to a grand piano, which I guessed would be for Stu, and before I could say his name, there he was. "What have you been up to?" I told him I'd been working on Bonnie Raitt's record. "Oh, yeah. She plays slide guitar doesn't she? Yeah, she's quite good." That was fair praise from Stu.

Instead of the 1978 tour, when rehearsals began and finished on the same day for me, this time round I had three weeks to get it together. And it was just as well, because the other difference from that tour was that Mick didn't want me to play organ, only piano and synthesizers, as both he and Bill had experimented with them while finishing *Tattoo You,* their new album.

Unfortunately, I knew nothing about synthesizers, and except for Stevie Wonder, and Ray Charles' playing on "Game Number 9" I wasn't crazy about the sounds they made. In fact, on the subject of synths, I was as blinkered as Stu. Mick was insistent though and he brought in Todd Rundgren's synth man, Roger Powell, who was an expert in the field. He turned up one morning carrying a Prophet 10, just as I was about to go to bed after being up all night with Keith and Woody. Roger was a nice bloke, and patient too, but my state of inebriation and the subject matter were like oil and water. I watched befuddled as he adjusted knobs and flicked switches on the machine until I became mesmerized and confused.

I offered him a drink but he recoiled in horror, it being so early, but as I needed to think and it being very late in my time zone, I poured myself a large one and sat down ready to concentrate on this strange instrument.

I wasn't sure what sounds Mick wanted other than the sound on "Heaven" from *Tattoo You* and I thought if the Prophet was any good it ought to be able to at least give me a good B3 sound, as I wouldn't be using one on the road. Well, we were at odds from the start. He knew how to make sounds on the synth, but I didn't like any that he made for me, and I soon realized the nearest noise to an organ was just that—a noise! I thanked him for his time and his trouble and went to bed.

My rig was set up next to Woody's and if he had some blow, he'd put some my way. Occasionally though, when his nose was out of action, he'd roll a Marlboro between his fingers until the tobacco fell out. He'd pour blow on the leaves and suck it back into the empty cigarette and smoke it. He was quite a professional at it and one day, during a break in rehearsals, he made up a couple of them and handed one to me. I lit it and instantly recognized the taste of base amongst the tobacco. I looked at it, then at him, and he snapped at me. "Don't say anything to Keith!"

He would have been satisfied if I'd smoked it with him, but as I wouldn't then his big worry was that I'd tell Keith, because Keith had hated base from the start, and had enough experience with heroin not to want one of his friends to go down a similar road. It had been tough for me to stop and I certainly wasn't going to start again. But I would never have told Keith either, because Woody was my friend. I told Woody not to worry, but from then until he stopped doing it, I couldn't be trusted, and our friendship suffered. I found out later that the rest of The Stones had told him he had to quit base or quit the band and, looking back, it was quite a gamble on their part inviting me on the tour, since Keith was well aware of my struggles with it in the past.

One night after a long day at the keyboard, Keith, Woody, and I were playing a three-sided game of pool. It was actually a one-sided game, because Keith moved the balls to suit him if they didn't end up where he'd planned. Cheating might be too strong a word; let's just call it fiddling about. Anyway, while he was fiddling with his balls, we were listening to a cassette of rough mixes from the 1977 Paris sessions and a version of "Claudine" came on that I hadn't heard before. He'd given me a cassette copy after he played it for me in Paris, but this wasn't the same one. It was slower, it had Stu on piano, but it wasn't anywhere near as electrifying as the track I had played over and over. When I mentioned the other version, Keith and Woody couldn't remember it, so I said I'd dig it out and play it for them, because I carried it with me.

Keith said something about it to Mick, because the next afternoon all the lads came to the poolroom to have a listen. They were impressed at how tight it was, but Mick's main concern was where I got the tape. I just wanted them to hear how good it was.

One day, Mick came over to the piano and told me there was a phone call for me in the house. There was an old-fashioned phone booth next to the kitchen. I went in, sat down, and picked up the phone. Prince Rupert Loewenstein, The Stones' financial advisor, was on the other end and wanted to know what my price would be for the tour. Here we go again, I thought. Well, as I didn't have any real idea, I thought of a high number, doubled it, and told him. "Oh, they won't be able to pay you that much," he said politely. I thought about it for a second. Here I'd been rehearsing for three weeks, everybody seemed to be happy with what I was doing, and they're about to collect millions of dollars up front from a perfume company, Jovan, for doing nothing more than signing a piece of paper. Surely they wouldn't feel the pinch of another few thousand dollars? I told him I thought it was fair, and that I wasn't prepared to come down in price. He said he'd talk to the boys and get back to me. My legs were wobbling when I walked out of the phone booth, and I thought I'd probably blown it, and that Kim would see me sooner than we'd planned.

I sat down at the piano with the certain knowledge that everybody in the band knew I'd been talking to Rupert about money, and they would soon know how much I'd asked for, even though it would never be discussed between us. Meanwhile, I considered packing my bags just in case, but Rupert called back later to say it was all agreed, so the worst part being over, now I could get down to playing the piano and enjoying myself again.

The first show was to be JFK Stadium in Philadelphia, on September 25, but a secret opening bash at Sir Morgan's Cave, a tiny club in Worcester, was planned for September 14. We were advertised as Blue Monday and The Cockroaches, and the club reminded me of the old Station Hotel days, all sweaty and packed with people.

There were no monitors, the stage was minuscule, and I couldn't even see Charlie, who was behind the amps, with Stu and me stuck in one corner. Everyone knew The Stones were rehearsing locally, so word soon got around about the gig, and before long there were thousands of fans out in the street trying to get in. It was a loose show for us, but JC, Bob Bender, and Joe Seabrook, the security guys, had a hell of a job keeping people away from the stage. It was even worse outside. Police eventually had to bring in helicopters to control the crowd. After that the Mayor of Boston banned The Stones from playing the two other warm-up gigs that were planned for The Orpheum, but The Stones weren't bothered. It was all good press for the tour.

I remember the day at JFK Stadium in Philadelphia for one thing only. A famous tennis player, the late Vitas Gerulaitis, knocked on my hotel room door. When I opened it, he was singing, "Little troublemaker, always on the run...," at the top of his voice. We shook hands, then he broke out a huge line of coke on the table and handed me a straw, and though I'd never met him before, he became my instant pal.

For me, the tour was much the same as before. I'd generally go straight to Keith's room after the gig. But when we arrived at the hotel in Chicago, Alan Dunn, the tour manager, handed us our keys as usual, but said his brother Arnold would be a little while with the baggage. So I stepped into the bar to check it out.

"Hello," I said. "I'm Mac. We're staying here for a few days and you'll probably be seeing a lot of me."

"That sounds good to me, Mac. My name's Jack. What'll it be?"

"I'll have a Stoli greyhound please, Jack." I paid for the drink and went to my room. A little later, Keith called to say he'd arranged for us all to eat together in the restaurant, and he'd see me in the bar in five minutes. When I left my room, an extremely dapper Charlie Watts was standing at the elevator, so we walked into the bar together and spotted Mick, Keith, Bill, and Woody sitting at a table in the centre of the room. As soon as Jack saw me, he shouted across the bar:

"Will you be having your usual, Mac?"

Charlie was astonished, he couldn't believe his ears. Amazed, he turned to his bandmates at the table. "How does he do it? We've only been in the hotel five minutes, and already the barman knows what he drinks!" Of course, it wasn't planned, but Charlie was impressed.

Charlie is the best-dressed man in rock 'n' roll, without a doubt, but he's also the most unlikely person to be in a rock 'n' roll band. If any hotel maid walking into his room had heard horror stories about drummers like Keith Moon and John Bonham, they'd been sadly disappointed with Charlie. He unpacks his suits and hangs them up, lines his shoes up with the laces either side, and even makes the bed when he gets out of it in the morning. He's a maid's dream.

Keith's a different kettle of fish altogether. He'd been given a fancy stage shirt, which he liked but immediately set about adjusting it to his own preferred punk style. He tore off the collar, cut the buttons off, then ripped the sleeves and the body of it to shreds, until there wasn't much left but the knots he'd tied in it to keep it from falling off his shoulders. He seemed satisfied in the end, although I didn't ever see him wear it after that.

Some time during the early hours, bent over straight-legged, his bum in the air, Keith was shuffling through a pile of cassettes that were strewn in a heap around his cassette machine on the floor. He was getting more, and more frustrated, not being able to find the sound he was looking for and Freddie Sessler's son, Larry, who acted as Keith's helper, wasn't acting helpful enough. In a split second Keith was on his feet, his .38 was out of its holster, and he fired once into the floor, narrowly missing Larry's foot. I was sitting between the two of them and there'd been no warning. He just went for it. He hadn't lost it completely, but he was angry and was proving a point. Larry, on the other hand, was more than a little upset, because it really shook him up, and I'm sure he was thinking a kick in the pants would've been just as effective. Freddie and I searched without finding a bullet hole in the shag carpet. It must have stopped short of the room below, but in my stoned state I imagined someone lying there in a pool of blood.

Even now it seems incredible that a gun could be fired in the middle of the night in a five-star hotel in a big city like Chicago without alerting anyone in authority. I can only assume the city that Al Capone made famous had heard it all before.

I was on a bender when we played three nights at the Brendan Byrne Arena in New Jersey. We stayed at the Omni Berkshire Place in New York, but I hadn't slept since the night before we arrived. I was doing fine until the drive to the gig on the last night. I sat in the back of one of the vans with the window open so I could get some fresh air, but the driver took us through the Lincoln Tunnel. When we arrived I thought I was going to pass out. Bill Wyman noticed how pale I was as soon as I walked into the dressing room, where John McEnroe and Vitas Gerulaitis were waiting. Three days and nights of coke were no problem, but a few lungfuls of carbon monoxide was the last straw for me. Of all the luck, those three nights were recorded and used for the soundtrack of The Stones' tour movie *Let's Spend the Night Together.*

Bill is a dry old codger. Whenever people think of The Stones, they imagine the "Sex and Drugs and Rock and Roll" that Ian Dury sang about. They wouldn't be far wrong up to a point, though Bill never took drugs. But when it came to sex, he was the boy. You'd never think it to look at him. Butter wouldn't melt in his mouth. But I've seen girls lined up along the corridor two-deep, just waiting for a chance to get a good shagging from him. We were watching ZZ Top perform from the skybox at the Astrodome in Houston, and I said to him, "Zee Zee Top are fuckin' great, aren't they?" He turned slowly and said quietly:

"They were Zed Zed Top when they opened for us in 1972, and they're Zed Zed Top tonight. All right?"

One of the highlights of that tour was when Freddie Sessler wheeled Ronnie Lane into the dressing room in Orlando, Florida. I hadn't seen him since that awful night at Joe Brown's house, but had learned he'd got multiple sclerosis some time later, and I believe he already had the disease then. There weren't any bad feelings between us and although he looked weaker he was as sarcastic and feisty as ever and enjoyed all the attention The Stones and the crew paid him.

Freddie had generously paid for his flight from England and for a course of injections of snake venom that a doctor believed could cure MS, or at least slow down the disease's grip on the body. In the end, it didn't work, but he was game enough to try anything.

We played two nights at Hampton Roads Coliseum in Virginia. The first night, December 18, was Keith's birthday, and that's always a bash, especially as he shares his birthday with Bobby Keys. That night's show went out live to paying cable customers. The great Hal Ashby, director of *Harold and Maude, The Last Detail, Coming Home,* and *Being There,* directed the telecast and had a lot of fun. His cameras were backstage in the dressing rooms, behind the amps and anywhere you'd least expect, and it was all going out live. He had nude women in body paint, goats and sheep in the toilets, and before you knew what was happening the camera would be in your face. When one of the camera crews appeared in our dressing room suddenly, the two drug dealers who'd been sitting quietly in the corner until that moment, ran for the door as if their clothes were on fire.

I never got to see how it came out, as it was broadcast live, but I saw *Let's Spend the Night Together,* the movie Hal made of the whole tour, and I don't think it captured any of the excitement or fun of the show. I didn't expect to see much of me in it, but when you consider there are only five guys in the band and there wasn't ONE shot of Charlie Watts on his own, I thought it was a disgrace. I think Hal must have had something other than the movie on his mind.

I had one starring moment as a result of that movie though. Some months after the tour, Kim, Mandy, and I were driving along Pacific Coast Highway when I stopped to get gas. A car pulled up behind me and a young woman ran up to me excitedly.

"Hey, are you Ian?"

"Yes," I said smiling, fully expecting to be asked to sign an autograph.

"I knew it was you. I recognized the back of your head."

She wasn't a fan at all, just one of Hal Ashby's team of editors and her job had been to edit out the miles of film taken from the back of the stage that showed the back of my head. She'd just taken a lunch break and thought she must be hallucinating when she saw "that" head in the car in front of her.

CHAPTER THIRTY-TWO

Close to the Edge

After The Stones, I went back and toured with Bonnie Raitt for about three years until 1984, and she was very good to me, and very good for me. And although I've got a ton of good memories of those times, I was doing altogether too much blow, and wasn't playing at the top of my game. My mind just wasn't focused. Although she gave me a lot of slack, I was oblivious to it at the time.

Also, I'd never been paid wages before I toured with The Stones, and I wasn't used to being a hired hand. In The Muleskinners, Boz People, Small Faces, and The Faces, I was an equal member, and even with The Stones I wasn't working for just one person, it was for a band. But with Bonnie, she was the boss, and to her credit, a generous and fair one, but it was still a new experience for me. It rankled that though I'd formed The Bump Band in the first place, now it was her band. Plus, all the years of being able to say "fuck the gig" and having people wait around for me had left me totally ignorant and unaware that other people's feelings mattered.

Much worse, I was ignorant of Kim's feelings too, but that's another story. It took me a long time to figure it out, but on a professional level Bonnie finally took me aside and explained it was time I shaped up. She was very straight and to the point.

"Mac, for Christ's sake, you're late again!"

Apart from my lateness, the band was rocking. The Bump Band had cut "Green Light" with her, but Ricky Fataar didn't want to tour, partly because his wife, Penelope Tree, the model, had just given birth to their little girl, Paloma. So Johnny Lee, Ray, and I rehearsed with her old drummer, Dennis Whitted, and her horn player, David Woodford, and we became Bonnie and The Bump Band. These were good times at first, and she paid me well at a point in her career that would be seen later as the beginning of a slump. But eventually, I wanted to play my own songs with my band, so I told her I would be leaving.

Ray decided to stay with me and give The Bump Band another try, but when I told Bonnie we were both leaving, she was very upset. I knew she could get Marty Grebb to play keyboards with her as he'd done in the past, and my only saving grace was suggesting "Hutch" Hutchinson from The Neville Brothers, who's still playing great bass with her to this day. Ray and I didn't bother getting a drummer in at the outset, as we were using drum machines while we worked up the songs. But Rob Fraboni suggested Blondie Chaplin to play guitar, as well as sing. Blondie is a ginger-haired, black South African, who was Ricky Fataar's partner in Flame and who toured with The Beach Boys before joining the group. In fact, it's Blondie's soaring voice you hear singing lead on "Sail On Sailor."

Well, it seemed fine at first; we worked up several tunes and cut demos at Shangri-La, which sounded okay, but it wasn't rocking and I wasn't excited. Also, I wanted to rehearse as often as possible, but Blondie didn't have transport so we always had to rehearse at his apartment, which meant carrying keyboards, amps, drum machines, and cassette players across town instead of working at my place where everything was already set up. I started to lose interest in the project, but the last straw was when I told Ray I'd stopped doing blow and, although I had no objection to anyone else doing it, I didn't want it around me.

Ray always had a healthy supply in his blender and kept leaving it open in front of me, and in the end I told them I'd had enough, packed up my equipment and left.

It felt good to be free of the situation as I drove north on the Hollywood Freeway back to the San Fernando Valley. But as I got nearer to that gloomy little house with the swimming pool in the backyard, I began to feel so disillusioned about my band that I got more and more depressed. I was miserable and I was at the end of my tether. I didn't know what to do or how to go about it anymore. I had to think, but I couldn't think straight. I had no manager since Moke's illness and subsequent retirement from the business. I had no record deal, money was very tight, and I seemed to be alienated from all my musician friends.

Woody was back east in New York, Ricky had moved to Australia, Johnny was on tour with Bonnie, and I'd just blown out Ray and Blondie. I still had Kim, but I didn't know what she was going to make of me leaving my own group. Worst of all, I seemed to have lost all interest in music. I was doubting any talent I might have and regretted moving to the States where we were illegal, broke, and I was apparently unemployable.

Kim, bless her, stood by me and understood like no one else ever could. She saw that I was near the edge but sensed something I didn't, that I would come back stronger than ever. Though I couldn't see the wood for the wallpaper at that moment, she said I should take a vacation.

She advised me that I should sit out by the pool and do whatever I wanted, have a drink, play sounds, listen to the radio, whatever I wanted to do, but above all stop worrying. She told me that if I wanted to give up music and I ended up sweeping the streets, she'd stay with me. I know I'd have gone crazy without her. I was feeling suicidal, and my whole world seemed to have crumbled around me. Without her love, I might just have found a way to do it.

But I didn't jump in the lake. I did what Kim told me and jumped into the pool instead. I poured myself a Red Stripe and lazed in the sun. I dug up a book of Bob Dylan's words that I'd had for years and never read. I'd always loved his music ever since Nick, my mate in The Muleskinners, had turned me on to his first album, but to be able to have the words in front of me was such a different experience. I didn't know what was happening, but I was becoming rejuvenated. Kim wasn't much of a Dylan fan. She could never get past his whining voice, but as I read out whole songs to her by the pool, she grew to love them as much as I did, and we passed many an afternoon drinking, swimming, reading his lyrics, and occasionally listening to the BBC plays on KCRW, the local public radio station.

There was an old shack next to the pool that had two small rooms, and I'd put the upright piano and my studio gear in one of the rooms and used the other for storage. The inside walls were dark with fake wood panels, so I painted the whole place white to brighten it up and make it appear larger. I found this to be therapeutic, and without consciously knowing what I was doing, I began to set up my studio again. I began to play the piano just for fun. Before I knew what was happening I'd written and recorded several demos on my little four-track cassette machine, which sounded pretty good to my ear, and I began to feel good about myself again.

Just as I started to get above my depression I got a phone call out of the clear blue sky that changed my life. This time it was Gary Shafner, one of Bob Dylan's people, wanting to know if I'd have a play with Bob at his house on Point Dume the next day. I was blown away, and it was exactly what I needed, but I could hardly believe how strange it was, that I'd been poring through his book of writings and drawings for weeks and would be playing some of those songs the very next day. When I hung up, I realized I wasn't really strong enough yet, but I'd get stronger by the day, because this was just what the doctor ordered. Kim was so pleased for me, and I was running around like a chicken with its head cut off, digging up his *Greatest Hits* cassettes and learning as many of his songs as I possibly could. I hardly slept a wink, I was so excited. I'd actually stopped thinking of myself as a musician, and yet all of a sudden, because I'd been asked to play, I found I was one—after all.

The next afternoon, I drove through Malibu Canyon, past our old house and pulled up at a ramshackle gate on a quiet street on Point Dume. There was a large tattooed and hairy Hell's Angel on guard, and after I told him my name, he let me through, pointing to one of several houses in the compound, and showed me where to park. I could just see the dome of Bob's house beyond the trees over a rise, and carefully avoiding the chickens and chicken shit in the yard, I stepped through the door of a modern house into a large high-ceilinged room, unfurnished except for a P.A., amps, drum kit, and a Hammond organ. Mick Taylor saw me as I walked in and beamed as he stepped around the cables that were all over the floor. I hadn't realized he'd played on Bob's new album, *Infidels,* so I was pleasantly surprised to see him there. He told me Bob was getting a band together to promote his new album in Europe, and the tour was due to start in ten days' time.

Now I was really excited. I hadn't seen Mick since he sat in with The Stones in Kansas City in 1981. They'd plugged his guitar cord into an amp directly behind me that night, but as he was at least thirty feet away at the front of the stage, he could hardly hear it, so he cranked the volume all the way up. I've never heard anything louder than the sound that came from that amp in my whole life, and I ran from the stage to protect my ears and wouldn't go back on until he left the stage.

That aside, I'd always liked Mick. He's an affable, unpretentious soul without a bad bone in his body. Colin Allen was sitting at the drums, and the last time I'd seen him was in a cafe on the M1 in 1966, when I was in the Small Faces and he and Andy Summers were in Zoot Money's Big Roll Band. It helped knowing a couple of the guys because, although I'd been introduced to Bob a couple of times before, I was still nervous, not having played for a while. Greg Sutton was on the bass and Tim Drummond, who'd played bass with Bob before, introduced himself and prepared me for the moment Bob would give me a steely glance. Tim said, "It's not a personal thing, he just won't wear glasses on stage and he's only trying to focus on you."

I'd just checked out the Hammond when Bob walked in and gave me what has to be the weakest handshake in the business. But he was friendly enough as he picked up his old Fender Strat and plugged it into his amp. He started playing "Jokerman" off the new album, which I hadn't heard yet, and as I started to find my way through the chords, listening to his scratchy guitar playing, it all came back to me. Years before, when Kim, Mandy, and I had lived on Point Dume, we used to hear a guitarist playing every afternoon at the top of the hill above us. It was so annoyingly loud we actually considered calling the police. Just as well we didn't because it might have been Bob. That afternoon, we went through many of the older songs as well as the new ones from *Infidels,* and I spent the whole day jotting down titles and chords as I played along.

It must have sounded half-decent because I was asked to come back the next day, and at the end of that day's rehearsals I was told I'd got the job. Hoo-fuckin'-ray! I was a professional musician again after the seemingly endless dark days, and I felt good about myself for the first time in months. I found out later that one of the reasons I had been called was that my old pal Nicky Hopkins had been there the previous day. Although he could play practically anything on the piano, he wasn't as comfortable on the organ, and Bob had particularly wanted to take an organist on the tour.

Bob was sitting at the table in the kitchen chatting with Mick and I went over to him. "Thanks, Bob. It's an honour and a privilege to work with you," I said. His comeback was too sharp for me. He said quietly, "I hope you feel the same when the tour's over." I think, looking back, that he was really only being honest, that he thought I might feel differently when it was all done, but I'd have to wait and see for myself. Nothing could be that bad, could it?

The following day we went into full production rehearsals at the Beverly Theater on Wilshire Boulevard, and thrashed out many, many songs, working long and hard without a break. Bob would turn up every day wearing the same straw hat, old Harley jacket, jeans, boots, and a white T-shirt he'd worn at his house. He wasn't very communicative; he'd just pick up his guitar and start playing without a word. He'd say nothing all day to you unless you spoke to him first. But he wasn't unfriendly either. He was just focused on performing. Occasionally, he'd come over to the Hammond to point out a line he wanted to hear or to throw me a solo. And as the organ was set up at the front of the stage to his right, I soon saw the look that Tim Drummond had warned me about, but at least now I knew what was really going on.

Kim came up to the theatre for lunch one day and I won't forget how proud and happy I felt walking down Wilshire Boulevard in the sunshine with her by my side. She looked gorgeous, and I was employed–a winning combination! Plus, I felt like I was finally off drugs for good and that everything was all coming together, at long last. On the way home that day, we got stuck at a traffic light next to Bob. He was driving a red, convertible Cadillac, and I didn't want him to turn round and see us there, in case he thought we were following him. But as he sat in his car squinting in the sunshine, waiting for the light to change, he appeared oblivious to the huge Great Dane behind him in the back seat, panting and slobbering at us. I squirmed in the passenger seat, hoping he wouldn't bark at me, and luckily the traffic eased up and Bob drove off without turning round. The scene was like a Norman Rockwell painting of a typical day in Beverly Hills in 1984.

I'd known Bill Graham from The Faces days, and as well as being the promoter he also managed Carlos Santana, who was going to be opening for Bob on the tour. Bill brought Carlos down to the theatre one day so that he could work up a couple of songs with Bob for the encore. But instead of one of Bob's many hits, Carlos was determined to teach Bob a really naff pop song that Jimmy Cliff had recently released. Bob was going along with it in a docile way, while Mick and I were pulling "Stu" faces at each other across the stage. Jesus, I could hardly believe Bob was going to be singing this crap at the end of his show. He might as well do a couple of Abba's hits while he was at it. It was an odd situation and after Carlos left Bob asked us what we thought about the song. Cautiously, I said it was up to him, and luckily it was never mentioned again. We ended up doing a singalong version of "Blowing in the Wind" for the encore instead, which wasn't that much better.

Our first stop was Verona, Italy, where we were to open the tour a couple of nights later, on May 28, 1984. The Hotel Regina Adelaide Palace was a few miles out of town on Lake Garda, and it was only when I got to my room that I realized I didn't have a room list. I'd have to call the front desk and ask for the person by name to get through to anyone. But it was no accident. There were no tour managers to look after the band as such, just Bob's helpers, and we found it was to be the pattern for the whole tour. We had to fend for ourselves. It became more difficult as we went along because we'd have to get the other's room numbers as we checked into a hotel. Otherwise, we wouldn't be able to get in touch with each other at all, especially if it was late at night and the night manager couldn't speak English. You'd be stuck in a hotel room looking at the wallpaper, which is one of the reasons I started a series of self-portraits, out of boredom. It gave me something to do with my time while I was wide awake with jet lag.

CHAPTER THIRTY-THREE

"Bloody Folk Singers..."

As it was a vacation area and still not quite in season, we had the hotel pretty much to ourselves, and Mick, Colin Allen, Greg Sutton, and I spent a lot of time in the bar and quickly made friends with Gino, the hotel's friendly barman. Since Mick knew Bob better than any of us, I asked him if he thought Bob would come and have a drink with us, as we hadn't seen hide nor hair of him since we'd arrived in Italy. Mick said it was unlikely, and we didn't want to bother Bob, but he went off to see if he could find him anyway. It seems Bob would take three rooms at a time in a hotel, and he might move from one to the other during the night, like a gypsy, and only his right hand man would know where he was. To my surprise, a half-hour later he wandered into the bar and came over to our table.

"Hey, Ian, Mick tells me you wanted to buy me a drink." He was still wearing the same clobber he had on at Point Dume, and I couldn't help wondering if he slept in his clothes.

"Yes, of course. What would you like?"

"Well, what are you drinking?" I think I'd been on the "greyhounds," a vodka and grapefruit combination that I'd been kidding myself was a health drink. He said he'd have one of those too and sat down with us. I was really chuffed to finally get to talk to him, and while Gino fixed the drinks the conversation went back and forth between all of us, just small talk. There were so many questions we wanted to ask him, but neither of us wanted to be the first to start the avalanche that would be impossible to stop if we asked him about his songs. Naturally, we couldn't ask the questions we really wanted to know the answers for, so we were very careful to keep the conversation light. Surprisingly, it was him who started it all.

"Mick tells me that there were some songs you thought I might do?" Oh boy, here we go, downhill all the way. I asked him why he wasn't doing "Sweetheart like You" from the new album, and he said maybe we should do it after all. I asked him if he ever considered doing "Positively 4th Street," one of my favourites, and we had another drink. He said, "Let's make a list of the songs that you want me to do."

We didn't know it yet, but we were being suckered. We wrote them down on a napkin as we got drunker and drunker. We were remembering all the old chestnuts from his early days, and I was so knocked out to be having this moment with Bob Dylan, and him drinking one for one with us, that I got very drunk, very quickly. We asked all the questions that we'd been waiting years to ask, all the questions that my old pal from The Muleskinners, Nick Tweddell, would've wanted to ask. I mean, he was talking plain and pulling no punches, he was answering all our questions, but it was much too much all in one go. The next day, I could hardly remember anything about the heartfelt conversation I'd looked forward to for years, all I had was a list on the back of a hotel postcard, another bleary self-portrait, and a bad hangover. Of the seven songs he wrote down, we did at least play two of them, "It's All Over Now, Baby Blue" and "Forever Young."

Late that night, we drove into Verona to check the equipment and sound before the big day, but when we arrived I was told we were now a three-piece band, as Mick had been fired earlier that evening. He was zonked out in his room and even his wife Valerie couldn't rouse him. It was bad enough trying to remember all the songs, but now I was terrified at the prospect of playing without Mick, since he took most of the solos and, more important, Bob needed him to lean on. With just organ, bass, and drums behind Bob's scratchy electric guitar, we would sound like a garage band or worse. Also, I'd been listening to "Positively 4th Street" and studying the songs on the new list all day, expecting to work on them that night, so I was a little frazzled.

Of course, as it turned out, Bob had no intention of doing any of the songs on that list that day, he was just having fun, and since he now knew exactly what we wanted to play, they wouldn't be mentioned. Talk about contrary.

The next day, after a sleepless night brought on as much by fear of playing the gig without him as by jet lag, Mick was reinstated in the band, with no hard feelings from Bob and great relief from the rest of us.

JC was head of security for Bob, and I knew him well from The Stones' tours. He's got a dry sense of humour, and you'd think he had ears at the back of his head, the way he cases the joint for nutters, groupies, or problems about to happen. He'll see the funny side of a potentially sticky situation if there is one to be seen, and as we drove in to Verona in the pouring rain that first night, he chuckled at the antics of the police in the unmarked car that was supposed to be protecting Bob. They had positioned themselves between our two motors, which wasn't very practical. So for a laugh, JC told our driver to slow down to a crawl. And as they didn't know whether to follow Bob's car or slow down for us to catch up, they braked, then raced ahead to catch Bob, who by then was long gone. A couple of minutes later, they raced past us in the other direction and that was the last we saw of them.

The coliseum in Verona is the largest in Italy, larger than the more famous one in Rome, and though it was built for gladiators and chariot races, it's used primarily for opera and classical concerts now. It's an awe-inspiring place and it absolutely reeks of history and bad plumbing. The backstage area was under construction when we were there. It was a mess, with ancient, squatting toilets that are probably as old as the building and a complete mystery to us. We went to our dressing room and Bob went to his, and after a while it became apparent that Bob wasn't going to see us before the show, and even worse, we weren't going to get a set list. Now, Bob must have written about a thousand songs, all of which he knew word perfect, so he'd probably forgotten that we were only human and merely knew about forty or so of them. When Bill Graham came into the dressing room, I asked if he could have a word in Bob's ear, and soon after he came back and brought Bob with him. He was still wearing the same clobber, and before we got to the question of a set list, he said:

"Hey, Ian, what are they wearing out there?"

"Bob, it's raining. They're wearing raincoats."

"What colours are they wearing?"

"Black, some yellow, a few red. You know, raincoats." I couldn't believe I was having this conversation.

"Hey, I like your shirt." He was pointing at me. This was my chance to show solidarity with my hero.

"Would you like it? It's yours," I said, unbuttoning it and handing it to him.

"Thanks." He put it on over his T-shirt.

"Hey, Greg, I like your jacket."

Now, Greg Sutton, our bass player, was wearing a purple satin jacket, and as far as I can remember, not the finest jacket in the world, but a nice bit of stage gear nonetheless. Bob, on the other hand was wearing a genuine old, worn, black leather Harley-Davidson motorcycle jacket. It was a classic. It might even have been the one he was wearing the day of his famous and mysterious motorcycle accident. Maybe it was just his way to show solidarity with us on that opening night, I don't know, but they swapped jackets and you get no prizes for guessing who made out like a bandit on the deal.

The conversation turned to Buddy Holly, and Bob told me that he'd seen him on stage once when he was very young. Being a big fan of Buddy's, I asked him what it was like, and he said that he was transfixed by him, that it was as if there was a halo around Buddy's head. It was a strange picture that he'd conjured up, and I tried to imagine Bob Dylan as a teenager looking up at the only slightly older Buddy Holly, and I couldn't. They seemed to come from different worlds, but in reality were just branches of the same tree. After Bob went back to his room, Bill brought us a set list, which consisted of five or six song titles in a box at the top of the page, some more in another box over to the right, and yet another box of maybe ten songs at the bottom. It wasn't very helpful, though it was well intentioned, and only served to throw us into more confusion.

While we were waiting to go on, Mitch Fennell, Bill's stage manager, told me that ancient Romans would build a mound of earth in the centre of this coliseum, lead a blind poet up to the top of it, and while he recited his poetry pump water in, leaving him standing on an island. Then they would unleash alligators. The poet would be totally unaware of the danger he was in, and eventually as the water lapped around his feet the alligators would crawl up onto the island and eat him alive, while the crowd roared their approval.

I told Bob the story as we were about to go on and the irony of it wasn't lost on him, him being a shortsighted poet himself. The show went well, but like most first nights it was a case of "hopefully most of the mistakes have now been made. It's over. Let's get on to the next one." Bob never wore my shirt again after that night in Verona, but for some reason he kept it with him, and carried it over his shoulder every day as he walked to the bus and to the plane.

It was odd, but the following year I saw a photograph of him wearing it on the back cover of his next album, *Empire Burlesque.*

We hardly ever knew which song would come next, and sometimes we wouldn't even know the song at all. There was one beautiful song he played occasionally that he'd never recorded and never rehearsed with us either. It was a tricky little number—we never knew the title—but he'd launch into it from time to time, leaving us totally in the dark. We would have loved to learn the tune, and I was in the best position to keep up with the chord changes, as I was the only one in the band who could see his hands. Greg was behind Bob so he'd try and follow me, whereas Mick could hardly make anything out of Greg's playing, as he was on the other side of the stage. One night Mick got really annoyed, threw his guitar down in desperation, and walked off the stage. I'm not sure Bob even noticed, but Mick ambled on a couple of minutes later, with a fresh drink and a cigarette in his hand, picked up his guitar and strapped it on, throwing me a "Stu" chin across the stage and miming the words: "Tsk, bloody folk singers. They're all the same."

Stu would have had a field day, as he had no patience with folk singers. It was only a problem for us in the band, though. When Eric Clapton sat in at the Wembley Stadium show, Bob turned his back on the audience and went through it for him, showing him each chord, the bridge, the chorus, everything. Naturally, we couldn't see what he was doing, so we were fucked again. He played and we fumbled away as usual, looking like a bunch of bloody amateurs. It was nothing compared to the night he started a song in the wrong key, and after a long introduction he played the next chord, which was correct but sounded completely wrong against the first one. He glared at me as if I'd just farted, and then carried on as if nothing had happened.

It was high summer when we got to Rome, and with three shows to play at Mussolini's Palais de Sports over five days, we had time to wander around the city, shopping and sightseeing. We stayed at the Lord Byron Hotel, an exclusive smaller hotel that had once been Byron's home. Bob had the master bedroom. When he came into our dressing room before the show, looking very dapper in a black drape jacket with a white high collar shirt, I said in a friendly way, just making conversation, "Hey, Bob, you're looking very 'Byronic' tonight," thinking he'd dressed that way intentionally. Six days later in Barcelona, I was mixing a drink when he walked into our dressing room. He came straight over to me and said, "Hey, Ian, at the show in Rome, why did you call me moronic?" I was bewildered for a second, and then realized he'd got the wrong end of the stick altogether, so I reminded him about the Byron Hotel, and the penny finally dropped. "Oh" was all he said. He'd been stewing for days wondering why I would call him moronic. I could think of much better ways to hand in my cards.

Even with all my good intentions, and after leaving my own band partly because I wanted to get away from drugs, I'd now found myself in a band of heavy users and got back onto coke in no time. It's Murphy's law, I suppose, but I had no strength to fight it and resolved to clean up after the tour. As for Bob, if he was using anything, he kept it to himself, but as soon as he got to the hotel he was gone until the next day anyway. There were always doctor's offices at the gigs in Europe, and Mick was a professional at squeezing prescription drugs out of them. He'd go in with a pained expression on his face, holding his back, complaining of old war wounds, and as he knew which symptoms would convince them to dish out painkillers or stimulants, he'd usually be successful. Then I'd go in after him saying, "Me too." It often worked.

Almost without exception, the people who worked close to Bob were well meaning, but unqualified or ill equipped to do the work they were assigned. They were an odd bunch. He appointed his American dentist as head of security, although JC actually did the job, and there were Italians, French, and Germans getting under your feet everywhere you went. The most useless individual of them all was a Frenchman called Roland Grivell. He was a "gofer" whose main job was to take care of the bags, but he was also supposed to pour drinks for us while we were onstage. He wasn't dim, but it proved to be too difficult for him. I'd ask for a vodka and he'd pour me gin. He was an annoying little man and his days were numbered.

We travelled all over Europe in a leased Vickers Viscount, an ancient propeller job I knew well from my early days in Hounslow. Living only three miles from Heathrow airport, and directly on the flight path, planes would roar over our house coming in to land every two minutes, and I could tell a Stratocruiser from a Super Constellation without looking up. Bob generally sat towards the front of the plane with the odd bunch, but on one flight he came up to the back where we were sprawled out recovering from the night before. He said he needed to look for a phone number he thought might still be in the Harley jacket, which Greg hadn't taken off since they swapped jackets in Verona. Greg assumed he was going to take the jacket back there and then, but Bob was definitely after something. He went through pockets Greg hadn't even discovered, but without finding whatever he was looking for. I think Bob was trying to figure a way to get the jacket back without losing face, but he gave it back to Greg without comment.

When we arrived at Nantes airport and stepped off the Viscount, it was such a beautiful sunny day we knew it had to be an indoor show. We were unlucky with the weather for most of the tour. Bob seemed to have his own rain clouds that followed us across Europe. We stayed at a hotel better known for its restaurant than its rooms, which were small and cramped. As the weather was so pleasant Mick, Greg, Colin, and I decided to enjoy a fine meal in the garden, where the tables were laid out beneath the overhanging branches of the trees. We sat down, ordered the food and a bottle of wine, and sat back to enjoy the evening while waiting for the meal to arrive.

The waiter brought bread and the wine, and after half an hour brought another bottle of wine. An hour had gone by and still we had no food, and by then we were starving and were getting pretty sloshed. Bob came out and sat down at a table with some people, while Grivell fussed and farted about, whispering to the waiter as he took their orders. Within fifteen minutes, their food was on the table and they were tucking in. It was too much; we'd had nothing to eat, but we'd had enough, and we knew Grivell was responsible. I went inside and asked the waiter what was going on, and he said that Grivell had particularly asked for Bob to be served before us, even though our meals were ready. He apologized for the misunderstanding and told me he'd serve us immediately.

Afterwards, I spotted Grivell walking towards me in the doorway of the restaurant and punched him on the nose before I knew what I was doing. It was a reflex action. I saw his face, I punched it, and the next moment he was flat on his back. It was very gratifying. As I hit him, Bob walked out of the restaurant behind him. He must have seen him fall, but he said nothing as he passed by.

It wasn't a happy tour by any means, and we made our fun out of desperation. By the time we got to Paris with about two weeks of the tour left to go, I'd had enough. I was doing too much blow, I was a nervous wreck all over again, and I was ready to jump ship and go home. I called Kim and poured my heart out to her but she convinced me to stick it out. As we were about to get on the bus outside the hotel, Bob came over to me. "Hey, Ian, I bought you a shirt," he said quietly. He handed me a really cool jazzy, pink shirt. I was touched that he'd thought of me and as I thanked him I couldn't help wondering whether he'd bought it to replace the shirt I'd given him in Verona—or was it for decking Grivell? That was a bit unlikely, but, whatever, it was a nice shirt and I wore it when we played at Wembley Stadium a few nights later.

The last night of the tour, on June 8, 1984, we played outside Slane Castle, near Dublin, on the banks of the river Boyne. Van Morrison sat in and sang "It's All Over Now, Baby Blue," as he had at the chateau outside Paris, and it was a beautiful, magic moment the crowd loved. For the encore, as well as having Van, from the north of Ireland, onstage, Bob introduced Bono of U2, from the south, to sing on "Blowing in the Wind." It was a lovely touch and the crowd went crazy. After Bob sang a verse and a chorus, Bono came up to the microphone and sent my head spinning because his voice was much louder than Bob's or even Van's. I was stuck at the organ and couldn't get away from the monitor speaker, and it was killing me, so I was shoving it away with my foot while I played, in a vain attempt at aiming it anywhere but at me. Bono was a crowd pleaser, but he hadn't done his homework the night before the gig.

"The answer my friend, the answer my friend, the answer my friend, the answer my friend…" He didn't know the answer, and he would've gone on all night if Bob hadn't taken the song home.

"…is blowing in the wind."

Bob came to the back of the bus on the drive back to the hotel and told us how pleased he was with the band, and said he'd love to do more shows if we were going to stay together. This was very unlikely, but it seemed like a good idea. I half expected an end-of-tour gathering, but Bob didn't surface. I was so glad to be going home and I partied all night with Mick, Valerie, and B.P. Fallon, who was Bob's P.R. in Ireland and an old friend. At the end of the night, I wrote Bob a short note telling him that it had indeed been an honour and a privilege, as I'd told him during rehearsals, and slipped it under his door, but I had to admit to myself that it hadn't been at all easy. I had my last line of coke on the Aer Lingus flight to London, and I was back in Kim's arms and back on track the following day in Los Angeles.

We celebrated being back together by flying to London two weeks later for a lightning visit with friends and relations, and then on to Harare, Zimbabwe, for a three-week holiday with Kim's stepmother Heather, and her brother, Dermot, who was now eighteen years old. Bill Kerrigan and Heather had been married for less than two years when he'd died of throat cancer in December 1982. Although Kim had been at their wedding in Zimbabwe, it was my first time in that part of Africa.

On the subject of smoking and cancer, I had been a decent long-distance runner at the age of twelve and represented Spring Grove Grammar School in cross-country runs at County meetings. But before I reached thirteen, I'd joined the elite smokers club in the boys' toilets and become a professional cigarette smoker instead of an athlete. Managing to get the smoke to billow out of my mouth and up into my nose the way the film stars took some practice, but after throwing up a few times I got the hang of it. What an Oscar-winning moment!

I happily chain-smoked between two and three packs of Pall Malls every day for twenty-five years until Kim's dad died. Mandy had tried to get me to quit, but I never really got motivated until he died. A tough man's man, I thought if it can cut him down then I had no chance, so I decided to quit by Christmas Day as a present to Kim and Mandy, and it was only then I began to realize how difficult it was going to be. I just couldn't stop lighting the damn things.

I was still smoking on February 5, 1983, when I came home after a late recording session with Bonnie Raitt. Kim and Mandy were fast asleep, so I poured myself a drink, lit a cigarette, and turned on the TV. A James Cagney movie, *Come Fill the Cup,* had just started. I love Cagney, but this was a different role for him. He played an alcoholic battling with the bottle, and James Gleason's character, another alcoholic, teaches him the "one day at a time" method. It was a revelation, and I thought I might adapt it to "one hour at a time" and quit smoking that way.

The following morning, I decided to wait for an hour after eating breakfast before I smoked my first of the day. It was easier than I thought, so I waited another hour and then another. I lasted for six hours that first day and felt pretty good about myself, but not confident enough to mention it to Kim and Mandy, who strangely hadn't even noticed the lack of smoke in the air. That night I smoked as usual at the studio, but the next day I held back for seven hours, and when the time came I put it back another hour, then another, and I've never smoked since!

My mum died of cancer later that year, and my dad died of a broken heart soon after. He'd quit smoking when I was a lad, but I still blame cigarettes because he'd be alive now if Mum hadn't died first. In 1993, Kim's mum, Joan, died of cancer too, so Kim and I are orphans thanks to that foul-smelling drug. Four out of four is a rotten result.

Meanwhile, after the gruelling ten-hour flight, we showed our passports and travel documents and went on to the baggage claim area, where a purple-clad Heather greeted us by smiling sweetly and asking Kim, "And is this the article you married?"

Although we'd seen photographs of each other, we hadn't met until that moment, and I must have been quite a sight, as my hair was dyed burgundy red and stuck out like a lavatory brush. Just as I was getting a warm hug from Heather, the young black official who'd stamped my passport a minute before put his hand on my shoulder and told me my visa had been denied. It was a quick hello, and an even quicker goodbye! He took me into an office where his white superior said I was going to be deported because of my criminal record, details of which I'd written on the back of the immigration form as requested. I'd written, "Possession of marijuana. Fined fifty pounds, Uxbridge Court, 1967." Under that I'd put as an afterthought, "U.S. Immigration has since waived ineligibility."

My bringing the U.S. Immigration into it was taken as an insult, and the officer made it clear that the U.S. government could do whatever it liked, but this was Zimbabwe, not the United States of America. As a drug offender I couldn't be allowed in the country, and I would be deported and put on the next available plane to London. Heather bulldozed her way into the office, introduced herself as my stepmother, and demanded to know what the problem was. Meeting a red spiky-haired person was one thing, but to find he was a drug addict as well was more than she had bargained for. However, as a schoolteacher, she recognized the senior official as the father of one of her pupils, and he recognized her too, and he smiled.

From then on, Heather was in charge. I was given a visa for three weeks and warned never to come back to Zimbabwe, as I couldn't be allowed in under any circumstances in the future.

With the drama behind us, we had the holiday of holidays, touring God's country in Heather's trusty car. Her old tyres would blow every few hundred miles and as new tyres were rarer than white people in the country at that time, we got into a routine of fixing flats by the side of the road that would make a Grand Prix mechanic green with envy. We visited the tea plantation Bill had once managed and dropped in on a host of friends and relatives, before we went on to Victoria Falls and Hwange Game Reserve. Until recently, it had been called by the name the British gave it years before, Wanke, which surely must have been a joke.

We watched silently from the grounds of Hwange Lodge, as a bull elephant appeared out of the bush and strode towards the watering hole, not fifty yards away. After ensuring there was no danger, he signalled to the herd, and forty-three other elephants came out of the dust to drink and wallow in the mud. What was most impressive was that the youngest were allowed to drink first while the grown-ups watched and waited. This was no movie or zoo, this was their world, and we were only getting a small glimpse. Americans go wild for Europe because it's so old compared to the New World, but Africa is ancient, and the feeling of the place stays with you.

CHAPTER THIRTY-FOUR

Ronnie

By 1985, Ronnie Lane had moved to Houston, Texas, where the ARMS America office was based and run by a woman called Mae Nacol. ARMS stood for "Action for Research into Multiple Sclerosis." When Ronnie asked me to play at a benefit for ARMS, I was more than happy to help out. He was living in a cheap apartment building in the suburbs next to the freeway with a character called "Big Bucks" looking after him. Though Ronnie spent most of his time in a wheelchair, he could still walk with some difficulty, and Big Bucks was seeing to it that he exercised with weights every morning and swam regularly at the YMCA. Big Bucks kept him busy and kept him amused, and Ronnie enjoyed being tortured to health. He was also getting hyperbaric oxygen treatment, which he said helped him a great deal. He would lie on a bed in an airtight chamber for an hour or more, during which the air was gradually replaced with oxygen.

He got quite high on it and said I should try it because, he explained with a twinkle in his eye, "If it makes me feel good, think how great you'll feel, man."

I spent ten days with him and saw how he lived, exercised, and ate–doing everything he could to improve his health. A little doozie every now and then kept him smiling, which was medicinal in my eyes.

One of the duties he performed was to go up to Mae Nacol's office in downtown Houston every day to answer the ARMS hot lines. That was where Nacol put on a show for us that boggles my mind to this day. She claimed that she had MS, but that it was in remission, and she gave us such a stirring speech about the research needed to cure this terrible disease that I began to wonder if maybe I was listening to a preacher. In fact, she was the head of a charitable organization that collected research funds in the region of $1,200,000 from people who'd been moved by Ronnie's plight and who'd seen stars like Eric Clapton, Jeff Beck, Jimmy Page, Steve Winwood, Kenney Jones, Charlie Watts, and Bill Wyman give their support.

Nacol assumed Ronnie would continue to ask his friends to play at benefit concerts, but Ronnie hadn't planned on being ARMS' poster boy and couldn't wait to get away from her and her demands. So he left Houston and moved to Austin, where the music community eagerly took him to their hearts.

But just spending time with Ronnie was my reward and rehearsing his songs with local hero Little Screaming Kenny was a lot of fun. A benefit at Fitzgerald's raised some cash and gave Ronnie a great night out. After ten days in Houston, he gave me a set of seven-pound weights to take back with me so I could continue the workouts. I could think of lighter gifts to carry on a plane flight, but it was a lovely thought.

Frustrated by the lack of work, I recorded an EP, *Last Chance to Dance*, with Paul Warren's production help. He also played guitar on the sessions. Johnny X engineered and mixed. My old mate from The Vagabonds, Phil Chen, played bass and David Kemper played drums. I thought it turned out very well and was almost as proud of the cover and label copy, because I designed them myself. A friend, Leslie Lian, had been at Oxford for the summer and had sent me a postcard that showed a carved head from one of the college walls. I thought it was odd, but when I showed it to Kim she got it straightaway and burst out laughing. It could have been carved from my likeness. It looked exactly like me. Although I didn't get it at first, I liked it so much I used it as the basis for the cover.

By this time, I had a new manager, Mike Jacobs, who got me a deal with Greenworld Records. I thought I was up and running, but the record company folded before the ink was dry on the contract, and unfortunately very few copies were sold before they went belly up.

When Albert Lee called to ask if I'd be interested in playing on The Everly Brothers' 1985 world tour, there was nothing to think about. I'd been a fan since "Bye Bye Love" in 1957. My first romantic moments were accompanied by their later records on Warner Brothers, and I'd loved their Albert Hall reunion show in London when I saw it on TV in 1984.

I hadn't met Albert, but I knew him from his days with the group Heads, Hands, and Feet back in England, and knew he'd been lead guitarist and musical director since the Brothers had got back together. Though I didn't have their most recent album, I boned up as quickly as possible on all the early songs that I had and drove to the Hollywood rehearsal room the next day. Of course, I knew some of the songs well enough to sing along, but it was a bigger thrill to be able to play the Floyd Cramer piano parts from the records. Phil and Don never came to the rehearsals, but Albert and Phil Donnelly, the other guitarist, helped me and the new drummer, Ron Krasinski, work out the arrangements, while they sang the "Everly" harmonies.

The old expression "it never rains but it pours" comes to mind, because we had only rehearsed for four days when, while I was packing for the flight to Hawaii, Jackson Browne called for me to play organ on a track of his soon to be released album, *Lives in the Balance*. I'd recorded it once before, but he'd recut the track since and wanted me to play the same part on it again. Though I was concerned I'd miss the flight and lose my new job, I didn't want to pass on the opportunity of being on his new record. So I drove to his home studio in the hills above the Hollywood Freeway and put it down as quickly as my fingers would allow. Knowing I had a flight to catch as soon as I'd finished, he drove us to his bank in Hollywood in an old Buick convertible to get the cash. A gentleman pays on the same day, but a real gentleman pays in cash. As we crossed Sunset Boulevard, a redheaded girl in a passing car called out to us, "Hey, boys, are you looking for a good time?" I thought my luck had changed, but it was just Bonnie Raitt messing with us. A quick hello and goodbye, and with cash in hand, I drove home. After which Kim took me to the airport. A kiss, a cuddle, and an "I'll call you."

I finally got to meet Don and Phil in the first-class lounge at LAX. They were very natural, and were really easy to be around, no airs and graces at all, and they chatted, drank with us, and told stories in the upstairs compartment of the 747 for most of the flight to Honolulu. There was a day off, and then we played the first gig on the beach at Waikiki the following day. It was a relief to get it over. First gigs are always very stressful. I missed a couple of chord changes here and there, and a couple of endings went west, but on the whole it was okay. The best part of the show was being able to listen to Don and Phil's sweet harmonies on "Cathy's Clown" and "All I Have to Do Is Dream" in person for the first time ever.

We flew to Australia the next day and checked into the Sebel Town House in the notorious King's Cross area of Sydney. Phil Donnelly, Ron, and I walked out for a drink as soon as the bags arrived, and we were only a short distance from the hotel when I spotted Reneé Geyer doing a left in her Mercedes. It was unbelievable luck, because another second and she'd have been gone. I shouted at her and she almost had a baby when she saw me. I'd intended to call her the next day to see if she might be in town, but this was much better. After hugs and kisses, she told me she was on her way to some trendy magazine's opening party, and that of all things Ricky Fataar and Penelope would be there. We all jumped into her car and she took us to meet the fashionable, the fortunate, and the filthy rich! It was an unexpectedly interesting night and it was great to see Ricky and Penelope again. They invited me, Albert, and his wife, Karen, to dinner on our next day off. Although you might think travelling is its own reward, one of the few joys of touring around the world is seeing old pals again, especially when you have the opportunity of a home-cooked meal.

On previous Australian tours with Small Faces and The Faces, we'd never played in Perth, so I was interested to see something of the city while I was there. Ron and I spent a very pleasant afternoon wandering around the city, shopping, eating, and drinking. On the second day I began to notice that a lot of the girls had thick ankles, and he eventually had to agree there was something in my theory. When I mentioned it to the other guys in the band they just laughed. "You're mad," the bass player, Phil Cranham, said. As we were leaving the hotel for the airport the following morning, Albert said he had something interesting he wanted to show me when we got on the plane to Adelaide.

He'd been carrying a very large book around with him for some days, and I'd been intrigued by its size and title–*The Farthest North of Humanness, Letters of Percy Grainger 1901-1914*. He was a long-dead Australian classical composer and I couldn't have imagined a more boring book to take on the road, and a heavy one as well. But Albert had found it fascinating and was grinning from ear to ear when we got to the airport. Once inside the terminal, he opened the book at a page he'd marked and handed it to me. Percy had toured Australia in 1908, and on the day he sailed from Perth, he wrote to his Danish girlfriend:

"It is lovely to see the tight-shaped legs of the small English girls on board here; I cannot deny that I think my race (Australians) are very ugly, in any case compared with the English. The girls' ankles, here at home, are so thick and ignobly formed, that there is nothing noble, concentrated, or fine about them."

Well, I'd been vindicated. I wasn't mad at all. Maybe a little crazy, but not mad.

Adelaide's hotels and motels were fully booked when we arrived, because the scene of the Mod scootercade for The Who/Small Faces tour in 1968 would become the track for Adelaide's first Grand Prix in two days. A cheap motel was found out of town on Christies Beach, and the flat sandy beaches with kangaroos running wild in the fields suited me fine. George Harrison was in town for the racing, being a formula one fanatic, but he came to the Friday night show at the Memorial Drive Tennis Stadium because he was a long-time fan and friend of The Everly Brothers. He came backstage afterwards and invited us all to his hotel, where he, Don, Phil, Albert and Phil Donnelly sat around playing the old songs, while the rest of us drank and sang along. He arranged for Don and Phil to get gold cards for the big race the next day, but when the time came to leave, the thought of having their ears blasted by a lot of high performance cars didn't appeal to them, so the band got to use them instead.

George met us at the track and showed us around the pit area, introducing us to Barry Sheen, the world motorcycling champion. Royalty couldn't have been treated better, and the gold cards gave us access everywhere, even the pits. But we could watch the pit crews, scurrying about in matching overalls in the hospital-like conditions, better from above, as the bar and restaurant overlooked them. It was the perfect place to watch the race. The cars zoomed past in a blur of colour at breakneck speeds, and as colourful as it was, it was far noisier than any Deep Purple concert and I couldn't work out who was in the lead. At my elbow was Australia's Prime Minister, Bob Hawke, who wanted to know the same thing. So I went inside to the bar to ask someone and bumped into a chubby man in a panama hat who looked strangely familiar. It was none other than Billy Gaff, ex-manager to the stars.

It had been nine years since I'd seen him, and it was no more of a thrill then than the last time. It was as much as I could do not to chin him, but instead I asked him the question on everybody's lips. He didn't know who was in the race, never mind who was in the lead. As I said before, a useless person.

I hadn't been back to Belfast since Small Faces played there in 1968. The place looked very beaten up and though everybody I met seemed friendly enough, there were barriers around the Forum Hotel, and you had to be escorted by a policeman through a checkpoint every time you went out or came back in. It didn't look as if it would be conducive to fun, but I hadn't counted on the loyalty of the fans, which hadn't diminished over the years because The Everlys always came to Ireland when they toured Europe.

Belfast audiences are arguably among the best in the world, along with Glasgow, Detroit, and Berlin before the wall came down. Where life is hard, people need to be entertained, and the crowd at Grosvenor Hall showed The Everly Brothers how much they appreciated and loved them.

We played two really good shows, The Brothers excelled themselves, and we drank pint after lovely pint of Guinness with members of Clannad in the hotel bar until I dragged myself to my room for a few hours of restless sleep.

The Belfast Festival was in full swing while we were there, and comedians, actors, playwrights, and musicians filled the restaurant as I sat down to a cup of tea and a hearty breakfast of eggs, bacon, sausage, tomato, black pudding, and fried bread. Glorious hangover food! As I was tucking in, I spotted Michael Palin walking in the door. I'd met him once at Woody's house, The Wick, in Richmond, but it was a brief encounter and I didn't think he would remember me. But as I looked up, him being such a polite, nice chap, he smiled as if we knew each other. It was an awkward moment because my brain wasn't properly awake, and I had nothing to say anyway, but as he passed the table I blurted out, "How's it going?" in a knee-jerk reaction. Innocent enough, but he stopped and proceeded to tell me that he'd had a bit of a rough night actually, and that he was re-thinking the whole piece. I, of course, had no idea what "piece" he was talking about and had no comment to offer in reply. But he went into great detail, and the whole time I was thinking, "I've got a hangover, which isn't going to allow me to say anything sensible to this lovely man." About this time, I think it started to dawn on him that he didn't know me after all, and that there was no good way to end the conversation with any grace, except by saying he was going to get his breakfast, which he did. At which point I got up and left the restaurant. It's one of a few embarrassing moments that I'll talk about. Sorry about that, Michael.

Not unlike the time I played the L.A. Coliseum with The Stones in 1981. Chuch had built a small bar behind the amps on our side of the stage, and while Stu barrel-housed "All Down the Line," I would step around the back of the amps for a drink. Being in Los Angeles meant the sides of the stage were thick with stars, and some were allowed to hang out at the most private bar in the world. I'd read recently that Richard Harris had undergone heart surgery and had been recuperating in the West Indies. And though I'd never met the man, my first thought when I saw him at the bar was to tell him how good it was to see him up and about. My friendly comment was met with a stony silence, and he turned and walked away without a word. I couldn't think why he should be annoyed until about halfway through the next song, when I realized I'd been talking to Peter O'Toole, not Richard Harris. But I'm sure they've been mistaken for each other before. They are both, after all, Irish actors who've been known to take a drink or two.

We took the train from Belfast and stayed at the Gresham Hotel on O'Connell Street in Dublin. This time round there was to be no taxi ride to Gran's house in Mountrath though, as both Gran and Uncle Ned were no longer living. But I was in another heaven, being less than a mile from the Guinness brewery. But as we had a gig at the RDS Hall that night, followed by a day off, we had an early flight the next morning, so I had to box clever.

To my complete surprise, the promoter brought a full keg of Guinness backstage before the show, slammed it on a table, and poured himself a pint. "Come on!" He ordered. "I'm not taking it back full."

Phil Donnelly was the local hero, of course. Every solo he played brought the house down. He was known in Ireland as the Clontarf Cowboy, because he'd come from his hometown of Clontarf, near Dublin, and settled in Nashville. It may have been the warm reception that the crowd gave him that convinced him to get into politics, but the thought passed quickly. After the show, Heather's sister Hazel and her family came backstage. Between them, Don and Phil, and the guys in the band, we emptied the keg dutifully for the promoter before we left for the Gresham, where we drank and chatted until the bar closed, very much later, early flight be damned!

The Everly Brothers played two nights at Hammersmith Odeon in London. It's now owned by a beer company and called Labatt's Apollo these days, but it was the site of many great shows I've seen, including the Stax Volt Revue, Aretha Franklin's first London appearance, and several of Muhammad Ali's great fights via satellite. I got a message after the first show that Linda was waiting outside the stage door, but it couldn't have been Keith Moon's sister Linda, because I'd already called to ask if any of the family wanted tickets, and they'd had other plans. I thought it was a mistake, and I was having a drink in the hospitality room when the doorman handed me a note. It said, "Hello, Mac, do you remember me? I was your first lover, Linda."

Oh boy! Of course I remembered Linda Fogden. How could I forget her, even though it was twenty-three years since we'd last seen each other? I popped my head around the stage door and recognized her immediately. It was a wonderful surprise, and she hadn't changed a bit. We used to make love at her parent's house in Chiswick while "Cathy's Clown" and "Ebony Eyes" played in the background, and her mum and dad were at the pub. I wasn't in a band then. I was still at art school. But later, after we'd broken up, she knew I'd joined the Small Faces and then The Faces, but she was married, with a child, and the music just hadn't interested her. She'd gone to see The Everly Brothers out of nostalgia for the old days, and until the part of the show where Don introduced us one by one, she still hadn't realized I was on the stage. It was only when he said my name that she fell out of her seat!

I walked the rainy streets of Oxford all afternoon on the day we played at the city's Apollo Theatre. I was searching for the gremlin in the postcard that I'd used for the cover of *Last Chance to Dance,* but got nothing but rain in my face for my troubles. I couldn't find the postcard at any of the newsagents either. But about a year later, I received one in the mail, signed, "With love from Albert." I don't know how Albert Lee ever found it, but it was a lovely surprise.

We did a Sunday night television show live from the stage of Her Majesty's Theatre in London. Whoever organized the bill must have been playing a joke because The Beverly Sisters were on the show too.

But at least it gave me the opportunity of meeting Joy Beverly, who I'd had a crush on ever since I was a small boy. She was still gorgeous, and she smiled sweetly at her greying fan. It was like being back in the early Sixties. Jimmy Tarbuck, the comedian, brought the acts on one by one, and it was a tired old show all round except for The Everly Brothers, who sang as sweet as ever.

Sacha Distel, the French singer and guitarist, sang a really lame version of John Lennon's incredibly beautiful "Imagine." Now I can't imagine why anyone would ever bother to try and sing that song, as it's John's personal statement, and it's been done perfectly well, thank you. My advice would be to leave it alone. I feel the same way about Hank Williams' "I'm So Lonesome I Could Cry," and Ray Charles' version of "Georgia on My Mind." There doesn't seem to be any point in singing them again, ever. Especially not by the likes of Michael Bolton or Sacha Distel. Our dressing room was up on the fifth floor, and when he started squawking the line "You may say I'm a dreamer…" I lost control and screamed out, "You're fuckin' dreaming, mate!"

CHAPTER THIRTY-FIVE

A Death in the Family

After The Faces dream turned into a nightmare in 1975, I didn't speak to Rod Stewart until Woody passed me the phone one day at the Getty house at the end of the 1978 Stones tour. I had nothing much to say, as I still mistakenly put all the blame for The Faces demise on him, but no threatening language was used and it was good to talk to him again. A few months later, when we moved to Malibu, I discovered that he and his current wife, Alana, were living only a mile up the beach from us, but whether he knew we were there or not, neither of us made contact. Then, some years later, I was surprised to get an invitation to his birthday party at his house in Bel Air. It was slightly disconcerting for me because he behaved as if no time had passed, and as if we'd always been pals. Yet it had been years since we'd seen each other and in all that time I'd still never got my Hammond organ and Leslies back. But putting that aside, it was very good to see him and Kelly Emberg, his model of the moment. We had a great evening. It was quite like the old days, except this time he bought the booze.

His people called in 1986 and this time it was to get The Faces back together at his show at Wembley Stadium. As Ronnie spent most of his time in a wheelchair by then and couldn't play bass anymore, Woody got Bill Wyman to fill in for him. Kim and I flew in from Los Angeles, and Ronnie and his assistant Jo Rae Dimenno, came in from Austin, Texas, where he'd moved from Houston after the ARMS fiasco. The Wembley get-together seemed like a grand idea at the time, but Rod never even came to the rehearsal room in Hammersmith and we were left to sort it out for ourselves. It was a classic Faces situation, really. Poor old Bill had one day to rehearse the songs with us, and the sound check at Wembley ended up as little more than a photo session. Rod would call from home to discuss what we should play, and then he'd change his mind, so in the end we just got on with it, rehearsing the songs we wanted to play.

All this time, Ronnie was under the impression he was going to sing a couple of his own songs, so we rehearsed them as well. Just as Bill was getting really confused, we went down to the pub. As Woody had said on the phone the week before we flew over, "We'll wack it out in the dressing room." It was typical Faces "fuck the gig" mentality; we were only playing five songs to 70,000 people, and we went down a storm anyway!

While on vacation in San Diego, I called home to get my messages. There were three from Chesley Millikin, who'd managed Terry Reid, Stevie Ray Vaughan, and Ronnie Lane amongst others, but he was an old pal first and foremost, and a very, very dear pal of Jerry Garcia's. He'd called to let me know Grateful Dead was looking for a new keyboard player after the recent death of Brent Mydland and they intended sending me a tape. All I had to do was to play along with the tape and send it back to them. Chesley said if I got the gig it could be worth at least $250,000 a year and that I could live wherever I liked because they'd fly me in from anywhere.

The only trouble was, I didn't like what I'd heard of the music. But when I rang him he said, "It doesn't matter, kid, just send that tape back and you'll make a small fortune!"

I was excited by the thought of the money, so I stopped at a record store and bought their newest CD. While Kim took the dog out for a pee, I put the CD in the player. Oh, what a disappointment. I wasn't enjoying the music, and when Kim came back in the room I was in a severe state of depression, staring blankly at the wall.

"Whatever's wrong!" she said.

"I can't do it, not even for that money," I said. "I just don't fuckin' get it."

However, I played on sessions with Bruce Springsteen, Melissa Etheridge, Stray Cats, Joe Cocker, Izzy Stradlin, Buddy Guy, Otis Rushn and Taj Mahal, as well as many young bands in the coming months and years, and I also played a lot of gigs around Los Angeles. I toured with Bernie Larsen's Cry on Cue and Pat McLaughlin, a soulful singer and songwriter. We recorded his amazing album, *Get Out And Stay Out,* which was shelved for five long years, and only a few people could have heard it when it did finally get released. I toured with David Lindley for a whole year after that. He's a total nut and a giant of a guitarist, and it was rewarding musically, spiritually, and financially, which is extremely rare in this business. I put several of my own bands together, including Ian McLagan's Loco, Barking Dogs, The Thump Band, and even The Four Kinells–for a joke. But it was only when Craig Ross and Jimmy Ashhurst, guitarist and bass player from The Broken Homes, popped round to see me that I formed another band.

As their band was falling apart at the time, they offered me their services. I called Nick Vincent, a brilliant drummer I'd seen a year before, and we became the newest version of The Bump Band. I'd missed singing and playing my songs more than I thought. There's nothing quite like the feeling you get when you play a new tune for the first time live and the audience applauds. We played regularly at The Mint on Pico Boulevard and The Coconut Teazer on Sunset in Hollywood, and we'd always get members of up-and-coming bands in the audience who'd come down to check me out. At the end of the night, I'd often be asked if I ever considered doing sessions. I'd have to explain that playing on recording sessions was what I did for a living, and as a result I got a lot of session work from young bands who'd come to see me play.

One night Chris Robinson and Johnny Colt from The Black Crowes popped in to say hello. George Drakoulias, their producer, had asked me to play on their first record, *Shake Your Money Maker,* a year before and when he'd played me their rehearsal tapes in his office at Def American, I was really impressed with Chris's voice and was eager to do the record. But when he told me they wanted to rehearse in Atlanta for ten days before going in the studio, I said I could do it in a day, which is what I'd done before with The Georgia Satellites. I explained it would be cheaper for them as well. But he said, "They want you to become part of the band." I called him back later and left a figure with his secretary, but he never called back. Luckily, my friend Chuck Leavell got the phone call instead, and naturally, he did the whole record in a day, which just goes to show I was right, and you can't win 'em all.

Since their album had been released, reviewers had been quick to name Rod as one of Chris's influences, and while it was certainly true, I appreciated and thanked him for mentioning Steve Marriott as his main man in a

Rolling Stone interview. Steve gets overlooked sometimes and he's still not in The Rock and Roll Hall of Fame, whatever that is. It suddenly dawned on me that as Steve and Pam had lived in Atlanta for several years, it would have been almost impossible for Chris not to have bumped into Steve.

Looking at me pitifully, he said, "Mac, I was twelve." I forget sometimes how fast time passes.

While I was on stage with The Bump Band at The Teazer one night, a stranger handed me a scrap of paper with Steve's phone number. He'd been recording tracks with Pete Frampton in Los Angeles and was returning to London in a couple of days, but wanted to get in touch with me before he flew back. I flinched when I saw his name on the piece of paper, and as we hadn't been in contact since 1978, I could only imagine how exhausting it would be to spend time with him, so I never called.

Two days later, on April 20, 1991, the night he arrived back in England, he died in a fire at his home. Jet-lagged, he'd apparently fallen asleep with a cigarette in his hand. It was a horrible way to die.

He'd lived so many lives already, the fact that he was finally dead wasn't totally unexpected, but if he'd died of a heart attack or an overdose I wouldn't have been surprised. The surprise was that he lived so long. Though he could be hell to be around, he had a pure heart and I loved him as a brother. He never stopped rocking, whichever band he had at the time—Small Faces, Humble Pie, Packet of Three, The Official Receivers or Steve Marriott and the DTs. Steve's band names in themselves tell you something about his attitude to fame and fortune. He was already famous, and the fortune slipped easily through his fingers. For years, he'd played hard in pubs, giving it all he had, but above all, I think he just wanted to be liked. God Bless him, you can't fault a man for that.

Woody came to town to finish his fifth album, *Slide on This,* at A&M Studios, and I managed to get on the record by the skin of my teeth. He'd cut all the tracks at his home studio in Ireland, but he and I cut a tender version of his beautiful song, "Breathe On Me," sitting at the piano. Bernard Fowler, who Woody called "The Foul One," had been singing background with The Stones since the Steel Wheels tour, and was producing the album with him. Woody even had a keg of Guinness in the control room, where he and Bernard were tossing them back as I played. Woody sat in with my band at The Teazer one night, and the place went berserk. I was surprised at how they reacted, but I tend to forget how famous he is. The security at the club wasn't impressed, though, and even grabbed the unfinished drink out of his hand at 1:50 A.M. the way they do with everybody.

Woody planned a six-week American club tour in October to promote *Slide on This,* and as he'd been asked to take part in a tribute show for Bob Dylan at Madison Square Garden on October 16, he decided to stay and rehearse in New York for ten days after it. Johnny Lee Schell had been asked to play rhythm guitar on the tour as well, so Johnny Lee and I flew out a couple of days early so we could go to the "Bobfest" with him. I'd had a few drinks on the plane and couldn't digest the meal, so I was already pretty wasted when I arrived in New York. With stars like Neil Young, Stevie Wonder, George Harrison, Eric Clapton, Roger McGuinn, Tom Petty, and The Clancy Brothers celebrating Bob's music, you'd think that would have been enough to please anyone. But the backing band for the night was Booker T. and the MG's, so I was in my element. Booker T. Jones, Steve Cropper, Donald "Duck" Dunn, and Jim Keltner replacing the late, great Al Jackson, played magnificently all night. Woody sang Bob's "Seven Days," which we'd cut on his *Gimme Some Neck* album, and he came over really well.

Apart from the obvious choices, Neil Young put on an electrifying performance, sweating up the stage like a teenager. It was a truly magical night, and I got to shake Booker T.'s hand again, and although we'd met several times before, it always seems to be the first time for him.

There was to be an after-show gathering at Tommy Makem's bar on 57th Street, and as I'd done nothing more than listen to great music and drink vodka all night, the idea of a couple of pints of Guinness to round it off appealed to me. I stepped out of Woody and Jo's limousine, wobbled through the door, and Jim Callahan greeted me.

"Are you gonna 'ave a pint, Mac?"

"Yes please, JC. How are you doin'?"

"Not bad, mate. Does Woody want one?"

"I reckon so."

"Here you are, mate." And with that, he handed me a Guinness. Life was good. "Wolfie's down there, he'll show you where to go." Jim pointed to the back of the bar, where Wofie Horgan, one of JC's team of security men, was keeping the public out of the roped-off area.

Many of the musicians who'd played that night were there, and Bob Dylan sat with a girl at a table on one side, against the wall. I said hello and Woody suggested he might try a pint and he said, "Sure." It was all very civilized and friendly and you might even say low-key, but it soon started to unravel for me. I remember going to the bathroom for a pee, and it must have been at the same time as Bob, because when I got back up the stairs and sat back down, Chuch was all over me.

"What was going on down there between you two? Man, that was funny! You were telling him you wanted a million dollars in cash and as I walk in Bob turns to me and says, 'I'll give you a million dollars in cash if you'd get him outta here.' Then I see a girl sitting on the floor, naked from the waist down with her legs wide open, and I'm thinking, What the fuck is going on?"

It was already too long ago for me. I didn't remember seeing Bob in the toilet, never mind the naked girl. The fact is, I often ask people for a million dollars in cash, as a joke, figuring that one day someone's going to give it to me. I had a bite to eat and fell asleep soon after. The next thing I remember, someone was telling a very boring story, and then I nodded off again.

When I woke up the next afternoon, Woody told me I'd interrupted the storyteller by singing a song that Steve Marriott once taught me at the top of my voice. Bill, Kim's dad, used to sing the same little ditty too, but only when he was really pissed.

It begins: "I love my wife, I love her dearly, I love the hole she pisses through."

"Oh my God!" I said in horror, not remembering anything, and not knowing how the story was going to end. "Did anyone laugh?"

"I laughed," said Woody quietly. I groaned. I could just imagine the horrified looks on the faces of my idols as I made a complete arse of myself in front of them.

"Jesus! Thank God I didn't sing it again...I didn't sing it again, did I?" A faint memory filtered through the headachy haze of my hangover.

"Yeah, you did," he said, quieter this time.

"Oh no! Did anyone laugh the second time?"

"No, nobody."

CHAPTER THIRTY-SIX

Slide on This

Rehearsals began whenever Woody walked into the main room at Studio Instrument Rentals' building on West 25th Street. And as we both liked the bangers and mash at Kennedy's on 57th Street, we generally had the first meal of the day there and washed it all down with a couple of pints poured by Michael Glynn, the proprietor, before we got to work. Apart from Woody, Johnny Lee, and myself, Bernard Fowler sang, Wayne P. Sheehy, who'd also played on the album, was on drums, and Shaun Solomon, a funky player from New York, was on bass. Chuck Leavell had played keyboards on the record and he rehearsed with us and played the first few gigs before getting called back to his Christmas tree farm near Macon, Georgia. For the three Texas dates, Bobby Keys joined and played. I always call Bobby "Wide" because he's always been a chubby chap and he usually calls me "Short stuff" or "Jimminy Cricket" because I'm small. But now that he's lost weight, I can't call him anything other than Bobby and he can still call me anything he damn well likes!

One of the highlights of Woody's tour was the night we played at The Terrace in Austin, Texas. Chesley Millikin threw a party for us and for Ronnie Lane the night before the show at Manor Downs, the racetrack he managed on the east side of town. He laid on free booze and a Texas barbecue. Ronnie was puffing at a joint one minute, munching on a rib the next, and sipping my vodka whenever I wasn't looking. It was a blast and we were all pretty blitzed when we got back to the Driskill Hotel.

The next night, Ronnie came on in his wheelchair to a roar from the crowd and sang "Ooh La La" with Woody. It would be the last time Ronnie Lane would grace any stage, and he took over that night, starting the verse before Woody had even finished playing the intro. The song ended with Woody sitting in his lap and giving him a big kiss, much to Ronnie's and everyone else's amusement.

Although The Faces never played in Austin, having the three of us onstage that night was pretty exciting for members of the audience, but it was a far bigger thrill for me and Woody to see Ronnie singing again.

Usually on a club tour, you'd use the "in-house" P.A. and lights, but Woody carried full production, which meant trucks carrying our own sound and lights, and catering too. Eoghan McCarron, the sound engineer who'd recorded and co-produced the album, recorded every show as well. The idea was to put out a live album later. For Woody, it was very different from any tour he'd ever been on. With Faces and Stones tours, there had always been a private jet; we even had one on The New Barbarians tour. He'd paid the album costs out of earnings from sales of his paintings, and to keep touring costs down, we travelled on buses instead of planes. These weren't ordinary buses though, they were "top of the line," luxurious coaches with leather upholstery and a double bed in the back for Woody and Jo. Another wonderful thing about this extremely jolly tour was that Nick Cowan, Woody's manager, had made a deal with Guinness to supply the brand new cans they'd just brought out in every area, and in selected places they even supplied a keg and a cold box for the dressing room! Now, it's always been fun to play with Woody, but now it was harder to leave the dressing room after the show than ever before!

The first few drives were quite short, but the long drive from Miami to New Orleans, a distance of some nine hundred miles, was the real test for Woody. Nick hoped he'd take advantage of the bed and sleep, because he wanted him to get some rest on the tour, but he was only in bed for ten minutes before he got up again, and we carried on drinking all the way. It was to be the pattern for the whole tour and, after all, we could always rest when we got home, couldn't we?

Jim Sullivan was our swagman, or merchandiser. He'd worked on The Stones tours and was a big fan and friend of The Replacements, a band who I'd been told were influenced by The Faces. Although I hadn't heard much of their stuff, I'd heard enough to know they were an irreverent bunch of rascals. Tony Berg had produced one of their albums, and he invited me to meet them at a gig at the Hollywood Palladium in 1990. I wasn't prepared for them at all. I was in the hospitality room when they came bounding in, bouncing off the walls, and dressed in grubby boiler suits. They were high, on speed I guessed, and they were really drunk as well. They reminded me of The Faces so much; they were wrecked, and ready to hit the stage just like we used to be. During a tour in those days, I'd notice my alcohol and drug intake increase until there were nights without sleep and days without food, and I imagine it was like that with them. But whereas I'd walked in fresh from a bath and a home-cooked meal, they were in the middle of a gruelling tour, and I was the alien, not them.

Paul Westerberg and Tommy Stinson shook my hand, and Paul offered me a drink. They were buzzing about and they couldn't keep still.

"D'you wanna sit in?" Paul asked.

"Er, yeah, okay."

"D'you know any of our songs?" Tommy said.

"Well…er, no, actually I don't. Do you have a keyboard?"

"No." That seemed to be that.

"Well, have a great show anyway," I said, and they bounded out of the room and left me to go back out front and watch them play. They were frightening, but great, and I could see why people loved them. They rocked, but they had fun with it, and even played Petula Clark's "Downtown" and made it sound like one of their own songs.

Since that time I'd bought several of their CDs, but the one that impressed me the most was the last group album they made before Paul left and went solo. Called *All Shook Down,* it was a classic record and should have been the one that made them international rock gods. Jim Sullivan had tried to get me to play on Paul's record, since he was recording in New York during our rehearsals, but he'd left town before we could get together. When we arrived in Los Angeles, Jim heard that Paul was recording in San Francisco, and as that was our next stop, he called ahead and arranged for us to go over to the studio on the day of the gig.

Rod came to the Palace show in Hollywood, but I hardly recognized him because he had a full beard. I thought he must have retired from the business and opened up a health food shop, but he hadn't. My Hammond broke down in the first number, but the keyboard tech, Andy Topeka, managed to change the bottom speaker in the Leslie and switch amplifiers in the space of three minutes and I was back in on the intro of "Flying" before Woody could say "Where've you been?" I think Rod had to be impressed by Bernard's singing of that song. It had been The Faces' first single, but we never played it after 1970 and doing it on Woody's tour had proved to me just how strong it is. After the show, The Edge came backstage and Rod took great delight in taking the piss out of him, and everybody else, for that matter.

We got to San Francisco on the day off before the show at The Warfield, and the Irish bunch. Wayne and Eoghan, found an Irish pub only a short walk from the hotel and dragged me with them, kicking and screaming.

By the time the second pint arrived, I'd forgotten all about Paul's session, and we carried on drinking until they shut up shop. When I heard Jim's voice on the phone in the horrible morning, I groaned and told him I was hung over like a pair of trousers, and although I knew I'd be fine by the time of the gig, a session would be too much like hard work. He wouldn't hear of it, and eventually I had to give in and we set off for Coast Recorders. It was a blisteringly sunny day, but mercifully, the studio was cool and dark, and I watched as Paul put a bass on a track as Matt Wallace worked the board. Paul played as if he was tracking on a demo, goofs were instantly forgiven in favour of the feel. These days he was sober and relaxed, unlike our first meeting, and this time he was the alien. It would be nice to be around him when we're both stone-cold sober, or drunk.

There were two songs he wanted me on, and after I played the slower and beautiful "First Glimmer," Matt put "Silver Naked Ladies" on and turned the speakers up loud. It was a rocker, and it was right up my street. I think I only went through it a couple of times, but I was a sweating mess of Guinness and piano hammer dust by the time I'd finished and the hangover was long gone.

Paul came to the sound check, and spotting Van Morrison backstage he asked if I'd introduce him, as he was a fan. After the show, I cornered Van in Woody's tiny dressing room and introduced Paul, mentioning that he was a great songwriter. Van had been drinking wine and took exception to him, for no apparent reason.

"Who are you? A songwriter? Play me a song. Do you have a tape?" He said in Paul's general direction.

"No, Van," I said. "He hasn't got a tape. He just wanted to meet you."

"Hand me the tape. Come on, play it!" He kept on about this nonexistent tape, pointing at the cassette player on the table, but he meant no harm, and Paul let it slide. It was an unusual meeting of the minds.

The tour ended on December 5 at The Chestnut Cabaret in Philadelphia, but we got into town the night before. Wayne and I went to the club to watch NRBQ play. They are, in my humble opinion, one of the all-time best bands to ever hit a stage. They play every style of music, not just rhythm and blues, and Terry Adams, the keyboardist, plays dirty blues, rock, and bebop in a combination that defies categorization. He's a piano magician! So it was a very proud moment when he asked me to sit in on piano at their show in Philly and one that I'll treasure forever.

One of the best shows I've ever seen Bonnie Raitt put on was when Charles Brown and NRBQ opened for her at The Universal in North Hollywood in the early Nineties. Kim and I had seen Charles in the intimate setting of The Cinegrill at the Roosevelt Hotel in Los Angeles the year before and it was a fabulous show. But at The Universal, NRBQ came on first and took no prisoners! The fact that Charles Brown followed them only made them work harder and when Bonnie came onstage it was the best I've ever seen her perform, and I've seen a few of her shows in my time.

After Christmas 1991 at home, we flew to Japan for the last leg of Woody's tour, and on the last night at Budokan in Tokyo, everyone in the band except Woody and I got a severe case of food poisoning. At one point during the show, Bernard had to run from the stage in the middle of a verse. After the show, Slash from Guns N' Roses came to Woody's room for a few drinks and asked Woody to sit in with them the following night at Budokan. I said good-bye to everyone about 2 A.M. because my flight to Los Angeles was early the next day and I still had to pack. About 4 A.M. I woke up and had to run to the bathroom. It had got to me too, but delayed by a few hours. The flight back home was miserable because I couldn't eat or drink and kept having to use the bathroom. Woody didn't catch it, whatever it was, and I suspect his system has so much alcohol in it, no bug could survive!

Rod was to receive a lifetime achievement award at The Brit Awards in London in February, and he flew me in to play "Stay with Me" with Woody and Kenney at the end of the show. Bill Wyman played bass, like before, but this time he got the chords all wrong. It wasn't totally his fault though, because we only rehearsed for an hour at John Henry's before we went down the pub. As a laugh, we went into "Sweet Little Rock and Roller," at the end of the show when the credits were rolling, but they cut it out when it was broadcast in England. My brother, who lived in Toronto, sent me a video of the whole thing as it was shown there, and it was pretty good, but "Stay with Me" really sucked!

Craig Ross left The Bump Band to join Lenny Kravitz's band, so Jimmy's other best mate, Marc Ford, joined. Then he got offered a job with The Black Crowes after only a few gigs, and so when Craig called me from New York and told me Lenny was looking for a keyboard player for an eighteen-month tour, I jumped at the chance of some steady loot. Two days later, I was back at SIR, but this time the music wasn't doing as much for me. Lenny seemed to be stuck in the sound and the music from the early Seventies, and I'd already done that. He carted in an old beaten up Mellotron he wanted me to play. Thankfully, after only a few days of rehearsal, I heard a band playing "Pinball Wizard" in the next room and discovered it was Pete Townshend. It was a breath of fresh air to see him again, the first time since Keith's funeral in 1978. He was rehearsing a makeshift band for a little show for the cast and crew of *Tommy* to be held in a small restaurant, and he invited me to come along. The premiere was the following day, but we squeezed in a few drinks, several reminiscences, and many laughs that night.

I flew to Orlando the next day for two schmooze gigs at NARM, the record manufacturers' convention. At the rehearsal, a stranger came up and stood next to me while I played. He watched me like a ferret, and at the end of the song, I turned and asked him sarcastically if I was playing it all right for him. "Well, it's close," he said without emotion. This was my introduction to Lenny's engineer, Henry Hirsch. As cold a fish as you'll find wide-eyed on a fishmonger's slab.

While Henry had played keyboards on all of Lenny's records, he fully expected me to play every note of his on stage. I learned he'd never even been on the road, so I realized he couldn't know that what works on tape doesn't necessarily work live. When he said we'd go back to his studio in New York after the two shows in Orlando, and go through all the recordings, one by one, track by track, so I could learn all of his parts, I knew I wasn't long for these parts.

If I thought I wasn't having any fun, Lenny was probably unhappier than me, but at least I could quit. He was stuck with it. When he found his guitar was out of tune he threw a plastic water bottle at the roadie responsible, which narrowly missed me. It wasn't that I might have been hurt, it was that his behaviour would be excusable in a small child, but he was old enough to know better. When he screamed obscenities at the monitor guy over the P.A. system at the sound check, it was as much as I could do not to walk off the stage, especially as I knew a few of the people waiting in the wings. Bruce Hornsby and John Mollo, his drummer, Buddy Guy, and Greg Rzab, his bass player, were embarrassed for me and I didn't like being seen with Lenny after that. I called Kim as soon as I got to my room and told her I couldn't take anymore of it, and even though we needed the dosh, she said the magic words that only a wife who truly loves and understands her husband could say: "Come home, Mac."

I called Craig aside after the gig, and told him I was going to quit and thanked him anyway for thinking of me. Tony Selinger, the tour manager, booked me on the first available flight back to L.A. and then I went to my room and called Lenny.

"Are you leaving because of my tantrums?" Lenny asked. I told him it wasn't that at all, but that it was an insult to expect me to play note for note keyboard parts, when they could get a young kid in instead. "Failing that," I said, "get Henry to do it. No hard feelings, okay?"

"Sure. Hey, if I called you and asked you to play on my next record, would you do it?" Lenny was a gent, after all.

"In a New York minute. Thanks, I'll look forward to that."

I was up bright and early the next day, and followed breakfast with a Bloody Mary at the bar in the airport. As Jeff Ayeroff, Virgin Records boss, walked past me, he said knowingly, "You've got a smile on your face of a man who's just been paroled." He was dead right, and although I had no plans and had just passed on eighteen months of steady paychecks, I didn't have a care in the world. I was going home to my baby.

A few days later I worked on a session with Melissa Etheridge that made me more than I would have earned in two weeks on the road with Lenny Kravitz, so that helped. Craig called a week later to get Nicky Hopkins phone number. I told him Nicky would be as insulted as I was, but gave it to him anyway and wasn't surprised when I heard Nicky turned him down too.

Rod's album *Unplugged...And Seated* had just come out and to promote it Woody and Rod were going to be interviewed live from New York on a radio programme broadcast nationally called Rockline. Early in May, Jim Vallenueva from Rockline called and asked if I'd surprise them during the show by pretending I was a fan calling in with a question. When Kim turned on the radio they'd already started, and were both quite piddled.

The phone rang soon after. Beau Riles, the host was already talking as I picked it up.

"Guys, let's go locally one more time, Pasadena, California, talk to Ian, a listener of 97.1 KLSX..."

"I bet it's Mac," Woody interrupted him drunkenly.

"Yeah, I've got a question," I said, and started singing, "What is the weather like in Paris?" It's the theme from Jacques Tati's *Monsieur Hulot's Holiday* and well known to the pair of them.

"It is Mac! Mac, you filthy swine..." Meanwhile, Rod was mumbling in the background. I couldn't hear him because I was still singing. Then they both joined in and it became very loud and raucous. Beau interrupted the rabble rousing by introducing me.

"Former Faces ace, Ian McLagan. Welcome to the show, Ian."

"How're you doin'?" Woody interrupted again before he could get a word in.

"Mac…Mac, you're gonna do the tour, aren't you? Rod wants you to do it."

"Oh, does he? He hasn't called me." Rod came on, very drunk.

"No, I want you to sing that song about 'I love my wife, I love her dearly…' Go on, go on."

It was the song I'd sung at Tommy Makem's. Woody had obviously told him about my embarrassing moment and Rod was dying for me to sing the next line: "I love the hole she pisses through" over the air.

"How you doin', Rod?"

"Yeaagh! I'm doin' all right, my old mate." Screaming and shouting and then after a commercial break, Beau tried to get things back on track.

"You do have a question for them, Ian, right?" But Rod interrupted boisterously.

"No, he's got a question for you, Beau. Are you queer?" Woody saved the day.

"Here, Mac, before they cut you off, Rod wants to ask you if you're gonna do his tour?"

"Yeah, I'd love to."

"Now, are you serious?" Rod asked me. "It's just the organ and piano and the old songs. You know 'em."

"Lovely, oh that'll be great! Are you kidding me?"

"Right, we've struck a deal!" Rod shouted, and they sang the next line of the song very loudly together on the air. "Her lily white tits, tiddly-it-tit-tits, and her nut brown arsehole. I eat her shit, gobble-gobble-chomp-chomp, with a rusty spoon!" They collapsed, screaming with laughter. And that's how I started touring with Rod again after all those years.

We began rehearsing in June 1993 with Rod promising me he'd never, ever play "Do You Think I'm Sexy" and "Passion" on the tour. We were only a few weeks into the tour before he wanted us to play the intro of "Sexy" for a joke, and before I knew it, we were playing the whole damn song, and then "Passion" crept in as well. We played festivals in Europe with Prince, Tina Turner, and

Joe Cocker for a couple of weeks, then came back and carried on touring around the States until the middle of December, when we took a break until the beginning of February. My son Lee, who by then was twenty-three years old, and Dermot, who'd just turned twenty-eight, came to Los Angeles to spend Christmas and the New Year with us. I was feeling flush, so I rented a Cadillac and a four-bedroom house on a cliff facing the Pacific Ocean near Cambria, on the central California coast. We had the Christmas of Christmases, drinking, eating, and walking on the beach. Then my brother Mike, who lived in Toronto, his wife Pat, and their sons, Shaun and Anthony, touched down in Los Angeles for two days on their way from Toronto to Baja California, in Mexico, to spend New Year's Eve with us. It was perfect.

At 4 A.M. on January 17, 1994, like everybody else in Los Angeles, we awoke to a jarring and a shaking that I hope we never experience again in our lifetimes. Truckers call Los Angeles "Shakeytown" and although we were a good ten miles from the epicentre, it was enough to make me think seriously for the first time about leaving. We were up, out of bed, and under the dining table with our two dogs in seconds flat. When the house stopped rolling on its foundations, I turned the radio on and heard that this had been the "Big One." Finally, it had happened, and it was an incredible feeling of relief.

Kim had been trying to convince me we should leave Los Angeles for a while, but because my work was there, I couldn't see how we could. I'd talked vaguely about a five-year plan, but as I was on the road for the last half of 1993, she was having to deal with living there, not me. I'd called from the road one Sunday afternoon, when she'd just heard gunfire outside in the street in broad daylight, and could actually smell the gunpowder. I agreed that we had to get out and we had spent every vacation since looking for areas away from the city. The trouble was, you had to leave California entirely to avoid the earthquakes, so it wasn't an easy decision for me.

During the sixteen years we'd lived in Southern California we'd breathed the smog, avoided wildfires by a change in the wind direction, driven miles out of our way for months at a time because of landslides in Malibu, been constantly scared by the random gunfire and violence, and driven in some of the busiest traffic on the face of the earth, too scared to make eye contact with other drivers. We had almost learned to live with the earthquakes. But the day after the quake, when the voice on the radio calmly said it had NOT been the "Big One," Kim and I knew this was the time to get out of Los Angeles. Enough was enough.

Deciding where to move was merely a matter of elimination, it seemed. It was important to live in a city with a healthy music scene. San Francisco was out because of the earthquakes, New York, Chicago, and Seattle were out because of crime rates and weather, and Nashville was too bland for my palate. That left Austin. Two days later, over a drink and a game of darts, it came to me in a blinding flash of alcoholic clear thinking. Although we'd had no experience running a bar, I said, "Let's open an English pub in Austin, Texas!" And Kim agreed, as her friend Susie Barker-Benfield lived there. I had several musician friends there too, not to mention my dear old pal Ronnie Lane. We learned that the crime rate was very low, there was no smog, no problem with landslides as it was quite flat, and there was "Zero Geological Activity" too, which in layman's terms meant no earthquakes. Though we later decided against running a bar, since we preferred being this side of it, we decided to move there anyway. It also meant we'd be able to put "The Sweethearts" print back up on our bedroom wall, as now there'd be no danger of it falling on us while we slept.

CHAPTER THIRTY-SEVEN
The Passing Show

Rod's *Unplugged* album was doing such great business, we began another trek round the States in February, with Kim flying to meet me in Austin at the end of March, so we could have a good look at properties. She'd already done her research, looking through the listings of houses on the market in our price range and faxing the good ones to me on the road. On the day of the gig at the Erwin Centre, after spending the day driving around Austin, we made an offer on the house we now live in.

Rod hadn't seen Ronnie since the Wembley concert in 1986, but even I could tell that his health had deteriorated, even since Woody's tour. His eyesight was much weaker and one eye drifted slightly. Rod and his band and crew made a big fuss of him in the dressing room, but he wasn't his old cheeky self that night. When I told him we were definitely moving to Austin and had found a house that day, I expected a better reaction than the one I got. I was a little surprised he wasn't more excited, but I put it down to the fact he was tired. When I told him Kim and I wanted to take him to lunch the following day, as it would be his birthday, April 1, he brightened up and said, "That would be lovely."

In the past, we had often tortured Ronnie on his birthday. We'd forget some years, but we got him good when we played the Mar Y Sol Festival in San Juan, Puerto Rico, in 1972. We stayed on the other side of the island from the festival, at a large hotel that had a nightclub, a casino, two outdoor pools, and a fully equipped spa, with masseurs, facialists, sauna, steam, gym, the works. We'd taken the girls with us for that trip, and they'd huddle in the beauty salon in the afternoon, getting facials, massages, and manicures, while we spent the time kicking a ball around in the gym and swimming. As we were there for five days, we got into the habit of having a morning massage most days.

On the morning of April 1, we asked the masseur to work on Ronnie first, and once he'd turned him over onto his front, he gave us a signal and Woody, Rod, Kenney, and I slipped through the curtains that separated the booths. As he took one hand off him, I put mine on and then one by one we were all over him, and the masseur left us to grope, slap, and pinch his bum as he screamed, face down into the towel.

By 1994, all the tricks life had to offer had been played on him. He sat in his wheelchair at the table in the Four Seasons, looking very weak, and before we ordered the food, I asked him if he'd like a drink. I meant a glass of water or juice because I knew he shouldn't drink alcohol, but when he said, "I'll have a bourbon and coke, please," I thought, What the hell, I'm not his minder. He had a sip through a straw, and I asked him if it was all right. With a sour expression on his face, he said quietly:

"It's bleedin' rocket fuel!" He'd had all he wanted.

Ronnie came to the house for lunch soon after we moved in and broke the sad news that he and his wife, Susan, would be leaving Austin for Trinidad, Colorado, in July. The summers had become too uncomfortable for him, and though they'd made their plans earlier in the year, when I'd told him we were moving to Austin at Rod's gig, he hadn't had the heart to mention it to me. I'd looked forward to seeing a lot more of him, but it wasn't meant to be.

We arrived at our new house on May 19, only four months after the earthquake, and we thought that was fast, but Nicky Hopkins and his wife Moira had flown to Nashville the very next day. He'd come to see my band at The Mint soon after he'd moved to Los Angeles, and had let me know he was there by shouting from the back of the room, "Hello, silly person!" He sat in with us that night and the place went wild. He called from Nashville, and after being referred to our Austin number, left a message on the answering machine. "You fucker, you did it! Well done! So glad you moved and got the hell out of there!" He went on to say how happy he and Moira were in Nashville, but tragically, it wasn't to last. He died unexpectedly on September 6, 1994, of Crohn's disease. Although he'd suffered with intestinal problems since he was a young man, he'd had an operation in 1993 that seemed to sort him out. But it was discovered the day he died that part of his intestine hadn't healed properly and gangrene had already set in. He was a master of the piano and a lovely, funny man, and I was lucky to have known him.

On the day Nicky died, Kim and I were shopping in the city, and I spotted a bar called Lovejoys across the street. I remembered seeing an ad for the place in the *Austin Chronicle* that showed a pretty girl holding a pint of Guinness. That's good advertising for you. Well, it was only 2 P.M., but when I suggested we had a pint for Nicky, Kim readily agreed.

We walked into the strangest place. There were coffins for tables and pews for seats, and it was empty except for a couple in one corner. I ordered two pints at the bar and the jukebox came to life. It was "Street Fighting Man," by The Stones, which for us meant classic Nicky Hopkins. I took the pints and sat down next to Kim. She'd noticed how odd the furnishings were, but pointed to a mural on the wall, in front of which there was a low stage. It depicted two angels wearing purple velvet shrouds, hovering in midair, and pulling back the curtains from the heavens. It was strange, but the only music we heard on the jukebox was early Stones recordings with Nicky on piano.

When I ordered the next pint, I asked the bored barmaid if she knew who Nicky Hopkins was. She didn't. I asked her who chose the music. She said the jukebox was on automatic, and if no one put money in, it played something anyway. It was how the manufacturer made sure there was always music playing, it was the same with all jukeboxes.

We eventually stayed for three pints, because I didn't want the moment to end but we never heard anything other than Nicky while we were there. People came and went, and they were all oblivious to it. I think he would have liked that silly touch.

We listened, though, and we felt his presence and drank to his future. God Bless him.

I'd bought a computer in 1994 with the intention of composing and recording songs, but as I was constantly on the road with Rod and his band I never had the time to learn how to use it for that. I soon got the hang of the word processor though, and after so many years of people telling me I should write a book, I thought I'd give it a go. In 1995, I treated myself to an Apple Powerbook, a laptop computer, and on a flight from Austin to Los Angeles to rehearse for Rod's European tour, I wrote my first five hundred words. It was a revelation to me that I could write just about anywhere I wanted. I bought three extra batteries and I was set. Hardly a day went by when I didn't write something, and I worked on gig days and on days off. I think Rod would appreciate the irony of the fact he was paying me and yet I was taking care of my own business on his time.

Touring with him was good fun, even though I wasn't convinced I'd be content as his sideman after the years of being an equal member of the band, but it turned out to be fine. I just checked my ego in at the door. As with any tour, the worst part was being away from Kim. Touring with Rod could be tortuous sometimes, though. In July 1995, an opportunity arose for him to appear in front of all the MTV station affiliates at a convention in San Francisco as a way of saying, "Thank you very much. Now play my video and make my record a hit." The only problem was we had an outdoor show in Bucharest, Romania, the night before and another show in Istanbul the day after, and the two cities were only about 250 miles apart.

Rod flew home to Rachel and his own bed that night, but as the promoter, Marcel Avram, was Romanian, he threw a small party for us at his club in Bucharest. I got to bed at 4 A.M. and had to be back up again at 5 A.M. The band, all the instruments and a reduced crew, took off for Stansted Airport at 6 A.M. where we picked up Rod as well as lots of English bangers, bacon, cans of Guinness and Caffreys, and the English newspapers. We had plenty of room to stretch out, but it was long and tiring. The plane was a luxurious large jet with regular seats up front, a bar, and dining area in the centre, and a bedroom that even had a shower in the back of the plane for Rod and Rachel.

We landed in Newfoundland to refuel, then took off for San Francisco and drove straight to The Marriott downtown. Then after a quick shower we had a sound check.

There was just time for a sandwich in the room, and it was "showtime." Boy, you've never seen a band that sparkled less! I never yawned so much during a show, and Rod even came over to the Hammond a couple of times with his back to the audience and stood yawning, cross-eyed at me!

The crowd loved the show though, and after a forty-five minute set, we jumped into the vans and went directly to the airport and took off for Newfoundland and another fill-up. Twenty minutes later we were airborne, drinking, eating, and sleeping in any particular order we liked. We were on World time. It was right now!

I didn't tell anyone about the book on the tour for some time because I wasn't confident about my writing and didn't want anyone criticizing it, and I certainly didn't want Rod to know, in case he thought I was writing something scandalous. But as I was pecking at the computer on the flight to Stansted, Rod slid into the seat beside me in a jovial mood.

"What's 'at?"

"It's my computer."

"What are you writin', then?"

"It's *The Autobiography of a Short Arse.*" Pete Townshend had given it that title after I'd asked for his advice and sent him some early chapters. Rod laughed.

"Let's 'ave a look then, come on."

I handed him the computer and showed him how to move the next page up and down, and he read quietly for about an hour. This, and the fact he laughed out loud occasionally, gave me confidence.

"You're gonna keep all the filthy stuff in, aren't you?" he said. "As I told a reporter the other day, 'The Faces would shag anything with a pulse!'" Then he reminded me how Ronnie Lane used to stand on an orange box on stage when they sang "Maybe I'm Amazed" together. He cracked up laughing at the thought of Ronnie straining for the notes as well as the microphone. I'd forgotten about it, and promised I'd put it in.

We dropped him and Rachel off at Stansted, picked up more newspapers and beer, and then flew on to Istanbul, the last stop on the longest journey. We'd flown fifteen thousand miles for a forty-five-minute show, on a day off, and when we landed, we discovered we couldn't even collect frequent flier miles because it was a rented plane!

While touring Japan with Rod, I found a bootleg video of Muddy Waters and his band at a bootleg store. When I got it back to the hotel room I was surprised and thrilled to find it was the same performance as on the *Muddy Waters at Newport* album that Rod, Woody, and I had treasured for years, though we hadn't dreamed there was film of it too. There were other tunes not included on the record, like "Rolling Stone," some rocking piano instrumentals from Otis Spann, and John Lee Hooker guesting with Muddy's band. It was such a find, but after looking at the album cover photograph again, I spotted the cameraman behind Muddy's head, which should have tipped me off that it was being filmed. There are many magical moments, but during James Cotton's harp solo in "Tiger in My Tank," Muddy runs across the stage and starts dancing cheek to cheek with James, to shrieks of laughter from the band and audience! We found Rod a copy the next time we were in Japan, but Woody already had a primo copy of it, the swine!

My proudest moment came on May 30, 1996, when Small Faces were presented with an Ivor Novello Award sponsored by the Performing Right Society for "Outstanding Contribution to British Music." Ray Davies of The Kinks did the honours. "It's about bloody time, Mac," he said.

The luncheon was held at the Grosvenor House Hotel in London, and Kay Marriott, Steve's mum, accepted his award with grace. She hardly looked a day older than when I'd first joined the group thirty-one years before. Woody came up to accept Ronnie Lane's award, as Ronnie was too weak to travel, and brought Ronnie's brother Stan up to say a few words. I hadn't seen Stan in years and remembered how we used to stop in at his sandwich shop, Tasty Snacks, in the East End for a "sarnie" on our way out of London. I thanked everybody and mentioned that it would be nice to be paid record royalties as well. Kenney said his bit and then we all went round the pub. But without Steve and Ronnie there it was a bittersweet occasion.

Woody and Jo, Rod and Rachel, Kenney, Kim, and I went out for a meal at Langan's the night before Kim and I flew back to the States. It was a silly evening of much high hilarity, eating, and drinking. At one point Rod, Kenney, Woody, and I moved to the table next to us and sat with a couple that were dining alone, but they took it all in good sport. The subject got around to the finished and unfinished Faces' tracks Woody had discovered in his vaults. We all agreed to meet at Woody's home studio in Ireland at the end of July to record a couple of songs and listen to what we had, the idea being to put out a *Best of Faces* album to include the new and unreleased tracks. Rod was to get there first, to go through all the tracks, but it never happened. Rod eventually told Woody some weeks later, "I never said I was going to Ireland!" He can be hard to love sometimes.

As Woody had started cutting tracks with Willie Weeks and Andy Newmark for his new album, I flew over to work on them instead, and my son, Lee, grabbed the opportunity to see me and flew in specially from London. We met at the Westbury Hotel and after a hearty Irish breakfast we had a couple of pints together and caught up on all the news. I'm so proud of him, he's a lovely man, and we've become really good pals in recent years. I eventually got in a cab to go to Woody's house and Lee caught one to the airport, and as Woody was still en route from Richmond, I took the opportunity of getting my head down for a couple of hours before he arrived.

His Georgian house is set among fields that stretch to the horizon in every direction. There's a courtyard surrounded by cow sheds on three sides at the back of the house that have been converted into an artist's studio, a recording studio, and a billiard room and bar. The bar is called Yer Father's Yacht and the pub sign hangs outside the door, complete with a portrait of Woody's dad, Arthur, who said it first. When Woody was a teenager living at home with his parents, his then-girlfriend, Krissie, had come back to the house for a shagging after a gig and they both fell asleep in Woody's bed afterwards. When his dad came in with a cup of tea in the morning, he muttered disgustedly, "Where d'you think you are, on yer father's yacht?" A right character, he'd raise his glass and say, "Good 'ealth, Alf." The reply being, "Not 'alf, Arfur."

Woody arrived later that afternoon, excitedly wanting me to guess who was sleeping in the bedroom next to the bar. Typically, it could be just about anybody living. He said it was Bob Dylan. "Oh no!" I thought, remembering my embarrassment after the night in Tommy Makem's bar. He was just passing through on tour, Woody said, and as Rod wasn't coming, we could always cut some stuff with Bob, or failing that, get on with his record. And so, burying the ghost for me, we recorded a dozen new Bob Dylan tunes that may never see the light of day and cut three new Ronnie Wood tunes with a similar view.

On April 12, 1997, Ronnie Lane's wife, Susan, called in great distress, and left a tearful message on the answering machine. "Ronnie's dyin'! You gotta come out and see him. He's dyin', Mac! I need you!"

I wasted no time and caught a 7 A.M. flight the next day to Albuquerque, rented a car, and drove north through the desert to the little town of Trinidad, Colorado, among the snow covered mountains. I found the hospital easily, it being the only one in town. Ronnie was very weak, his arms and legs were painfully thin, but he responded to me, though he could hardly speak above a whisper. He had a full moustache, like Clement Atlee's, and I told him not to shave it off, it was probably the only thing holding him together, which made him smile. Susan told me over dinner that he'd caught a virus, and the MS had taken over and he'd passed out. She said he wasn't in any pain, that he was being fed intravenously and that he had his good moments and bad. She said she thought it would be best to let him go if, and when, it happened again, and I understood and sympathized with her.

He'd brightened up considerably when we went back, his voice was clearer and most important, his sense of humour had returned. Friends in Austin had asked me to pass on their love and good wishes, and I could tell he was in better spirits because he called me a "barsteed." The next morning, he looked a little better again, and the doctors said he would be able to leave the hospital in a few days, so eventually I gave him a kiss and was on my way.

He lasted a little more than a month, after twenty-one years of battling multiple sclerosis. Susan called me on June 4 and told me the sad news. I called Kenney immediately, and though we'd both known it would happen before very long, he broke down, and when I told him Ronnie was to be buried that same day in Trinidad, he was even more saddened at not being able to pay his respects in person. Kenney has fought valiantly and tirelessly for years to get the companies who owed royalties to the Small Faces to pay up, and he'd helped to organize and played on a CD release, *Long Agos and Worlds Apart,* which, apart from being a tribute to the Small Faces, was a source of much needed income for Ronnie. Somehow, we're still brothers after thirty-one odd years still looking out for each other.

Susan said that in the years that she and Ronnie were together, "He never complained once." He was finally at peace and wasn't suffering anymore and I wasn't sad for him, but not to be able to see him again in this life brought me down hard. I'll miss him always, because he'll always be my brother.

Kim was at work, but Kim's brother, Dermot, had arrived from England some days before and was sunning himself at the pool when I broke the bad news. He hugged me and, taking matters into hand, decided we'd have a Guinness or two together, even though it was still morning. We drank, I reminisced, and when Kim came home, we played Small Faces and Faces records and videos all night, hugging and kissing, crying and laughing. It helped to see him shuffling across the stage and laughing his contagious laugh, but the next day when I turned on the portable radio and "Glad and Sorry," one of my favourite Ronnie Lane songs, came on, it broke me up again. Jody Denberg, the DJ at KGSR, had been Ronnie's best man at the wedding, and was one of the "barsteeds" lacking the opportunity I'd had to say goodbye to him in person.

A very small, red fly landed on the radio as I listened to the song. It didn't seem to be bothered by my presence at all, and I thought of swatting it, but didn't have the heart, it was so little. It shuffled about on the top of the radio looking for a bite to eat while the song blared out of the speakers. I thought it was odd that it didn't fly off, and I called Dermot over to have a look. When I finally got it, I laughed out loud. Of course, it was Ronnie! The Hungry Intruder from *Ogdens' Nut Gone Flake.* You can say what you like, but in my heart I know that little red fly was Ronnie Lane on another journey.

My own journey has taken me around the world and to countries I'd never heard of when I first started playing. Performing in front of audiences as small as five and as large as five million, I've worked constantly for the last thirty-five years and have made lasting friendships around the world. I've been fortunate enough to have met and played with many of my musical idols and to have seen many of the greats perform live.

It surprised me when in 1963 a girlfriend told me she thought Mick Jagger was sexy. "It's the way he moves his hips," she'd said, and where I thought I'd seen a singer in front of a great band, she'd seen a star in the making. But he'd be a lonely man up there on that stage without Keith Richards as his bandleader, believe me. When people criticize Rod Stewart for not making challenging records anymore, they forget that his biggest influences were Al Jolson and Sam Cooke, and that he's an entertainer first and foremost, and a star as a result. Of course, the main reason is he hasn't got The Faces to kick him up the arse anymore! Steve Marriott was another natural star, and in Ronnie Lane he had the perfect songwriting partner, but he wanted so much to be accepted as a serious musician that he fought stardom all the way to relative obscurity.

Bob Dylan is still making the most challenging records of anyone from my generation and constantly tours and puts out new releases, and he's a star because of his great writing. But of all the people I've performed with, Bonnie Raitt can give everyone a lesson in humanity. She is a star in the truest sense because she shines on others.

My love for the music hasn't dimmed. If anything, it's increased, as drugs now play no part in my life, only in my past. My only regret is the amount of time it took to wake up to my addictions and to face them.

With that little lot off my chest, I can honestly say I'm a happier person today than I used to be in the old days. I'm not as angry. And though I'm still "hungry and looking," the difference is that now I'm up with the larks instead of being up all night, like an owl. Kim and I will have been married for twenty-one years by the time this book is published, so we've been together for twenty-six years all told. That's not bad for a rock and roller, and I'll be happy if I can keep her happy until we're in our nineties.

When I was asked by a journalist in *Beat Instrumental* back in 1965 how I imagined it would be when "the big time" came along, I said that I had an image of myself playing a medium-sized club playing music with "a soul flavour." Well, that old chestnut, "Be careful what you wish for," applies, because that's what I do with my band here in Austin, Texas, when I'm not touring with other artists.

Drummer Don Harvey, guitarist "Scrappy" Jud Newcomb, bass player Sarah Brown, and guitarist Gurf Morlix are the latest version of The Bump Band, and early in 1998 I hooked up with a new manager who I'll call A. Wanker to save him any embarrassment. He told me he'd definitely got me a record deal and to go ahead and book studio time. Having enjoyed working with Gurf as both a producer and guitarist on Lucinda Williams' album, I asked him to produce mine, and we started rehearsing immediately. Although I thought it a little odd that Wanker didn't reply to any of my calls, I was so busy that I figured he was too, and we ploughed ahead.

One night around that time, Kim and I saw Billy Bragg on television and were absolutely riveted by his performance. I'd told my son, Lee, that we'd met Billy in Los Angeles some years before, and Lee had said he often saw him in the street near where he lived in London. I'd asked him to say hello from me the next time he saw him, but we never discussed it again. Watching Billy that night reminded me of our conversation, and got me thinking nostalgically about London, and wondering how Lee was doing. Inspired, the song "Best of British" popped into my head that night and gave me the title for the album.

I never heard from A. Wanker again, which left me struggling to finish the record under considerable stress. I couldn't pay the studio's bills, or my band members', producer's, and engineer's fees because I was broke and I didn't know what to do. There seemed to be no one to turn to, and "Best of British" wouldn't have seen the light of day if it hadn't been for the kindness and benevolence of Ronnie and Jo Wood. They lent me the money in double quick time and with no questions asked, the way only very good friends might. I grabbed the tapes and jumped on a plane to Ireland where Ronnie played guitar on a couple of tracks and sang from his heart on "Hello Old Friend," a tribute to another dear friend of ours, Ronnie Lane. On the same trip Billy Bragg did the honours on "Best of British," the tune he'd inspired, with Lee and me smiling our silly heads off in front of him. The CD "Best of British" was released on

Gadfly Records in March 2000, but if you can't find it, check my Website: www.macspages.com. Have a look, have a laugh, have a listen.

Billy and I have kept in touch ever since, and when he asked me to tour with him and his excellent band, The Blokes, I jumped at the chance, and I've toured around the world with him ever since. But now The Bump Band are starting to take off, I'm looking forward to seeing even more of the world with them too.

There's been talk of getting The Faces back together for some years now, and when I played with Rod and his band at The Point in Dublin in December 1995, Woody and Kenney came to the gig and played a couple of songs at the end of the show. It was a blast, and we talked of doing a tour and made plans, and then…absolutely nothing happened.

But I haven't given up, and when it happens I'll be the happiest man on that stage, because when The Faces played it was always fun. And when it was good, it was bloody marvellous.

Cheers, good health, and I hope to see you at the show.

Big Love,

Mac

P.S. Where have all the managers gone? Don Arden is retired and lives in Los Angeles, where if the earthquakes, smog, and general violence in the streets don't get him, then there's no justice. I haven't any idea where Tony Calder lives and that's fine with me. When The Stones' Steel Wheels tour rolled into the Coliseum in Los Angeles in 1989, I heard someone calling for me as I walked towards the backstage area. I recognized the voice immediately as the originator of the term "Happy to Be a Part of the Industry of Human Happiness," and what a lot of old bollocks that was.

"Andrew, you thieving bastard, how the hell are you?" I shouted over my shoulder. He wasn't even fazed. Yes, it was Andrew Loog Oldham, same as ever, no shame or remorse. They don't change, and they never apologize or pay the money due. The money's long gone now, but let me set the record straight once and for all.

Fact 1: Small Faces has never received any royalties from Don Arden or Contemporary Records, the company in his wife's name to which we were signed.

Fact 2: Small Faces had never received any royalties from Decca Records until Steve Marriott's death in 1991, when a Small Faces account was found in their files. They are still pissing and moaning about paying us current royalties, never mind what we're owed.

Fact 3: Small Faces has never received any royalties from Immediate Records.

Fact 4: In 1996, Small Faces reached an agreement with Castle Communications, the company that now has the rights to the Immediate Records catalogue in the U.K., and they are currently paying us royalties.

Fact 5: Charly Records, the company that releases the Small Faces Immediate catalogue worldwide, has yet to provide us with royalty statements.

Fact 6: The Small Faces songwriting and publishing contracts are currently under review.

P.P.S.

I'd always known Rod had my old "Faces" B3 stashed away somewhere, and in early 1998, twenty-two years after The Faces broke up, I finally convinced him to give it back to me. Naturally, I had to foot the bill for shipping it from California to Texas, but when it arrived and that combination of furniture polish and Hammond oil wafted up my nose, I got a flashback to 1964, when I caught that odd mixture for the first time.

Wait a minute, this is where I came in!

Discography

THE MULESKINNERS
(Dave Pether, Pete Brown, Nick Tweddell, Mick Carpenter,
Terry Brennan, and Ian McLagan)

Single
Back Door Man/Need Your Lovin'	1965	Fontana EP
Why Don't You Write Back to Me/		
Back Door Man/Untie Me/Need Your Lovin'	1973	Keepoint

SMALL FACES
(Steve Marriott, Ronnie Lane, Ian McLagan, and Kenney Jones)

Singles
Sha-La-La-La-Lee/Grow Your Own	1966	Decca
Hey Girl/Almost Grown	1966	Decca
All or Nothing/Understanding	1966	Decca
My Mind's Eye/I Can't Dance with You	1966	Decca
I Can't Make It/Just Passing	1967	Decca
Patterns/E to D	1967	Decca
Here Comes the Nice/Talk to You	1967	Immediate
Itchycoo Park/I'm Only Dreaming	1967	Immediate
Itchycoo Park (US)	1968	Immediate
Tin Soldier/I Feel Much Better	1968	Immediate
Tin Soldier (US)	1968	Immediate
Lazy Sunday/Rollin' Over	1968	Immediate
The Universal/Donkey Rides a Penny a Glass	1968	Immediate
Afterglow/Wham Bam, Thank You Ma'am	1969	Immediate
Itchycoo Park	1976	NEMS
Lazy Sunday	1976	NEMS

Albums
Small Faces	1966	Decca
From the Beginning	1967	Decca
Small Faces	1967	Immediate
There Are but Four Small Faces (US only)	1968	Immediate
Ogdens' Nut Gone Flake	1968	Immediate
Ogdens' Nut Gone Flake (US)	1968	Immediate
The Autumn Stone (originally titled In Memorium)	1969	Immediate

SMALL FACES (Second Round)
(Steve Marriott, Ian McLagan, Kenney Jones, and Rick Wills)

Singles

Lookin' for a Love/Kayoed (By Luv)	1977	Atlantic
Stand by Me (Stand by You)/Hungry and Looking	1977	Atlantic
Filthy Rich/Over Too Soon	1978	Atlantic

Albums

Playmates	1977	Atlantic
78 in the Shade	1978	Atlantic

THE FACES
(Ronnie Lane, Ronnie Wood, Rod Stewart, Ian McLagan, and Kenney Jones)

Singles

Flying/Three Button Hand Me Down	1970	Warner Bros
Had Me a Real Good Time/Rear Wheel Skid	1970	Warner Bros
Stay with Me/You're So Rude	1971	Warner Bros
Maybe I'm Amazed/Oh Lord I'm Browned Off	1972	Warner Bros
Dishevelment Blues/Borstal Boys/ Silicone Grown/Ooh La La	1973	Warner Bros/NME
Cindy Incidentally/Skewiff (Mend The Fuse)	1973	Warner Bros
Cindy Incidentally/Memphis/Stay with Me/ Pool Hall Richard	1973	Warner Bros
Pool Hall Richard/ I Wish It Would Rain (with a trumpet)	1973	Warner Bros
You Can Make Me Dance/As Long As You Tell Him	1974	Warner Bros
Stay with Me/Cindy/Memphis/ You Can Make Me Dance (EP)	1977	Riva

Albums

First Step (Small Faces in US)	1970	Warner Bros
Long Player	1971	Warner Bros
A Nod's As Good As a Wink (to a Blind Horse)	1971	Warner Bros
Various Artists/Reading Festival	1973	GM
Ooh La La	1973	Warner Bros
Coast to Coast/Overture and Beginners	1974	WB/Mercury
Snakes and Ladders (Best of)	1975	Warner Bros
The Best of the Faces	1977	Riva
Good Boys...When They're Asleep...	1999	Warner Bros/Rhino

ROD STEWART

Singles

It's All Over Now/Jo's Lament	1970	Vertigo
Reason to Believe/Maggie May	1971	Mercury
You Wear It Well/Lost Paraguayos	1972	Mercury
Oh No Not My Baby/Jodie	1973	Mercury
Farewell/Bring It On Home to Me/You Send Me	1974	Mercury
It's All Over Now/Jo's Lament	1975	Mercury

Albums

The Rod Stewart Album (Thin)	1969	Mercury
Gasoline Alley	1970	Mercury
Every Picture Tells a Story	1971	Mercury
Never a Dull Moment	1972	Mercury
Smiler	1974	Mercury
Handbags and Gladrags	1995	Polygram

RONNIE WOOD

Singles

I Can Feel the Fire/Breathe on Me	1974	Warner Bros
If You Don't Want My Love/I Got a Feeling	1974	Warner Bros
Big Bayou/Sweet Baby Mine	1975	Warner Bros
Show Me/Breathe on Me	1992	Continuum

Albums

I've Got My Own Album to Do	1974	Warner Bros
Now Look	1975	Warner Bros
Gimme Some Neck	1979	Warner Bros
1234	1981	Warner Bros
Slide on This	1992	Continuum
Slide on This Live (Plugged In and Standing)	1993	Continuum
Slide On Live	1998	BMG

RONNIE WOOD AND RONNIE LANE

Mahoney's Last Stand	1976	Atco

RONNIE LANE WITH SLIM CHANCE

You Never Can Tell (BBC Sessions)	1997	New Millenium
Anymore for Anymore	1997	New Millenium
April Fool	1997	New Millenium
Mahoney's Last Stand	1978	New Millenium

IAN MCLAGAN

Singles

Little Troublemaker/Hold On	1980	Mercury
La De La/Hold On	1980	Mercury
Little Girl	1981	Mercury
Pictures of Lily (Who Covers Who)	1994	Rip Off
Hello, Old Friend (KGSR Broadcasts, Volume 6)	1998	107.1 KGSR

Albums

Troublemaker	1979	Mercury
Bump in the Night	1981	Mercury
Last Chance to Dance (EP)	1985	Greenworld
Best of British	1999	Maniac
Best of British	2000	Gadfly

WITH OTHER ARTISTS

Billy Nicholls Would You Believe	1968	Immediate
P.P. Arnold (If You Think You're) Groovy	1968	Immediate
Marsha Hunt Woman Child	1971	Track
Juicy Lucy Pieces	1972	Polydor
Chuck Berry The London Chuck Berry Sessions	1972	Chess
Billy Nicholls Love Songs	1974	GM
Thin Lizzy Fighting	1975	Vertigo
Ted Wood Am I Blue/Shine	1975	Penny Farthing
Rich Kids Ghosts of Princes in Towers	1978	EMI
Rolling Stones Some Girls	1978	Rolling Stones
Carly Simon Spy	1979	Electra/Asylum
Reneé Geyer So Lucky	1981	Mushroom
Rolling Stones Sucking in the Seventies	1981	Rolling Stones
Bonnie Raitt Green Light	1982	Warner Bros
Rolling Stones "Still Life" (American Concert Tour 1981)	1982	Rolling Stones
Gary Panter Pray for Smurph	1983	Overheat
Bob Dylan Real Live	1984	CBS
Bonnie Raitt Tongue and Groove	1984	Warner Bros
Stray Cats Let's Go Faster	1985	Toshiba/EMI
Bernie Larsen Cry on Cue	1986	RCI
Jackson Browne Lives in the Balance	1986	Electra/Asylum
John Eddie John Eddie	1986	CBS
Marsha Hunt Walk on Gilded Splinters	1987	See For Miles
The Textones Cedar Creek	1987	Enigma

John Goodwin Behind the Palace Walls	1987	Heartline
Broken Homes Straight Line Through Time	1988	MCA
Cry on Cue Rhythm of Life	1988	Spinout
Georgia Satellites Open All Night	1988	Elektra/Asylum
Pontiac Brothers Johnson	1988	Frontier
Georgia Satellites In the Land of Salvation and Sin	1989	Elektra
Steel Magnolias Movie Soundtrack	1989	Polydor
Little Women Pretty Wiped Out	1989	Outerspace
Lions and Ghosts Wild Garden	1989	EMI
Bruce Springsteen Viva Las Vegas (The Last Temptation of Elvis)	1990	NME
Michael Anderson Michael Anderson	1990	A&M
Carla Olson and Mick Taylor Live	1990	Demon
Joe Cocker Night Calls	1991	Capitol
Paul Kelly Wanted Man	1991	White
Warren Zevon and David Lindley Deadicated (Grateful Dead Tribute)	1991	Arista
Bonnie Raitt Luck of the Draw	1991	Capitol
Flies on Fire Outside Looking Inside	1991	Atco
Izzy Stradlin Izzy Stradlin and the Ju Ju Hounds	1992	Geffen
The Sextants Lucky You	1992	Imago
Melissa Etheridge Never Enough	1992	Island
Buffy the Vampire Slayer Movie Soundtrack	1992	CBS
Miracle Legion Drenched	1992	Morgan Creek
Bruce Springsteen HumanTouch/Lucky Town	1992	Columbia
Hanoi Rocks Jerusalem Slim	1992	Mercury
Arc Angels Arc Angels	1992	Geffen
Taj Mahal Dancing the Blues	1993	Private Inc.
Crash Vegas Stone	1993	Polygram
TV In Flames Drool	1993	Reprise
Melissa Etheridge Yes I Am	1993	Island
Carla Olson Within an Ace	1993	Demon
Brian Joens Omaha	1993	House
Paul Westerberg 14 Songs	1993	Sire
Buddy Guy Feels Like Rain	1993	Silvertone
Idha Ovelius Melody Inn	1994	Creation
Michael Fracasso When I Lived in the Wind	1994	Bohemia Beat
Lee Rocker's Big Blue Big Blue	1994	Black Top
Carla Olson Reap the Whirlwind	1994	Watermelon
Otis Rush Ain't Enough Comin' In	1994	Quicksilver
Idha Get Undressed	1994	Creation

Art Wood Moneydue	1995	Nippon Crown
Marcia Ball Band with Ian McLagan		
Various Artists–KGSR Broadcasts Volume 6	1995	107.1 KGSR
Pat McLaughlin Get Out and Stay Out	1995	Dos
Carla Olson Wave of the Hand	1995	Watermelon
Art Wood Quiet Melon	1995	Lost Moment
Chris Gaffney Loser's Paradise	1995	Hightone
Lenny McDaniel Bad for Me	1996	Renegade
Sarah Brown Sayin' What I'm Thinkin'	1996	Blind Pig
Wyckham Porteous Looking for Ground	1996	Bohemia Beat
Calvin Russell Dream of the Dog	1997	Last Call
Charlie Burton Charlie Burton and the		
Texas Twelve Steppers	1997	Lazy S.O.B.
Caroline Wonderland and the		
Imperial Monkeys Bursting with Flavor	1997	Justice
Troy Dillinger and Del Dragons		
Crazy About Tori	1998	Stinky Derringer
Hurricane #1 Only the Strongest Will Survive	1998	Creation
John Hiatt The Best of John Hiatt	1998	Capitol
Robert Earl Keen Walking Distance	1998	Arista
Toni Price Low Down and Up	1999	Antones
Billy Bragg Billy Bragg and the Blokes–		
Mermaid Avenue Tour	1999	Billy Bragg
Van Wilks Koko's Hideaway	1999	Texas
Rainravens Rose of Jericho	1999	Blue Rose
Dumptruck Terminal	1999	Devil in the Woods
Billy Nicholls Snapshot	1999	Southwest
Slaid Cleaves Broke Down	2000	Rounder/Philo
Gurf Morlix The Toad of Titicaca	2000	Catamount

Index